Contents

Part 2 Genres 19

Part 3   Processes *193*

Part 4   Strategies   *237*

Part 5   Doing Research   *329*

Part 6   Media / Design   451

part 1

Rhetorical Situations

Whenever we write, whether it's email to a friend or a toast for a wedding, an English essay or a résumé, we face some kind of rhetorical situation. We have a **PURPOSE**, a certain **AUDIENCE**, a particular **STANCE**, a **GENRE**, and a **MEDIUM** to consider—and often as not a **DESIGN.** All are important elements that we need to think about carefully. The following chapters offer brief discussions of those elements of the rhetorical situation, along with questions that can help you make the choices you need to as you write. See also the fifteen **GENRES** chapters for guidelines for considering your rhetorical situation in specific kinds of writing.

Rhetorical Situations

Purpose 1

All writing has a purpose. We write to explore our thoughts and emotions, to express ourselves, to entertain; we write to record words and events, to communicate with others, to try to persuade others to believe as we do or to behave in certain ways. In fact, we often have several purposes at the same time. We may write an essay in which we try to persuade an audience of something, but as we write, we may also be exploring our thoughts on the subject. Look, for example, at this passage from a 2002 *New York Time's Magazine* essay about the compensation of chief executive officers by economist and editorial columnist Paul Krugman:

> Is it news that C.E.O.'s of large American corporations make a lot of money? Actually, it is. They were always well paid compared with the average worker, but there is simply no comparison between what executives got a generation ago and what they are paid today.
>
> Over the past 30 years most people have seen only modest salary increases: the average annual salary in America, expressed in 1998 dollars (that is, adjusted for inflation), rose from $32,522 in 1970 to $35,864 in 1999. That's about a 10 percent increase over 29 years — progress, but not much. Over the same period, however, according to *Fortune* magazine, the average real annual compensation of the top 100 C.E.O.'s went from $1.3 million — 39 times the pay of an average worker — to $37.5 million, more than 1,000 times the pay of ordinary workers.
>
> The explosion in C.E.O. pay over the past 30 years is an amazing story in its own right, and an important one. But it is only the most spectacular indicator of a broader story, the reconcentration of income and wealth in the U.S. The rich have always been different from you and me, but they are far more different now than they were not long ago — indeed, they are as different now as they were when F. Scott Fitzgerald made his famous remark.
>
> — Paul Krugman, "For Richer"

rhetorical situations ▪ genres ▲ processes ○ strategies ◆ research mla/apa ● media/ design □

Krugman is reporting information here, outlining how top business executives' pay has increased over the last thirty years. He is also making an argument, that their pay is far greater than it was not too long ago and that this difference in income resembles the disparity that characterized the United States right before the Great Depression. (Krugman, writing for a magazine, is also using a style—dashes, contractions, rhetorical questions that he then answers—that strives to be entertaining while it informs and argues.)

Even though our purposes may be many, knowing our primary reason for writing can help us shape that writing and understand how to proceed with it. Our purpose can determine the genre we choose, our audience, even the way we design what we write.

Identify your purpose. While writing often has many purposes, we usually focus on one. When you get an assignment or see a need to write, ask yourself what the primary purpose of the writing task is: to entertain? to inform? to persuade? to demonstrate your knowledge or your writing ability? What are your own goals? What are your audience's expectations, and do they affect the way you define your purpose?

Thinking about Purpose

- *What do you want your audience to do, think, or feel?* How will they use what you tell them?

- *What does this writing task call on you to do?* Do you need to show that you have mastered certain content or skills? Do you have an assignment that specifies a particular **STRATEGY** or **GENRE**—to compare two things, perhaps, or to argue a position?

- *What are the best ways to achieve your purpose?* What kind of **STANCE** should you take? Should you write in a particular genre? Do you have a choice of **MEDIUM,** and does your text require any special **DESIGN** elements?

237–328 ◆
19–192 ▲
12–14 ■
451–84 ☐

rhetorical situations ■   genres ▲   processes ○   strategies ◆   research mla/apa ●   media/ design ☐

Audience   2

Who will read (or hear) what you are writing? A seemingly obvious but crucially important question. Your audience affects your writing in various ways. Consider a piece of writing as simple as a note left on the kitchen table:

> Jon —
> *Please take the chicken out to thaw,*
> *and don't forget to feed Annye.*
> *Remember: Dr. Wong at 4.*
> *Love,*
> *Mom*

On the surface, this brief note is a straightforward reminder to do three things. But in fact it is a complex message filled with compressed information for a specific audience. The writer (Mom) counts on the reader (her son) to know a lot that can be left unsaid. She expects that Jon knows that the chicken is in the freezer and needs to thaw in time to be cooked for dinner; she knows that he knows who Annye is (a pet?), what he or she is fed, and how much; she assumes that Jon knows who (and where) Dr. Wong is. She doesn't need to spell any of that out because she knows what Jon knows and what he needs to know — and in her note she can be brief. She understands her audience. Think how different such a reminder would be were it written to another audience — a babysitter, perhaps, or a friend helping out while Mom is out of town.

What you write, how much you write, how you phrase it, even your choice of genre (memo, essay, email, note, speech) — all are influenced by the audience you envision. And your audience will interpret your writing according to their expectations and experiences.

When you are a student, your teachers are most often your audience, so you need to be aware of their expectations and know the conventions (rules, often unstated) for writing in specific academic fields. You may make statements that seem obvious to you, not realizing that your instructors may consider them assertions that must be proved with evidence of one sort or another. Or you may write more or less formally than teachers expect. Understanding your audience's expectations — by asking outright, by reading materials in a related field, by trial and error — is important to your success as a writer.

This point is worth dwelling on. You are probably reading this text for a writing course. As a student, you will be expected to produce essays with few or no errors. If you have a job in an office or correspond using email, you may question such standards; after all, much of the email you get at work or from friends is not grammatically perfect. But in a writing class, the instructor needs to see your best work. Whatever the rhetorical situation, your writing must meet the expectations of your audience.

Identify your audience.   Audiences may be defined as *known, multiple,* or *unknown. Known audiences* can include people with whom you're familiar as well as people you don't know personally but whose needs and expectations you do know. You yourself are a known, familiar audience, and you write to and for yourself often. Class notes, to-do lists, reminders, and journals are all written primarily for an audience of one: you. For that reason, they are often in shorthand, full of references and code that you alone understand. Other known, familiar audiences include anyone you actually know — friends, relatives, teachers, classmates — and whose needs and expectations you understand. You can also know what certain readers want and need, even if you've never met them personally, if you write for them within a specific shared context. Such a known audience might include computer gamers who read instructions for beating a game that you have posted on the Internet; you don't know those people, but you know roughly what they know about the game and what they need to know, and you know how to write about it in ways they will understand.

You often have to write for *multiple audiences.* Business memos or reports may be written initially for a supervisor, but he or she may pass them along to others. Grant proposals are a good example: the National Cancer Institute Web site advises scientists applying for grants to bear in

mind that the application may have six levels of readers — each, of course, with its own expectations and perspectives. Even writing for a class might involve multiple audiences: your instructor and your classmates.

Unknown audiences can be the most difficult to address since you can't be sure what they know, what they need to know, how they'll react. Such an audience could be your downstairs neighbor, whom you say hello to but with whom you've never had a real conversation; how will she respond to your letter asking her to sponsor you in an upcoming charity walk? Another unknown audience — perhaps surprisingly — might be many of your instructors, who want — and expect! — you to write in ways that are new to you. While you can benefit from analyzing any audience, you need to think most carefully about those you don't know.

Thinking about Audience

- **Whom do you want to reach?** To whom are you writing (or speaking)?
- **What is your audience's background — their education and life experiences?** It may be important for you to know, for example, whether your readers attended college, fought in a war, or have young children.
- **What are their interests?** What do they like? What motivates them? What do they care about?
- **Is there any demographic information that you should keep in mind?** Consider whether race, gender, sexual orientation, disabilities, occupations, religious beliefs, economic status, and so on, should affect what or how you write. For example, writers for *Men's Health*, *InStyle*, and *Out* must consider the particular interests of each magazine's readers.
- **What political circumstances may affect their reading?** What attitudes — opinions, special interests, biases — may affect the way your audience reads your piece? Are your readers conservative, liberal, or middle of the road? Politics may take many other forms as well — retirees on a fixed income may object to increased school taxes, so a letter arguing for such an increase would need to appeal to them differently than would a similar letter sent to parents of young children.

- *What does your audience already know — or believe — about your topic? What do you need to tell them? What is the best way to do so?* Those retirees who oppose school taxes already know that taxes are a burden for them; they may need to know why schools are justified in asking for more money every few years when other government organizations do not. A good way to explain this may be with a bar graph showing how good schools with adequate funding benefit property values. Consider which **STRATEGIES** will be effective — narrative, comparison, something else?

237–328 ◆

- *What's your relationship with your audience, and how does it affect your language and tone?* Do you know them, or not? Are they friends? colleagues? mentors? adversaries? completely unknown to you? Will they likely share your **STANCE?** In general, you need to write more formally when you're addressing readers you don't know, and you may address friends and colleagues more informally than you would a boss.

12–14 ■

- *What does your audience need and expect from you?* Your history professor, for example, may need to know how well you can discuss the economy of the late Middle Ages in order to assess your learning; that same professor may expect you to write a carefully reasoned argument, drawing conclusions from various sources, with a readily identifiable thesis in the first paragraph. Your boss, on the other hand, may need an informal email that briefly lists your sales contacts for the day; she may expect that you list the contacts in the order in which you saw them, that you clearly identify each one, and that you give a few words about how well each contact went. What **GENRE** is most appropriate?

19–192 ▲

- *What kind of response do you want?* Do you want to persuade readers to do or believe something? to accept your information on a topic? to understand why an experience you once had matters to you?

451–84 ▫
451–84 ▫

- *How can you best appeal to your audience?* Is there a particular **MEDIUM** that will best reach them? Are there any **DESIGN** requirements? (Elderly readers may need larger type, for instance.)

Genre 3

Genres are kinds of writing. Letters, profiles, reports, position papers, poems, Web pages, instructions, parodies — even jokes — are genres. Genres have particular conventions for presenting information that help writers write and readers read. For example, here is the beginning of a profile of a mechanic who repairs a specific kind of automobile:

> Her business card reads Shirley Barnes, M.D., and she's a doctor, all right — a Metropolitan Doctor. Her passion is the Nash Metropolitan, the little car produced by Austin of England for American Motors between 1954 and 1962. Barnes is a legend among southern California Met lovers — an icon, a beacon, and a font of useful knowledge and freely offered opinions.

A profile offers a written portrait of someone or something that informs and sometimes entertains, often examining its subject from a particular angle — in this case, as a female mechanic who fixes Nash Metropolitans. While the language in this example is informal and lively ("she's a doctor, all right"), the focus is on the subject, Shirley Barnes, "M.D." If this same excerpt were presented as a poem, however, the new genre would change our reading:

> Her business card reads
> Shirley Barnes, M.D.,
> and she's a doctor, all right
> — a Metropolitan Doctor.
> Her passion is the Nash Metropolitan,
> the little car produced by Austin of England
> for American Motors between 1954 and 1962.
> Barnes is a legend
> among southern California Met lovers
> — an icon,

a beacon,
and a font of useful knowledge and
freely offered opinions.

The content and words haven't changed, but the presentation invites us to read not only to learn about Shirley Barnes but also to explore the significance of the words and phrases on each line, to read for deeper meaning and greater appreciation of language. The genre thus determines how we read and how we interpret what we read.

Genres help us write by defining features for conveying certain kinds of information. They give readers clues about what sort of information they're likely to find and so help them figure out how to read ("Ah! A letter from Brit!" or "Thank goodness! I found the instructions for programming this DVD player"). At the same time, writers sometimes challenge genre conventions, reshaping them as communicative needs and technologies change. For example, computers have enabled us to add visuals to texts that we never before thought to illustrate.

19–192
Identify your genre. Does your writing situation call for a certain **GENRE?** A memo? A report? A proposal? A letter? Academic assignments generally specify the genre ("take a position," "analyze the text"), but if the genre isn't clear, ask your instructor.

Thinking about Genre

- *What is your genre, and does it affect what content you can or should include?* Objective information? Researched source material? Your own opinions? Personal experience?

237–328
- *Does your genre call for any specific* **STRATEGIES?** Profiles, for example, usually include some narration; lab reports often explain a process.

- *Does your genre require a certain organization?* Most proposals, for instance, first identify a problem and then offer a solution. Some genres leave room for choice. Business letters delivering good news might be organized differently than those making sales pitches.

rhetorical situations genres processes strategies research mla/apa media/ design

- *Does your genre affect your tone?* An abstract of a scholarly paper calls for a different tone than a memoir. Should your words sound serious and scholarly? brisk and to the point? objective? opinionated? Sometimes your genre affects the way you communicate your STANCE.

12–14

- *Does the genre require formal (or informal) language?* A letter to the mother of a friend asking for a summer job in her bookstore calls for more formal language than does an email to the friend thanking him for the lead.

- *Do you have a choice of medium?* Some genres call for print; others for an electronic medium. Sometimes you have a choice: a résumé, for instance, can be mailed (in which case it must be printed), or it may be emailed. Some teachers want reports turned in on paper; others prefer that they be emailed or posted to a class Web site. If you're not sure what MEDIUM you can use, ask.

451–84

- *Does your genre have any design requirements?* Some genres call for paragraphs; others require lists. Some require certain kinds of type-faces—you wouldn't use **Impact** for a personal narrative, nor would you likely use DrSeuss for an invitation to Grandma's sixty-fifth birthday party. Different genres call for different DESIGN elements.

451–84

4 Stance

Whenever you write, you have a certain stance, an attitude toward your topic. The way you express that stance affects the way you come across as a writer and a person. This email from a college student to his father, for example, shows a thoughtful, reasonable stance for a carefully researched argument:

> Hi Dad,
> I'll get right to the point: I'd like to buy a car. I saved over $2500 from working this summer, and I've found three different cars that I can get for under $2000. That'll leave me $400 to cover the insurance. I can park in Lot J, over behind Monte Hall, for $75 for both semesters. And I can earn gas and repair money by upping my hours at the cafeteria. It won't cost you any more, and if I have a car, you won't have to come and pick me up when I want to come home.
> Love,
> Michael

While such a stance can't guarantee that Dad will give permission, it's more likely to produce results than this version:

> Hi Dad,
> I'm buying a car. A guy in my Western Civ course has a cool Chevy he wants to get rid of. I've got $2500 saved from working this summer, it's mine, and I'm going to use it to get some wheels. Mom said you'd blow your top if I did, but I want this car.
> Michael

The writer of the first email respects his reader and offers reasoned arguments and evidence of research to convince him that buying a car is an action that will benefit them both. The writer of the second, by contrast, seems impulsive, ready to buy the first car that comes along, and defiant—he's picking a fight. Each email reflects a certain stance that shows the writer as a certain kind of person dealing with a situation in a certain way and establishing a certain relationship with his audience.

Identify your stance. What is your attitude about your topic? Critical? Curious? Opinionated? Objective? Passionate? Indifferent? You convey your attitude about your topic (and your audience) in the tone your writing takes. And your tone may be affected by your relationship to your audience. How do you want them to see you? As a colleague sharing information? As a good student showing what you can do? As an advocate for a position? Often your stance is affected by your GENRE: for example, lab reports require an objective, unemotional stance that emphasizes the content and minimizes the writer's own attitudes. Memoir, by comparison, allows you to reveal your feelings about your topic. As a writer, you communicate your stance through your tone, in the words you choose.

▲ 19–192

Just as you likely alter what you say depending on whether you're speaking to a boss, an instructor, a parent, or a good friend, so you need to make similar adjustments as a writer. It's a question of appropriateness: we behave in certain ways in various social situations, and writing is a social situation. You might sign email to a friend with an x and an o, but in an email to your supervisor you'll likely sign off with a "Many thanks" or "Regards." To write well, you need to write with integrity, to say what you wish to say, yet you also must understand that in writing, as in speaking, your voice needs to suit your purpose, your relationship to your audience, the way in which you wish your audience to perceive you, and your medium. In writing as in other aspects of life, the Golden Rule applies: "Do unto audiences as you would have them do unto you." Address readers respectfully if you want them to respond to your words with respect.

Thinking about Stance

- *What is your stance, and how can you present it best to achieve your purpose?* If you're writing about something you take very seriously, be

sure that your language and even your typeface reflect that serious-
3–4 ◼
ness. Make sure your stance is appropriate to your **PURPOSE.**

- *What tone will best convey your stance?* Do you want to be seen as reasonable? angry? thoughtful? gentle? funny? ironic? What aspects of your
personality do you want to project? Check your writing for words that
reflect that tone—and for ones that do not (and revise as necessary).

- *How is your stance likely to be received by your audience?* Your tone and
5–8 ◼
especially your attitude toward your **AUDIENCE** will affect how willing
they are to take your argument seriously.

- *Should you openly reveal your stance?* Do you want or need to announce
your own perspective on your topic? Will doing so help you reach your
audience, or would it be better to make your argument without saying directly where you're coming from?

◼ ▲ ○ ◆ ● ☐
rhetorical
situations   genres   processes   strategies   research
mla/apa   media/
design

Media/Design **5**

In its broadest sense, a *medium* is a go-between: a way for information to be conveyed from one person to another. We communicate through many media, verbal and nonverbal: our bodies (we catch someone's eye, wave, nod), our voices (we whisper, talk, shout, groan), and various technologies, including handwriting, print, telephone, radio, CD, film, and computer.

Each medium has unique characteristics that influence both what and how we communicate. As an example, consider this message: "I haven't told you this before, but I love you." Most of the time, we communicate messages like that one in person, using the medium of voice (with, presumably, help from eye contact and touch). A phone call will do, though most of us would think it a poor second choice, and a handwritten letter or note would be acceptable, if necessary. Few of us would break such news on a Web site or during a radio call-in program.

By contrast, imagine whispering the following sentence in a darkened room: "By the last decades of the nineteenth century, the territorial expansion of the United States had left almost all Indians confined to reservations." That sentence starts a chapter in a history textbook, and it would be strange indeed to whisper it into someone's ear. It is available in the medium of print, in the textbook, but it may also be read on a Web site, in promotional material for the book, or on a PowerPoint slide accompanying an oral presentation. Each medium has different uses and takes different forms, and each has distinctive characteristics. As you can see, we can choose various media depending on our purpose and audience. *The Norton Field Guide* focuses mostly on three media: **PRINT**, **SPOKEN**, and **ELECTRONIC**.

453–63
464–75
476–84

Because we now do most of our writing on computers, we are increasingly expected to pay close attention to the look of the material we write. No matter the medium, a text's *design* affects the way it is received and understood. A typed letter on official letterhead sends a different message than the same letter handwritten on pastel stationery, whatever the words on the page. Classic type sends a different message than *flowery italics*. Some genres and media (and audiences) demand photos, diagrams, color. Some information is easier to explain—and read—in the form of a pie chart or a bar graph than in the form of a paragraph. Some reports and documents are so long and complex that they need to be divided into sections, which are then best labeled with headings. Those are some of the elements to consider when you are thinking about how to design what you write.

Identify your media and design needs. Does your writing situation call for a certain medium and design? A printed essay? An oral report with visual aids? A Web site? Academic assignments often assume a particular medium and design, but if you're unsure about your options or the degree of flexibility you have, check with your instructor.

Thinking about Media

453–63

- *What medium are you using—* PRINT? SPOKEN? ELECTRONIC?—*and how does it affect the way you will write your text?* A printed résumé is usually no more than one page long; a scannable résumé sent via email has no length limits. An oral presentation should contain detailed information; accompanying PowerPoint slides should provide only an outline.

237–328

- *Does your medium affect your organization and* STRATEGIES? Long paragraphs are fine on paper but don't work well on the Web. On PowerPoint slides, phrases or key words work better than sentences. In print, you need to define unfamiliar terms; on the Web, you can sometimes just add a link to a definition found elsewhere.

- *How does your medium affect your language?* Some print documents require a more formal voice than spoken media; email often invites greater informality.

- *Should you use a combination of media?* Should you include audio or video in Web text? Do you need PowerPoint slides, handouts, or other visuals to accompany an oral presentation?

rhetorical situations   genres   processes   strategies   research mla/apa   media/design

Thinking about Design

- *What's the appropriate look for your* RHETORICAL SITUATION? Should your text look serious? whimsical? personal? something else? What design elements will suit your audience, purpose, genre, and medium?

1–17

- *Does your text have any elements that need to be designed?* Is there any information you would like to highlight by putting it in a box? Are there any key terms that should be bold?

- *What typeface(s) are appropriate* to your audience, purpose, genre, and medium?

- *Are you including any illustrations?* Should you? Is there any information in your text that would be easier to understand as a chart or graph? Will your AUDIENCE expect or need any?

5–8

- *Should you include headings?* Would they help you organize your materials and help readers follow the text? Does your GENRE require them?

9–11

part 2

Genres

When we make a shopping list, we automatically write each item we need in a single column. When we email a friend, we begin with a salutation: "Hi, Brian." Whether we are writing a letter, a résumé, a lab report, or a proposal, we know generally what it should contain and what it should look like because we are familiar with each of those genres. Genres are kinds of writing, and texts in any given genre share goals and features—a proposal, for instance, generally starts out by identifying a problem and then suggests a certain solution. The chapters in this part provide guidelines for writing in fifteen common academic genres. First come detailed chapters on four genres often assigned in writing classes: LITERACY NARRATIVES, essays ANALYZING TEXTS, REPORTS, and ARGUMENTS, followed by brief chapters on ELEVEN OTHER GENRES.

Genres

Writing a Literacy Narrative   6

Narratives are stories, and we read and tell them for many different purposes. Parents read their children bedtime stories as an evening ritual. Preachers base their Sunday sermons on Bible stories to teach the importance of religious faith. Grandparents tell how things used to be (sometimes the same stories year after year). Schoolchildren tell teachers that their dog ate their homework. College applicants write about significant moments in their lives. Writing students are often called upon to compose literacy narratives to explore how they learned to read or write. This chapter provides detailed guidelines for writing a literacy narrative. We'll begin with three good examples.

Readings

RICK BRAGG
All Over But the Shoutin'

This narrative is from All Over But the Shoutin,' *a 1997 autobiography by Rick Bragg, a former reporter for the* New York Times *and author of* I Am a Soldier, Too: The Jessica Lynch Story *(2003). Bragg grew up in Alabama, and in this narrative he recalls when, as a teenager, he paid a final visit to his dying father.*

> He was living in a little house in Jacksonville, Alabama, a college and mill town that was the closest urban center—with its stoplights and a high school and two supermarkets—to the country roads we roamed in our raggedy cars. He lived in the mill village, in one of those houses the mills subsidized for their workers, back when companies still did things like

21

rhetorical situations   genres   processes   strategies   research mla/apa   media/ design

that. It was not much of a place, but better than anything we had ever lived in as a family. I knocked and a voice like an old woman's, punctuated with a cough that sounded like it came from deep in the guts, told me to come on in, it ain't locked. It was dark inside, but light enough to see what looked like a bundle of quilts on the corner of a sofa. Deep inside them was a ghost of a man, his hair and beard long and going dirty gray, his face pale and cut with deep grooves. I knew I was in the right house because my daddy's only real possessions, a velvet-covered board pinned with medals, sat inside a glass cabinet on a table. But this couldn't be him.

He coughed again, spit into a can and struggled to his feet, but stopped somewhere short of standing straight up, as if a stoop was all he could manage. "Hey, Cotton Top," he said, and then I knew. My daddy, who was supposed to be a still-young man, looked like the walking dead, not just old but damaged, poisoned, used up, crumpled up and thrown in a corner to die. I thought that the man I would see would be the trim, swaggering, high-toned little rooster of a man who stared back at me from the pages of my mother's photo album, the young soldier clowning around in Korea, the arrow-straight, good-looking boy who posed beside my mother back before the fields and mophandle and the rest of it took her looks. The man I remembered had always dressed nice even when there was no cornmeal left, whose black hair always shone with oil, whose chin, even when it wobbled from the beer, was always angled up, high.

I thought he would greet me with that strong voice that sounded so fine when he laughed and so evil when, slurred by a quart of corn likker, he whirled through the house and cried and shrieked, tormented by things we could not see or even imagine. I thought he would be the man and monster of my childhood. But that man was as dead as a man could be, and this was what remained, like when a snake sheds its skin and leaves a dry and brittle husk of itself hanging in the Johnson grass.

"It's all over but the shoutin' now, ain't it, boy," he said, and when he let the quilt slide from his shoulders I saw how he had wasted away, how the bones seemed to poke out of his clothes, and I could see how it killed his pride to look this way, unclean, and he looked away from me for a moment, ashamed.

He made a halfhearted try to shake my hand but had a coughing fit again that lasted a minute, coughing up his life, his lungs, and after

5

that I did not want to touch him. I stared at the tops of my sneakers, ashamed to look at his face. He had a dark streak in his beard below his lip, and I wondered why, because he had never liked snuff. Now I know it was blood.

I remember much of what he had to say that day. When you don't see someone for eight, nine years, when you see that person's life red on their lips and know that you will never see them beyond this day, you listen close, even if what you want most of all is to run away.

"Your momma, she alright?" he said.

I said I reckon so.

"The other boys? They alright?"

I said I reckon so.   10

Then he was quiet for a minute, as if trying to find the words to a question to which he did not really want an answer.

"They ain't never come to see me. How come?"

I remember thinking, fool, why do you think? But I just choked down my words, and in doing so I gave up the only real chance I would ever have to accuse him, to attack him with the facts of his own sorry nature and the price it had cost us all. The opportunity hung perfectly still in the air in front of my face and fists, and I held my temper and let it float on by. I could have no more challenged him, berated him, hurt him, than I could have kicked some three-legged dog. Life had kicked his ass pretty good.

"How come?"

I just shrugged.   15

For the next few hours — unless I was mistaken, having never had one before — he tried to be my father. Between coughing and long pauses when he fought for air to generate his words, he asked me if I liked school, if I had ever gotten any better at math, the one thing that just flat evaded me. He asked me if I ever got even with the boy who blacked my eye ten years ago, and nodded his head, approvingly, as I described how I followed him into the boys' bathroom and knocked his dick string up to his watch pocket, and would have dunked his head in the urinal if the aging principal, Mr. Hand, had not had to pee and caught me dragging him across the concrete floor.

He asked me about basketball and baseball, said he had heard I had a good game against Cedar Springs, and I said pretty good, but it was two years ago, anyway. He asked if I had a girlfriend and I said,

"One," and he said, "Just one?" For the slimmest of seconds he almost grinned and the young, swaggering man peeked through, but disappeared again in the disease that cloaked him. He talked and talked and never said a word, at least not the words I wanted.

He never said he was sorry.

He never said he wished things had turned out different.

He never acted like he did anything wrong.

20

Part of it, I know, was culture. Men did not talk about their feelings in his hard world. I did not expect, even for a second, that he would bare his soul. All I wanted was a simple acknowledgment that he was wrong, or at least too drunk to notice that he left his pretty wife and sons alone again and again, with no food, no money, no way to get any, short of begging, because when she tried to find work he yelled, screamed, refused. No, I didn't expect much.

After a while he motioned for me to follow him into a back room where he had my present, and I planned to take it and run. He handed me a long, thin box, and inside was a brand-new, well-oiled Remington .22 rifle. He said he had bought it some time back, just kept forgetting to give it to me. It was a fine gun, and for a moment we were just like anybody else in the culture of that place, where a father's gift of a gun to his son is a rite. He said, with absolute seriousness, not to shoot my brothers.

I thanked him and made to leave, but he stopped me with a hand on my arm and said wait, that ain't all, that he had some other things for me. He motioned to three big cardboard egg cartons stacked against one wall.

Inside was the only treasure I truly have ever known.

I had grown up in a house in which there were only two books, the King James Bible and the spring seed catalog. But here, in these boxes, were dozens of hardback copies of everything from Mark Twain to Sir Arthur Conan Doyle. There was a water-damaged Faulkner, and the nearly complete set of Edgar Rice Burroughs's Tarzan. There was poetry and trash, Zane Grey's Riders of the Purple Sage, and a paperback with two naked women on the cover. There was a tiny, old copy of Arabian Nights, threadbare Hardy Boys, and one Hemingway. He had bought most of them at a yard sale, by the box or pound, and some at a flea market. He did not even know what he was giving me, did not recognize most of the writers. "Your momma said you still liked to read," he said.

25

There was Shakespeare. My father did not know who he was, exactly, but he had heard the name. He wanted them because they were pretty, because they were wrapped in fake leather, because they looked like rich folks' books. I do not love Shakespeare, but I still have those books. I would not trade them for a gold monkey.

"They's maybe some dirty books in there, by mistake, but I know you ain't interested in them, so just throw 'em away," he said. "Or at least, throw 'em away before your momma sees 'em." And then I swear to God he winked.

I guess my heart should have broken then, and maybe it did, a little. I guess I should have done something, anything, besides mumble "Thank you, Daddy." I guess that would have been fine, would not have betrayed in some way my mother, my brothers, myself. But I just stood there, trapped somewhere between my long-standing, comfortable hatred, and what might have been forgiveness. I am trapped there still.

Bragg's narrative illustrates all the features that make a narrative good: how the son and father react to each other creates the kind of suspense that keeps us reading; vivid details and rich dialogue bring the scene to life. His later reflections make the significance of that final meeting very clear—and the carton of books reveals the story's complex connection to Bragg's literacy.

RICHARD BULLOCK

How I Learned about the Power of Writing

I wrote this literacy narrative, about my own experience learning to read, as a model for my students in a first-year writing course.

When I was little, my grandmother and grandfather lived with us in a big house on a busy street in Willoughby, Ohio. My grandmother spent a lot of time reading to me. She mostly read the standards, like *The Little Engine That Could,* over and over and over again. She also let me help her plant African violets (I stood on a chair in her kitchen, carefully placing fuzzy violet leaves into small pots of soil) and taught me to tell time (again in her kitchen, where I watched the minute hand move slowly around the dial and tried in vain to see the hour hand move). All that attention and time spent studying the pages as Grandma read them again and again led me to start reading when I was around three years old.

My family was blue-collar, working-class, and — my grandmother excepted — not very interested in books or reading. But my parents took pride in my achievement and told stories about my precocious literacy, such as the time at a restaurant when the waitress bent over as I sat in my booster chair and asked, "What would you like, little boy?" I'm told I gave her a withering look and said, "I'd like to see a menu."

There was a more serious aspect to reading so young, however. At that time the murder trial of Dr. Sam Sheppard, a physician whose wife had been bludgeoned to death in their house, was the focus of lurid coverage in the Cleveland newspapers. Daily news stories recounted the grisly details of both the murder and the trial testimony, in which Sheppard maintained his innocence. (The story would serve as the inspiration for both *The Fugitive* TV series and the Harrison Ford movie of the same name.) Apparently I would get up early in the morning, climb over the side of my crib, go downstairs and fetch the paper, take it back upstairs to my crib, and be found reading about the trial when my parents got up. They learned that they had to beat me to the paper in the morning and remove the offending sections before my youthful eyes could see them.

The story of the Sheppard murder had a profound effect on me: it demonstrated the power of writing, for if my parents were so concerned that I not see certain things in print, those things must have had great importance. At the same time, adults' amazement that I could read was itself an inducement to continue: like any three-year-old, I liked attention, and if reading menus and the *Plain Dealer* would do it, well then, I'd keep reading.

As I got older, I also came to realize the great gift my grandmother had given me. While part of her motivation for spending so much time with me was undoubtedly to keep me entertained in a house isolated from other children at a time when I was too young for nursery school, another part of her motivation was a desire to shape me in a certain way. As the middle child in a large family in rural West Virginia, my

5

grandmother had received a formal education only through the eighth grade, after which she had come alone to Cleveland to make a life for herself, working as a seamstress while reading the ancient Greeks and Etruscans on her own. She had had hopes that her daughter (my mother) would continue her education as she herself hadn't been able to, but Mom chose instead to marry Dad shortly after graduating from high school, and Dad hadn't even gotten that far—he had dropped out of school three days before graduation. So Grandma decided that I was going to be different, and she took over much of my preschool life to promote the love of learning that she herself had always had. It worked, and at ninety she got to see me graduate from college, the first in our family to do so.

In my literacy narrative, the disconnect between my age and my ability to read provides a frame for several anecdotes. The narrative's significance comes through in the final paragraph, in which I explore the effects of my grandmother's motivation for teaching me.

SHANNON NICHOLS

"Proficiency"

In the following literacy narrative, Shannon Nichols, a student at Wright State University, describes her experience taking the standardized writing proficiency test that high school students in Ohio must pass to graduate. She wrote this essay for a college writing course, where her audience included her classmates and instructor.

The first time I took the ninth-grade proficiency test was in March of eighth grade. The test ultimately determines whether students may receive a high school diploma. After months of preparation and anxiety, the pressure was on. Throughout my elementary and middle school years, I was a strong student, always on the honor roll. I never had a GPA below 3.0. I was smart, and I knew it. That is, until I got the results of the proficiency test.

Although the test was challenging, covering reading, writing, math, and citizenship, I was sure I had passed every part. To my surprise, I did pass every part—except writing. "Writing! Yeah right! How did I manage to fail writing, and by half a point, no less?" I thought to myself in disbelief. Seeing my test results brought tears to my eyes. I honestly could not believe it. To make matters worse, most of my classmates, including some who were barely passing eighth-grade English, passed that part.

Until that time, I loved writing just as much as I loved math. It was one of my strengths. I was good at it, and I enjoyed it. If anything, I thought I might fail citizenship. How could I have screwed up writing? I surely spelled every word correctly, used good grammar, and even used big words in the proper context. How could I have failed?

Finally I got over it and decided it was no big deal. Surely I would pass the next time. In my honors English class I worked diligently, passing with an A. By October I'd be ready to conquer that writing test. Well, guess what? I failed the test again, again with only 4.5 of the 5 points needed to pass. That time I did cry, and even went to my English teacher, Mrs. Brown, and asked, "How can I get A's in all my English classes but fail the writing part of the proficiency test twice?" She couldn't answer my question. Even my friends and classmates were confused. I felt like a failure. I had disappointed my family and seriously let myself down. Worst of all, I still couldn't figure out what I was doing wrong.

I decided to quit trying so hard. Apparently—I told myself—the people grading the tests didn't have the slightest clue about what constituted good writing. I continued to excel in class and passed the test on the third try. But I never again felt the same love of reading and writing.

This experience showed me just how differently my writing could be judged by various readers. Obviously all my English teachers and many others enjoyed or at least appreciated my writing. A poem I wrote was put on television once. I must have been a pretty good writer. Unfortunately the graders of the ninth-grade proficiency test didn't feel the same, and when students fail the test, the state of Ohio doesn't offer any explanation.

After I failed the test the first time, I began to hate writing, and I started to doubt myself. I doubted my ability and the ideas I wrote

rhetorical situations   genres   processes   strategies   research mla/apa   media/ design

about. Failing the second time made things worse, so perhaps to protect myself from my doubts, I stopped taking English seriously. Perhaps because of that lack of seriousness, I earned a 2 on the Advanced Placement English Exam, barely passed the twelfth-grade proficiency test, and was placed in developmental writing in college. I wish I knew why I failed that test, because then I might have written what was expected on the second try, maintained my enthusiasm for writing, and continued to do well.

Nichols's narrative focuses on her emotional reaction to failing a test that she should have passed easily. The contrast between her demonstrated writing ability and her repeated failures creates a tension that captures readers' attention. We want to know what will happen to her.

Key Features / Literacy Narratives

A well-told story.   As with most narratives, those about literacy often set up some sort of situation that needs to be resolved. That need for resolution makes readers want to keep reading. We want to know whether Nichols ultimately will pass the proficiency test. Some literacy narratives simply explore the role that reading or writing played at some time in someone's life—assuming, perhaps, that learning to read or write is a challenge to be met.

Vivid detail.   Details can bring a narrative to life for readers by giving them vivid mental images of the sights, sounds, smells, tastes, and textures of the world in which your story takes place. The details you use when describing something can help readers picture places, people, and events; dialogue can help them hear what is being said. We get a picture of the only treasure Bragg has ever known through the details he provides: "a water-damaged Faulkner," "a paperback with two naked women on the cover," books "wrapped in fake leather." Similarly, we hear a three-year-old's exasperation through his own words: "I'd like to see a menu." Dialogue can help bring a narrative to life.

Some indication of the narrative's significance. By definition, a literacy narrative tells something the writer remembers about learning to read or write. In addition, the writer needs to make clear why the incident matters to him or her. You may reveal its significance in various ways. Nichols does it when she says she no longer loves to read or write. Bragg is more direct when he tells us he would not trade the books for a gold monkey. The trick is to avoid tacking onto the end a statement about your narrative's significance as if it were a kind of moral of the story. Bragg's narrative would have far less power if he'd said, "Thus did my father teach me to value books of all kinds."

A GUIDE TO WRITING A LITERACY NARRATIVE

Choosing a Topic

In general, it's a good idea to focus on a single event that took place during a relatively brief period of time. For example:

- any early memory about writing or reading that you recall vividly
- someone who taught you to read or write
- a book or other text that has been significant for you in some way
- an event at school that was interesting, humorous, or embarrassing
- a writing or reading task that you found (or still find) difficult or challenging
- a memento that represents an important moment in your literacy development (perhaps the start of a LITERACY PORTFOLIO)
- the origins of your current attitudes about writing or reading
- perhaps more recent challenges: learning to write instant messages, learning to write email appropriately, learning to construct a Web page

234–35 ○

Make a list of possible topics, and then choose one that you think will be interesting to you and to others — and that you're willing to share with others. If several seem promising, try them out on a friend or classmate.

rhetorical situations
genres
processes
strategies
research mla/apa
media/ design

Or just choose one and see where it leads; you can switch to another if need be. If you have trouble coming up with a topic, try **FREEWRITING, LISTING, CLUSTERING,** or **LOOPING.**

199–202

Considering the Rhetorical Situation

PURPOSE   Why do you want to tell this story? To share a memory with others? To fulfill an assignment? To teach a lesson? To explore your past learning? Think about the reasons for your choice and how they will shape what you write.

3–4

AUDIENCE   Are your readers likely to have had similar experiences? Would they tell similar stories? How much explaining will you have to do to help them understand your narrative? Can you assume that they will share your attitudes toward your story, or will you have to work at making them see your perspective? How much about your life are you willing to share with this audience?

5–8

STANCE   What attitude do you want to project? Affectionate? Neutral? Critical? Do you wish to be sincere? serious? humorously detached? self-critical? self-effacing? something else? How do you want your readers to see you?

12–14

MEDIA / DESIGN   Will your narrative be in print? presented orally? on a Web site? Will photos or other illustrations help you present your subject? Is there a typeface that conveys the right tone?

15–17

Generating Ideas and Text

Good literacy narratives share certain elements that make them interesting and compelling for readers. Remember that your goals are to tell the story as clearly and vividly as you can and to convey the meaning the incident has for you today. Start by writing out what you remember about the setting and those involved, perhaps trying out some of the methods in the chapter on **GENERATING IDEAS AND TEXT.** You may also want to **INTERVIEW** a teacher or parent who figures in your narrative.

199–204
350–52

Describe the setting. Where does your narrative take place? List the places where your story unfolds. For each place, write informally for a few minutes, **DESCRIBING** what you remember:

285–93

- *What do you see?* If you're inside, what color are the walls? What's hanging on them? What can you see out any windows? What else do you see? Books? Lined paper? Red ink? Are there people? Places to sit?

- *What do you hear?* A radiator hissing? Air conditioners? Leaves rustling? The wind howling? Rain? Someone reading aloud? Shouts? Cheers? Children playing? Music? The zing of an instant message arriving?

- *What do you smell?* Sweat? White paste? Perfume? Incense? Food cooking?

- *How and what do you feel?* Nervous? Happy? Cold? Hot? A scratchy wool sweater? Tight shoes? Rough wood on a bench?

- *What do you taste?* Gum? Mints? Graham crackers? Juice? Coffee?

Think about the key people. Narratives include people whose actions play an important role in the story. In your literacy narrative, you are probably one of those people. A good way to develop your understanding of the people in your narrative is to write about them:

- *Describe each person in a paragraph or so.* What do the people look like? How do they dress? How do they speak? Quickly? Slowly? With an accent? Do they speak clearly, or do they mumble? Do they use any distinctive words or phrases? You might begin by **DESCRIBING** their movements, their posture, their bearing, their facial expressions. Do they have a distinctive scent?

285–93

- *Recall (or imagine) some characteristic dialogue.* A good way to bring people to life and move a story along is with **DIALOGUE,** to let readers hear

294–98

them rather than just hearing about them. Try writing six to ten lines of dialogue between two people in your narrative. If you can't remember an actual conversation, make up one that could have happened. (After all, you are telling the story, and you get to decide how it is to be told.) If you don't recall a conversation, try to remember (and write down) some of the characteristic words or phrases that the people in your narrative used.

Write about "what happened." At the heart of every good narrative is the answer to the question "What happened?" The action in a literacy **NARRATIVE** may be as dramatic as winning a spelling bee or as subtle as a conversation between two friends; both contain action, movement, or change that the narrative tries to capture for readers. A good story dramatizes the action. Try **SUMMARIZING** the action in your narrative in a paragraph—try to capture what happened. Use active and specific verbs (*pondered, shouted, laughed*) to describe the action as vividly as possible.

◆ 304–12

◆ 321–22

Consider the significance of the narrative. You need to make clear the ways in which any event you are writing about is significant for you now. Write a page or so about the meaning it has for you. How did it change or otherwise affect you? What aspects of your life now can you trace to that event? How might your life have been different if this event had not happened or had turned out differently? Why does this story matter to you?

Ways of Organizing a Literacy Narrative

Start by **OUTLINING** the main events in your narrative. Then think about how you want to tell the story. Don't assume that the only way to tell your story is just as it happened. That's one way—starting at the beginning of the action and continuing to the end. But you could also start in the middle—or even at the end. Shannon Nichols, for example, could have begun her narrative by telling how she finally passed the proficiency test and then gone back to tell about the times she tried to pass it, even as she was an A student in an honors English class. Several ways of organizing a narrative follow.

⬤ 203–04

[Chronologically, from beginning to end]

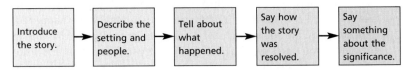

Introduce the story. → Describe the setting and people. → Tell about what happened. → Say how the story was resolved. → Say something about the significance.

[Beginning in the middle]

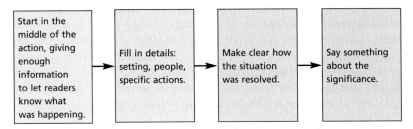

Start in the middle of the action, giving enough information to let readers know what was happening. → Fill in details: setting, people, specific actions. → Make clear how the situation was resolved. → Say something about the significance.

[Beginning at the end]

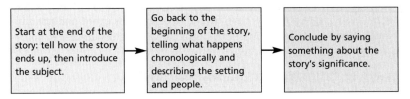

Start at the end of the story: tell how the story ends up, then introduce the subject. → Go back to the beginning of the story, telling what happens chronologically and describing the setting and people. → Conclude by saying something about the story's significance.

Writing Out a Draft

205–07

Once you have generated ideas and thought about how you want to organize your narrative, it's time to begin **DRAFTING.** Do this quickly—try to write a complete draft in one sitting, concentrating on getting the story on paper or screen and on putting in as much detail as you can. Some writers find it helpful to work on the beginning or ending first.

rhetorical situations ▲ genres ○ processes ◆ strategies ● research mla/apa □ media/design

Draft a beginning. A good narrative grabs readers' attention right from the start. Here are some ways of beginning; you can find more advice in the chapter on BEGINNING AND ENDING. 239–49

- *Jump right in.* Sometimes you may want to get to the main action as quickly as possible. Nichols, for example, begins as she takes the ninth-grade proficiency test for the first time.
- *Describe the context.* You may want to provide any background information at the start of your narrative, as I decided to do, beginning by explaining how my grandmother taught me to read.
- *Describe the setting, especially if it's important to the narrative.* Bragg begins by describing the small Alabama town where his father lived.

Draft an ending. Think about what you want your readers to read last. An effective ending helps them understand the meaning of your narrative. Here are some possibilities; look also at the chapter on BEGINNING AND ENDING. 239–49

- *End where your story ends.* It's up to you to decide where a narrative ends. Bragg's story ends with him standing in front of a pile of books; mine ends several years after it begins, with my graduation from college.
- *Say something about the significance of your narrative.* Nichols observes that she no longer loves to read or write, for example. The trick is to touch upon the narrative's significance without stating it too directly, like the moral of a fable.
- *Refer back to the beginning.* My narrative ends with my grandmother watching me graduate from college; Nichols ends by contemplating the negative effects of failing the proficiency test.
- *End on a surprising note.* Bragg catches our attention when his father gives him the boxes of books—and leaves us with a complicated image to ponder.

Come up with a title. A good title indicates something about the subject of your narrative—and makes readers want to take a look. Nichols's title states her subject, "Proficiency," but she also puts the word in quotes, calling it into question in a way that might make readers wonder — and read on. I focus on the significance of my narrative: "How I Learned about the Power of Writing." Bragg takes his title from something memorable his father said: "It's all over but the shoutin.' " See the chapter on **GUIDING YOUR READER** for more advice on titles.

250–54

Considering Matters of Design

You'll probably write your narrative in paragraph form, but think about the information you're presenting and how you can design it to enhance your story and appeal to your audience.

454–55

- What would be an appropriate **TYPEFACE?** Something serious, like Times Roman? Something whimsical, like Comic Sans? Something else?

456–57

- Would it help your readers if you added **HEADINGS** in order to divide your narrative into shorter sections?

458–62

- Would photographs or other **VISUALS** show details better than you can describe them with words alone? If you're writing about learning to read, for example, you might scan in an image of one of the first books you read in order to help readers picture it. Or if your topic is learning to write, you could include something you wrote.

Getting Response and Revising

The following questions can help you study your draft with a critical eye. **GETTING RESPONSE** from others is always good, and these questions can guide their reading, too. Make sure they know your purpose and audience.

213–14

- Do the title and first few sentences make readers want to read on? If not, how else might you begin?

- Does the narrative move from beginning to end clearly? Does it flow, and are there effective transitions? Does the narrative get sidetracked at any point?

- Is anything confusing?
- Is there enough detail, and is it interesting? Is there enough information about the setting and the people? Can readers picture the characters and sense what they're like as people? Would it help to add some dialogue, so that readers can "hear" them? Will they be able to imagine the setting?
- Have you made the situation meaningful enough to make readers wonder and care about what will happen?
- Do you narrate any actions clearly? vividly? Does the action keep readers engaged?
- Is the significance of the narrative clear?
- Does the narrative end in a satisfying way? What are readers left thinking?

The preceding questions should identify aspects of your narrative you need to work on. When it's time to **REVISE,** make sure your text appeals to your audience and achieves your purpose as successfully as possible.

○ 214–16

Editing and Proofreading

Readers equate correctness with competence. Once you've revised your draft, follow these guidelines for **EDITING** a narrative:

○ 219–22

◆ 304–12
◆ 254

- Make sure events are **NARRATED** in a clear order and include appropriate time markers, **TRANSITIONS,** and summary phrases to link the parts and show the passing of time.
- Be careful that verb tenses are consistent throughout. If you write your narrative in the past tense ("he *taught* me how to use a computer"), be careful not to switch to the present ("So I *look* at him and *say* . . . ") along the way.
- Check to see that verb tenses correctly indicate when an action took place. If one action took place before another action in the past, you should use the past perfect tense: "I forgot to dot my i's, a mistake I *had made* many times."

294–98

- Punctuate **DIALOGUE** correctly. Whenever someone speaks, surround the speech with quotation marks ("No way," I said.). Periods and commas go inside quotation marks; exclamation points and question marks go inside if they're part of the quotation, outside if they're part of the whole sentence:

    Inside: Opening the door, Ms. Cordell announced, "Pop quiz!"
    Outside: It wasn't my intention to announce, "I hate to read"!

222–23

- **PROOFREAD** your finished narrative carefully before turning it in.

Taking Stock of Your Work

- How well do you think you told the story?
- What did you do especially well?
- What could still be improved?
- How did you go about coming up with ideas and generating text?
- How did you go about drafting your narrative?
- Did you use photographs or any other graphics? What did they add? Can you think of graphics you might have used?
- How did others' responses influence your writing?
- What would you do differently next time?

224–35

See Chapter 27 if you are required to submit your literacy narrative as part of a writing **PORTFOLIO.**

147–52

168–73

> See also **MEMOIRS** (Chapter 15), a kind of narrative that focuses more generally on a significant event from your past, and **REFLECTIONS** (Chapter 18), a kind of essay for thinking about a topic in writing.

■ rhetorical situations
▲ genres
○ processes
◆ strategies
● research mla/apa
□ media/ design

Both *Time* and *U.S. News and World Report* cover the same events, but each magazine interprets them differently. All toothpaste ads claim to make teeth "the whitest." Saddam Hussein was supporting terrorists—or he wasn't, depending on which politician is speaking. Those are but three examples that demonstrate why we need to be careful, analytical readers of magazines and newspapers, ads, political documents, even textbooks. Not only does text convey information, but it also influences how and what we think. We need to read, then, to understand not only what texts say but also how they say it. Because understanding how texts say what they say is so crucial, assignments in many disciplines ask you to analyze texts. You may be asked to analyze sensory imagery in James Joyce's "Araby" for a literature class or, for an art history course, to analyze the use of color and space in Edward Hopper's *Nighthawks*. In a statistics course, you might analyze a set of data—a numerical text—to find the standard deviation from the mean. This chapter offers detailed guidelines for writing an essay that closely examines a text both for what it says and for how it does so, with the goal of demonstrating for readers how—and how well—the text achieves its effects. We'll begin with three good examples.

Readings

DAVID S. RUBIN

It's the Same Old Song

In this analysis of a painting, David Rubin, curator of visual arts at the Contemporary Arts Center in New Orleans, analyzes how a painting uses themes from the Eagles' song "Hotel California" to critique California culture. This analysis comes from a book that accompanied a museum exhibition on rock music's influence on contemporary art.

> Whether one has been consciously or subliminally affected by the music, the mention of "Respect," "Hotel California," or "Stayin' Alive," to name a few of the song titles appropriated by artists, conjures up instant associations and pangs of nostalgia. Yet, when attached to an artwork, such titles may take on any number of new meanings, at times reflective of the musical source, but often equally remote from it. . . .

Alfred Leslie, Hotel California *(Wadsworth Atheneum, Hartford, Connecticut)*

Initially an abstract expressionist painter, Alfred Leslie turned to figuration in the 1960s because he felt that "modern art had, in a sense, killed figure painting. Painting the figure could become the most challenging subject one could undertake." By the 1970s, Leslie had developed a distinctive figural style in which subjects are shown in frontal, confrontational poses, at close range, and bathed in sharp, dramatic lighting that was inspired by baroque artists such as Caravaggio. While many of Leslie's paintings deal with events drawn from personal experience, such as his self-portraits and a cycle of paintings concerning the death of a friend, poet Frank O'Hara, others, such as *Hotel California* (1980), are purely fictional.

As with all of Leslie's paintings, the figures in *Hotel California* are based on drawings structured on a geometric grid—a useful formal device for developing stiff, awkward poses. Although they remain anonymous, the man and woman depicted are a generic breed of displaced traveler. They arrive in Los Angeles in search of Eden only to find it as described in the Eagles song. As [sociologist Robert G.] Pielke explains, "The 'hotel' is obviously a metaphorical reference to California and the state of mind that accompanies it. After checking in for the night, a traveler comes to the realization that 'this could be Heaven or this could be Hell'; it turns out to be both. On the one hand it's 'such a lovely place,' but on the other 'we are all prisoners here of our own device' " (189). Leslie, who is a New Yorker, communicates this vision of California through incongruity of scale between the figures and the setting, which is a broad vista with expansive blue skies, as well as through carefully articulated iconographic details, such as the styles of clothing and luggage, the Pepsi can, and the *Hotel California* album cover, shown propped against a wall. Taken together, these minutiae present a disconcerting time capsule of Los Angeles in the 1970s.

Work Cited

Pielke, Robert G. <u>You Say You Want a Revolution: Rock Music in American Culture</u>. Chicago: Nelson-Hall, 1986.

Rubin focuses on several textual elements in the painting: the relative size of people and setting, "iconographic details"; in addition, he discusses contextual elements, including the lyrics of the song that inspired the painting and the artist's method, as evidence to support his analysis.

WILLIAM SAFIRE

A Spirit Reborn

Just before the first anniversary of September 11, 2001, New York Times columnist William Safire analyzed the Gettysburg Address for what it meant to Americans after 9/11.

Abraham Lincoln's words at the dedication of the Gettysburg cemetery will be the speech repeated at the commemoration of September 11 by the governor of New York and by countless other speakers across the nation.

The lips of many listeners will silently form many of the famous phrases. "Four score and seven years ago" — a sonorous way of recalling the founding of the nation eighty-seven years before he spoke — is a phrase many now recite by rote, as is "the last full measure of devotion."

But the selection of this poetic political sermon as the oratorical centerpiece of our observance need not be only an exercise in historical evocation, nonpolitical correctness, and patriotic solemnity. What makes this particular speech so relevant for repetition on this first anniversary of the worst bloodbath on our territory since Antietam Creek's waters ran red is this: now, as then, a national spirit rose from the ashes of destruction.

Here is how to listen to Lincoln's all-too-familiar speech with new ears.

In those 236 words, you will hear the word *dedicate* five times. The first two times refer to the nation's dedication to two ideals mentioned in the Declaration of Independence, the original ideal of "liberty" and the ideal that became central to the Civil War: "that all men are created equal."

The third, or middle, *dedication* is directed to the specific consecration of the site of the battle of Gettysburg: "to dedicate a portion of that field as a final resting place." The fourth and fifth times Lincoln repeated *dedicate* reaffirmed those dual ideals for which the dead being honored fought: "to the unfinished work" and then "to the great task remaining before us" of securing freedom and equality.

Those five pillars of dedication rested on a fundament of religious metaphor. From a president not known for his piety — indeed, often

criticized for his supposed lack of faith—came a speech rooted in the theme of national resurrection. The speech is grounded in conception, birth, death, and rebirth.

Consider the barrage of images of birth in the opening sentence. The nation was "conceived in liberty" and "brought forth"—that is, delivered into life—by "our fathers" with all "created" equal. (In the nineteenth century, both "men" and "fathers" were taken to embrace women and mothers.) The nation was born.

Then, in the middle dedication, to those who sacrificed themselves, come images of death: "final resting place" and "brave men, living and dead."

Finally, the nation's spirit rises from this scene of death: "that this 10 nation, under God, shall have a new birth of freedom." Conception, birth, death, rebirth. The nation, purified in this fiery trial of war, is resurrected. Through the sacrifice of its sons, the sundered nation would be reborn as one.

An irreverent aside: All speechwriters stand on the shoulders of orators past. Lincoln's memorable conclusion was taken from a fine oration by the Reverend Theodore Parker at an 1850 Boston antislavery convention. That social reformer defined the transcendental "idea of freedom" to be "a government of all the people, by all the people, for all the people."

Lincoln, thirteen years later, dropped the "alls" and made the phrase his own. (A little judicious borrowing by presidents from previous orators shall not perish from the earth.) In delivering that final note, the Union's defender is said to have thrice stressed the noun "people" rather than the prepositions "of," "by," and "for." What is to be emphasized is not rhetorical rhythm but the reminder that our government's legitimacy springs from America's citizens; the people, not the rulers, are sovereign. Not all nations have yet grasped that.

Do not listen on September 11 only to Lincoln's famous words and comforting cadences. Think about how Lincoln's message encompasses but goes beyond paying "fitting and proper" respect to the dead and the bereaved. His sermon at Gettysburg reminds "us the living" of our "unfinished work" and "the great task remaining before us"—to resolve that this generation's response to the deaths of thousands of our people leads to "a new birth of freedom."

Safire analyzed Lincoln's text for what it said to Americans on the anniversary of 9/11. His analysis focuses on patterns of specific words and images—he identifies *dedicate* as a key term and analyzes how its meaning changes and develops each time it is used. He shows how Lincoln shaped his text around images of birth, death, and resurrection to assert that although a nation's soldiers die, their deaths permit the rebirth of the nation. In doing so, Safire built an argument linking Lincoln's words to current circumstances.

DOUG LANTRY

"Stay Sweet As You Are": An Analysis of Change and Continuity in Advertising Aimed at Women

Doug Lantry wrote this analysis of three print ads for a first-year writing course at the University of Akron.

Magazine advertisements aimed at American women have a long history of pushing things like makeup, mouthwash, soap, and other products that reinforce men's roles in women's lives. The concept of personal hygiene has been used to convey the message that "catching" a man or becoming a wife is a woman's ultimate goal, and in advertisements from the 1920s, 1930s, and 1950s this theme can be traced through verbal and visual content.

For example, a 1922 ad for Resinol soap urges women to "make that dream come true" by using Resinol (see Fig. 1). The dream is marriage. The premise is that a bad complexion will prevent marriage even if a woman has attributes like wit and grace, which the ad identifies as positive. Blotchy skin, the ad says, will undermine all that. The word *repellent* is used for emphasis and appears in the same sentence as the words *neglected* and *humiliated*, equating the look of the skin with the state of the person within. Of course, Resinol can remedy the condition, and a paragraph of redemption follows the paragraph about being repellent. A treatment program is suggested, and the look and feel of "velvety" skin are only "the first happy effects," with eventual marriage (fulfillment) implied as the ultimate result of using Resinol soap.

Fig. 1.   A 1922 Resinol soap ad.

Visual content supports the mostly verbal ad. In a darkened room, a lone woman peers dreamily into a fireplace, where she sees an apparition of herself as a bride in a white veil, being fulfilled as a person by marriage to a handsome man. She lounges in a soft chair, where the glow of the image in the fireplace lights her up and warms her as much as the comforting fire itself. A smaller image shows the woman washing with Resinol, contentedly working her way toward clear skin and marriage over a water-filled basin suggestive of a vessel of holy water. This image is reinforced by her closed eyes and serene look and by the ad's suggestion that "right living" is a source of a good complexion.

A somewhat less innocent ad appeared more than a decade later, in 1934 (see Fig. 2). That ad, for Lux soap, like the one for Resinol, prescribes a daily hygiene regimen, but it differs significantly from the Resinol message in that it never mentions marriage and uses a clear-skinned movie star as proof of Lux's effectiveness. Instead of touting marriage, Lux teaches that "a girl who wants to break hearts simply must have a tea-rose complexion." Romance, not marriage, is the woman's goal, and competition among women is emphasized because "girls who want to make new conquests . . . [are] *sure* to win out!" by using Lux. Lux's pitch is more sophisticated than Resinol's, appealing to a more emancipated woman than that of the early 1920s and offering a kind of evidence based on science and statistics. The text cites "9 out of 10 glamorous Hollywood stars" and scientists who explain that Lux slows aging, but it declines to cite names, except that of Irene Dunne, the ad's star. The unnamed stars and scientists give the ad an air of untruthfulness, and this sense is deepened by the paradox of the ad's title: "Girls who know this secret always win out." If Lux is a secret, why does it appear in a mass-media publication?

Like Resinol, Lux urges women to seek love and fulfillment by enhancing their outward beauty and suggests that clear skin means having "the charm men can't resist." 5

The Lux ad's visual content, like Resinol's, supports its verbal message. Several demure views of Irene Dunne emphasize her "pearly-smooth skin," the top one framed by a large heart shape. In all the photos, Dunne wears a feathery, feminine collar, giving her a birdlike appearance: she is a bird of paradise or an ornament. At the bottom of the ad, we see a happy Dunne being cuddled and admired by a man.

The visual and verbal message is that women should strive, through steps actually numbered in the ad, to attain soft, clear skin

Fig. 2.   1934 Lux soap ad.

and hence charm and hence romance. Not surprisingly, the ad uses the language of battle to describe the effects of clear skin: girls who use Lux will "make new conquests!" and "win out!" Similar themes are developed for a younger audience in a 1954 ad for Listerine mouthwash (see Fig. 3). This time the target is no longer grown women but teenage girls: "If you want to win the boys . . . Stay Sweet As You Are!" Because attracting men would be inappropriate for teenagers, boys are the catch of the day in the Listerine ad. The idea of staying sweet means on the surface that girls should have nice breath, but the youthful context of the ad means that for women to be attractive they must stay young and "stay adorable," preferably with the girlish inno-cence of a teenager. The consequences of not staying sweet are clear: if you don't use Listerine every morning, every night, and before every

Fig. 3.   Listerine mouthwash ad.

date, "you're headed for boredom and loneliness." If you do use Listerine, there are "good times, good friends, and gaiety ahead."

Like Lux, Listerine relies on science as well as sex. With talk of "the bacterial fermentation of proteins," research, and clinical tests, the mouthwash props up its romantic and sexual claims by proclaiming scientific facts. Listerine is "4 times better than any tooth paste," the ad proclaims "With proof like this, it's easy to see why Listerine belongs in your home."

Visuals contribute to the message, as in the other ads. The central image is a photo of a perky, seemingly innocent teenage girl playing records on a portable phonograph. A vision of midcentury American femininity, she wears a fitted sweater, a scarf tied at the neck (like a wrapped present?), and a full, long skirt. She sits on the floor, her legs hidden by the skirt; she could be a cake decoration. Leaning forward slightly, she looks toward the reader, suggesting by her broad smile and submissive posture that perhaps kissing will follow when she wins the boys with her sweet breath. The record player affirms the ad's teenage target.

The intended consumers in the Resinol, Lux, and Listerine ads are 10 women, and the message of all three ads is that the product will lead to—and is required for—romantic or matrimonial success. Each ad implies that physical traits are paramount in achieving this success, and the ads' appearance in widely circulated magazines suggests that catching a man (whether or not she marries him) is the ultimate goal of every American woman. While there is a kind of progress over time, the ads' underlying assumptions remain constant. There is evidence of women's increasing sophistication, illustrated in the later ads' use of science and "objective" proof of the products' effectiveness. Women's development as individuals can also be seen in that marriage is not presupposed in the later ads, and in the case of Lux a single woman has a successful career and apparently has her pick of many partners.

Still, one theme remains constant and may be seen as a continuing debilitating factor in women's struggle for true equality in the world of sex roles: pleasing men is the prerequisite for happiness. Despite apparent advances on other levels, that assumption runs through all three ads and is the main selling point. The consumer of Resinol, Lux, and Listerine is encouraged to objectify herself, to become more physically attractive not for her own sake but for someone else's. The women in all three ads are beautifying themselves because they assume they must "make new conquests," "win the boys," and "make that dream come true."

Lantry summarizes each ad clearly and focuses his analysis on a theme run-ning through all three ads: the concept that to find happiness, a woman must be physically attractive to men. He describes patterns of images and language in all three ads as evidence.

Key Features / Textual Analysis

A summary of the text. Your readers may not know the text you are ana-lyzing, so you need to include it or tell them about it before you can analyze it. Because Safire's text is so well-known, he describes it only briefly as "Abra-ham Lincoln's words at the dedication of the Gettysburg cemetery." Texts that are not so well-known require a more detailed summary. Both Rubin and Lantry include the texts—and images—they analyze and also describe them in detail.

Attention to the context. Texts don't exist in isolation: they are influ-enced by and contribute to ongoing conversations, controversies, or debates, so to understand the text, you need to understand the larger context. Rubin describes Leslie's development and names several song titles that visual artists have "appropriated." Safire notes the source of the phrase "of the people, by the people, for the people" and is clearly writing in the context of the United States after 9/11.

A clear interpretation or judgment. Your goal in analyzing a text is to lead readers through careful examination of the text to some kind of inter-pretation or reasoned judgment, generally announced clearly in a thesis statement. When you interpret something, you explain what you think it means, as Lantry does when he argues that the consumers of the three beauty products are encouraged to "objectify" themselves. He might instead have chosen to judge the effectiveness of the ads, perhaps noting that they promise the impossible, that no mouthwash, soap, or other product can guar-antee romantic "success."

Reasonable support for your conclusions. Written analysis of a text is generally supported by evidence from the text itself and sometimes from

rhetorical situations

genres

processes

strategies

research mla/apa

media/ design

other sources. The writer might support his or her interpretation by quoting words or passages from a written text or referring to images in a visual text. Safire, for example, looks at Lincoln's repetition of the word "dedicate" in the Gettysburg Address as a way of arguing that the speech was still relevant in 2002, on the anniversary of the 9/11 attacks. Lantry examines patterns of both language and images in his analysis of the three ads. Note that the support you offer for your interpretation need only be "reasonable" — there is never any one way to interpret something.

A GUIDE TO ANALYZING A TEXT

Choosing a Text to Analyze

Most of the time, you will be assigned a text or a type of text to analyze: a poem in a literature class, the work of a political philosopher in a political science class, a speech in a history or communications course, a painting or sculpture in an art class, a piece of music in a music theory course. If you must choose a text to analyze, look for one that suits the demands of the assignment — one that is neither too large or complex to analyze thoroughly (a Dickens novel or a Beethoven symphony is probably too big) nor too brief or limited to generate sufficient material (a ten-second TV news brief or a paragraph from *Fast Food Nation* would probably be too small). Be sure you understand what the assignment asks you to do, and ask your instructor for clarification if you're not sure.

Considering the Rhetorical Situation

■ **PURPOSE** Why are you analyzing this text? To demonstrate that you understand it? To persuade readers that the text demonstrates a certain point? Or are you using the text as a way to make some other point?

3–4

■ **AUDIENCE** Are your readers likely to know your text? How much detail will you need to supply?

■ **STANCE** What interests you about your analysis? Why? What do you know or believe about your topic, and how will your own beliefs affect your analysis?

■ **MEDIA / DESIGN** Are you writing an essay for a class? to be published in a journal or magazine? something for the Web? If you are analyzing a visual text, you will probably need to include an image of the text.

Generating Ideas and Text

In analyzing a text, your goal is to understand what it says, how it works, and what it means. To do so, you may find it helpful to follow a certain sequence: read, respond, summarize, analyze, and draw conclusions from your analysis.

Read to see what the text says.   Start by reading carefully, to get a sense of what it says. This means first skimming to **PREVIEW THE TEXT,** rereading for the main ideas, then questioning and **ANNOTATING.**

Consider your **INITIAL RESPONSE.** Once you have a sense of what the text says, what do you think? What's your reaction to the argument, the tone, the language, the images? Do you find the text difficult? puzzling? Do you agree with what the writer says? Disagree? Agree *and* disagree? Your reaction to a text can color your analysis, so start by thinking about how you react—and why. Consider both your intellectual reaction and any emotional reactions. Identify places in the text that trigger or account for those reactions. If you think that you have no particular reaction or response, try to articulate why. Whatever your response, think about what accounts for it.

Next, consolidate your understanding of the text by **SUMMARIZING** (or, if it's a visual text, **DESCRIBING**) what it says in your own words. You may find it helpful to **OUTLINE** its main ideas. See, for instance, how Lantry care-

rhetorical situations   genres   processes   strategies   research mla/apa   media/ design

fully described what a soap ad he was analyzing shows and says. Some of this analysis ended up in his essay.

> Several demure views of Irene Dunne emphasize her "pearly-smooth skin," the top one framed by a large heart shape. In all the photos, Dunne wears a feathery, feminine collar, giving her a birdlike appearance: she is a bird of paradise or an ornament. At the bottom of the ad, we see a happy Dunne being cuddled and admired by a man.

Decide what you want to analyze.   Having read the text carefully, think about what you find most interesting or intriguing, and why. Does the language interest you? The imagery? The structure? The argument? The larger context? Something else? You might begin your analysis by exploring what attracted your notice.

Study how the text works.   Texts are made up of several components — words, sentences, images, even punctuation. Visual texts might be made up of images, lines, angles, color, light and shadow, and sometimes words. All these elements can be used in various ways. To analyze them, look for patterns in the way they're used and try to decide what those patterns reveal about the text. How do they affect its message? See the sections on THINKING ABOUT HOW THE TEXT WORKS and IDENTIFYING PATTERNS in Chapter 38 for specific guidelines on examining patterns this way.

◆ 319–24

Then write a sentence or two describing the patterns you've discovered and how they contribute to what the text says.

Analyze the argument.   Every text makes an argument. Both verbal and visual texts make certain assertions and provide some kind of support for those claims. An important part of understanding any text is to recognize its argument — what the writer or artist wants the audience to believe, feel, or do. Consider the text's purpose and audience, identify its thesis, and decide how convincingly it supports that thesis. See the section on ANALYZING THE ARGUMENT for help doing so.

◆ 324–27

Then write a sentence or two summarizing the argument the text makes, along with your reactions to or questions about that argument.

Think about the larger context. Texts are always part of larger, on-going conversations. To analyze a text's role in its larger context, you may need to do additional 329–449 **RESEARCH** to determine where the text was originally published, what else was happening or being discussed at the time the text was published or created, and whether or not the text responded directly to other ideas or arguments. You'll find detailed help doing so in the section on 327–28 **THINKING ABOUT THE LARGER CONTEXT** in Chapter 38.

Then write a sentence or two describing the larger context surrounding the text and how that context affects your understanding of the text.

Consider what you know about the writer or artist. What you know about the person who created a text can influence your understanding of that text. His or her other work, reputation, stance, and beliefs are all useful windows into understanding a text. See the guidelines on **AUTHORS' CREDENTIALS** 355 in Chapter 41.

Then write a sentence or two summarizing what you know about the writer and how that information affects your understanding of the text.

Come up with a thesis. When you analyze a text, you are basically arguing that the text should be read in a certain way. Once you've studied the text thoroughly, you need to identify your analytical goal: do you want to show that the text has a certain meaning? Uses certain techniques to achieve its purposes? Tries to influence its audience in particular ways? Relates to some larger context in some significant manner? Should be taken seriously—or not? Something else? Come up with a tentative 251–52 **THESIS** to guide your thinking and analyzing—but be aware that your thesis may change as you continue to work.

Ways of Organizing a Textual Analysis

Examine the information you have to see how it supports or complicates your thesis. Look for clusters of related information that you can use to 203–04 structure an **OUTLINE.** Your analysis might be structured in at least two ways. You might, as Safire does, discuss patterns or themes that run through the text. Alternatively, you might analyze each text or section of text separately, as Lantry does. Following are graphic representations of some ways of organizing a textual analysis.

[Thematically]

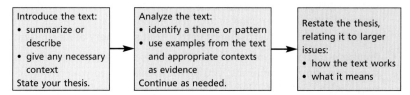

[Part by part, or text by text]

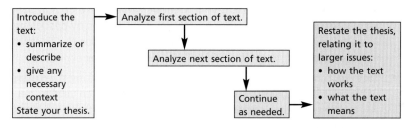

Writing Out a Draft

In drafting your analysis, your goal should be to integrate the various parts into a smoothly flowing, logically organized essay. However, it's easy to get bogged down in the details. Consider writing one section of the analysis first, then another and another until you've drafted the entire middle; then draft your beginning and ending. Alternatively, start by summarizing the text and moving from there to your analysis and then to your ending. However you do it, you need to support your analysis with evidence: from the text itself (as Lantry's analysis of advertisements does), or from **RESEARCH** on the larger context of the text (as Rubin and Safire do).

329–449

Draft a beginning.   The beginning of an essay that analyzes a text generally has several tasks: to introduce or summarize the text for your readers, to offer any necessary information on the larger context, and to present your thesis.

- *Summarize the text.* If the text is one your readers don't know, you need to give a brief **SUMMARY** early on that introduces it to them and shows that you understand it fully. For example, Lantry begins each analysis of a soap advertisement with a brief summary of its content.

321–22

- *Provide a context for your analysis.* If there is a larger context that is significant for your analysis, you might mention it in your introduction. Safire does this when he begins his analysis of Lincoln's Gettysburg Address by describing its status as a "centerpiece" of 9/11 commemorations.

- *Introduce a pattern or theme.* If your analysis centers on a certain pattern of textual or contextual elements, you might begin by describing it, as Rubin does in his first sentence when he mentions the "instant associations and pangs of nostalgia" certain song titles evoke.

251–52

- *State your thesis.* Lantry ends his first paragraph by stating the **THESIS** of his analysis: "The concept of personal hygiene has been used to convey the message that 'catching' a man or becoming a wife is a woman's ultimate goal, and in advertisements from the 1920s, 1930s, and 1950s this theme can be traced through verbal and visual content."

239–49

- See Chapter 28 for more advice on **BEGINNING AND ENDING**.

Draft an ending.   Think about what you want your readers to take away from your analysis, and end by getting them to focus on those thoughts.

- *Restate your thesis — and say why it matters.* Lantry, for example, ends by pointing out that "one theme remains constant" in all the ads he analyzes: that "pleasing men is the prerequisite for happiness."

- *Say something about the implications of your findings.* If your analysis has any general implications, you might end by stating them as Rubin does: "Taken together, these minutiae present a disconcerting time capsule of Los Angeles in the 1970s."

239–49

- See Chapter 28 for more advice on ways of **BEGINNING AND ENDING**.

Come up with a title.   A good title indicates something about the subject of your analysis — and makes readers want to see what you have to

say about it. Rubin's title "It's the Same Old Song," uses a cliché to refer to the "old song" on which the painting he analyzes is based. Safire's title may seem cryptic but would have made sense when it was published, shortly before the first anniversary of 9/11: "A Spirit Reborn." And Lantry's title uses an eye-catching headline from one ad with a clear statement of his essay's content: " 'Stay Sweet As You Are': An Analysis of Change and Continuity in Advertising Aimed at Women." See Chapter 29 on GUIDING YOUR READER for more tips on writing titles.

250–54

Considering Matters of Design

- If you cite written text as evidence, be sure to set long quotations and DOCUMENTATION according to the style you're using.

375–449

- If your essay is lengthy, consider whether HEADINGS would make your analysis easier for readers to follow.

456–57

- If you're analyzing a visual text, you may need to include a reproduction, along with a caption identifying it.

Getting Response and Revising

The following questions can help you study your draft with a critical eye. GETTING RESPONSE from others is always good, and these questions can guide their reading, too. Make sure they know your purpose and audience.

213–14

- Is the beginning effective? Does it make a reader want to continue?
- Does the introduction provide an overview of your analysis and conclusions? Is your thesis clear?
- Is the text described or summarized clearly and sufficiently?
- Is the analysis well organized and easy to follow? Do the parts fit together coherently? Does it read like an essay rather than a collection of separate bits of analysis?

- Does each part of the analysis relate to the thesis?
- Is anything confusing or in need of more explanation?
- Are all quotations accurate and correctly documented?
- Is it clear how the analysis leads to the interpretation? Is there adequate evidence to support the interpretation?

 Then it's time to **REVISE.** Make sure your text appeals to your audience and achieves your purpose as successfully as possible.

Editing and Proofreading

Readers equate correctness with competence. Once you've revised your draft, edit carefully:

- Is your thesis clearly stated?
- Does the **BEGINNING** make readers want to read on?
- Check all **QUOTATIONS, PARAPHRASES,** and **SUMMARIES** for accuracy and form. Be sure that each has the required **DOCUMENTATION.**
- Make sure that your analysis flows clearly from one point to the next and that you use **TRANSITIONS** that help readers move through your text.
- Does the **ENDING** make clear what your findings mean?
- **PROOFREAD** your finished analysis carefully before turning it in.

Taking Stock of Your Work

Take stock of what you've written and learned by writing out answers to these questions:

- How did you go about analyzing the text? What methods did you use—and which ones were most helpful?
- How did you go about drafting your essay?

214–16

239–40
358–69
375–449

254

245
222–23

 rhetorical situations
 genres
 processes
 strategies
 research mla/apa
media/ design

- How well did you organize your written analysis? What, if anything, could you do to make it easier to read?
- Did you provide sufficient evidence to support your analysis?
- What did you do especially well?
- What could still be improved?
- Did you use any visuals, and if so, what did they add? Could you have shown the same thing with words?
- How did other readers' responses influence your writing?
- What would you do differently next time?
- Are you pleased with your analysis? What did it teach you about the text you analyzed? Did it make you want to study more works by the same writer or artist?

See also Chapter 14 on LITERARY ANALYSES if you are analyzing a work of poetry, fiction, or drama. See Chapter 27 if you are required to submit your analysis as part of a writing PORTFOLIO.

▲ 137–46

○ 224–35

8 Reporting Information

Many kinds of writing report information. Newspapers report on local and world events; textbooks give information about biology, history, writing; Web sites provide information about products (jcrew.com), people (johnnydepp.com), institutions (smithsonian.org). We write out a lot of information ourselves, from a note we post on our door saying we've gone to choir practice to an essay we're assigned to write for a history class, reporting what we've learned about the state of U.S. diplomacy in the days before the bombing of Pearl Harbor. This chapter focuses on reports that are written to inform readers about a particular topic. Very often this kind of writing calls for some kind of research: you need to know your subject in order to report on it! When you write to report information, you are the expert. This chapter offers guidelines for writing essays that inform. We'll begin with three good examples.

THE 9/11 COMMISSION
The Hijacking of United 175

In 2004, the National Commission on Terrorist Attacks upon the United States published The 9/11 Commission Report, *a detailed account of the "facts and circumstances" of the terrorist attacks on September 11, 2001, with recommendations for "protecting against and preparing for" future terrorist attacks. The audience for the report was the President, Congress, and the American people. To begin, the report lays out the facts of the attacks, one plane at a time. Since it is reporting on an event, the* 9/11 Commission Report *begins with a narrative, relating what the Commission was able to learn about what happened. Here is the report on the hijacking of United 175.*

rhetorical situations · genres · processes · strategies · research mla/apa · media/ design

United Airlines Flight 175 was scheduled to depart for Los Angeles at 8:00. Captain Victor Saracini and First Officer Michael Horrocks piloted the Boeing 767, which had seven flight attendants. Fifty-six passengers boarded the flight.[1]

United 175 pushed back from its gate at 7:58 and departed Logan Airport at 8:14. By 8:33, it had reached its assigned cruising altitude of 31,000 feet. The flight attendants would have begun their cabin service.[2]

The flight had taken off just as American 11 was being hijacked, and at 8:42 the United 175 flight crew completed their report on a "suspicious transmission overheard from another plane (which turned out to have been Flight 11) just after takeoff. This was United 175's last communication with the ground.[3]

The hijackers attacked sometime between 8:42 and 8:46. They used knives (as reported by two passengers and a flight attendant), Mace (reported by one passenger), and the threat of a bomb (reported by the same passenger). They stabbed members of the flight crew (reported by a flight attendant and one passenger). Both pilots had been killed (reported by one flight attendant). The eyewitness accounts came from calls made from the rear of the plane, from passengers originally seated further forward in the cabin, a sign that passengers and perhaps crew had been moved to the back of the aircraft. Given similarities to American 11 in hijacker seating and in eyewitness reports of tactics and weapons, as well as the contact between the presumed team leaders, Atta and Shehhi, we believe the tactics were similar on both flights.[4]

The first operational evidence that something was abnormal on United 175 came at 8:47, when the aircraft changed beacon codes twice within a minute. At 8:51, the flight deviated from its assigned altitude, and a minute later New York air traffic controllers began repeatedly and unsuccessfully trying to contact it.[5]

At 8:52, in Easton, Connecticut, a man named Lee Hanson received a phone call from his son Peter, a passenger on United 175. His son told him: "I think they've taken over the cockpit—An attendant has been stabbed—and someone else up front may have been killed. The plane is making strange moves. Call United Airlines—Tell them it's Flight 175, Boston to LA." Lee Hanson then called the Easton Police Department and relayed what he had heard.[6]

Also at 8:52, a male flight attendant called a United office in San Francisco, reaching Marc Policastro. The flight attendant reported that the flight had been hijacked, both pilots had been killed, a flight attendant had been stabbed, and the hijackers were probably flying the plane. The call lasted about two minutes, after which Policastro and a colleague tried unsuccessfully to contact the flight.[7]

At 8:58, the flight took a heading toward New York City.[8]

At 8:59, Flight 175 passenger Brian David Sweeney tried to call his wife, Julie. He left a message on their home answering machine that the plane had been hijacked. He then called his mother, Louise Sweeney, told her the flight had been hijacked, and added that the passengers were thinking about storming the cockpit to take control of the plane away from the hijackers.[9]

At 9:00, Lee Hanson received a second call from his son Peter:

> It's getting bad, Dad—A stewardess was stabbed—They seem to have knives and Mace—They said they have a bomb—It's getting very bad on the plane—Passengers are throwing up and getting sick—The plane is making jerky movements—I don't think the pilot is flying the plane—I think we are going down—I think they intend to go to Chicago or someplace and fly into a building—Don't worry, Dad—If it happens, it'll be very fast—My God, my God.[10]

The call ended abruptly. Lee Hanson had heard a woman scream just before it cut off. He turned on a television, and in her home so did Louise Sweeney. Both then saw the second aircraft hit the World Trade Center.[11]

At 9:03:11, United Airlines Flight 175 struck the South Tower of the World Trade Center.[12] All on board, along with an unknown number of people in the tower, were killed instantly.

Notes

[1] The 56 passengers represented a load factor of 33.33 percent of the airplane's seating capacity of 168, below the 49.22 percent for Flight 175 on Tuesdays in the three-month period prior to September 11, 2001. See UAL report, Flight 175 BOS-LAX Load Factors, undated (from June 1, 2001, to Sept. 11, 2001). Nine passengers holding reservations for Flight 175 did not show for the flight. They were interviewed and cleared by the FBI. FAA report, "Executive Summary," Sept. 12, 2001; FAA report, "Executive Summary, Chronology of a Multiple Hijacking Crisis, September 11, 2001," Sept. 17, 2001; UAL record, Flight 175 ACARS report, Sept. 11, 2001; UAL record, Flight 175 Flight Data Recap, Sept. 11, 2001.

[2] FAA report, "Executive Summary," Sept. 12, 2001; FAA report,

rhetorical situations | genres | processes | strategies | research mla/apa | media/ design

"Executive Summary, Chronology of a Multiple Hijacking Crisis, September 11, 2001," Sept. 17, 2001; NTSB report, "Flight Path Study — United Airlines 175," Feb. 19, 2002; NTSB report, Air Traffic Control Recording — United Airlines Flight 175, Dec. 21, 2001. At or around this time, flight attendants Kathryn Laborie and Alfred Marchand would have begun cabin service in first class; with Amy King and Robert Fangman in business class; and with Michael Tarrou, Amy Jarret, and Alicia Titus in economy class. See UAL report, "Flight 175 Flight Attendant Positions/Jumpseats," undated. United flight attendants, unlike those at American, did not carry cockpit keys. Instead, such keys were stowed in the cabin — on Flight 175, in the overhead bin above seats 1A and 1B in first class. See Don Dillman briefing (Nov. 18, 2003); Bob Jordan briefing (Nov. 20, 2003).

[3] Asked by air traffic controllers at 8:37 to look for an American Airlines 767 (Flight 11), United 175 reported spotting the aircraft at 8:38. At 8:41, the flight crew reported having "heard a suspicious transmission" from another aircraft shortly after takeoff, "like someone keyed the mike and said everyone stay in your seats." See NTSB report, Air Traffic Control Recording — United Airlines Flight 175, Dec. 21, 2001.

[4] See Marc Policastro interview (Nov. 21, 2003); FBI reports of investigation, interview of Lee Hanson, Sept. 11, 2001; interview of Marc Policastro, Sept. 11, 2001; interview of Louise Sweeney, Sept. 28, 2001; interview of Ronald May, Sept 11, 2001. On both American 11 and United 175, Boeing 767 double-aisled aircraft, the hijackers arrayed themselves similarly: two seated in first class close to the cockpit door, the pilot hijacker seated close behind them, and at least one other hijacker seated close behind the pilot hijacker. Hijackers were seated next to both the left and right aisles. On American 77 and United 93, Boeing 757 single-aisle aircraft, the pilot hijacker sat in the first row, closest to the cockpit door. See FBI report, "Summary of Penttbom Investigation," Feb. 29, 2004, pp. 67–69; AAL schematics for Flight 11 and Flight 77; UAL schematics for Flight 175 and Flight 93.

[5] NTSB report, "Flight Path Study — United Airlines 175," Feb. 19, 2002; NTSB report, Air Traffic Control Recording — United Airlines Flight 175, Dec. 21, 2001.

[6] See FBI report of investigation, interview of Lee Hanson, Sept. 11, 2001.

[7] Flight crew on board UAL aircraft could contact the United office in San Francisco (SAMC) simply by dialing *349 on an airphone. See FBI report of investigation, interview of David Price, Jan. 24, 2002. At some

point before 9:00, SAMC notified United's headquarters of the emergency call from the flight attendant. See Marc Policastro interview (Nov. 21, 2003); FBI report of investigation, interview of Marc Policastro, Sept. 11, 2001; Rich Miles interview (Nov. 21, 2003).

[8] NTSB report, "Flight Path Study—United Airlines 175," Feb. 19, 2002.

[9] See FBI reports of investigation, interview of Julie Sweeney, Oct. 2, 2001; interview of Louise Sweeney, Sept. 28, 2001.

[10] See FBI report of investigation, interview of Lee Hanson, Sept. 11, 2001.

[11] See ibid.; interview of Louise Sweeney, Sept. 28, 2001.

[12] NTSB report, "Flight Path Study—United Airlines 175," Feb. 19, 2002.

This report on the events aboard the airliner provides a minute-by-minute narrative, along with direct quotations from passengers as they described the events and came to realize what the hijackers intended to do. The notes provide additional details, including source information; they are reproduced here as they are presented in the original report.

CATHI EASTMAN AND BECKY BURRELL

The Science of Screams: Laws of Physics Instill Thrills in Roller Coasters

The following account, written in 2002 for the Dayton Daily News *by two staff members of a science museum, provides information about how a roller coaster works.*

For roller coasters, being the star of summer amusement park rides certainly has its ups and downs. Ever wonder how they get the energy to deliver thrill after thrill?

A roller coaster uses a motor or other mechanical force to pull or propel the cars to the top of the first hill. After that, it rises and falls, slowing down and speeding up—all on its own.

Whether they're built from wood and ride on steel wheels or follow steel paths on air-cushioned tires, roller coasters work because of two main principles: the laws of conservation of energy and gravity.

The law of conservation of energy states that energy can change from one form to another but cannot be created or destroyed. At rest, a roller coaster represents potential energy, that is, energy that is stored for later use. As the coaster travels to the top of the first hill, it is storing potential energy. That potential energy is then changed into kinetic energy as gravity pulls it down the first hill. Kinetic energy is energy that is being used: in this case, it's the energy caused by motion.

Gravity is the force that pulls all objects in the universe toward one another and that pulls a roller coaster to the bottom of a hill. The farther it goes down the hill, the more potential energy is changed into kinetic energy, which makes the ride go faster. 5

As it goes up the next hill, kinetic energy is changed back into potential energy and the ride slows down. This changing of kinetic energy to potential energy and back again continues as It continues to go up and down hills. Remember, the energy does not increase, decrease, or disappear; it just changes from one form to the other.

In this brief explanation, the writers define and explain processes to help a general audience understand a complex set of concepts. Their focus on a well-known process—riding a roller coaster—gives them a concrete example with which to illustrate abstract scientific principles. Notice how they use a forecasting statement—"roller coasters work because of two main principles: the laws of conservation of energy and gravity"—to cue readers to the topics they then discuss.

JEFFREY DeROVEN

The Greatest Generation: The Great Depression and the American South

The following essay was written in 2001 by a student for a history course at the Trumbull Campus of Kent State University. It was first published in Etude and Techne, a journal of Ohio college writing.

Tom Brokaw called the folks of the mid-twentieth century the great-est generation. So why is the generation of my grandparents seen as this country's greatest? Perhaps the reason is not what they accom-plished but what they endured. Many of the survivors feel people today "don't have the moral character to withstand a depression like that."[1] This paper will explore the Great Depression through the eyes of ordi-nary Americans in the most impoverished region in the country, the American South, in order to detail how they endured and how the gov-ernment assisted them in this difficult era.

President Franklin D. Roosevelt (FDR) announced in 1938 that the American South "represented the nation's number one economic prob-lem." He commissioned the National Emergency Council to investigate and report on the challenges facing the region. Though rich in physi-cal and human resources, the southern states lagged behind other parts of the nation in economic development.[2]

Poor education in the South was blamed for much of the prob-lem. Young children attending school became too costly for most fam-ilies. In the Bland family, "when Lucy got to the sixth grade, we had to stop her because there was too much to do."[3] Overcrowding of schools, particularly in rural areas, lowered the educational standards. The short school terms further reduced effectiveness. As Mrs. Aber-crombie recalls, "Me and Jon both went to school for a few months but that wa'n't enough for us to learn anything."[4] Without the proper education, the youth of the South entered the work force unprepared for the challenges before them.

Southern industries did not have the investment capital to turn their resources into commodities. Manufacturers were limited to pro-ducing goods in the textile and cigarette industries and relied heav-ily on the cash crops of cotton and tobacco for the economy. Few facilities existed in the South for research that might lead to the devel-opment of new industries. Hampered by low wages, low tax revenue, and a high interest rate, Southerners lacked the economic resources to compete with the vast industrial strength of the North. As Aber-crombie indicates, "Penalized for being rural, and handicapped in its efforts to industrialize, the economic life of the South has been squeezed to a point where the purchasing power of the southern people does not provide an adequate market for its own industries nor an attractive market for those of the rest of the country."[5] The

Franklin Delano Roosevelt (1882–1945)
Photo from Bettmann / Corbis

South had an untapped market for production and consumption. However, without adequate capital, it did not have the means to profit from them.

Southern industries paid their employees low wages, which led to a low cost of living. "You could live very cheaply because . . . you couldn't make a great deal of money," remembers Rita Beline."[6] Most families did not have much left for themselves after bills and living expenses. "Nobody had much money, you know," recalls June Atchetce. "Everybody kind of lived at home, had gardens and raised their own produce, raised their own meat and had chickens and eggs and such as that." The needs of the families "were very small as far as purchases were concerned." What they could not grow, they did not have a need for, except for basic staples such as coffee, flour, sugar, and honey. To save on the cost of clothes, families "had a lot of hand-me-downs from the oldest to the baby. We did not throw them away. We patched them up and sent them down the line."[7] Luxury items, like radios, cost too much money, and "only the [aristocrats] had radios because the poor did not stay at home long enough to enjoy them."[8] The fact was that Southerners wanted modern consumer items but did not have the purchasing power to pay for them. "The people of the South need to buy, they want to buy, and they would buy — if they had the money." Without paying laborers a fair wage, industry had forced upon itself a lower living standard, thus perpetuating losses in local revenue resulting in a decline in purchasing power.[9]

The Federal government had to step in and help, as historians David L. Carlton and Peter A. Coclanis note:

> Some of the South's credit difficulties have been slightly relieved in recent years . . . by the Public Works Administration, . . . the Works Progress Administration, [and] the Soil Conservation Service, [which] have brought desperately needed funds into the South.[10]

Along with other New Deal projects like the Tennessee Valley Authority (TVA) and the Civilian Conservation Corps [CCC], President Roosevelt was able to prime the pump into a seemingly dead Southern economy.

Other ways the federal government primed the pump was with the WPA [Works Progress Administration]. This New Deal measure gave jobs to those who wanted to work. Local governments benefited too. The WPA provided new roads, buildings, hospitals, and schools. Rita Beline remembers her "father came very short of money, . . . took a job with the WPA, in which he helped in building a road across a lagoon."[11] President Roosevelt knew "cheap wages mean low buying power."[12] The WPA ensured a fair wage for good work. Warren Addis remembers that "workers were tickled to death with it because it gave so many people jobs. It started out at eight cents an hour for common labor, and it finally went to thirty cents an hour."[13]

FDR also created the CCC. The concept of putting the American youth to work yielded an economic stimulus by having them send home twenty-five dollars a month. That money worked itself back into local economies as families spent the money on needed goods. Young men across the South "left home to go and do this work. They got paid a little bit of money, which they sent home to their families."[14] The CCC created recreation habitats as well. Jefferson Brock recalls, "They came and built brush poles for the fish to live in the lake near my cottage."[15] The CCC became an outlet for young men who could not find work in their hometowns. Jesse Brooks remembers:

> They did a great lot of good. For instance, they built Vogel State Park and raised the wall up on the national cemetery. Just put people to work. Gave them their pride back. A man's not going to feel very good about himself if he can't feed his family. So, that was the

rhetorical situations

genres

processes

strategies

research mla/apa

media/ design

New Deal itself — to put people back to work and get the economy growing again.[16]

The South did not enjoy the United States' economic successes in [10] the early part of the twentieth century and in many ways was a third world country within our own nation. The federal action that fueled the Southern economy during the Great Depression changed the way of life for the better and helped Southerners endure a time of great despair. Programs like the TVA, WPA, and CCC planted the seeds for a prosperous future. I still do not know if they were the greatest generation, but they did overcome tremendous obstacles to bring forth other "greatest generations."

Notes

1. Allen Furline in Kenneth J. Bindas, "Oral History Project," Kent State University, Trumbull Campus, Trumbull, OH. Dr. Bindas has a collection of 476 oral-history interviews from western Georgia and eastern Alabama, from which the information for this paper is derived. (Hereafter cited in Notes as BOHP.)

2. David L. Carlton and Peter A. Coclanis, *Confronting Southern Poverty in the Great Depression: The Report on Economic Conditions of the South with Related Documents* (New York: Bedford / St. Martin's Press, 1996), 92.

3. Vera Bland in BOHP.

4. M. Abercrombie in BOHP.

5. Carlton and Coclanis, *Confronting Southern Poverty*, 76–78.

6. Rita Beline in BOHP.

7. June Romero Atchetce in BOHP.

8. Ruby Girley in BOHP.

9. Carlton and Coclanis, *Confronting Southern Poverty*, 62–65.

10. Ibid., 73.

11. Rita Beline in BOHP.

12. David M. Kennedy, *Freedom from Fear: The American People in Depression and War, 1929–1945* (New York: Oxford University Press, 1999), 346.

13. Warren Addis in BOHP.

14. Jane Berry in BOHP.

15. Jefferson Brock in BOHP.

16. Jesse Brooks in BOHP.

DeRoven's essay reports information about how the American South got through the Great Depression. His information is based on both library research and interviews with people who lived through the period he describes. He documents his sources according to The Chicago Manual of Style, *the preferred style in history classes.*

Key Features / Reports

A tightly focused topic. The goal of this kind of writing is to inform readers about something without digressing—and without, in general, bringing in the writer's own opinions. All three examples focus on a particular topic—the hijacking of United 175, the physics of roller coasters, and the Great Depression in the American South—and present information about the topics evenhandedly.

Accurate, well-researched information. Reports usually require some research. The kind of research depends on the topic. Library research to locate scholarly sources may be necessary for some topics—DeRoven, for example, uses an archive available only at his university's library. Other topics may require field research—interviews, observations, and so on. The 9/11 Commission interviewed "more than 1,200 people, in ten countries"—and also reviewed more than 2.5 million pages of documents.

Various writing strategies. Presenting information usually requires various organizing patterns—defining, comparing, classifying, explaining processes, analyzing causes and effects, and so on. Eastman and Burrell explain the process that makes roller coasters work; the portion of the *9/11 Commission Report* reprinted here provides a detailed narrative; DeRoven analyzes some of the causes of the Great Depression in the South.

Clear definitions. Reports need to provide clear definitions of any key terms that their audience may not know. Eastman and Burrell define several terms—"potential energy" and "gravity," among others—as they explain how coasters work.

rhetorical situations　　genres　　processes　　strategies　　research mla/apa　　media/ design

Appropriate design.   Reports often combine paragraphs with information presented in lists, tables, diagrams, and other illustrations. When you're presenting information, you need to think carefully about how to DESIGN it—numerical data, for instance, can be easier to understand and remember in a table than in a paragraph. And see how the *9/11 Commission Report* shows us the flight path of United 175 on a map, along with a minute-by-minute account of the events on the plane (laid out as a list to make the chronology easy to see).

453–63

United Airlines Flight 175 (UA 175)
Boston to Los Angeles

8:14	Takeoff
8:42	Last radio communication
8:42–8:46	Likely takeover
8:47	Transponder code changes
8:52	Flight attendant notifies UA of hijacking
8:54	UA attempts to contact the cockpit
8:55	New York Center suspects hijacking
9:03:11	Flight 175 crashes into 2 WTC (South Tower)
9:15	New York Center advises NEADS that UA 175 was the second aircraft crashed into WTC
9:20	UA headquarters aware that Flight 175 had crashed into WTC

A GUIDE TO REPORTING INFORMATION

Choosing a Topic

If you are working with an assigned topic, see if you can approach it from an angle that interests you. If you get to choose your topic, the following guidelines should help:

If you get to choose.   What interests you? What do you wish you knew more about? The possible topics for informational reports are limitless, but the topics that you're most likely to write well on are those that engage you. They may be academic in nature or reflect your personal interests or both. If you're not sure where to begin, here are some places to start:

- an intriguing technology: file sharing, Google, cell phones, roller coasters
- sports: soccer, snowboarding, ultimate Frisbee, skateboarding, basketball
- an important world event: 9/11, the fall of Rome, the Black Death
- a historical period: the African diaspora, medieval Europe, the Ming dynasty, the Great Depression
- a common object: hooded sweatshirts, gel pens, mascara, Post-it notes
- a significant environmental issue: Arctic oil drilling, the Clean Air Act, mercury and the fish supply
- the arts — hip-hop, outsider art, the J. Paul Getty Museum, Savion Glover, Mary Cassatt

200–01 ○
LIST a few possibilities, and then choose one that you'd like to know more about — and that your audience might find interesting, too. You might start out by phrasing your topic as a question that your research will attempt to answer. For example:

> How is Google different from Yahoo!?
>
> How was the Great Pyramid constructed?
>
> Why did the World Trade Center towers collapse on themselves rather than fall sideways?
>
> What kind of training do football referees receive?

If your topic is assigned. Some assignments are specific: "Explain the physics of roller coasters." If, however, your assignment is broad — "Explain some aspect of the U.S. government" — try focusing on a more limited topic within the larger topic: federalism, majority rule, political parties, states' rights, division of powers. Even if an assignment seems to offer little flexibility, your task is to decide how to research the topic — and sometimes even narrow topics can be shaped to fit your own interests and those of your audience.

Considering the Rhetorical Situation

■ **PURPOSE**	Why are you presenting this information? To teach readers about the subject? To demonstrate your research and writing skills? For some other reason?	3–4
■ **AUDIENCE**	Who will read this report? What does your audience already know about the topic? What background information do they need in order to understand it? Will you need to define any terms? What do you think they want or need to know about it? Why should they care or want to know about it? How can you attract their interest?	5–8
■ **STANCE**	What is your own attitude toward your subject? What interests you most about it? What about it seems important?	12–14
■ **MEDIA / DESIGN**	What medium are you using? What is the best way to present the information? Will it all be in paragraph form, or is there information that is best presented as a chart or a table? Do you need headings? Would diagrams, photographs, or other illustrations help you explain the information?	15–17

Generating Ideas and Text

Good reports share certain features that make them useful and interesting to readers. Remember that your goal is to present information clearly and accurately. Start by exploring your topic.

Explore what you already know about your topic.   Write out whatever you know or want to know about your topic, perhaps by **FREEWRITING, LISTING,** or **CLUSTERING.** Why are you interested in this topic? What questions do you have about it? Such questions can help you decide what you'd like to focus on and how you need to direct your research efforts.

199–202

Narrow your topic.   To write a good report, you need to narrow your focus—and to narrow your focus, you need to know a fair amount about your subject. If you are assigned to write on a subject like biodiversity, for example, you need to know what it is, what key issues are, and so on. If you do, you can simply list or brainstorm possibilities, choose one, and start your research. If you don't know much about the subject, though, you need to do some research to discover focused, workable topics. This research may shape your thinking and change your focus. Start with **SOURCES** that can give you a general sense of the subject, such as an encyclopedia entry, a magazine article, an Internet site, perhaps an interview with an expert. Your goal at this point is simply to find out what issues your potential topic might include and then to focus your efforts on an aspect of the topic you will be able to cover.

340–53

Come up with a tentative thesis.   Once you narrow your topic, write out a statement that explains what you plan to report or explain. A good **THESIS** is potentially interesting (to you and your readers) and limits your topic enough to make it manageable. Eastman and Burrell state their thesis in the form of a direct statement—"roller coasters work because of two main principles: the laws of conservation of energy and gravity"—

251–52

assuming that readers will know that in the essay that follows those two principles will be explained. DeRoven, on the other hand, lays out exactly what will be discussed: "This paper will explore the Great Depression through the eyes of ordinary Americans in the most impoverished region in the country, the American South, in order to detail how they endured and how the government assisted them in this difficult era." At this point, however, you need only a tentative thesis that will help focus any research you do.

Do any necessary research, and revise your thesis. To focus your research efforts, **OUTLINE** the aspects of your topic that you expect to discuss. Identify any aspects that require additional research and **DEVELOP A RESEARCH PLAN.** Expect to revise your outline as you do your research, since more information will be available for some aspects of your topic than others, some may prove irrelevant to your topic, and some may turn out to be more than you need. You'll need to revisit your tentative thesis once you've done any research, to finalize what your statement will be.

○ 203–04
● 331–39

Ways of Organizing a Report

Reports can be organized in various ways. Here are three common ones:

[Reports on topics that are unfamiliar to readers]

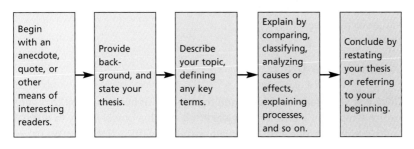

Begin with an anecdote, quote, or other means of interesting readers. → Provide background, and state your thesis. → Describe your topic, defining any key terms. → Explain by comparing, classifying, analyzing causes or effects, explaining processes, and so on. → Conclude by restating your thesis or referring to your beginning.

[Reports on an event]

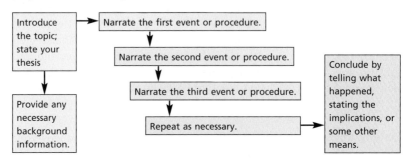

[Reports that compare and contrast]

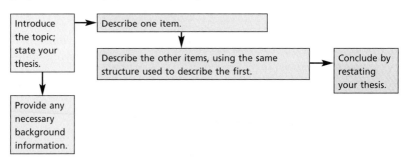

Many reports use a combination of organizational structures; don't be afraid to use whatever method of organization best suits your material and your purpose.

Writing Out a Draft

205–07 ⦾

Once you have generated ideas and thought about how you want to organize your report, it's time to start **DRAFTING**. Do this quickly—try to write a complete draft in one sitting, concentrating on getting the report on paper or screen and on putting in as much detail as you can.

Writing that reports information often calls for certain writing strategies. The report on the hijacking of United 175, for example, uses **NARRATION,**
telling readers what happened, minute by minute. The article about roller
coasters requires the **DEFINITION** of concepts such as "gravity" and "conservation of energy." When you're reporting on a topic your readers aren't
familiar with, you may wish to **COMPARE** it with something more familiar;
you can find useful advice on these and other writing strategies in Part 4
of this book.

304–12
275–84
266–74

Draft a beginning.   Essays that report information often need to begin
in a way that will get your audience interested in the topic. Here are a few
ways of **BEGINNING:**

239–45

- *Simply state your thesis.* DeRoven begins his essay about "the greatest
  generation" this way. Opening with a thesis works well when you can
  assume your readers have enough familiarity with your topic that you
  don't need to give detailed background information.

- *Open by asking a question.* Eastman and Burrell open this way, asking
  a question about roller coasters that their report then answers: "Ever
  wonder how they get the energy to deliver thrill after thrill?"

- *Jump right in.* The writers of the report on the hijacking of United 175
  can assume their audience is familiar with the events they are reporting on, so they open by saying simply that "United Airlines Flight 175
  was scheduled to depart for Los Angeles at 8:00."

Draft an ending.   Think about what you want your readers to read last.
An effective **ENDING** leaves them thinking about your topic.

245–48

- *Summarize your main points.* This is a good way to end when you've
  presented several key points you want readers to remember. Eastman
  and Burrell end this way when they write "Remember, the energy does
  not increase, decrease, or disappear; it just changes from one form to
  the other."

- *Point out the implications of your report.* DeRoven concludes with a paragraph explaining that "The federal action that fueled the Southern

economy during the Great Depression changed the way of life for the better and helped Southerners endure a time of great despair."

- *Frame your report by referring to its introduction.* DeRoven begins and ends his report by mentioning "the greatest generation."

- *Tell what happened.* If you are reporting on an event, you could conclude by telling how it turns out. The report on the hijacking of United 175 ends powerfully by simply saying that "All on board, along with an unknown number of people in the tower, were killed instantly."

Come up with a title. You'll want a title that tells readers something about your subject—and makes them want to know more. Eastman and Burrell, for instance, get our interest in their report on how roller coasters work with the title "The Science of Screams," and tell us something about the subject of their report in a subtitle, "Laws of Physics Instill Thrills in Roller Coasters." 250–54 See the chapter on **GUIDING YOUR READER** for tips on coming up with titles that are informative and enticing enough to make readers wish to read on.

Considering Matters of Design

You'll probably write your report in paragraph form, but think about the information you're presenting and how you can design and format it to make it as easy as possible for your readers to understand. You might ask yourself these questions:

- 454–55 What is an appropriate **TYPEFACE?** Something serious like Times Roman, something traditional like Courier, something else?

- 456–57 Would it help your readers if you divided your report into shorter sections and added **HEADINGS?**

- 455–56 Is there any information that would be easier to follow if it were in a **LIST?**

- 458–60 Could any of your information be summarized in a **TABLE?**

- 458–62 Do you have any data that readers would more easily understand in the form of a bar **GRAPH,** line graph, or pie chart?

- Would **ILLUSTRATIONS** — diagrams, photos, drawings, and so on — help you explain anything in your report?

458–62

Getting Response and Revising

The following questions can help you study your draft with a critical eye. **GETTING RESPONSE** from others is always good, and these questions can guide their reading, too. Make sure they know your purpose and audience.

213–14

- Do the title and opening sentences get readers' interest? If not, how might they do so?

- What information does this text provide, and for what purpose?

- Does the introduction explain why this information is being presented? Does it place the topic in a larger context?

- Are all key terms defined?

- As you read, do you have any questions? Is more information or explanation needed? Where might an example help you understand something?

- Is any information presented visually, with a chart, graph, table, drawing, or photograph? If so, is it clear how these illustrations relate to the larger text? Is there any text that would be more easily understood if it were presented visually?

- Does the organization help make sense of the information? Does the text include description, comparison, definition, or any other writing strategies? Does the topic or rhetorical situation call for any particular strategies?

- If the report cites any sources, are they quoted, paraphrased, or summarized effectively (and with appropriate documentation)?

- Does the report end in a satisfying way? What are readers left thinking?

These questions should identify aspects on your report you need to work on. When it's time to **REVISE,** make sure your report appeals to your audience and achieves your purpose as successfully as possible.

214–16

Editing and Proofreading

Readers equate correctness with the writer's competence. Once you've revised your draft, follow these guidelines for **EDITING** a report:

219–22 ⊙

- Check your use of key terms. Repeating key words is acceptable in reports; synonyms for unfamiliar words may confuse readers while the repetition of key words or the use of clearly identified pronouns can be genuinely helpful.

254 ◆

- Check your use of **TRANSITIONS** to be sure you have them where you need them.

456–57 ☐

- If you have included **HEADINGS,** make sure they're parallel in structure and consistent in design.

458–62 ☐

- Make sure that any photos or other **ILLUSTRATIONS** have captions, that charts and graphs have headings — and that all are referred to in the main text. Have you used white space effectively to separate sections of your report and to highlight graphic elements?

375–449 ●

- Check any **DOCUMENTATION** to see that it follows the appropriate style without mistakes.

222–23 ⊙

- **PROOFREAD** and spell-check your report carefully.

Taking Stock of Your Work

- How well did you convey the information? Is it complete enough for your audience's needs?
- What strategies did you rely on, and how did they help you achieve your purpose?
- How well did you organize the report?
- How did you go about researching the information for this piece?
- How did you go about drafting this piece?

■ rhetorical situations ▲ genres ○ processes ◆ strategies ● research mla/apa ☐ media/ design

- Did you use any tables, graphs, diagrams, photographs, illustrations, or other graphics effectively?
- How did others' responses influence your writing?
- What did you do especially well?
- What could still be improved?
- What would you do differently next time?

See Chapter 27 if you are required to submit your report in a writing **PORTFOLIO.** See also Chapter 10 on **ABSTRACTS** if your report requires one; Chapter 13 on **LAB REPORTS,** a kind of report written in the sciences; and Chapter 16 on **PROFILES,** a report based on firsthand research.

224–35
107–11

127–36

153–59

9 Arguing a Position

Everything we say or do presents some kind of argument, takes some kind of position. Often we take overt positions: "Everyone in the United States is entitled to affordable health care." "The university needs to offer more language courses." "Ice-T shouldn't have gone into acting." Some scholars claim that everything makes some kind of argument, from yellow ribbons that honor U.S. troops to a yellow smiley face, which might be said to argue for a good day. In college course work, you are constantly called on to argue positions: in an English class, you may argue for a certain interpretation of a poem; in a business course, you may argue for the merits of a flat tax; in a linguistics class, you may argue that English should not be made the official language of the United States. All of those positions are arguable — people of goodwill can agree or disagree with them and present reasons and evidence to support their positions. This chapter provides detailed guidelines for writing an essay that argues a position. We'll begin with three good examples.

Readings

ANNA QUINDLEN
Still Needing the F Word

Anna Quindlen is a columnist for Newsweek, *where this essay appeared in October 2003. In it, she argues that the goals defined by the feminist movement have not yet been achieved.*

> Let's use the F word here. People say it's inappropriate, offensive, that it puts people off. But it seems to me it's the best way to begin, when it's simultaneously devalued and invaluable.

Feminist. Feminist, feminist, feminist.

Conventional wisdom has it that we've moved on to a postfeminist era, which is meant to suggest that the issues have been settled, the inequities addressed, and all is right with the world. And then suddenly from out of the South like Hurricane Everywoman, a level '03 storm, comes something like the new study on the status of women at Duke University, and the notion that we're post-anything seems absurd. Time to use the F word again, no matter how uncomfortable people may find it.

Fem-i-nism n. 1. Belief in the social, political, and economic equality of the sexes.

That wasn't so hard, was it? Certainly not as hard as being a female 5 undergraduate at Duke, where apparently the operative ruling principle is something described as "effortless perfection," in which young women report expending an enormous amount of effort on clothes, shoes, workout programs, and diet. And here's a blast from the past: they're expected "to hide their intelligence in order to succeed with their male peers."

"Being 'cute' trumps being smart for women in the social environment," the report concludes.

That's not postfeminist. That's prefeminist. Betty Friedan wrote *The Feminine Mystique* exactly forty years ago, and yet segments of the Duke report could have come right out of her book. One seventeen-year-old girl told Friedan, "I used to write poetry. The guidance office says I have this creative ability and I should be at the top of the class and have a great future. But things like that aren't what you need to be popular. The important thing for a girl is to be popular."

Of course, things have changed. Now young women find themselves facing not one but two societal, and self-imposed, straitjackets. Once they obsessed about being the perfect homemaker and meeting the standards of their male counterparts. Now they also obsess about being the perfect professional and meeting the standards of their male counterparts. In the decades since Friedan's book became a best seller, women have won the right to do as much as men do. They just haven't won the right to do as little as men do. Hence, effortless perfection.

While young women are given the impression that all doors are open, all boundaries down, empirical evidence is to the contrary. A study from Princeton issued at the same time as the Duke study showed that faculty women in the sciences reported less satisfaction in their jobs and less of a sense of belonging than their male counterparts. Maybe that's because they made up only 14 percent of the faculty in those disciplines or because one out of four reported their male colleagues occasionally or frequently engaged in unprofessional conduct focusing on gender issues.

[In the 2003 election for governor,] Californians were willing to 10 ignore Arnold Schwarzenegger's alleged career as a serial sexual bigot, despite a total of sixteen women coming forward to say he thought nothing of reaching up your skirt or into your blouse. (Sure, they're only allegations. But it was Arnold himself who said that where there's smoke, there's fire. In this case, there was a conflagration.) The fact that one of the actor's defenses was that he didn't realize this was objectionable — and that voters were OK with that — speaks volumes about enduring assumptions about women. What if he'd habitually publicly humiliated black men, or Latinos, or Jews? Yet the revelation that the guy often demeaned women with his hands was written off as partisan politics and even personal behavior. Personal behavior is when you have a girlfriend. When you touch someone intimately without her consent, it's sexual battery.

The point is not that the world has not changed for women since Friedan's book lobbed a hand grenade into the homes of pseudohappy housewives who couldn't understand the malaise that accompanied sparkling Formica and good-looking kids. Hundreds of arenas, from government office to the construction trades, have opened to working women. Of course, when it leaks out that the Vatican is proposing to scale back on the use of altar girls, it shows that the forces of reaction are always waiting, whether beneath hard hats or miters.

But the world hasn't changed as much as we like to tell ourselves. Otherwise *The Feminine Mystique* wouldn't feel so contemporary. Otherwise Duke University wouldn't find itself concentrating on eating disorders and the recruitment of female faculty. Otherwise the governor-elect of California wouldn't be a guy who thinks it's "playful" to grab and grope, and the voters wouldn't ratify that attitude. Part fair game, part perfection: that's a tough standard for 51 percent of everyone. The first women's rights activists a century ago set out to prove, in Friedan's words, "that woman was not a passive empty mirror." How dispiriting it would be to those long-ago heroines to read of the women at Duke focused on their "cute" reflections in the eyes of others. The F word is not an expletive but an ideal—one that still has a way to go.

Quindlen offers evidence from a variety of sources—feminist scholarship, current events, a research study—to argue her position that the ideals of feminism have still not been met. She adopts an informal tone, which may help readers identify with her as she discusses values they may think they do not share with her. Since this essay appeared in a newsmagazine, Quindlen follows the convention of citing her sources only informally in the text, rather than offering exact citations and a list of references, as academic writers are expected to do.

LAWRENCE LESSIG

Some Like It Hot

This essay on electronic piracy appeared in Wired *magazine in March 2004. Lawrence Lessig is an authority on copyright law. He teaches at Stanford Law School, where he founded its Center for Internet and Society.*

If piracy means using the creative property of others without their permission, then the history of the content industry is a history of piracy. Every important sector of big media today—film, music, radio, and cable TV—was born of a kind of piracy. The consistent story is how each generation welcomes the pirates from the last. Each generation—until now.

The Hollywood film industry was built by fleeing pirates. Creators and directors migrated from the East Coast to California in the early twentieth century in part to escape controls that film patents granted the inventor Thomas Edison. These controls were exercised through the Motion Pictures Patents Company, a monopoly "trust" based on Edison's creative property and formed to vigorously protect his patent rights.

California was remote enough from Edison's reach that filmmakers like Fox and Paramount could move there and, without fear of the law, pirate his inventions. Hollywood grew quickly, and enforcement of federal law eventually spread west. But because patents granted their holders a truly "limited" monopoly of just seventeen years (at that time), the patents had expired by the time enough federal marshals appeared. A new industry had been founded, in part from the piracy of Edison's creative property.

Meanwhile, the record industry grew out of another kind of piracy. At the time that Edison and Henri Fourneaux invented machines for reproducing music (Edison the phonograph; Fourneaux the player piano), the law gave composers the exclusive right to control copies and public performances of their music. Thus, in 1900, if I wanted a copy of Phil Russel's 1899 hit, "Happy Mose," the law said I would have to pay for the right to get a copy of the score, and I would also have to pay for the right to perform it publicly.

But what if I wanted to record "Happy Mose" using Edison's phono- 5 graph or Fourneaux's player piano? Here the law stumbled. If I simply sang the piece into a recording device in my home, it wasn't clear that I owed the composer anything. And more important, it wasn't clear whether I owed the composer anything if I then made copies of those recordings. Because of this gap in the law, I could effectively use someone else's song without paying the composer anything. The composers (and publishers) were none too happy about this capacity to pirate.

In 1909, Congress closed the gap in favor of the composer and the recording artist, amending copyright law to make sure that composers would be paid for "mechanical reproductions" of their music. But rather than simply granting the composer complete control over the right to make such reproductions, Congress gave recording artists a right to record the music, at a price set by Congress, after the composer allowed it to be recorded once. This is the part of copyright law that makes cover songs possible. Once a composer authorizes a recording of his song, others are free to record the same song, so long as they pay the original composer a fee set by the law. So, by limiting musicians' rights—by partially pirating their creative work—record producers and the public benefit.

A similar story can be told about radio. When a station plays a composer's work on the air, that constitutes a "public performance." Copyright law gives the composer (or copyright holder) an exclusive right to public performances of his work. The radio station thus owes the composer money.

Both photos from Bettmann / Corbis

But when the station plays a record, it is not only performing a copy of the *composer's* work. The station is also performing a copy of the *recording artist's* work. It's one thing to air a recording of "Happy Birthday" by the local children's choir; it's quite another to air a recording of it by the Rolling Stones or Lyle Lovett. The recording artist is adding to the value of the composition played on the radio station. And if the law were perfectly consistent, the station would have to pay the artist for his work, just as it pays the composer.

But it doesn't. This difference can be huge. Imagine you compose a piece of music. You own the exclusive right to authorize public performances of that music. So if Madonna wants to sing your song in public, she has to get your permission.

Imagine she does sing your song, and imagine she likes it a lot. 10 She then decides to make a recording of your song, and it becomes a top hit. Under today's law, every time a radio station plays your song, you get some money. But Madonna gets nothing, save the indirect effect on the sale of her CDs. The public performance of her recording is not a "protected" right. The radio station thus gets to pirate the value of Madonna's work without paying her a dime.

No doubt, one might argue, the promotion artists get is worth more than the performance rights they give up. Maybe. But even if that's the case, this is a choice that the law ordinarily gives to the creator. Instead, the law gives the radio station the right to take something for nothing.

Cable TV, too: When entrepreneurs first started installing cable in 1948, most refused to pay the networks for the content that they hijacked and delivered to their customers — even though they were basically selling access to otherwise free television broadcasts. Cable companies were thus Napsterizing broadcasters' content, but more egregiously than anything Napster ever did — Napster never charged for the content it enabled others to give away.

Broadcasters and copyright owners were quick to attack this theft. As then Screen Actors Guild president Charlton Heston put it, the cable outfits were "free riders" who were "depriving actors of compensation."

Copyright owners took the cable companies to court. Twice the Supreme Court held that the cable companies owed the copyright owners nothing. The debate shifted to Congress, where almost thirty years later it resolved the question in the same way it had dealt with phonographs and player pianos. Yes, cable companies would have to pay for the content that they broadcast, but the price they would have to pay was not set by the copyright owner. Instead, lawmakers set the price so that the broadcasters couldn't veto the emerging technologies of cable. The companies thus built their empire in part upon a piracy of the value created by broadcasters' content.

As the history of film, music, radio, and cable TV suggest, even if   15 some piracy is plainly wrong, not all piracy is. Or at least not in the sense that the term is increasingly being used today. Many kinds of piracy are useful and productive, either to create new content or foster new ways of doing business. Neither our tradition, nor any tradition, has ever banned all piracy.

This doesn't mean that there are no questions raised by the latest piracy concern — peer-to-peer file sharing. But it does mean that we need to understand the harm in P2P sharing a bit more before we condemn it to the gallows.

Like the original Hollywood, P2P sharing seeks to escape an overly controlling industry. And like the original recording and radio indus-

tries, it is simply exploiting a new way of distributing content. But unlike cable TV, no one is selling the content that gets shared on P2P services. This difference distinguishes P2P sharing. We should find a way to protect artists while permitting this sharing to survive.

Much of the "piracy" that file sharing enables is plainly legal and good. It provides access to content that is technically still under copyright but that is no longer commercially available — in the case of music, some four million tracks. More important, P2P networks enable sharing of content that copyright owners want shared, as well as work already in the public domain. This clearly benefits authors and society.

Moreover, much of the sharing — which is referred to by many as piracy — is motivated by a new way of spreading content made possible by changes in the technology of distribution. Thus, consistent with the tradition that gave us Hollywood, radio, the music industry, and cable TV, the question we should be asking about file sharing is how best to preserve its benefits while minimizing (to the extent possible) the wrongful harm it causes artists.

The question is one of balance, weighing the protection of the law 20 against the strong public interest in continued innovation. The law should seek that balance, and that balance will be found only with time.

Lessig argues that the "piracy" that Napster and other peer-to-peer music-sharing services are accused of is similar to that practiced by every other electronic medium in the last one hundred years. He offers a clear definition of piracy and carefully supports his assertions with historical evidence for each one.

ANDY MᴄDONIE

Airport Security: What Price Safety?

Here is an argument written in 2002 by Andy McDonie for his first-year writing course at Wright State University, in Dayton, Ohio.

We all want to feel safe. Most Americans lock their doors at night, lock their cars in parking lots, try to park near buildings or under lights, and wear seat belts. Many invest in expensive security systems, carry pepper spray or a stun gun, keep guns in their homes, or take self-defense classes. Obviously, safety and security are important issues in American life. But there are times when people are unable to protect themselves.

Air travel is one such situation. There is nowhere to run, and no one is allowed to carry weapons that could be used for self-defense on board an aircraft. Therefore, it is important that no one at all be allowed on board an airplane with a gun or any other weapon.

Unfortunately, this is much more easily said than done.

Though airlines and the U.S. government are taking many steps to ensure the safety of passengers, there is still a risk. In light of recent hijackings by militant Islamic Arabs, it would be very easy and economically sensible to target Middle Easterners for security checks at airports and anywhere else security could be an issue. This would allow everyone else who is statistically less likely to be a terrorist to travel more freely without long delays. However, as sensible and economical as this solution could be, it must never be allowed here in the United States.

One airline that targets passengers for security checks based on ethnicity and gender is El Al, Israel's national airline. In "Unfriendly Skies Are No Match for El Al," Vivienne Walt, a writer for *USA Today*, describes her experience flying with this airline. Before anyone gets on any one of El Al's aircraft, he or she has to go through an extensive interview process. The intensity of the process depends on categories into which passengers fit. Jews are in the low-risk category. Most foreigners are medium risk, while travelers with Arabic names are very high-risk. Women traveling alone are considered high risk as well, because authorities fear that a Palestinian lover might plant a bomb in their luggage. Screening passengers takes time; El Al passengers must arrive three hours before their scheduled departure, and even so flights are sometimes delayed because of the screening process.

El Al is secretive about what goes on in its interviews, and company spokespersons admit that the airline will deny boarding privileges to certain ticket holders, but their security record is the best in the world. Since these and other policies took effect over twenty years ago, not one terrorist act has occurred on an El Al plane (Walt 1D–2D). El Al's anti-terrorist system is indisputably effective. But is it ethical?

Here in the United States, airports and airlines are racing to meet new security standards set by the federal government. As travelers are

5

rhetorical situations

genres

processes

strategies

research mla/apa

media/ design

flying and as new regulations are being implemented, more and more air travelers are getting pulled aside for "random" security checks. In my experience, these checks may not be as random as the airports would like the public to think. Since September 11, 2001, I have spent several hours at airport gates and have boarded eight separate flights. Not once have I been delayed at the gate for a random security check. I am a young white male. However, I have seen who does get checked. I have seen some middle-class Caucasians checked, but at least from what I have observed, that is not the norm. Minorities are a target, especially minorities traveling alone. I have seen a seemingly disproportionate number of nonwhites delayed at gates. I have also noticed that women traveling alone or with other women are often picked out.

History has many examples of the U.S. government's suspending or abridging the rights of certain groups during wartime. In the Civil War, Abraham Lincoln suspended the right of habeas corpus (which allows prisoners to have their detention reviewed by a court of law), an act that was later ruled unconstitutional. During the First World War, freedom of speech was restricted by the Supreme Court, which declared, "When a nation is at war, many things that might be said in time of peace are such a hindrance to its effort that their utterance will not be endured so long as men fight and that no Court could regard them as protected by any constitutional right." During the same war, Pittsburgh banned Beethoven's music; the Los Angeles Board of Education forbade discussions of peace in school; and in many states German could not be taught. Perhaps the worst example of American wartime discrimination occurred during World War II, when Japanese Americans had their property seized and were forced to live in internment camps. Lieutenant General John L. DeWitt, one commander enforcing the internment, justified this policy by saying that "in the war in which we are now engaged, racial affiliations are not severed by migration. The Japanese race is an enemy race. . . . A jap is a jap" (O'Brien 419–25).

What can we learn from this grim history? Ben Franklin said that if we sacrifice freedom for security, we get neither. Though safety is important, at what price should it be bought? And if we sacrifice our freedoms for it, are we really safe? It would be easy for most Americans to justify restricting the rights of just one minority group. After all, most people would not be affected. But if we can oppress people from the Middle East during a time of crisis, we can do the same to any other group of people at any time. That is not the way Americans should have to live.

There is an additional point here: not all terrorists are of Middle Eastern descent. If we were to target Middle Easterners for security checks, many Muslims might have difficulty boarding an aircraft, but the Unabomber or Timothy McVeigh would have had little or no trouble. Acts of murder, political turmoil, and terrorism are carried out by persons of all races and nationalities. Focusing on one group might only simplify the process for non-Arab terrorists.

New security measures exist in many European airports. Some use retinal scans, a high-tech way of identifying passengers by scanning their eyes. Most screen checked baggage and match checked baggage to passenger lists. Many airports interview all passengers. According to one German frequent flier, "The level of scrutiny at a checkpoint says a lot about security at the whole airport to me. I feel safer flying to the United States than flying back" (Davis).

Clearly more changes need to be made at airports worldwide. Though it would be more economically sensible to target certain groups, doing so would be unethical. If the rights of one group of people are jeopardized, then the rights of all Americans are jeopardized. Freedom must not be sacrificed for security.

Discriminating against a single group would also be ineffective. Many people of Arab descent would have difficulty boarding an aircraft, but white, black, or Asian terrorists could move through security easily. Targeting certain groups would be easier but less than fair. Instead of focusing on one or more groups, airlines should treat all passengers equally, using technology that is currently available.

Works Cited

Davis, Aaron. "Guarding Europe's Airports—Future of Air Travel Visible in Tight Security Terminal." *San Jose Mercury News.* 22 Nov. 2001: A1+.

O'Brien, Ed. "In War, Is Law Silent?" *Social Education* 65 (2001) 419–25.

Walt, Vivienne. "Unfriendly Skies Are No Match for El Al." *USA Today* 1 Oct. 2001: 1D–2D.

This argument offers a clear statement of its position: people of Middle Eastern descent must not be targeted for airport security checks. McDonie organizes his essay carefully: after introducing the topic, he contrasts El Al's procedures with

those of U.S. air carriers, provides examples of suspended rights in the United States during wartime, presents the core of his argument against targeted searches, and concludes by acknowledging the need for improved security.

Key Features / Arguments

A clear and arguable position.   At the heart of every argument is a claim with which people may reasonably disagree. Some claims are not arguable because they're completely subjective, matters of taste or opinion ("I hate sauerkraut"), because they are a matter of fact ("The first *Star Wars* movie came out in 1977"), or because they are based on belief or faith ("There is life after death"). To be arguable, a position must reflect one of at least two points of view, making reasoned argument necessary: Internet file sharing should (or should not) be considered fair use; airport security should target certain groups (or should treat everyone the same). In college writing, you will often argue not that a position is correct but that it is plausible — that it is reasonable, supportable, and worthy of being taken seriously.

Necessary background information.   Sometimes we need to provide some background on a topic we are arguing so that readers can understand what is being argued. McDonie establishes the need for special measures to ensure airline passengers' safety before launching his argument against targeting specific groups for security checks; Quindlen offers a characterization of the current connotations of the term *feminism* and provides its historical context as context for her argument that it's a term we're "still needing."

Good reasons.   By itself, a position does not make an argument; the argument comes when a writer offers reasons to back the position up. There are many kinds of good reasons. Some are a matter of defining — Quindlen bases her argument about feminism on a dictionary definition of the word. Lessig makes his argument by comparing, showing many examples of so-called piracy in other media. McDonie's main reason for his position that we should not target Middle Easterners for airport security checks is that doing so is unethical.

Convincing support for each reason.   It's one thing to give reasons for your position. You then need to offer support for your reasons: facts, statistics, expert testimony, anecdotal evidence, case studies, textual evidence. All three essays use a mix of these types of support. Quindlen uses statistics from a Princeton study to support her claim that women do not yet have job equality in comparison with men; Lessig offers facts from the history of the broadcast media to support his argument for file sharing.

Appeals to readers' values.   Effective arguers try to appeal to readers' values and emotions. Both Quindlen and McDonie appeal to basic values — Quindlen to the value of equality, McDonie to the values of freedom and security. These are deeply held values that we may not think about very much and as a result may see as common ground we share with the writers. And some of Quindlen's evidence appeals to emotion — the examples she offers from Duke University and the state of California are likely to evoke an emotional response in many, if not all, readers.

A trustworthy tone.   Arguments can stand or fall on the way readers perceive the writer. Very simply, readers need to trust the person who's making the argument. One way of winning this trust is by demonstrating that you know what you're talking about. Lessig offers plenty of facts to show his knowledge of copyright history — and he does so in a self-assured tone. There are many other ways of establishing yourself (and your argument) as trustworthy — by showing that you have some experience with your subject (as McDonie does), that you're fair (as Quindlen suggests when she says that "hundreds of arenas . . . have opened to working women"), and of course that you're honest.

Careful consideration of other positions.   No matter how reasonable and careful we are in arguing our positions, others may disagree or offer counterarguments or hold other positions. We need to consider those other views and to acknowledge and, if possible, refute them in our written arguments. Quindlen, for example, acknowledges that women today have more employment opportunities than they did forty years ago, but she refers to the Duke study to refute any argument that women have attained complete equality with men.

rhetorical situations | genres | processes | strategies | research mla/apa | media/ design

A GUIDE TO ARGUING A POSITION

Choosing a Topic

A fully developed argument requires significant work and time, so choosing a topic in which you're interested is very important. Students find that widely debated topics such as "animal rights" or "gun control" can be difficult to write on because they seldom have a personal connection to them. Better topics include those that

- interest you right now,
- are focused, but not too narrowly,
- have some personal connection to your life.

One good way to **GENERATE IDEAS** for a topic that meets those three criteria is to explore your own roles in life.

199–204

Start with your roles in life.   On a piece of paper, make four columns with the headings "Personal," "Family," "Public," and "School." Below each heading, **LIST** the roles you play that relate to it. Here is a list one student wrote:

200–01

Personal	Family	Public	School
gamer	son	voter	college student
dog owner	younger	homeless-shelter	work-study
old-car owner	brother	volunteer	employee
male	grandson	American	dorm resident
white		resident	primary-education
middle-class		of Ohio	major

Identify issues that interest you. Think, then, about issues or controversies that may concern you as a member of one or more of those groups. For instance, as a primary-education major, this student cares about the controversy over whether kids should be taught to read by phonics or by whole language methods. As a college student, he cares about the costs of a college education. Issues that stem from these subjects could include the following: Should reading be taught by phonics or whole language? Should college cost less than it does?

Pick four or five of the roles you list. In five or ten minutes, identify issues that concern or affect you as a member of each of those roles. It might help to word each issue as a question starting with *Should*.

Choose one issue to write about. Remember that the issue should be interesting to you and have some connection to your life. It is a tentative choice; if you find later that you have trouble writing about it, simply go back to your list of roles or issues and choose another.

Considering the Rhetorical Situation

3–4 · **PURPOSE** — Do you want to persuade your audience to do or think something? change their minds? consider alternative views? accept your position as plausible — see that you have thought carefully about an issue and researched it appropriately?

5–8 · **AUDIENCE** — Who is your intended audience? What do they likely know and believe about this issue? How personal is it for them? To what extent are they likely to agree or disagree with you? Why? What common ground can you find with them?

12–14 · **STANCE** — How do you want your audience to perceive you? As an authority on your topic? As someone much like them? As calm? reasonable? impassioned or angry? something else? What's your attitude toward your topic, and why?

■ **MEDIA / DESIGN**   What media will you use, and how do your media affect your argument? If you're writing on paper, does your argument call for photos or charts? If you're giving an oral presentation, should you put your reasons and support on slides? If you're writing on the Web, should you add links to counterarguments?

15–17

Generating Ideas and Text

Most essays that successfully argue a position share certain features that make them interesting and persuasive. Remember that your goal is to stake out a position and convince your readers that it is plausible.

Explore what you already know about the issue.   Write out whatever you know about the issue by freewriting or as a **LIST** or **OUTLINE.** Why are you interested in this topic? What is your position on it at this point, and why? What aspect do you think you'd like to focus on? Where do you need to focus your research efforts? This activity can help you discover what more you need to learn. Chances are you'll need to learn a lot more about the issue before you even decide what position to take.

○ 199–201
○ 203–04

Do some research.   At this point, try to get an overview. Start with one **GENERAL SOURCE** of information that will give you a sense of the ins and outs of your issue, one that isn't overtly biased. *Time, Newsweek,* and other national weekly newsmagazines can be good starting points on current issues; encyclopedias are better for issues that are not so current. For some issues, you may need to **INTERVIEW** an expert. For example, one student who wanted to write about chemical abuse of animals at 4H competitions interviewed an experienced show competitor. Use your overview source to find out the main questions your issue raises and to get some idea about the various ways in which you might argue it.

● 344

● 351–52

Explore the issue strategically.   Most issues may be argued from many different perspectives. You'll probably have some sense of the different views that exist on your issue, but you should explore multiple perspectives before deciding on your position. The following methods are good ways of exploring issues:

275–84 ◆
- As a matter of **DEFINITION.** What is it? How should it be defined? How can *phonics* or *whole language* be defined? How do backers of phonics define it—and how do they define *whole language*? How do advocates of whole language define it—and how do they define *phonics*? Considering these definitions is one way to identify different perspectives on the topic.

260–65 ◆
- As a matter of **CLASSIFICATION.** Can the issue be further divided? What categories might it be broken into? Are there different kinds of "phonics" and "whole language"? Do various subcategories suggest various positions or perhaps a way of supporting a certain position? Are there other ways of categorizing the teaching of reading?

266–74 ◆
- As a matter of **COMPARISON.** Is one way better than another? Is whole language a better way of teaching children to read than phonics? Is phonics a better way than whole language? Is the answer somewhere in the middle?

299–303 ◆
- As a matter of **PROCESS.** Should somebody do something? What? Should teachers use whole language to teach reading? Should they use phonics? Should they use a mix of the two methods?

Reconsider whether the issue can be argued.   Is this issue worth discussing? Why is it important to you and to others? What difference will it make if one position or another prevails? At this point, you want to be sure that your topic is worth arguing about.

Draft a thesis.   Having explored the possibilities, decide your position, and write it out as a complete sentence. For example:

> Pete Rose should not be eligible for the Hall of Fame.
>
> Reading should be taught using a mix of whole language and phonics.
>
> Genetically engineered foods should be permitted in the United States.

Qualify your thesis.   Rarely is a position on an issue a matter of being for or against; in most cases, you'll want to qualify your position—in cer-

rhetorical situations

genres

processes

strategies

research mla/apa

media/ design

tain circumstances, with certain conditions, with these limitations, and so on. This is not to say that we should settle, give in, sell out; rather, it is to say that our position may not be the only "correct" one and that other positions may be valid as well. Qualifying your **THESIS** also makes your topic manageable by limiting it. For example:

◆ 251–52

> Pete Rose should not be eligible for the Hall of Fame, though he should be permitted to contribute to major league baseball in other ways.
>
> Reading should be taught using a mix of phonics and whole language, but whole language should be the dominant method.
>
> Genetically engineered foods should be permitted in the United States if they are clearly labeled as such.

Some questions for qualifying a thesis

- Can it be true in some cases?
- Can it be true at some times?
- Can it be true for some groups or individuals?
- Can it be true under certain circumstances?

Come up with good reasons.   Once you have a thesis, you need to come up with good reasons to convince your readers that it's plausible. Start by stating your position and then answering the question "Why?"

> **Thesis:** Pete Rose should not be eligible for the Hall of Fame. **Why?**
>
> **Underlying reason (because):** He bet on professional baseball games, an illegal practice. **Why?**
>
> **Underlying reason (because):** Professional athletes' gambling on the outcome of games will cause fans to lose faith in professional sports.

As you can see, this exercise can continue indefinitely as the underlying reasons grow more and more general and abstract. You can do the same with other positions:

> **Thesis:** Pete Rose should be eligible for the Hall of Fame. **Why?**
>
> **Underlying reason (because):** He's one of the greatest baseball players of all time. **Why?**

Underlying reason (because): Few players have played with more hustle and passion than Rose.

Write out your position, and then, below it, list several reasons. Think about which reasons are best for your purposes: Which seem the most persuasive? Which are most likely to be accepted by your audience? Which seem to matter the most now? If your list of reasons is short or you think you'll have trouble developing them enough to write an appropriate essay, this is a good time to rethink your topic — before you've invested too much time in it.

Develop support for your reasons. Next, you have to come up with support for your reasons. Here are some of the ways you can offer support:

- facts
- statistics ("A national study found that X percent of . . . ")
- testimony by authorities and experts ("According to X, . . . ")
- anecdotal evidence ("This happened . . . ")
- scenarios ("What if . . . ?")
- case studies and observation ("This is what happened when . . . ")
- textual evidence ("I found this in . . . ")

Some kinds of support are acceptable to certain audiences but not to others. For example, case studies may be readily accepted in certain social sciences but not in the physical sciences; anecdotes or stories may be accepted as evidence in humanities courses but not in engineering. Some audiences will be persuaded by emotional appeals while others will not. You may well need to consult **SOURCES.**

340–53

Identify other positions. Now, think about positions that differ from yours and about the reasons people are likely to give for those positions. Be careful to represent their points of view as accurately and fairly as

rhetorical situations   genres   processes   strategies   research mla/apa   media/design

you can. Then decide whether you need to acknowledge or refute the position.

Acknowledging other positions.   Some positions can't be refuted, but still you need to acknowledge readers' doubts, concerns, and objections to show that you've considered them. Rather than weakening your argument, acknowledging possible objections shows that you've thought about and researched your argument thoroughly. For example, in an essay about his experience growing up homosexual, writer Andrew Sullivan acknowledges that not every young gay man or woman has the same experience: "I should add that many young lesbians and homosexuals seem to have had a much easier time of it. For many, the question of sexual identity was not a critical factor in their life choices or vocation, or even a factor at all." Thus does he qualify his assertions, making his own stance appear to be reasonable. In addition to acknowledging other views, though, you may sometimes shape other views to incorporate them into your own argument.

Refuting other positions.   State the position as clearly and as fairly as you can, and then show why you believe it is wrong. Are the values underlying the position questionable? Is the reasoning flawed? Is the supporting evidence inadequate or faulty? If the argument has some merit but fails on some points, say so, but emphasize its shortcomings. Avoid the **FALLACY** of attacking the person making the argument or bringing up a competing position that no one seriously entertains.

◆ 325–27

Ways of Organizing an Argument

Readers need to be able to follow the reasoning of your argument from beginning to end; your task is to lead them from point to point as you build your case. Sometimes you'll want to give all the reasons for your argument first, followed by discussion of any other positions. Alternatively, you might discuss each reason and any counterargument together.

[Reasons to support your argument, followed by counterarguments]

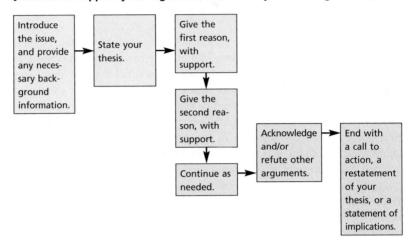

[Reason / counterargument, reason / counterargument]

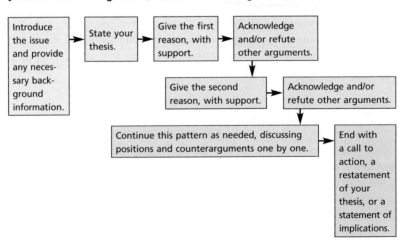

Consider the order in which you discuss your reasons. Usually what comes last is the most emphatic and what comes in the middle is the least emphatic, so you might want to put your most important or strongest reasons first and last.

Writing Out a Draft

Once you have generated ideas, done some research, and thought about how you want to organize your argument, it's time to start **DRAFTING**. Your goal in the initial draft is to develop your argument—you can fill in support and transitions as you revise. You may want to write your first draft in one sitting, so that you can develop your reasoning from beginning to end. Or you may write the main argument first and the introduction and conclusion after you've drafted the body of the essay; many writers find that beginning and ending an essay are the hardest tasks they face. Here is some advice on how you might **BEGIN AND END** your argument:

○ 205–07

◆ 239–49

Draft a beginning. There are various ways to begin an argument essay, depending on your audience and purpose. Here are a few suggestions.

- *Offer background information.* You may need to give your readers information to help them understand your position. McDonie provides a rationale for Americans' desire to fly safely in dangerous times before stating his own position that safety must not be achieved through selective airport security checks.

- *Define a key term.* You may need to show how you're using certain key words. Lessig, for example, defines piracy as "using the creative property of others without their permission" in his first sentence, a definition that is central to his argument.

- *Begin with something that will get readers' attention.* Quindlen's first sentence does just that: "Let's use the F word here." From there, she goes on to argue that feminism "is not an expletive but an ideal."

- *Explain the context for your position.* All arguments are part of a larger, ongoing conversation, so you might begin by showing how your position fits into the arguments others have made. Quindlen does this in her third paragraph when she refers to the "conventional wisdom" that sees feminism as having accomplished all it set out to accomplish.

Draft an ending.   Your conclusion is the chance to wrap up your argument in such a way that readers will remember what you've said. Here are a few ways of concluding an argument essay.

- *Summarize your main points.* Especially when you've presented a complex argument, it can help readers to SUMMARIZE your main point. McDonie sums up his argument with the sentence "Freedom must not be sacrificed for security."

321–22

- *Call for action.* Lessig does this when he concludes by saying the law should seek a balance between copyright law and the need for continued innovation.

- *Frame your argument by referring to the introduction.* Quindlen does this when she ends by saying that "The F word is not an expletive but an ideal—one that still has a way to go."

Come up with a title.   Most often you'll want your title to tell readers something about your topic—and, if possible, to make them want to read on. McDonie covers both bases with his title and subtitle, "Airport Security: What Price Safety?" Quindlen's title doesn't quite tell us what she's writing about, but she probably makes a lot of readers continue reading to see what "Still Needing the F Word" is all about. See the chapter on GUIDING YOUR READER for more advice on composing a good title.

250–54

Considering Matters of Design

You'll probably write your essay in paragraph form, but think about the information you're presenting and how you can design it in such a way as to make your argument as easy as possible for your readers to understand. Think also about whether any visual elements would be more persuasive than plain words.

454–55

- What would be an appropriate TYPEFACE? Something serious like Times Roman? Something traditional like Courier? Something else?

rhetorical situations

genres

processes

strategies

research mla/apa

media/ design

- Would it help your readers if you divided your argument into shorter sections and added **HEADINGS**?

  456–57

- If you're making several points, would they be easier to follow if you set them off in a **LIST**?

  455–56

- Do you have any supporting evidence that would be easier to understand in the form of a bar **GRAPH**, line graph, or pie chart?

  458–60

- Would **ILLUSTRATIONS**—photos, diagrams, or drawings—add support for your argument?

  458–62

Getting Response and Revising

At this point you need to look at your draft closely, and if possible **GET RESPONSE** from others as well. The following are some questions for looking at an argument with a critical eye.

213–14

- Is there sufficient background or context?
- Is the thesis clear and appropriately qualified?
- Are the reasons plausible?
- Is there enough support for these reasons? Is that support appropriate?
- Have you cited enough sources, and are these sources credible?
- Can readers follow the steps in your reasoning?
- Have you considered potential objections or other positions? Are there any others that should be addressed?
- Are source materials documented carefully and completely, with in-text citations and a works cited or references section?

Next it's time to **REVISE**, to make sure your argument offers convincing support, appeals to readers' values, and achieves your purpose.

214–16

Editing and Proofreading

Readers equate correctness with competence. Once you've revised your draft, follow these guidelines for **EDITING** an argument:

219–22

- Make sure that every assertion you make is well supported.

- Check to see that your tone is appropriate and consistent throughout, reflects your **STANCE** accurately, and enhances the argument you're making.

12–14

- Be sure readers will be able to follow the argument; check to see you've provided **TRANSITIONS** and summary statements where necessary.

254

- Make sure you've smoothly integrated **QUOTATIONS, PARAPHRASES,** and **SUMMARIES** from source material into our writing and **DOCUMENTED** them accurately.

358–69
375–449

- Make sure that **ILLUSTRATIONS** have captions and that charts and graphs have headings—and that all are referred to in the main text.

458–62

- **PROOFREAD** and spell-check your essay carefully.

222–23

Taking Stock of Your Work

Take stock of what you've written by writing out answers to these questions:

- What did you do well in this piece?
- What could still be improved?
- How did you go about researching your topic?
- How did others' responses influence your writing?
- How did you go about drafting this piece?
- Did you use graphic elements (tables, graphs, diagrams, photographs, illustrations) effectively? If not, would they have helped?
- What would you do differently next time?
- What have you learned about your writing ability from writing this piece? What do you need to work on in the future?

224–35
120–26
137–46
160–67

See Chapter 27 if you are required to submit your argument as part of a writing **PORTFOLIO.**
See also Chapter 12 on **EVALUATIONS,** Chapter 14 on **LITERARY ANALYSES,** and Chapter 17 on **PROPOSALS** for advice on writing those specific types of arguments.

rhetorical situations   genres   processes   strategies   research mla/apa   media/ design

Abstracts 10

Abstracts are summaries written to give readers the gist of a report or presentation. Sometimes they are published in conference proceedings or databases. In some academic fields, you may be required to include an abstract in a REPORT or as a preview of a presentation you plan to give at an academic or professional conference. Abstracts are brief, typically 100–200 words, sometimes even shorter. Three common kinds are *informative abstracts*, *descriptive abstracts*, and *proposal abstracts*.

▲ 60–81

INFORMATIVE ABSTRACTS

Informative abstracts state in one paragraph the essence of a whole paper about a study or a research project. That one paragraph must mention all the main points or parts of the paper: a description of the study or project, its methods, the results, and the conclusions. Here is an example of the abstract accompanying a seven-page essay that appeared in 2002 in *The Journal of Clinical Psychology*:

> The relationship between boredom proneness and health-symptom reporting was examined. Undergraduate students (N = 200) completed the Boredom Proneness Scale and the Hopkins Symptom Checklist. A multiple analysis of covariance indicated that individuals with high boredom-proneness total scores reported significantly higher ratings on all five subscales of the Hopkins Symptom Checklist (Obsessive–Compulsive, Somatization, Anxiety, Interpersonal Sensitivity, and Depression). The results suggest that boredom proneness may be an important element to consider when assessing symptom reporting. Implications for determining the effects of boredom proneness on psychological- and physical-health symptoms, as well as the application in clinical settings, are discussed.
>
> —Jennifer Sommers and Stephen J. Vodanovich,
> "Boredom Proneness"

The first sentence states the nature of the study being reported. The next summarizes the method used to investigate the problem, and the following one gives the results: students who, according to specific tests, are more likely to be bored are also more likely to have certain medical or psychological symptoms. The last two sentences indicate that the paper discusses those results and examines the conclusion and its implications.

DESCRIPTIVE ABSTRACTS

Descriptive abstracts are usually much briefer than informative abstracts and provide much less information. Rather than summarizing the entire paper, a descriptive abstract functions more as a teaser, providing a quick overview that invites the reader to read the whole. Descriptive abstracts usually do not give or discuss results or set out the conclusion or its implications. A descriptive abstract of the boredom-proneness essay might simply include the first sentence from the informative abstract plus a final sentence of its own:

> The relationship between boredom proneness and health-symptom reporting was examined. The findings and their application in clinical settings are discussed.

PROPOSAL ABSTRACTS

Proposal abstracts contain the same basic information as informative abstracts, but their purpose is very different. You prepare proposal abstracts to persuade someone to let you write on a topic, do a project, conduct an experiment, or present a paper at a scholarly conference. This kind of abstract is not written to introduce a longer piece but rather to stand alone, and often the abstract is written before the paper itself. Titles and other aspects of the proposal deliberately reflect the theme of the proposed work, and you may use the future tense, rather than the past, to describe work not yet completed. Here is a possible proposal for doing research on boredom:

Undergraduate students will complete the Boredom Proneness Scale and the Hopkins Symptom Checklist. A multiple analysis of covariance will be performed to determine the relationship between boredom-proneness total scores and ratings on the five subscales of the Hopkins Symptom Checklist (Obsessive–Compulsive, Somatization, Anxiety, Interpersonal Sensitivity, and Depression).

Key Features / Abstracts

A summary of basic information. An informative abstract includes enough information to substitute for the report itself, a descriptive abstract offers only enough information to let the audience decide whether to read further, and a proposal abstract gives an overview of the planned work.

Objective description. Abstracts present information on the contents of a report or a proposed study; they do not present arguments about or personal perspectives on those contents. The informative abstract on boredom proneness, for example, offers only a tentative conclusion: "The results *suggest* that boredom proneness *may* be an important element to consider."

Brevity. Although the length of abstracts may vary, journals and organizations often restrict them to 120–200 words—meaning you must carefully select and edit your words.

A BRIEF GUIDE TO WRITING

Considering the Rhetorical Situation

▦ **PURPOSE**	Are you giving a brief but thorough overview of a completed study? only enough information to create interest? or a proposal for a planned study or presentation?	3–4
▦ **AUDIENCE**	For whom are you writing this abstract? What information about your project will your readers need?	5–8
▦ **STANCE**	Whatever your stance in the longer work, your abstract must describe it objectively.	12–14

15–17

■ **MEDIA / DESIGN**   How will you set your abstract off from the rest of the paper? If you are publishing it online, will you devote a single Web page to it or make it a preface to the longer work? What format does your audience require?

Generating Ideas and Text

Write the paper first, the abstract last.   You can then use the finished work as the guide for the abstract, which should follow the same basic structure. *Exception:* You may need to write a proposal abstract months before the work it describes will be complete.

Copy and paste key statements.   If you've already written the work, highlight your thesis, objective, or purpose; basic information on your methods; statements of your results; and your conclusion. Copy and paste those sentences into a new document to create a rough version of your abstract.

321–22 ◆

Pare down the information to key ideas.   **SUMMARIZE** the report, editing out any nonessential words and details. In your first sentence, introduce the overall scope of your study. Also include any other information that seems crucial to understanding your paper. Avoid phrases that add unnecessary words, such as "It is concluded that." In general, you probably won't want to use "I"; an abstract should cover ideas, not say what you think or will do.

Conform to any requirements.   In general, an informative abstract should be at most 10 percent as long as the original and no longer than the maximum length allowed. Descriptive abstracts should be shorter still, and proposal abstracts should conform to the requirements of the organization calling for the proposal.

■ rhetorical situations
▲ genres
○ processes
◆ strategies
● research mla/apa
□ media/ design

Ways of Organizing an Abstract

[An informative abstract]

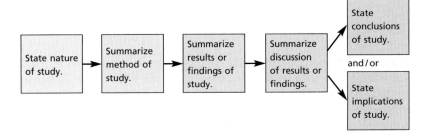

[A descriptive abstract]

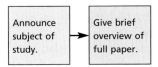

[A proposal abstract]

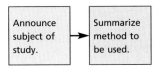

If You Need More Help

See Chapter 23 for guidelines on **DRAFTING,** Chapter 24 on **ASSESSING YOUR DRAFT,** Chapter 25 on **GETTING RESPONSE AND REVISING,** and Chapter 26 on **EDITING AND PROOFREADING.**

○ 205–07
○ 213–18
○ 219–23

11 Annotated Bibliographies

Annotated bibliographies describe, give publication information for, and sometimes evaluate each work on a list of sources. When we do research, we may consult annotated bibliographies to evaluate potential sources. You may also be assigned to create annotated bibliographies to weigh the potential usefulness of sources and to document your search efforts so that teachers can assess your ability to find, describe, and evaluate sources. There are two kinds of annotations, *descriptive* and *evaluative*; both may be brief, consisting only of phrases, or more formal, consisting of sentences and paragraphs. Sometimes an annotated bibliography is introduced by a short statement explaining its scope.

Descriptive annotations simply summarize the contents of each work, without comment or evaluation. They may be very short, just long enough to capture the flavor of the work, like the following excerpt from a bibliography of books and articles on teen films, published in 1997 in the *Journal of Popular Film and Television*.

MICHAEL BENTON, MARK DOLAN, AND REBECCA ZISCH

Teen Film$

In the introduction to his book *The Road to Romance and Ruin*, Jon Lewis points out that over half of the world's population is currently under the age of twenty. This rather startling fact should be enough to make most Hollywood producers drool when they think of the potential profits from a target movie audience. Attracting the largest demographic group is, after all, the quickest way to box-office success. In fact, almost from its beginning, the film industry has recognized the importance of the teenaged audience, with characters such as Andy Hardy and locales such as Ridgemont High and the 'hood.

rhetorical situations

genres

processes

strategies

research mla/apa

media/ design

Beyond the assumption that teen films are geared exclusively toward teenagers, however, film researchers should keep in mind that people of all ages have attended and still attend teen films. Popular films about adolescents are also expressions of larger cultural currents. Studying the films is important for understanding an era's common beliefs about its teenaged population within a broader pattern of general cultural preoccupations.

This selected bibliography is intended both to serve and to stimulate interest in the teen film genre. It provides a research tool for those who are studying teen films and their cultural implications. Unfortunately, however, in the process of compiling this list we quickly realized that it was impossible to be genuinely comprehensive or to satisfy every interest.

Doherty, Thomas, <u>Teenagers and Teenpics: The Juvenilization of American Movies in the 1950s</u>. Boston: Unwin Hyman, 1988.
Historical discussion of the identification of teenagers as a targeted film market.

Foster, Harold M. "Film in the Classroom: Coping with Teen Pics." <u>English Journal</u> 76 (1987): 86-88.
Evaluation of the potential of using teen films such as <u>Sixteen Candles</u>, <u>The Karate Kid</u>, <u>Risky Business</u>, <u>The Flamingo Kid</u>, and <u>The Breakfast Club</u> to instruct adolescents on the difference between film as communication and film as exploitation.

Paul, William. <u>Laughing, Screaming: Modern Hollywood Horror and Comedy</u>. New York: Columbia UP, 1994.
Critical history and discussion of the "gross-out" movie, discusses <u>Porky's</u> and <u>Carrie</u>.

Rapping, Elayne. "Hollywood's Youth Cult Films." <u>Cineaste</u> 16 (1987-88): 14-19.
Historical and chronological assessment of the image of teenagers and the "cult of youth" in American movies from James Dean to the characters in <u>River's Edge</u>.

Washington, Michael, and Marvin J. Berlowitz. "Blaxploitation Films and High School Youth: Swat Superfly." <u>Jump Cut</u> 9 (1975): 23-24.
Marxist reaction to the trend of youth-oriented black action films. Article seeks to illuminate the negative influences the films have on

high school students by pointing out the false ideas about education, morality, and the black family espoused by the heroes in the films.

These annotations are purely descriptive; the authors express none of their own opinions. They describe works as "historical" or "Marxist" but do not indicate whether they're "good." The bibliography entries are documented in MLA style.

Sometimes annotations go into much more detail and are more formal, as the following entry from a bibliography on censorship in the United States illustrates:

> Downs, Robert Bingham, ed. <u>The First Freedom Today: Critical Issues Relating to Censorship and Intellectual Freedom</u>. Chicago: American Library Association, 1984.
> This book is an anthology of writings about censorship and intellectual freedom in the United States. It gives an overview of the history of the subject and examines some of the key issues in the field, especially those that developed during the 1960s and 1970s. It includes excerpts from Thomas Emerson's writings on the First Amendment and then devotes several chapters to exploring censorship topics, including school textbooks and libraries, obscenity and pornography, the teaching of evolution, and topics of special interest to the press, such as libel, privacy, free press, and fair trial.

Evaluative annotations offer opinions on a source as well as describing it. The following two annotations show how an evaluative annotation can differ from a descriptive one:

DESCRIPTIVE ANNOTATION

> Krakauer, Jon. <u>Under the Banner of Heaven: A Story of Violent Faith</u>. New York: Doubleday, 2003.
> Krakauer explores the beliefs and sometimes violent actions of fundamentalist Mormons in the western United States. He focuses his study on two brothers who murdered the wife and infant daughter of their younger brother, believing they were acting under orders from God. Krakauer claims that the beliefs motivating their actions have created a climate promoting violent actions against nonbelievers.

EVALUATIVE ANNOTATION

> Krakauer, Jon. <u>Under the Banner of Heaven: A Story of Violent Faith</u>.
>   New York: Doubleday, 2003.
> A chilling exploration of the beliefs and sometimes violent actions of funda-
> mentalist Mormons in the western United States. Krakauer focuses his study
> on two brothers who brutally murdered the wife and infant daughter of
> their younger brother, believing they were acting under orders from God.
> Krakauer argues that the beliefs that motivated their fanaticism have cre-
> ated a climate that leads to violent actions against nonbelievers and he
> invites comparisons with Islamic extremists. The book offers an unflattering
> portrait of Mormonism in general, as if all Mormons were somehow com-
> plicit in the brothers' extreme actions. It's an implication that's hard to credit.

Key Features / Annotated Bibliographies

A statement of scope.   You need a brief introductory statement to explain
what you're covering. The authors of the bibliography on teen films introduce their bibliography with three paragraphs establishing a context for
the bibliography and announcing their purpose for compiling it.

Complete bibliographic information.   Provide all the information about
the source following one documentation system (**MLA**, **APA**, or another
one) so that your readers or other researchers will be able to find each
source easily.

● 375–449

A concise description of the work.   A good annotation describes each
item as carefully and objectively as possible, giving accurate information
and showing that you understand the source. These qualities will help to
build authority — for you as a writer and for your annotations.

Relevant commentary.   If you write an evaluative bibliography, your
comments should be relevant to your purpose and audience. The best way
to achieve relevance is to consider what questions a potential reader might
have about the sources. The evaluative annotation of the Krakauer book,
for example, assumes readers will want to know more than just what the

book is about and gives some sense of the book's tone and the controversy surrounding it.

Consistent presentation. All annotations should follow a consistent pattern: if one is written in complete sentences, they should all be. Each annotation in the teen films bibliography, for example, begins with a phrase (not a complete sentence) characterizing the work.

A BRIEF GUIDE TO WRITING

Considering the Rhetorical Situation

3–4
■ **PURPOSE** Will your bibliography need to demonstrate the depth or breadth of your research? Will your readers actually track down and use your sources? Do you need or want to convince readers that your sources are good?

5–8
■ **AUDIENCE** For whom are you compiling this bibliography? What does your audience need or want to know about each source?

12–14
■ **STANCE** Are you presenting yourself as an objective describer or evaluator? Or are you expressing a particular point of view toward the sources you evaluate?

15–17
■ **MEDIA / DESIGN** If you are publishing the bibliography online, will you provide links from each annotation to the source itself? Online or off, do you need to distinguish the bibliographic information from the annotation by using a different font?

Generating Ideas and Text

Decide what sources to include. You may be tempted to include in a bibliography every source you find or look at. A better strategy is to include only those sources that you or your readers may find potentially useful in

rhetorical situations genres processes strategies research mla/apa media/design

researching your topic. For an academic bibliography, you need to consider these qualities:

- *Appropriateness.* Is this source relevant to your topic? Is it a primary source or a secondary source? Is it aimed at an appropriate audience? General or specialized? Elementary, advanced, or somewhere in between?
- *Credibility.* Is the author reputable? Is the publication or publishing company reputable? Do its ideas more or less agree with those in other sources you've read?
- *Balance.* Does the source present enough evidence for its assertions? Does it show any particular bias? Does it present countering arguments fairly?
- *Timeliness.* Is the source recent enough? Does it reflect current thinking or research about the subject?

If you need help FINDING SOURCES, see Chapter 40.

340–53

Compile a list of works to annotate. Give the sources themselves in whatever documentation style is required; see the guidelines for MLA and APA styles in Chapters 45 and 46.

378–416
417–49

Determine what kind of bibliography you need to write. Descriptive or evaluative? Will your annotations be in the form of phrases? complete sentences? paragraphs? The form will shape your reading and note taking. If you're writing a descriptive bibliography, your reading goal will be to understand and capture the writer's message as clearly as possible. If you're writing an evaluative bibliography, your annotations must also include your own comments on the source.

Read carefully. To write an annotation, you must understand the source's argument, but when you are writing an annotated bibliography as part of a PROPOSAL, you may have neither the time nor the need to read the whole text. Here's a way of quickly determining whether a source is likely to serve your needs:

160–67

- Check the publisher or sponsor (university press? scholarly journal? popular magazine? Web site sponsored by a reputable organization?).

- Read the preface (of a book), abstract (of a scholarly article), introduction (of an article in a nonscholarly magazine, or a Web site).
- Skim the table of contents or the headings.
- Read the parts that relate specifically to your topic.

Research the writer, if necessary.   If you are required to indicate the writer's credentials, you may need to do additional research. You may find information by typing the writer's name into a search engine or looking up the writer in *Contemporary Authors*. In any case, information about the writer should take up no more than one sentence in your annotation.

285–93 **Summarize the work in a sentence or two.**   **DESCRIBE** it as objectively as possible: even if you are writing an evaluative annotation, you can evaluate the central point of a work better by stating it clearly first. *If you're writing a descriptive annotation, you're done.*

120–26 **Establish criteria for evaluating sources.**   If you're **EVALUATING** sources for a project, you'll need to evaluate them in terms of their usefulness for 12–14 your project, their **STANCE,** and their overall credibility.

Write a brief evaluation of the source.   If you can generalize about the worth of the entire work, fine. You may find, however, that some parts are useful while others are not, and what you write should reflect that mix.

Be consistent — in content, sentence structure, and format.

- *Content.* Try to provide about the same amount of information for each entry; if you're evaluating, evaluate each source, not just some sources.
- *Sentence structure.* Use the same style throughout — complete sentences, brief phrases, or a mix.
- *Format.* Use one documentation style throughout; use consistent **TYPE** for each element in each entry — for example, italicize or underline all book titles.

454–55

rhetorical situations ▪ genres ▲ processes ○ strategies ◆ research mla/apa ● media/ design ☐

Ways of Organizing an Annotated Bibliography

Depending on their purpose, annotated bibliographies may or may not include an introduction. Most annotated bibliographies cover a single topic and so are organized alphabetically by author's or editor's last name. When a work lacks a named author, alphabetize it by the first important word in its title. Consult the documentation system you're using for additional details about alphabetizing works appropriately.

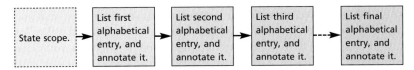

Sometimes an annotated bibliography needs to be organized into several subject areas (or genres, periods, or some other category) and the entries are listed alphabetically within each category. For example, a bibliography about terrorism breaks down into subjects such as "Global Terrorism" and "Weapons of Mass Destruction."

[Multi-category bibliography]

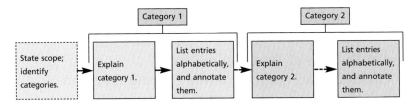

If You Need More Help

See Chapter 23 for guidelines on DRAFTING, Chapter 24 on ASSESSING YOUR DRAFT, Chapter 25 on GETTING RESPONSE AND REVISING, and Chapter 26 on EDITING AND PROOFREADING. See Chapter 27 if you are required to submit your bibliography in a writing PORTFOLIO.

○ 205–35

12 Evaluations

Consumer Reports evaluates MP3 players and laundry detergents. The *Princeton Review* and *US News and World Report* evaluate colleges and universities. You probably consult such sources to make decisions, and you probably evaluate things all the time—when you recommend a film (or not) or a teacher (ditto). An evaluation is at bottom a judgment; you judge something according to certain criteria, supporting your judgment with reasons and evidence. You need to give reasons for evaluating it as you do because often your evaluation will affect your audience's actions: they must see this movie, needn't bother with this book, should be sure to have the Caesar salad at this restaurant, and so on. In the following review, first done for a first-year writing class and later published in the *Dayton Daily News*, Ben Leever offers his evaluation of the TV drama *Dawson's Creek*.

BEN LEEVER

In Defense of Dawson's Creek: *Teen Heroes Inspire Youths Seeking Answers*

Ever since the Warner Brothers network began airing *Dawson's Creek*, religious and parental advocacy groups alike have criticized its sexually charged dialogue and have deemed it inappropriate for its target audience—teenagers and young adults.

The series, set in a small Massachusetts town and portraying the lives of high-school students, inarguably has embarked on controversial terrain. But rather than quick and thoughtless rebuke, the show deserves more serious analysis and even praise.

rhetorical situations | genres | processes | strategies | research mla/apa | media/ design

The first significant accomplishment of the show has been its commitment not to be a carbon copy of the rich-kids-with-petty-problems format (*Beverly Hills 90210*). Charting a riskier course for teen drama, creator Kevin Williamson has steered the series into delicate issues such as verbally abusive parents, manic depression, and, most recently, homosexuality.

The traditional themes of shows for this age group—maturing friendship, teenage rebellion, and romantic relationships—are still present. Gone, however, is the contrived backdrop of singularly happy, two-parent families living in upper-middle-class America.

One serious issue addressed this season is the "outing" of 17-year-old Jack McPhee (Kerr Smith). In recent episodes, he struggled to find his sexual identity as classmates ridiculed and ostracized him because they suspected him of being gay. Although the writers created an unlikely vehicle for this revelation (a teacher forcing Jack to read out loud a poem he composed), as a recent high-school graduate I can verify that had a similar incident occurred at my alma mater, the response would have been every bit as thoughtless and hurtful.

As the New York *Daily News* recently reported, parents groups claim such issues have no place in shows aimed at teenagers. Brent Bozell, chairman of the Parents Television Council, said: "When you know that your audience is young, you have to know presenting them with such difficult questions is wrong."

Quite to the contrary, it would seem to be wrong to avoid topics such as sex, divorce, and homosexuality when they are clearly the reality of modern society. Bringing these topics to center stage and stimulating discussion would seem a far more effective way of confronting them than denying their existence.

Williamson's greatest success, though, has been the characters he created to deal with these true-to-life scenarios. In an age when highly acclaimed literature proudly portrays the Quentin Tarantino anti-hero, Williamson presents characters not yet enveloped by cynicism, whom we can admire.

Dawson Leery (James Van Der Beek), the show's star, is an excellent student who aspires to be a movie director. In the wake of his parents' recent divorce, he didn't turn to drugs or alcohol but instead fell back on his friends and is now directing a movie he wrote. His co-star, Joey Potter (Katie Holmes), dreams of being an artist while she maintains a stellar grade-point average and works a part-time job. Both characters have difficult home lives, yet both deal with their dilemmas in mature manners that parents could only hope their children imitate.

Dawson's Creek, while better than average, is not by any meas-   10
ure great drama. The dialogue is often needlessly complex and awkward, and the writers haven't escaped many of the clichés that plague teen drama. Yet despite its flaws, the series unabashedly tackles serious issue after serious issue, almost always presenting them from multiple viewpoints. The show's greatest strength is painting backdrops with which all teenagers can identify and then superimposing characters who shine in these difficult scenarios.

At a time when young people can hardly find heroes among their elders, *Dawson's Creek* portrays the nearly unknown heroic teenager. In doing so, the show provides inspiration for a generation desperately seeking answers to questions critics say it should never even address.

Leever tells us briefly what the show is about and states his assessment, giving several reasons for his opinion.

Key Features / Evaluations

A concise description of the subject.   You should include just enough information to let readers who may not be familiar with your subject understand what it is; the goal is to evaluate, not summarize. Leever quickly describes *Dawson's Creek* as a TV series that focuses on youths in a small town and that contains "sexually charged dialogue."

Clearly defined criteria.   You need to determine clear criteria as the basis for your judgment. In reviews or other evaluations written for a broad audience, you can integrate the criteria into the discussion as reasons for your assessment, as Leever does in his evaluation of *Dawson's Creek.* In more formal evaluations, you may need to announce your criteria explicitly. Leever mentions several criteria for evaluating this television show: originality; realism; believable characters willingness to focus on serious, even controversial issues.

A knowledgeable discussion of the subject.   To evaluate something credibly, you need to show that you know it yourself and that you've researched what other authoritative sources say. Leever cites many examples, showing his knowledge of the plot and characters of *Dawson's Creek*. He does not cite anyone else's opinion of the show but does refer to what the chairman of the Parents Television Council has said about TV shows that tackle controversial issues.

A balanced and fair assessment.   An evaluation is centered on a judgment. Leever concludes that *Dawson's Creek* "while better than average, is not by any measure great" but goes on to say that it "provides inspiration for a generation." It is important that any judgment be balanced and fair. Seldom is something all good or all bad. A fair evaluation need not be all positive or all negative; it may acknowledge both strengths and weaknesses. For example, a movie's soundtrack may be wonderful while the plot is not. Leever is careful to point out some of *Dawson's Creek*'s shortcomings (clichés, dialogue that is often "complex and awkward") even as he judges it good overall.

Well-supported reasons.   Your need to give reasons for your judgment. Leever gives several reasons for his positive assessment of *Dawson's Creek*: that it tackles serious issues, that it does not present a "contrived back drop of . . . happy, two-parent families," and that it includes characters "we can admire," and he supports these reasons with examples from the show.

A BRIEF GUIDE TO WRITING

Choose something to evaluate.   You can more effectively evaluate a limited subject than a broad one: review certain dishes at a local restaurant rather than the entire menu; review one film or episode rather than all the films by Alfred Hitchcock or all eighty *Star Trek* episodes. The more specific and focused your subject, the better you can write about it.

Considering the Rhetorical Situation

■ **PURPOSE**   Are you writing to affect your audience's opinion of a subject? Do you want to evaluate something to help others decide what to see, do, or buy?

■ **AUDIENCE**   To whom are you writing? What will your audience already know about the subject? What will they expect to learn from your evaluation of it? Are they likely to agree with you or not?

■ **STANCE**   How will you show that you have evaluated the subject fairly and appropriately? Think about the tone you want to use: should it be reasonable? passionate? critical?

■ **MEDIA / DESIGN**   How will you deliver your evaluation? In print? Online? As a speech? Can you show an image or film clip? If you're submitting your text for publication, are there any format requirements?

Generating Ideas and Text

Explore what you already know.   FREEWRITE to answer the following questions: What do you know about this subject or subjects like it? What are your initial or gut feelings, and why do you feel as you do? How does this subject reflect or affect your basic values or beliefs? How have others evaluated subjects like this?

Identify criteria.   Make a list of criteria you think should be used to evaluate your subject. Think about which criteria will likely be important
to your AUDIENCE. You might find CUBING and QUESTIONING to be useful processes for thinking about your topic.

Evaluate your subject.   Study your subject closely to determine if it meets your criteria. You may want to list your criteria on a sheet of paper with space to take notes, or you may develop a grading scale for each criterion to help stay focused on it. Come up with a tentative judgment.

Compare your subject with others. Often, evaluating something involves **COMPARING AND CONTRASTING** it with similar things. We judge movies in comparison with the other movies we've seen and french fries with the other fries we've tasted. Sometimes those comparisons can be made informally. For other evaluations, you may have to do research — to try on several pairs of jeans before buying any, for example — to see how your subject compares.

266–74

State your judgment as a tentative THESIS statement. It should be one that balances both pros and cons. "*Fight Club* is a great film — but not for children." "Of the five sport-utility vehicles tested, the Toyota 4Runner emerged as the best in comfort, power, and durability, though not in styling or cargo capacity." Both of these examples offer a judgment but qualify it according to the writer's criteria.

251–52

Anticipate other opinions. I think Adam Sandler is a comic genius whose movies are first-rate. You think Adam Sandler is a terrible actor who makes awful movies. How can I write a review of his latest film that you will at least consider? One way is by acknowledging other opinions — and refuting those opinions as best I can. I may not persuade you to see Adam Sandler's next film, but I can at least demonstrate that by certain criteria he should be appreciated. You may need to **RESEARCH** how others have evaluated your subject.

329–449

Identify and support your reasons. Write out all the reasons you can think of that will convince your audience to accept your judgment. Review your list to identify the most convincing or important reasons. Then review how well your subject meets your criteria and decide how best to support your reasons: through examples, authoritative opinions, statistics, or something else.

Ways of Organizing an Evaluation

Evaluations are usually organized in one of two ways. One way is to introduce what's being evaluated, followed by your judgment, discussing your criteria along the way. This is a useful strategy if your audience may not be familiar with your subject.

[Start with your subject]

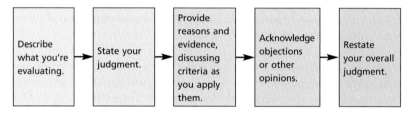

You might also start by identifying your criteria and then follow with a discussion of how your subject meets or doesn't meet those criteria. This strategy foregrounds the process by which you reached your conclusions.

[Start with your criteria]

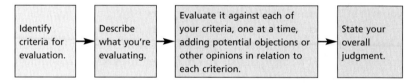

If You Need More Help

205–35

See Chapter 23 for guidelines on **DRAFTING,** Chapter 24 on **ASSESSING YOUR DRAFT,** Chapter 25 on **GETTING RESPONSE AND REVISING,** and Chapter 26 on **EDITING AND PROOFREADING.** See Chapter 27 if you are required to submit your report in a writing **PORTFOLIO.**

Lab Reports **13**

Lab reports describe the procedures and results of experiments in the natural sciences, the social sciences, and engineering. We write reports of lab work in school to show instructors that we have followed certain procedures, achieved appropriate results, and drawn accurate conclusions. On the job, lab reports not only describe what we did and what we learned; they may also present data and interpretations to attempt to persuade others to accept our hypotheses, and they become a record that others may refer to in the future. As an example, here is a lab report written by a student for a psychology class at Wittenberg University.

SARAH THOMAS

The Effect of Biofeedback Training on Muscle Tension and Skin Temperature

Purpose
The purpose of this lab was for subjects to train themselves to increase their skin temperature, measured on the index finger of their non-dominant hand, and to decrease their muscle tension, measured over the frontalis muscle by using biofeedback training. This study is based on the research of Miller and Brucker (1979), which demonstrated that smooth muscles could experience operant conditioning.

Methods
Subjects
Seven subjects were used in this study: five female and two male. The subjects were the undergraduate students of Dr. Jo Wilson in her hon-

ors psychophysiology class at Wittenberg University in Springfield, Ohio. All subjects were in their early twenties.

Apparatus

Equipment used in this lab included an Apple Microlab system configured to measure (1) skin temperature through a thermode taped with paper surgical tape onto the index finger of the subjects' nondominant hand and (2) frontalis muscle tension via three electrodes placed over the frontalis. When subjects' skin temperatures were more than the means for the previous 90-second intervals, the computer emitted a tone. It also emitted a tone when muscle tension in the frontalis was less than the mean of the previous interval. See the procedure section for exact electrode placement specifications.

Materials

Materials used in this lab included paper surgical tape, alcohol to clean off the forehead, conducting gel, wire, electrode collars, and a chair.

Procedure

Upon arriving at the lab, the researchers turned on the Apple Microlab computer. With the aid of Dr. Wilson, subjects had either electrodes attached to their forehead or a thermode attached to the nondominant hand's index finger. The treatment order was random for each subject, and it was reversed for his or her second biofeedback session. The forehead was swiped with alcohol to clean the skin. Electrodes with conducting gel were placed over the frontalis muscle by putting the ground electrode in the center of the forehead and the white electrodes two inches on either side of the center of the forehead. Premeasured electrode collars allowed the researchers to place the conducting gel on the electrodes, peel off the backing on the collar, and place it on the subjects' forehead. The researchers still made sure the electrodes were placed properly. The wire running from the electrodes to the computer was then taped to the subjects' back so it would be out of their way. They were then seated in a comfortable chair with their back to the computer.

Depending on the experimental condition, subjects were told to reduce their frontalis muscle tension by relaxing and even thinking of holding something warm in their hands. They were told that they

5

would know they were meeting the goal when they heard a tone emitted by the computer.

Each session began with a 90-second baseline period, followed by fifteen 90-second trial periods. During each trial period, a tone was emitted by the computer each time the subjects' frontalis muscle tension was below their mean tension for the previous trial; the tone served as the rewarding stimulus in the operant conditioning paradigm.

When skin temperature was to be measured, a thermode was attached to the index finger of the subjects' nondominant hand with surgical tape. The wire running from the thermode to the computer was taped to the back of their hand so it would be out of their way. Then a 90-second baseline period occurred, followed by fifteen 90-second trial periods. During each trial period, a tone was emitted by the computer each time the subjects' skin temperature was above their mean temperature for the previous trial; once again, the tone served as the rewarding stimulus in the operant conditioning paradigm.

Results

The results of this lab were generally similar (Tables 1 and 2). All subjects demonstrated the ability to increase their skin temperature and decrease the tension in their frontalis muscle in at least one of their sessions. Five subjects were able to increase their skin temperature in both sessions; the same number decreased their muscle tension in both trials.

The majority of subjects (five) were able to both increase the skin 10 temperature of the index finger of their nondominant hand and decrease the tension of their frontalis muscle more during the second trial than the first.

Specifically, subject 7 had atypical results. This subject's overall average skin temperature was less than the baseline value; the subject's overall average muscle tension was more than the baseline value.

Discussion

The bulk of the data collected in this study validated the research of Neal Miller; the subjects appeared to undergo operant conditioning of their smooth muscles in order to relax their frontalis muscles and increase their skin temperatures. Subjects 3 and 6 each failed to do this in one session; subject 7 failed to do this several times. This finding is difficult to explain precisely. It is possible that for subjects 3 and 6, this

Table 1: Skin Temperature in Degrees Fahrenheit during Sessions 1 and 2

	Subject 1	Subject 2	Subject 3	Subject 4	Subject 5	Subject 6	Subject 7
Baseline, Session 1	75.2	77.3	78.5	74.3	78.0	67.7	75.1
Mean skin temp, Session 1	79.3	85.6	78.5	74.4	83.2	73.5	72.6
Mean minus baseline, Session 1	4.1	8.3	0.0	0.1	5.2	5.8	−2.5
Baseline, Session 2	77.9	80.1	69.5	80.9	67.2	73.7	88.0
Mean skin temp, Session 2	79.9	86.3	70.7	84.6	76.8	79.7	88.8
Mean minus baseline, Session 2	2.0	6.2	1.2	3.7	9.6	6.0	0.8
Overall average of mean skin temp minus baseline	3.1	7.3	0.6	1.9	7.4	5.9	−0.85

data was a fluke. For subject 7, it is likely that the subject was simply stressed due to outside factors before arriving for the first trials of EMG and skin temperature, and this stress skewed the data.

The effect of biofeedback training was generally greater as the operant conditioning became better learned. Learning was indicated by the finding that the majority of the subjects performed better on the second trials than on the first trials. This finding shows the effectiveness of biofeedback on reducing factors associated with stress, like muscle ten-

rhetorical situations
genres
processes
strategies
research mla/apa
media/ design

Table 2: EMG of the Frontalis Muscle in Microvolts for Sessions 1 and 2

	Subject 1	Subject 2	Subject 3	Subject 4	Subject 5	Subject 6	Subject 7
Baseline, Session 1	4.4	4.5	2.8	3.8	7.9	3.1	2.4
Mean EMG, Session 1	2.1	1.4	1.7	3.2	2.0	3.7	3.2
Baseline minus mean, Session 1	2.3	3.1	1.1	0.6	5.9	−0.6	−0.8
Baseline, Session 2	4.1	2.3	3.0	2.9	11.1	6.5	1.9
Mean EMG, Session 2	1.3	1.3	1.4	2.3	2.5	3.2	1.4
Baseline minus mean, Session 2	2.8	1.0	1.6	0.6	8.6	3.3	0.5
Overall average of mean EMG minus baseline	2.6	2.1	1.4	0.6	7.3	1.4	−0.15

sion and low skin temperature; biofeedback's impact is even greater when it is administered over time. The implications of this information are without limits, especially for the treatment of a variety of medical disorders.

There were a few problems with this lab. The subjects all were at different levels of relaxation to begin with. It is impossible to determine the effects of outside events, like exams or other stresses, on their EMG and skin temperature levels. Skin temperature itself could have been altered by cold outside temperatures. Being in a lab may have altered the stress level of some subjects, and noises from outside the lab may have had an effect as well.

If this study were repeated, it would be a good idea to let sub- 15 jects simply be in the lab for a period of time before measures are taken. This would allow the effect of outside temperature to be minimized. It would also reduce the effect of getting used to the lab, decreasing the orienting response. Finally, it would also be good to do the lab in a soundproof room.

Reference

Miller, N. E., & Brucker, B. S. (1979). A learned visceral response apparently independent of skeletal ones in patients paralyzed by spinal lesions. In N. Birnbaumer & H. D. Kimmel (Eds.), *Biofeedback and self-regulation* (pp. 287–304). Hillsdale, NJ: Erlbaum.

This report includes categories commonly part of lab reports in the natural and social sciences: purpose, method, results, discussion, and references. Some reports keep results and discussion in one section; some reports include an abstract; and some reports include one or more appendices containing tables, calculations, and other supplemental material, depending on the audience and publication. In this example, the author assumes that her audience understands basic terms used in the report, such as frontalis muscle and biofeedback.

Key Features / Lab Reports

Most lab reports include the following strictly defined parts:

An explicit title. Lab report titles should describe the report factually and explicitly to let readers know exactly what the report is about and to provide key words for indexes and search engines. Avoid phrases like "an Investigation into" or "a Study of" and titles that are clever or cute. Thomas's title, "The Effect of Biofeedback Training on Muscle Tension and Skin Temperature," clearly describes the report's subject and includes the key words needed for indexing (*biofeedback training, muscle tension, skin temperature*).

rhetorical situations

genres

processes

strategies

research mla/apa

media/ design

Abstract. Some lab reports include a one-paragraph, 100–200-word ABSTRACT, a summary of the report's purpose, method, and discussion.

▲ 107–11

Purpose. Sometimes called an "Introduction," this section describes the reason for conducting the study: Why is this research important? What has been done by others, and how does your work relate to previous work? Why are you doing this research? What will your research tell us?

Methods. Here you describe how you conducted the study, including the materials and equipment you used and the procedures you followed. This is usually written as a narrative, explaining the process you followed in order to allow others to repeat your study, step-by-step. Your discussion should thoroughly describe the following:

- subjects studied and any necessary contextual information
- apparatus—equipment used, by brand and model number
- materials used
- procedures—including reference to the published work that describes any procedures you used that someone else had already followed; the techniques you used and any modifications you made to them; any statistical methods you used

Results and discussion. Here you analyze the results and present their implications, explain your logic in accepting or rejecting your initial hypotheses, relate your work to previous work in the field, and discuss the experiment's design and techniques and how they may have affected the results: what did you find out, and what does it mean? In longer reports, you may have two separate sections; "Results" should focus on the factual data you collected by doing the study; "Discussion" should speculate about what the study means: why the results turned out as they did, and what the implications for future studies may be.

References. List works cited in your report, alphabetized by author's last name and using the appropriate documentation style.

Appendices. Appendices are optional, presenting information that is too detailed for the body of the report.

Appropriate format. The design conventions for lab reports vary from discipline to discipline, so you'll need to check to see that yours meets the appropriate requirements. Find out whether any sections need to start their own page, whether you need to include a list of figures, whether you need to include a separate title page—and whether there are any other conventions you need to follow.

A BRIEF GUIDE TO WRITING

Considering the Rhetorical Situation

<table>
<tr>
<td>3–4</td>
<td>■ PURPOSE</td>
<td>Why are you writing? To demonstrate your ability to follow the appropriate methods and make logical inferences? To persuade others that your hypotheses are sound and your conclusions believable? To provide a record of the experiment for others?</td>
</tr>
<tr>
<td>5–8</td>
<td>■ AUDIENCE</td>
<td>Can you assume that your audience is familiar with the field's basic procedures? How routine were your procedures? Which procedures need to be explained in greater detail so your audience can repeat them?</td>
</tr>
<tr>
<td>12–14</td>
<td>■ STANCE</td>
<td>Lab reports need to have an impersonal, analytical stance. Take care not to be too informal, and don't try to be cute.</td>
</tr>
<tr>
<td>15–17</td>
<td>■ MEDIA / DESIGN</td>
<td>Are you planning to deliver your report in print or online? All lab reports have headings; choose a typeface that includes bold or italics so your headings will show clearly.</td>
</tr>
</table>

Generating Ideas and Text

Research your subject.   Researchers do not work in isolation; rather, each study contributes to an ever-growing body of information, and you need to situate your work in that context. **RESEARCH** what studies others have done on the same subject and what procedures those studies followed.

329–449

Take careful notes as you perform your study.   A lab report must be repeatable. Another researcher should be able to duplicate your study exactly, using only your report as a guide, so you must document every method, material, apparatus, and procedure very carefully. Break down procedures and activities into discrete parts, and record them in the order in which they occurred. **ANALYZE CAUSES AND EFFECTS;** think about whether you should **COMPARE** your findings with other studies. Take very careful notes so that you'll be able to **EXPLAIN PROCESSES** you followed.

255–59
266–74
299–303

DRAFT the report a section at a time.   You may find it easiest to start with the "Methods" or "Results" section first, then draft the "Discussion," followed by the "Purpose." Do the "Abstract" last.

205–07

- Write in complete sentences and paragraphs.
- Avoid using the first person *I* or *we*; keep the focus on the study and the actions taken.
- Use the active voice as much as possible ("the rats pushed the lever" rather than "the lever was pushed by the rats").
- Use the past tense throughout the report.
- Place subjects and verbs close together to make your sentences easy to follow.
- Use precise terms consistently throughout the report; don't alternate among synonyms.
- Be sure that each pronoun refers clearly to one noun.

Organizing a Lab Report

Lab reports vary in their details but generally include these sections:

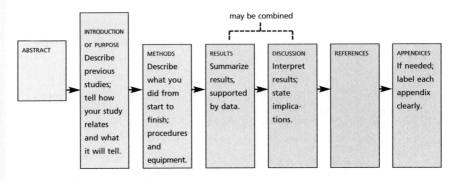

may be combined

| ABSTRACT | INTRODUCTION or PURPOSE Describe previous studies; tell how your study relates and what it will tell. | METHODS Describe what you did from start to finish; procedures and equipment. | RESULTS Summarize results, supported by data. | DISCUSSION Interpret results; state implications. | REFERENCES | APPENDICES If needed; label each appendix clearly. |

If You Need More Help

205–35 See Chapter 24 on ASSESSING YOUR DRAFT, Chapter 25 on GETTING RESPONSE AND REVISING, and Chapter 26 on EDITING AND PROOFREADING. See Chapter 27 if you are required to submit your report in a writing PORTFOLIO.

rhetorical situations

genres

processes

strategies

research mla/apa

media/ design

Literary Analyses **14**

Literary analyses are essays in which we examine literary texts closely to understand their messages, interpret their meanings, and appreciate their writers' techniques. You might read *Macbeth* and notice that Shakespeare's play contains a pattern of images of blood. You could explore the distinctive point of view in Ambrose Bierce's story "An Occurrence at Owl Creek Bridge." Or you could point out the differences between Stephen King's *The Shining* and Stanley Kubrick's screenplay based on that novel. In all these cases, you use specific analytical tools to go below the surface of the work to deepen your understanding of how it works and what it means. Here is a sonnet by the nineteenth-century English Romantic poet Percy Bysshe Shelley, followed by one student's analysis of it written for a literature course at Wright State University.

PERCY BYSSHE SHELLEY

Sonnet: "Lift Not the Painted Veil Which Those Who Live"

Lift not the painted veil which those who live
Call Life: though unreal shapes be pictured there,
And it but mimic all we would believe
With colours idly spread,—behind, lurk Fear
And Hope, twin Destinies; who ever weave   5
Their shadows, o'er the chasm, sightless and drear.
I knew one who had lifted it—he sought,
For his lost heart was tender, things to love,
But found them not, alas! nor was there aught

The world contains, the which he could approve. ₁₀
Through the unheeding many he did move,
A splendour among shadows, a bright blot
Upon this gloomy scene, a Spirit that strove
For truth, and like the Preacher found it not.

STEPHANIE HUFF

Metaphor and Society in Shelley's "Sonnet"

In his sonnet "Lift not the painted veil which those who live," Percy Bysshe Shelley introduces us to a bleak world that exists behind veils and shadows. We see that although fear and hope both exist, truth is dishearteningly absent. This absence of truth is exactly what Shelley chooses to address as he uses metaphors of grim distortion and radiant incandescence to expose the counterfeit nature of our world.

The speaker of Shelley's poem presents bold assertions about the nature of our society. In the opening lines of the poem, he warns the reader to "Lift not the painted veil which those who live / Call Life" (1–2). Here, the "painted veil" serves as a grim metaphor for life. More specifically, the speaker equates the veil with what people like to *call* life. In this sense, the speaker asserts that what we believe to be pure reality is actually nothing more than a covering that masks what really lies beneath. Truth is covered by a veil of falsehood and is made opaque with the paint of people's lies.

This painted veil does not completely obstruct our view, but rather distorts what we can see. All that can be viewed through it are "unreal shapes" (2) that metaphorically represent the people that make up this counterfeit society. These shapes are not to be taken for truth. They are unreal, twisted, deformed figures of humanity, people full of falsities and misrepresentations.

Most people, however, do not realize that the shapes and images seen through the veil are distorted because all they know of life is the veil—this life we see as reality only "mimic[s] all we would believe" (3), using "colours idly spread" (4) to create pictures that bear little resemblance to that which they claim to portray. All pure truths are covered up and painted over until they are mere mockeries. The lies that cloak the truth are not even carefully constructed, but are created

idly, with little attention to detail. The paint is not applied carefully, but merely spread across the top. This idea of spreading brings to mind images of paint slopped on so heavily that the truth beneath becomes nearly impossible to find. Even the metaphor of color suggests only superficial beauty—"idly spread" (4)—rather than any sort of pure beauty that could penetrate the surface of appearances.

What really lies behind this facade are fear and hope, both of which "weave / Their shadows, o'er the chasm, sightless and drear" (5–6). These two realities are never truly seen or experienced, though. They exist only as shadows. Just as shadows appear only at certain times of day, cast only sham images of what they reflect, and are paid little attention, so too do these emotions of hope and fear appear only as brief, ignored imitations of themselves when they enter the artificiality of this chasmlike world. Peering into a chasm, one cannot hope to make out what lies at the bottom. At best one could perhaps make out shadows and even that cannot be done with any certainty as to true appearance. The world is so large, so caught up in itself and its counterfeit ways, that it can no longer see even the simple truths of hope and fear. Individuals and civilizations have become sightless, dreary, and as enormously empty as a chasm.

This chasm does not include *all* people, however, as we are introduced to one individual, in line 7, who is trying to bring to light whatever truth may yet remain. This one person, who defies the rest of the world, is portrayed with metaphors of light, clearly standing out among the dark representations of the rest of mankind. He is first presented to us as possessing a "lost heart" (8) and seeking things to love. It is important that the first metaphor applied to him be a heart because this is the organ with which we associate love, passion, and purity. We associate it with brightness of the soul, making it the most radiant spot of the body. He is then described as a "splendour among shadows" (12), his purity and truth brilliantly shining through the darkness of the majority's falsehood. Finally, he is equated with "a bright blot / Upon this gloomy scene" (12–13), his own bright blaze of authenticity burning in stark contrast to the murky phoniness of the rest of the world.

These metaphors of light are few, however, in comparison to those of grim distortion. So, too, are this one individual's radiance and zeal too little to alter the warped darkness they temporarily pierce. This one person, though bright, is not bright enough to light up the rest of civilization and create real change. The light simply confirms the dark falsity that comprises the rest of the world. Shelley gives us one flame of hope, only to reveal to us what little chance it has under the suffocating veil. Both the metaphors of grim distortion and those of radiant incandescence work together in this poem to highlight the world's counterfeit nature.

Huff focuses her analysis on patterns in Shelley's imagery. In addition, she pays careful attention to individual words and to how, as the poem unfolds, they create a certain meaning. That meaning is her interpretation.

Key Features / Literary Analyses

An arguable thesis. A literary analysis is a form of argument; you are arguing that your analysis of a literary work is valid. Your thesis, then, should be arguable, as Huff's is: "[Shelley] uses metaphors of grim distortion and radiant incandescence to expose the counterfeit nature of our world." A mere summary—"Shelley writes about a person who sees reality and seeks love but never finds it"—would not be arguable and therefore is not a good thesis.

Careful attention to the language of the text. The key to analyzing a text is looking carefully at the language, which is the foundation of its meaning. Specific words, images, metaphors—these are where analysis begins. You may also bring in contextual information, such as cultural, historical, or biographical facts, or you may refer to similar texts. But the words, phrases, and sentences that make up the text you are analyzing are your primary source when dealing with texts. That's what literature teachers mean by "close reading": reading with the assumption that every word of a text is meaningful.

Attention to patterns or themes. Literary analyses are usually built on evidence of meaningful patterns or themes within a text or among several texts. These patterns and themes reveal meaning. In Shelley's poem, images of light and shadow and artifice and reality create patterns of meaning, while the poem's many half rhymes (*live/believe, love/approve*) create patterns of sound that may contribute to the overall meaning.

A clear interpretation.   A literary analysis demonstrates the plausibility of its thesis by using evidence from the text and, sometimes, relevant contextual evidence to explain how the language and patterns found there support a particular interpretation. When you write a literary analysis, you show readers one way the text may be read and understood; that is your interpretation.

MLA style.   Literary analyses usually follow MLA style. Even though Huff's essay has no works-cited list, it refers to line numbers using MLA style.

A BRIEF GUIDE TO WRITING

Considering the Rhetorical Situation

▦ **PURPOSE**	What do you need to do—show that you have examined the text carefully? offer your own interpretation? demonstrate a particular analytical technique? Or some combination? If you're responding to an assignment, does it specify what you need to do?	3–4
▦ **AUDIENCE**	What do you need to do to convince your readers that your interpretation is plausible and based on sound analysis? Can you assume that readers are already familiar with the text you are analyzing, or do you need to tell them about it?	5–8
▦ **STANCE**	How can you see your subject through interested, curious eyes—and then step back in order to see what your observations might *mean*?	12–14
▦ **MEDIA / DESIGN**	Will your analysis focus on a print text and take the form of a print text? If your subject is a visual or electronic medium, will you need to show significant elements in your analysis? Are you required to follow MLA or some other style?	15–17

Generating Ideas and Text

Look at your assignment.　Does it specify a particular kind of analysis? Does it ask you to consider a particular theme? to use any specific critical approaches? Look for any terms that tell you what to do, words like *analyze, compare, interpret,* and so on.

Study the text with a critical eye.　When we read a literary work, we often come away with a reaction to it: we like it, we hate it, it made us cry or laugh, it perplexed us. That may be a good starting point for a literary analysis, but students of literature need to go beyond initial reactions, to think about **HOW THE TEXT WORKS**: What does it *say*, and what does it *do*? What elements make up this text? How do those elements work together or fail to work together? Does this text lead you to think or feel a certain way? How does it fit into a particular context (of history, culture, technology, genre, and so on)?

319–21

Choose a method for analyzing the text.　There are various ways to analyze your subject. Three common focuses are on the text itself, on your own experience reading it, and on other cultural, historical, or literary contexts.

- *The text itself.* Trace the development and expression of themes, characters, and language through the work. How do they help to create the overall meaning, tone, or effect for which you're arguing? To do this, you might look at the text as a whole, something you can understand from all angles at once. You could also pick out parts from the beginning, middle, and end as needed to make your case, **DEFINING** key terms, **DESCRIBING** characters and settings, and **NARRATING** key scenes. The example essay about the Shelley sonnet offers a text-based analysis that looks at patterns of images in the poem. You might also examine the same theme in several different works.

275–84
285–93
304–12

- *Your own response as a reader.* Explore the way the text affects you or develops meanings as you read through it from beginning to end. By doing such a close reading, you're slowing down the process to notice how one element of the text leads you to expect something, confirming earlier suspicions or surprises. You build your analysis on your experience of reading the text—as if you were pretending to drive somewhere for the first time, though in reality you know the way intimately. By closely examining the language of the text as you experience it, you explore how it leads you to a set of responses, both intellectual and emotional. If you were responding in this way to the Shelley poem, you might discuss how its first lines suggest that while life is an illusion, a veil, one might pull it aside and glimpse reality, however "drear."

- *Context*. Analyze the text as part of some LARGER CONTEXT—as part of a certain time or place in history or as an expression of a certain culture (how does this text relate to the time and place of its creation?), as one of many other texts like it, a representative of a genre (how is this text like or unlike others of its kind? how does it use, play with, or flout the conventions of the genre?). A context-based approach to the Shelley poem might look at Shelley's own philosophical and religious views and how they may have influenced the poem's characterization of the world we experience as illusory, a "veil." 327–28

Read the work more than once. Reading literature, watching films, or listening to speeches is like driving to a new destination: the first time you go, you need to concentrate on getting there; on subsequent trips, you can see other aspects—the scenery, the curve of the road, other possible routes—that you couldn't pay attention to earlier. When you experience a piece of literature for the first time, you usually focus on the story, the plot, the overall meaning. By experiencing it repeatedly, you can see how its effects are achieved, what the pieces are and how they fit together, where different patterns emerge, how the author crafted the work. To analyze a literary work, then, plan to read it more than once, with the assumption that every part of the text is there for a reason. Focus on details, even on a single detail that shows up more than once: Why is it there? What can it mean? How does it affect our experience of reading or studying a text? Also, look for anomalies, details that *don't* fit the patterns: Why are they part of the text? What can they mean? How do they affect the experience of the text? See the READING STRATEGIES chapter for several different methods for reading a text. 313–28

251–52

Compose a strong thesis. The **THESIS** of a literary analysis should be specific, limited, and open to potential disagreement. In addition, it should be analytical, not evaluative: avoid thesis statements that make overall judgments, such as a reviewer might do: "Virginia Woolf's *The Waves* is a failed experiment in narrative" or "No one has equaled the achievement of *The Matrix* trilogy." Rather, offer a way of seeing the text: "The choice presented in Robert Frost's 'The Road Not Taken' ultimately makes no difference"; "The plot of *The Matrix Reloaded* reflects the politics of America after 9/11."

Do a close reading. When you analyze a text, you need to find specific, brief passages that support your interpretation. Then you should interpret those passages in terms of their language, their context, or your reaction to them as a reader. To find such passages, you must read the text closely, questioning it as you go, asking, for example:

- What language provides evidence to support your thesis?
- What does each word (phrase, passage) mean exactly?
- Why does the writer choose *this* language, *these* words? What are the implications or connotations of the language? If the language is dense or difficult, why might the writer have written it that way?
- What images or metaphors are used? What is their effect on the meaning?

322–24

- What **PATTERNS** of language, imagery, or plot do you see? If something is repeated, what significance does the repetition have?
- How does each word, phrase, or passage relate to what precedes and follows it?
- How does the experience of reading the text affect its meaning?

327–28

- What words, phrases, or passages connect to a larger **CONTEXT?** What language demonstrates that this work reflects or is affected by that context?
- How do these various elements of language, image, and pattern support your interpretation?

rhetorical
situations

genres

processes

strategies

research
mla/apa

media/
design

Your analysis should focus on analyzing and interpreting your subject, not simply summarizing or paraphrasing it. Many literary analyses also use the strategy of COMPARING two or more works.

266–74

Find evidence to support your interpretation. The parts of the text you examine in your close reading become the evidence you use to support your interpretation. Some think that we're all entitled to our own opinions about literature. And indeed we are. But when writing a literary analysis, we're entitled only to our own *well-supported* and *well-argued* opinions. When you analyze a text, you must treat it like any other ARGUMENT: you need to discuss how the text creates an effect or expresses a theme, and then you have to show evidence from the text — significant plot or structural elements; important characters; patterns of language, imagery, or action — to back up your argument.

82–106

Pay attention to matters of style. Literary analyses have certain conventions for using pronouns and verbs.

- In informal papers, it's okay to use the first person: "I believe Frost's narrator has little basis for claiming that one road is 'less traveled.'" In more formal essays, make assertions directly; claim authority to make statements about the text: "Frost's narrator has no basis for claiming that one road is 'less traveled.'"

- Discuss textual features in the present tense even if quotations from the text are in another tense: "When Nick finds Gatsby's body floating in the pool, he says very little about it: 'the laden mattress moved irregularly down the pool.'" Describe the historical context of the setting in the past tense: "In the 1920s, such estates as Gatsby's were rare."

Cite and document sources appropriately. Use MLA citation and documentation style unless told otherwise. Format QUOTATIONS properly, and use SIGNAL PHRASES when need be.

378–416
360–63
367–68

Think about format and design. Brief essays do not require HEADINGS; text divisions are usually marked by TRANSITIONS between paragraphs. In longer papers, though, heads can be helpful.

456–57
254

Organizing a Literary Analysis

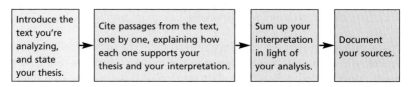

| Introduce the text you're analyzing, and state your thesis. | → | Cite passages from the text, one by one, explaining how each one supports your thesis and your interpretation. | → | Sum up your interpretation in light of your analysis. | → | Document your sources. |

If You Need More Help

205–35 ○

See Chapter 23 for guidelines on **DRAFTING,** Chapter 24 on **ASSESSING YOUR DRAFT,** Chapter 25 on **GETTING RESPONSE AND REVISING,** and Chapter 26 on **EDITING AND PROOFREADING.** See Chapter 27 if you are required to submit your analysis in a writing **PORTFOLIO.**

rhetorical situations

genres

processes

strategies

research mla/apa

media/ design

Memoirs 15

We write memoirs to explore our past — about shopping for a party dress with Grandma, or driving a car for the first time, or breaking up with our first love. *Memoirs* focus on events and people and places that are important to us. We usually have two goals when we write a memoir: to capture an important moment and to convey something about its significance for us. In the following example from *When Broken Glass Floats: Growing Up under the Khmer Rouge* (2001), a woman who grew up in Cambodia during the Vietnam War recalls her first experience of battle.

CHANRITHY HIM

When Broken Glass Floats

In 1969 war comes, and I am only four.

Loud rumbling noises wake me. I fumble in the dark, trying to open the mosquito netting around my bed. I run in the dark toward the living room, searching for my mother and father. *"Mak! Pa!"* I scream with all my might, trying to compete with the raucous sounds.

From the living room, I hear my oldest sister, twelve-year-old Chea, screaming: *"Mak! Pa! Yeakong chol srok Khmer! Yeakong chol srok Khmer!"* The Viet Cong are invading Cambodia! Her voice is itself a blast of terror.

Chea's hysterical warning makes me realize that the raging noise outside could be related to the word I had been wondering about: *war.* More than anything, I want to see my parents. Suddenly the light flips on, revealing my frightened sisters and brothers running around frantically, randomly — as disoriented as ants whose hill has been plowed under.

I see my mother clutching my baby sister, Avy, and my father standing at the wall where he has just turned on the light. I run to stand

5

beside *Mak*. My father reaches out to hold Chea's shoulders. He looks into her eyes and carefully says: "Achea, *koon,* take your brothers and sisters with you and hide in the bunker by the pond. Hunch and walk low, so you won't get hit by bullets. Hurry, *koon Pa!* [father's child]"

My brothers and sisters rush out the doorway, a small, traumatized herd of cattle. I clench my mother's hand, and my body rattles with each echo of gunfire. Carrying Avy and holding on to me, *Mak* hurries toward the door. She can't move quickly, for she is six months pregnant. Artillery explodes outside, and I scream and burst into tears. *Mak* shakes off my hand, then grabs onto it tightly.

"*Pa vea!*" She shouts to my father, who is running from one window to the next, sticking his head out and listening. "What are you doing? You'll get shot! Why aren't you careful? Help me with the children!" *Mak* is scared, and her tone frightens me even more than the artillery roaring in the night air.

Pa shouts back, "I just want to know where the gunfire is coming from."

Mak bends toward me. Her words come as hard and fast as an auctioneer's: "Athy, *koon,* wait for your father here." *Mak* takes Avy downstairs. My heart races when I see that she is scared for my father. After she hurries out, I cry, jumping up and down, anxious for *Pa* to take me to the bunker.

Pa runs over to comfort me, snatches me down from the peak of my hysteria. He carries me to the open bunker, a hole in the sticky clay soil ringed with sandbags. Safe at the bunker, he can't rest. He needs to go back to the house for *Yiey Tot,* his grandmother, who is blind and frail. He takes Chea and Tha with him to help carry her. Above the noise I can hear my great-grandmother's groans. 10

"Hunch, *koon!*" I hear *Pa* cry. "Don't you hear the flying bullets? Don't worry, *Yiey,* we won't drop you."

I'm relieved when everyone in my family, including Aunt Cheng, *Pa's* younger sister, finally hides by the pond. Lying beside my mother in the cold night, I wonder if everyone is as scared as I am as the bullets whiz over us—a fierce hiss and invisible whisper, so quick you wonder if you really heard it. Flares erupt like lightning, illuminating the dark sky.

So this is war. Will it ever stop?

Finally the gunfire belches its last round. Silence and relief. *Now we can go back home,* I think to myself, ready to be freed from wor-

ries about war. I look forward to the morning. I want to forget the adult world that pulled me from my dreams and into a nightmare.

What I don't know is that there is a world outside Cambodia—a world that will affect me, my family, and Cambodia as a nation. I do not know who owned the guns that night—only that they were aimed at me. It will be years before I begin to understand the causes and effects of war, the political gamesmanship. But by then my family will have become flotsam caught in the heave and thrust of its tide.

I look back now as a survivor educated in America. I've sought out answers to questions I raised as a little girl. Trying to make sense of what happened. Trying to understand the players in the Vietnam conflict and those who took advantage of the situation, pulling Cambodia—the pawn, they called it—into the whirlpool of destruction.

Him's memoir tells, first of all, a gripping story about a child in wartime trying to understand why an innocent family—hers—is being shot at. The significance of the event—for the family and for the world—she makes horrifyingly clear.

Key Features / Memoirs

A good story.   Your memoir should be interesting, to yourself and others. It need not be about a world-shaking event, but your topic—and how you write about it—should interest your readers. At the center of most good stories stands a conflict or question to be resolved. The most compelling memoirs feature some sort of situation or problem that needs resolution. That need for resolution is another name for suspense. It's what makes us want to keep reading.

Vivid details.   Details bring a memoir to life by giving readers mental images of the sights, sounds, smells, tastes, and textures of the world in which your story takes place. The goal is to show as well as tell, to take readers there. When Him's sister screams out, *"Mak! Pa! Yeakong chol srok Khmer!"* we don't at first know what she's saying, but we can hear her screaming. A memoir is more than simply a report of what happened; it uses vivid details and dialogue to bring the events of the past to life, much as good fiction brings to life events that the writer makes up or embellishes.

Clear significance.　Memories of the past are filtered through our view from the present: we pick out some moments in our lives as significant, some as more important or vivid than others. Over time, our interpretations change, and our memories themselves change.

A good memoir conveys something about the significance of its subject. As a writer, you need to reveal something about what the incident means to you. You don't, however, want to simply announce the significance as if you're tacking on the moral of the story. Him, for example, tells us at the end of the piece that she's trying "to make sense of what happened." She stops short, though, of telling us that that's why she wrote this narrative.

A BRIEF GUIDE TO WRITING

Deciding on a Topic

200–01 **Choose an event to write about.**　LIST several events or incidents from your past that you consider significant in some way. They do not have to be earthshaking; indeed, they may involve a quiet moment that only you see as important—a brief encounter with a remarkable person, a visit to a special place, a memorable achievement (or failure), something that makes you laugh whenever you think about it. Writing about events that happened at least a few years ago is often easier than writing about recent events because you can more easily step back and see those events with a clear perspective. To choose the event that you will write about, consider how well you can recall what happened, how interesting it will be to readers, and whether you want to share it with an audience.

Considering the Rhetorical Situation

3–4 ■ **PURPOSE**　　What important aspect of yourself are you trying to convey? How will this story help your readers (and you yourself) understand you, as you were then and as you are now?

rhetorical situations　　genres　　processes　　strategies　　research mla/apa　　media/ design

▧ **AUDIENCE**	Who are your readers? What do you want them to think of you after reading your memoir? How can you help them understand your experience?	5–8
▧ **STANCE**	What impression do you want to give, and how can your words contribute to that impression? What tone do you want to project? Sincere? Serious? Humorous? Detached? Self-critical?	12–14
▧ **MEDIA / DESIGN**	Will your memoir be a print document? a speech? Will it be posted on a Web site? Will you include illustrations, audio or video clips, or other visual texts?	15–17

Generating Ideas and Text

Think about what happened. Take a few minutes to write out an account of the incident: **WHAT** happened, **WHERE** it took place, **WHO** else was involved, what was said, how you feel about it, and so on. Can you identify any tension or conflict that will make for a compelling story? If not, you might want to rethink your topic.

○ 202–03

Consider its significance. Why do you still remember this event? What effect has it had on your life? What makes you want to tell someone else about it? Does it say anything about you? What about it might interest someone else? If you have trouble answering these questions, you should probably find another topic. But in general, once you have defined the significance of the incident, you can be sure you have a story to tell — and a reason for telling it.

Think about the details. The best memoirs connect with readers by giving them a sense of what it was like to be there, leading them to experience in words and images what the writer experienced in life. Spend some time **DESCRIBING** the incident, writing what you see, hear, smell, touch, and taste when you envision it. Do you have any photos or memorabilia or other **VISUAL** materials you might include in your memoir? Try writing out **DIALOGUE,** things that were said (or, if you can't recall exactly, things that

◆ 285–93

▢ 458–62
◆ 294–98

might have been said). Look at what you come up with—is there detail enough to bring the scene to life? anything that might be called vivid? If you don't have enough detail, you might reconsider whether you recall enough about the incident to write about it. If you have trouble coming 199–201 ◐ up with plenty of detail, try **FREEWRITING**, **LISTING**, or **LOOPING**.

Ways of Organizing Memoirs

[Tell about the event from beginning to end]

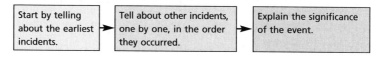

| Start by telling about the earliest incidents. | → | Tell about other incidents, one by one, in the order they occurred. | → | Explain the significance of the event. |

[Start at the end and tell how the event came about]

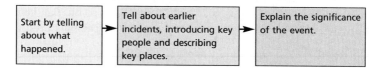

| Start by telling about what happened. | → | Tell about earlier incidents, introducing key people and describing key places. | → | Explain the significance of the event. |

If You Need More Help

205–35 ◐

See Chapter 23 for guidelines on **DRAFTING,** Chapter 24 on **ASSESSING YOUR DRAFT,** Chapter 25 on **GETTING RESPONSE AND REVISING,** and Chapter 26 on **EDITING AND PROOFREADING.** See Chapter 27 if you are required to submit your memoir in a writing **PORTFOLIO.**

rhetorical situations

genres

processes

strategies

research mla/apa

media/ design

Profiles 16

Profiles are written portraits—of people, places, events, or other things. We find profiles of celebrities, travel destinations, and offbeat festivals in magazines and newspapers, on radio and TV. A profile presents a subject in an entertaining way that conveys its significance, showing us something or someone that we may not have known existed or that we see every day but don't know much about. Here, for example, is an excerpt from a profile of a person. The excerpt is from Bob Merlis's, "Foster Cars: Orphan Makes and the People Who Love Them," an article published in *Automobile* magazine.

BOB MERLIS

Shirley Barnes, M.D.

Her business card reads Shirley Barnes, M.D., and she's a doctor, all right—a Metropolitan Doctor. Her passion is the Nash Metropolitan, the little car produced by Austin of England for American Motors between 1954 and 1962. Barnes is a legend among southern California Met lovers—an icon, a beacon, and a font of useful knowledge and freely offered opinions. She learned to drive on her brother's Met back in 1960 and really hasn't been the same since. She was a professional dancer—tap, ballet, acrobatic—but became a shade-tree mechanic of the highest order mostly out of necessity. Her first Met, a '59 purchased in 1966, needed service and she suffered a rude awakening when she couldn't find anyone willing to work on it. She met an elderly mechanic and became his apprentice. "He couldn't use his hands but he still had the brain," Barnes recalls. . . .

Like Fred Walker [who restores Kaiser-Frazer automobiles], she believes in keeping the cars as original as possible, which flies in the face of the current trend in Met circles to swap engines . . . and add automatic transmissions. . . . "My conviction is that if you put the right parts on the car, if they stay as stock as possible, you'll do fine."

Barnes tries hard to practice what she preaches in workshops where she teaches other Metheads how to do their own clutch and brake jobs. She has a sixth sense about the cars and can usually diagnose a problem over the phone. Her relationship with Metropolitans is not, strictly speaking, physical. She has an emotional bond with the cars and has given names to most of her personal fleet of thirteen. There's Daisy, the yellow convertible; Sheba, named by her mother-in-law; Misfit, the one she picked up on an April Fools' Day a while back. And Hannibal, Lady Bird, Homer, Omar, Clover, and Hercules, the one geared low, which pulled her trailer (a 1947 teardrop model named Beep-Beep) to Reno and back.

Shirley is completely involved with her cars. "I get upset when they don't run." She's convinced they have hearts and minds of their own. And she says good night to them, individually, before she, herself, turns in, visions of Met-shaped sugarplums dancing tap, acrobatic, or ballet in her head.

This profile starts with an unusual subject—a woman who fixes a kind of car that's no longer even made. The writer goes on to engage our interest by presenting details that help us understand her passion for these cars and her work.

Key Features / Profiles

An interesting subject. The subject may be something unusual, or it may be something very ordinary shown in an intriguing way. You might profile an interesting person (Shirley Barnes, for example, is someone who does something unusual), a place (Barnes's garage, perhaps), an event (a convention or rally for owners of Nash Metropolitans), or an activity (the workshops for other "Metheads").

Any necessary background or context. A profile usually includes just enough information to let readers know where the subject comes from or why it is what it is. For example, Merlis gives us minimal background on

Shirley Barnes: the Metropolitan is a little car once made in England, and Barnes became a Metropolitan specialist when she started working on hers and fell in love with the cars.

An interesting angle.   A good profile captures its subject from a particular angle. Merlis doesn't try to tell us all about Barnes; rather, he focuses on her as a specialized mechanic, ignoring other aspects of her life. Her relationships, her home, her other interests are irrelevant to Merlis's task: to provide a clear picture of a mechanic who fixes one brand of car.

A firsthand account.   Whether you are writing about a person, place, or event, you need to spend time observing and interacting with your subject. With a person, interacting means watching and conversing. Successful journalists tell us that "following the guy around"—getting a subject to do something and talk about it at the same time—yields excellent material for a profile. When a *Washington Post* writer met Theodor Geisel (Dr. Seuss) before profiling him, she asked him not only to talk about his characters but also to draw one—resulting in a colorful scene (and an illustration) for her profile. With a place or event, interacting may mean visiting and participating, although sometimes you may gather even more information by playing the role of the silent observer.

Engaging details.   You need to include details that bring your subject to life. These may include *specific information* (Shirley Barnes "learned to drive on her brother's Met back in 1960"); *sensory images* ("There's Daisy, the yellow convertible"); *figurative language,* including smile and metaphor ("She's convinced [her cars] have hearts and minds of their own"); *dialogue* (" 'He couldn't use his hands but he still had the brain' "); and *anecdotes* ("she says good night to them, individually"). Choose details that show rather than tell—that let your audience see and hear your subject rather than merely read an abstract description of it. And be sure all the details create some *dominant impression* of your subject; the impression we get of Shirley Barnes, for example, is of a colorful, whimsical person whose connection to Nash Metropolitans is more emotional than technical.

A BRIEF GUIDE TO WRITING

Choosing a Suitable Subject

200–01 ○

People, places, events, or activities—whatever you choose, you're likely to write a stronger piece if you choose something that arouses your curiosity but you're not too familiar with, because being too familiar with something can blind you to interesting details. **LIST** five to ten interesting subjects that you can see firsthand. Obviously, you can't profile a person who won't be interviewed or a place or activity that can't be observed. So before you commit to a topic, make sure you'll be able to carry out firsthand research and not find out too late that the people you need to interview aren't willing or that places you need to visit are off-limits.

Considering the Rhetorical Situation

3–4

■ **PURPOSE** Why are you writing the profile? What angle will best achieve your purpose? How can you inform *and engage* your audience?

5–8

■ **AUDIENCE** Who is your audience? How familiar are they with your subject? What expectations of your profile might they have? What background information or definitions do you need to provide? How interested will they be—and how can you get their interest?

12–14

■ **STANCE** What view of your subject do you expect to present? Sympathetic? Critical? Sarcastic? Will you strive for a carefully balanced perspective?

15–17

■ **MEDIA / DESIGN** Will your profile be a print document? Will it be published on the Web? Will it be an oral presentation? Can (and should) you include images or any other visuals?

Generating Ideas and Text

Visit your subject.   If you're writing about an amusement park, go there; if you're profiling the man who runs the carousel, make an appointment to meet and interview him. Get to know your subject—if you profile Ben and Jerry, sample the ice cream! Take along a camera if there's anything you might want to show visually in your profile. Find helpful hints for OBSERVING and INTERVIEWING in the chapter on finding sources.

351–53

Explore what you already know about your subject.   Why do you find this subject interesting? What do you know about it now? What do you expect to find out about it from your research? What preconceived ideas about or emotional reactions to this subject do you have? Why do you have them? It may be helpful to try some of the activities in the chapter on GENERATING IDEAS AND TEXT.

199–204

If you're planning to interview someone, prepare questions.   Merlis likely asked Shirley Barnes such questions as, "How did you become a mechanic? How did you end up specializing in a car that hasn't been made for forty years? Who influenced you?" See the INTERVIEWING guidelines in Chapter 40 for help with planning questions.

351–52

Do additional research.   You may be able to write a profile based entirely on your field research. You may, though, need to do some library or Web RESEARCH as well, to deepen your understanding, get a different perspective, or fill in gaps. Often the people you interview can help you find sources of additional information; so can the sponsors of events and those in charge of places. To learn more about a city park, for instance, contact the government office that maintains it.

329–449

Analyze your findings.   Look for patterns, images, recurring ideas or phrases, and engaging details. Compare your preconceptions with your findings. Look for contrasts or discrepancies: between a subject's words and actions, between the appearance of a place and what goes on there, between your expectations and your research findings. Merlis may have expected to meet a mechanic—not a former professional dancer who names each of her cars. You may find the advice in the READING STRATEGIES chapter helpful here.

313–28

Come up with an angle.   What's most memorable about your subject? What most interests you? What will interest your audience? Merlis wrote his profile for an automobile magazine, so he focused entirely on Barnes's relationship with cars—and on a female mechanic, a subject that might surprise some readers. Sometimes you'll know your angle from the start; other times you'll need to look further into your topic. You might try CLUSTERING, CUBING, FREEWRITING, and LOOPING, activities that will help you look at your topic from many different angles.

199–202

Note details that support your angle.   Use your angle to focus your research and generate text. Try DESCRIBING your subject as clearly as you can, COMPARING your subject with other subjects of its sort, writing DIALOGUE that captures your subject. Engaging details will bring your subject to life for your audience. Together, these details should create a dominant impression of your subject.

285–93
266–74
294–98

Ways of Organizing a Profile

[As a narrative]

304–12

One common way to organize a profile is by NARRATING. For example, if you are profiling a chess championship, you may write about it chronologically, creating suspense as you move from start to finish.

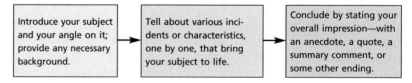

Introduce your subject and your angle on it; provide any necessary background.	→	Tell about various incidents or characteristics, one by one, that bring your subject to life.	→	Conclude by stating your overall impression—with an anecdote, a quote, a summary comment, or some other ending.

[As a description]

Sometimes you may organize a profile by **DESCRIBING**—a person or a place, for instance. The profile of Shirley Barnes is organized this way.

◆ 285–93

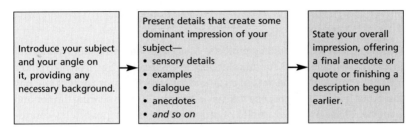

Introduce your subject and your angle on it, providing any necessary background.	Present details that create some dominant impression of your subject— • sensory details • examples • dialogue • anecdotes • and so on	State your overall impression, offering a final anecdote or quote or finishing a description begun earlier.

If You Need More Help

See Chapter 23 for guidelines on **DRAFTING,** Chapter 24 on **ASSESSING YOUR DRAFT,** Chapter 25 on **GETTING RESPONSE AND REVISING,** and Chapter 26 on **EDITING AND PROOFREADING.** See Chapter 27 if you are required to submit your profile in a writing **PORTFOLIO.**

◯ 205–35

17 Proposals

Contractors bid on building projects. Musicians and educators apply for grants. Researchers seek funding. Student leaders call for lights on bike paths. You offer to pay half the cost of a car and insurance if your parents will pay the other half. Lovers propose marriage; friends propose sharing dinner and a movie. These are all examples of proposals: ideas put forward for consideration that say, "Here is a solution to a problem" or "This is what ought to be done." All proposals are arguments: when you propose something, you are trying to persuade others to see a problem in a particular way and to accept your solution to the problem. For example, here is a proposal for reducing the costs of higher education, from a lengthy report prepared in 2004 by the Colorado student chapter of the Higher Education Project of the State Public Interest Research Groups (PIRGs). PIRGs are non-partisan, non-profit advocacy groups; this one focuses on increasing aid for college students.

TRACEY KING AND ELLYNNE BANNON

The Burden of Borrowing: A Proposal for Reducing Student Debt

Higher education is critical to the future success of Americans. In addition to the inherent benefits of a higher education, a college degree is worth 75 percent more than a high school diploma, or more than $1,000,000 over a lifetime in the workforce. However, as college costs continue to swell, students are increasingly shouldering high levels of debt to pay for a college education.

Thirty-nine percent of student borrowers now graduate with unmanageable levels of debt, meaning that their monthly payments are more than 8 percent of their monthly income. According to new

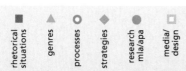

data from the Department of Education's National Postsecondary Student Aid Study (NPSAS), not only are the majority of students turning to loans to finance college, but debt levels are also escalating. In 1999–2000, 64 percent of students graduated with student-loan debt, and the average student-loan debt has nearly doubled over the past eight years, to $16,928.

There are several possible explanations for increases in student borrowing. First [according to a 2001 report of the Advisory Committee on Student Financial Assistance], the strength of the Pell grant has declined from covering 84 percent of tuition at a four-year public institution in 1975–76 to 39 percent today. While Congress has increased funding in recent years, the Pell grant maximum has not been able to keep up with inflation and rising tuition costs. As a result, low-income students are forced to borrow to cover that unmet need. Second, wealthy families may be shifting more of the cost of college from savings to student loans. Also, as tuition increases faster than inflation and median income, students overall are facing increasing levels of need.

We need to look for solutions that make college more affordable and protect students from unmanageable debt burden. Congress should increase grant-aid funding, reduce the cost of student loans, and provide flexibility within the student loan program to help make college more affordable for all Americans. . . .

Increase grant-aid funding: Federal need-based grant aid provides low-income students with access to a higher education. Without this aid, many low-income students take on unmanageable levels of debt burden or forgo a college education altogether. Recent increases in Pell grant funding may have kept some low-income students from borrowing and slowed the growth of debt levels among those who did borrow. Congress should increase need-based grant funding and, specifically, fully fund the Pell grant program.

Lower the cost of borrowing to students: With the typical senior graduating with $16,928 in federal loan debt, Congress should take the following steps to reduce the cost of borrowing:

- Congress should maintain low interest rates on student loans.
- Congress should pass the Affordable Student Loan Act (H.R. 1622), which would eliminate origination and insurance fees on student loans and save the typical student $677. These savings could be used to pay for tuition, books, and other living expenses.

- Congress should pass a tax credit of up to $1,500 for interest paid on student loans, which would help reduce the burden of debt after graduation.

Continue to provide flexible repayment options to borrowers: Congress should continue to provide flexibility within the student-loan program to help make college more affordable for all Americans. Repayment options such as deferment, loan forgiveness, forbearance, and income-contingent repayment help students who are facing unmanageable debt repay their loans without going into default.

Maintain current loan limits: Congress should not increase loan limits without reducing the current cost of borrowing. Raising loan limits will not solve the access problem. Instead, it will only make the situation worse, with more and more students falling into burdensome debt after college. Congress should continue to work toward increasing access to higher education while protecting students from unmanageable levels of debt.

This proposal clearly defines the problem, offers reasons for the increase in student debt, and proposes a set of actions to deal with the problem. It actually ends with the proposed actions, which function, therefore, as a call to action. Its tone, while forceful, is balanced and reasonable.

Key Features / Proposals

A well-defined problem. Some problems are self-evident or relatively simple, and you would not need much persuasive power to make people act — as with the problem "This university discards too much paper." While some people might see nothing wrong with throwing paper away, most are likely to agree that recycling is a good thing. Other issues are controversial: some people see them as problems while others do not, such as this one: "Motorcycle riders who do not wear helmets risk serious injury and raise health-care costs for everyone." Some motorcyclists believe that wearing or not wearing a helmet is a personal choice; you would have to present arguments to convince your readers that not wearing a helmet is indeed a problem needing a solution. Any written proposal must establish at the outset that there is a problem — and that it's serious enough to require a solution.

A recommended solution.   Once you have defined the problem, you need to describe the solution you are suggesting and to explain it in enough detail for readers to understand what you are proposing. Sometimes, as in the student-debt proposal in this chapter, you might suggest several solutions.

A convincing argument for your proposed solution.   You need to convince readers that your solution is feasible — and that it is the best way to solve the problem. Sometimes you'll want to explain in detail the steps needed to enact a proposal. See, for example, how the student-loan proposal details *how* Congress could lower the cost of borrowing.

Anticipate questions.   You may need to consider any questions readers may have about your proposal — and to show how its advantages outweigh any disadvantages. Had the student-loan proposal been written for a Congressional budget committee, it would have needed to anticipate and answer questions about the costs of the proposed solution.

A call to action.   The goal of a proposal is to persuade readers to accept your proposed solution. This solution may include asking readers to take action.

An appropriate tone.   Since you're trying to persuade readers to act, your tone is important — readers will always react better to a reasonable, respectful presentation than to anger or self-righteousness.

A BRIEF GUIDE TO WRITING

Deciding on a Topic

Choose a problem that can be solved.   When you are assigned to write a proposal for a writing class, you will need to choose a problem to write about. Complex, large problems, such as poverty, hunger, or terrorism, usually require complex, large solutions. Most of the time, focusing on a smaller problem or a limited aspect of a large problem will yield a more manageable proposal. Rather than tackling the problem of world poverty, for example, think about the problem faced by families in your community that have lost jobs and need help until they find employment.

Considering the Rhetorical Situation

3–4

■ **PURPOSE** Do you have a vested interest in the solution your readers adopt, or do you simply want to eliminate the problem, whatever solution might be adopted?

5–8

■ **AUDIENCE** How can you reach your readers? Do you know how receptive or resistant to change they are likely to be? Do they have the authority to enact your proposal?

12–14

■ **STANCE** How can you show your audience that your proposal is reasonable and should be taken seriously? How can you demonstrate your own authority and credibility?

15–17

■ **MEDIA / DESIGN** How will you deliver your proposal? In print? Online? As a speech? Would visuals help you to argue for your proposal?

Generating Ideas and Text

Explore potential solutions to the problem. Many problems can be solved in more than one way, and you need to show your readers that you've examined several potential solutions. You may develop solutions to your problem on your own; more often, though, you'll need to do

329–449 ●

RESEARCH to see how others have solved — or tried to solve — similar problems. Don't settle on a single solution too quickly — you'll need to

266–74 ◆

COMPARE the advantages and disadvantages of several solutions in order to argue convincingly for one.

Decide on the most desirable solution(s). One solution may be head and shoulders above others — but be open to rejecting all the possible solutions on your list and starting over if you need to, or to combining two or more potential solutions in order to come up with an acceptable fix.

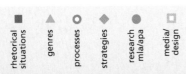

rhetorical situations   genres   processes   strategies   research mla/apa   media/ design

Think about why your solution is the best one. Why did you choose your solution? Why will it work better than others? What has to be done to enact it? What will it cost? What makes you think it can be done? Writing out answers to these questions will help you argue for your solution — to show that you have carefully and objectively outlined a problem, analyzed the potential solutions, and weighed their merits — and to show the reasons the solution you propose is the best.

Ways of Organizing a Proposal

You can organize a proposal in various ways, but always you will begin by establishing that there is a problem. You may then consider several solutions before recommending one particular solution. Sometimes, however, you might suggest only a single solution.

[Several possible solutions]

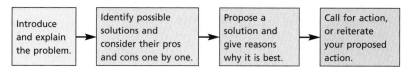

Introduce and explain the problem. → Identify possible solutions and consider their pros and cons one by one. → Propose a solution and give reasons why it is best. → Call for action, or reiterate your proposed action.

[A single solution]

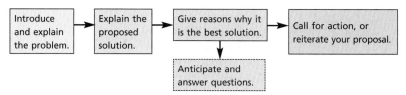

Introduce and explain the problem. → Explain the proposed solution. → Give reasons why it is the best solution. → Call for action, or reiterate your proposal.

Anticipate and answer questions.

If You Need More Help

See Chapter 23 for guidelines on **DRAFTING**, Chapter 24 on **ASSESSING YOUR DRAFT,** Chapter 25 on **GETTING RESPONSE AND REVISING,** and Chapter 26 on **EDITING AND PROOFREADING.** See Chapter 27 if you are required to submit your proposal in a writing **PORTFOLIO.**

○ 205–35

TOPIC PROPOSALS

Instructors often ask students to write topic proposals to ensure that their topics are appropriate or manageable. If you get your instructor's response to a good proposal before you write it, your finished product will likely be much better than if you try to guess the assignment's demands. Some instructors may also ask for an **ANNOTATED BIBLIOGRAPHY** showing that appropriate sources of information are available—more evidence that the project can be carried out. Here a first-year student proposes a topic for an assignment in a writing course in which she has been asked to take a position on a global issue.

112–19 ▲

JENNIFER CHURCH

Biodiversity Loss and Its Effect on Medicine

The loss of biodiversity—the variety of organisms found in the world—is affecting the world every day. Some scientists estimate that we are losing approximately one hundred species per day and that more than a quarter of all species may vanish within fifty years. I recently had the issue of biodiversity loss brought to my attention in a biological sciences course that I am taking this quarter. I have found myself interested in and intrigued by the subject and have found an abundance of information both in books and on the Internet.

In this paper, I will argue that it is crucial for people to stop this rapid loss of our world's biodiversity. Humans are the number-one cause of biodiversity loss in the world. Whether through pollution or toxins, we play a crucial role in the extinction of many different species. For example, 80 percent of the world's medicine comes from biological species and their habitats. One medicine vanishing due to biodiversity loss is TAXOL. Found in the Wollemi pine tree, TAXOL is one of the most promising drugs for the treatment of ovarian and breast cancer. If the Wollemi pine tree becomes extinct, we will lose this potential cure.

I will concentrate primarily on biodiversity and its effects on the medical field. If we keep destroying the earth's biodiversity at the cur-

rent rate, we may lose many opportunities to develop medicines we need to survive. The majority of my information will be found on the Internet, because there are many reliable Web sites from all around the world that address the issue of biodiversity loss and medicine.

Church defines and narrows her topic (from biodiversity loss to the impact of that loss on medicine), discusses her interest, outlines her argument, and discusses her research strategy. Her goal is to convince her instructor that she has a realistic writing project and a clear plan.

Key Features / Topic Proposals

You'll need to explain what you want to write about, why you want to explore it, and what you'll do with your topic. Unless your instructor has additional requirements, here are the features to include:

A concise discussion of the subject.   Topic proposals generally open with a brief discussion of the subject, outlining any important areas of controversy or debate associated with it and clarifying the extent of the writer's current knowledge of it. In its first two paragraphs, Church's proposal includes a concise statement of the topic she wishes to address.

A clear statement of your intended focus.   State what aspect of the topic you intend to write on as clearly as you can, narrowing your focus appropriately. Church does so by stating her intended topic — loss of biodiversity — and then showing how she will focus on the importance of biodiversity to the medical field.

A rationale for choosing the topic.   Tell your instructor why this topic interests you and why you want to write about it. Church both states what made her interested in her topic and hints at a practical reason for choosing it: plenty of information is available.

Mention of resources.   To show your instructor that you can achieve your goal, you need to identify the available research materials.

18 Reflections

Sometimes we write essays just to think about something—to speculate, ponder, probe; to play with an idea, develop a thought; or simply to share something. Reflective essays are our attempt to think something through by writing about it and to share our thinking with others. If such essays make an argument, it is about things we care or think about more than about what we believe to be "true." Have a look at one example by Bernard Cooper, an essayist and novelist who teaches at UCLA and Antioch University/Los Angeles.

BERNARD COOPER

The Fine Art of Sighing

You feel a gradual welling up of pleasure, or boredom, or melancholy. Whatever the emotion, it's more abundant than you ever dreamed. You can no more contain it than your hands can cup a lake. And so you surrender and suck the air. Your esophagus opens, diaphragm expands. Poised at the crest of an exhalation, your body is about to be unburdened, second by second, cell by cell. A kettle hisses. A balloon deflates. Your shoulders fall like two ripe pears, muscles slack at last.

My mother stared out the kitchen window, ashes from her cigarette dribbling into the sink. She'd turned her back on the rest of the house, guarding her own solitude. I'd tiptoe across the linoleum and make my lunch without making a sound. Sometimes I saw her back expand, then heard her let loose one plummeting note, a sigh so long and weary it might have been her last. Beyond our backyard, above telephone poles and apartment buildings, rose the brown horizon of the city; across it glided an occasional bird, or the blimp that advertised Goodyear tires. She might have been drifting into the distance,

or lamenting her separation from it. She might have been wishing she were somewhere else, or wishing she could be happy where she was, a middle-aged housewife dreaming at her sink.

My father's sighs were more melodic. What began as a somber sigh could abruptly change pitch, turn gusty and loose, and suggest by its very transformation that what begins in sorrow might end in relief. He could prolong the rounded vowel of *oy*, or let it ricochet like a echo, as if he were shouting in a tunnel or a cave. Where my mother sighed from ineffable sadness, my father sighed at simple things: the coldness of a drink, the softness of a pillow, or an itch that my mother, following the frantic map of his words, finally found on his back and scratched.

A friend of mine once mentioned that I was given to long and ponderous sighs. Once I became aware of this habit, I heard my father's sighs in my own and knew for a moment his small satisfactions. At other times, I felt my mother's restlessness and wished I could leave my body with my breath, or be happy in the body my breath left behind.

It's a reflex and a legacy, this soulful species of breathing. Listen   5 closely: My ancestors' lungs are pumping like bellows, men towing boats along the banks of the Volga, women lugging baskets of rye bread and pike. At the end of each day, they lift their weary arms in a toast; as thanks for the heat and sting of vodka, their a-h-h's condense in the cold Russian air.

At any given moment, there must be thousands of people sighing. A man in Milwaukee heaves and shivers and blesses the head of the second wife who's not too shy to lick his toes. A judge in Munich groans with pleasure after tasting again the silky bratwurst she ate as a child. Every day, meaningful sighs are expelled from schoolchildren, driving instructors, forensic experts, certified public accountants, and dental hygienists, just to name a few. The sighs of widows and widowers alone must account for a significant portion of the carbon dioxide released into the atmosphere. Every time a girdle is removed, a foot is submerged in a tub of warm water, or a restroom is reached on a desolate road . . . you'd think the sheer velocity of it would create mistrals, siroccos, hurricanes; arrows should be swarming over satellite maps, weathermen talking a mile a minute, ties flapping from their necks like flags.

Before I learned that Venetian prisoners were led across it to their execution, I imagined that the Bridge of Sighs was a feat of invisible engineering, a structure vaulting above the earth, the girders and trusses, the stay ropes and cables, the counterweights and safety rails connecting one human breath to the next.

Cooper explores a common but intriguing subject: the sigh. He begins by describing the physical experience of sighing and then compares two people doing so: his mother, standing at the kitchen window, sighing from disappointment, and his father, sighing with the pleasure of a moment. These memories lead Cooper to realize that his own sighs echo those of his parents and then lead him to reflect on the universality of the sigh. His final paragraph ties the essay together with an image of sighing as a bridge that connects "one human breath to the next."

Key Features / Reflections

A topic that intrigues you. A reflective essay has a dual purpose: to ponder something you find interesting or puzzling and to share your thoughts with an audience. Your topic may be anything that interests you. You might write about someone you have never met and are curious about, an object or occurrence that makes you think, a place where you feel comfortable or safe. Your goal is to explore the meaning that the person, object, event, or place has for you in a way that will interest others. One way to do that is by making connections between your personal experience and more general ones that readers may share. Cooper writes about the way he and his parents sigh but in doing so demonstrates the range of emotions that *everyone's* sighs represent.

Some kind of structure. A reflective essay can be structured in many ways, but it needs to *be* structured. It may seem to wander, but all its paths and ideas should relate, one way or another. The challenge is to keep your readers' interest as you explore your topic and to leave readers satisfied that the journey was pleasurable, interesting, and profitable. Cooper's essay is carefully structured to move us from particular to general, from the physical sensation of air moving in and out of the body to the abstraction of sighing as a bridge connecting human beings.

Specific details. You'll need to provide specific details to help readers understand and connect with your subject, especially if it's an abstract or unfamiliar one. Cooper's essay offers a wealth of figurative and concrete details: when you sigh, "your shoulders fall like two ripe pears," and "every day, meaningful sighs are expelled from schoolchildren, . . . certified public accountants, and dental hygienists, just to name a few." Anecdotes can bring your subject to life: seeing his mother standing at the kitchen sink, Cooper tells us, "I'd tiptoe across the linoleum and make my lunch without making a sound." Reflections may be about causes, such as why Cooper's mother sighed; comparisons, such as when Cooper compares his two parents' sighs; and examples, such as the simple things that evoke his father's sighs: "the coldness of a drink, the softness of a pillow."

A questioning, speculative tone. In a reflective essay, you are working toward answers, not providing them neatly organized and ready for consumption. So your tone is usually tentative, open; demonstrating willingness to entertain, accept, and reject various ideas as your essay progresses from beginning to end. Cooper achieves such a tone by looking at sighing from several perspectives, never settling on any one of them.

A BRIEF GUIDE TO WRITING

Deciding on a Topic

Choose a subject you want to explore. Write a list of things that you think about, wonder about, find puzzling or annoying. They may be big things—life, relationships—or little things—quirks of certain people's behavior, curious objects, everyday events. Try CLUSTERING one or more of those things, or begin by FREEWRITING to see what comes to mind as you write.

⊙ 201–02
◎ 199–200

Considering the Rhetorical Situation

| ▪ PURPOSE | What's your goal in writing this essay? To introduce a topic that interests you? Entertain? Provoke readers to | 3–4 |

think about something? What aspects of your subject do you want to ponder and reflect on?

■ **AUDIENCE** Who is the audience? How familiar are they with your subject? How will you introduce it in a way that will interest them?

■ **STANCE** What is your attitude toward the topic you plan to explore? Questioning? Playful? Critical? Curious? Something else?

■ **MEDIA / DESIGN** Will your essay be a print document? an oral presentation? Will it be posted on a Web site? Would it help to have any visuals?

Generating Ideas and Text

Explore your subject in detail. Reflections often start with descriptive details. Cooper opens his by **DESCRIBING** the physical feeling of sighing. Those details provide a base for the speculations to come. You may also make your point by **DEFINING, COMPARING,** even **CLASSIFYING.** Virtually any organizing pattern will help you explore your subject.

Back away. Ask yourself why your subject matters: why is it important or intriguing or significant? You may try **LISTING** or **OUTLINING** possibilities, or you may want to start **DRAFTING** to see where the writing takes your thinking. Your goal is to think on paper (or screen) about your subject, to play with its possibilities.

Think about how to keep readers with you. Reflections may seem loose or unstructured, but they must be carefully crafted so that readers can follow your train of thought. It's a good idea to sketch out a rough **THESIS** to help focus your thoughts. You may not include the thesis in the essay itself, but every part of the essay should in some way relate to it.

rhetorical situations | genres | processes | strategies | research mla/apa | media/ design

Ways of Organizing a Reflective Essay

Reflective essays may be organized in many ways because they mimic the way we think, associating one idea with another in ways that make sense but do not necessarily form a "logical" progression. In general, you might consider organizing a reflection using this overall strategy:

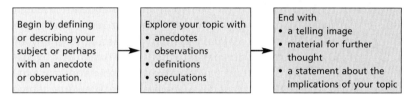

Another way to organize this type of essay is as a series of brief reflections that together create an overall impression:

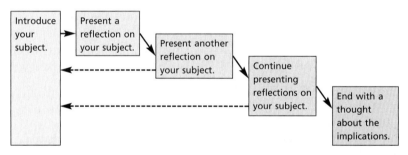

If You Need More Help

See Chapter 23 for GUIDELINES ON DRAFTING, Chapter 24 on ASSESSING YOUR DRAFT, Chapter 25 on GETTING RESPONSE AND REVISING, and Chapter 26 on EDITING AND PROOFREADING. See Chapter 27 if you are required to submit your reflection in a writing PORTFOLIO.

⊙ 205–35

19 Reviews of Scholarly Literature

Reviews of scholarly literature describe and evaluate important research ("literature") available on a topic. We consult literature reviews when we need an overview of such research. In writing a literature review, your goal is to give an overview of the literature on a topic. You do that by discussing the literature that is most relevant to your topic and your purposes, providing clear and accurate summaries of appropriate source material, and describing relationships among facts and concepts. Here is an example of a literature review that describes two methods of teaching reading. The review was prepared for the North Central Regional Educational Laboratory in 1999.

DEBRA JOHNSON

Balanced Reading Instruction: A Review of the Literature

In the history of education, few topics have sparked such public debate as the teaching of reading. Because reading is at the heart of every child's learning, it has been a principal educational focus for more than a century. Research on reading dates as far back as 1879, when a paper was published on eye movements in reading (Samuels & Kamil, 1984). In the mid-1960s, discussion of appropriate reading instruction gained prominence as a result of published research on models of reading instruction and comparative studies of the U.S. Office of Education's Cooperative Research Program in First Grade Reading Instruction (Venezky, 1984; Samuels & Kamil, 1984). Both of these research efforts sparked widespread interest in all aspects of the reading process, particularly at the beginning stages of learning to read. Two basic views

rhetorical situations

genres

processes

strategies

research mla/apa

media/ design

of reading instruction grew out of this activity: the skills-based approach (which emphasizes the use of phonics) and the meaning-based approach (which emphasizes reading comprehension and enrichment).

Skills-Based Approach. The skills-based approach to reading was highly influenced by the work of Jeanne S. Chall (Snow, Burns, & Griffin, 1998). In 1967, Chall discussed her efforts to identify effective practices in beginning reading instruction in *Learning to Read: The Great Debate.* She concluded that there are "consistent and substantial advantages to programs that included systematic phonics" (Snow, Burns, & Griffin, 1998). Phonics is an instructional strategy used to teach letter-sound relationships by having readers "sound out" words. In 1990, Marilyn J. Adams extended Chall's work with her review of research, *Beginning to Read: Thinking and Learning About Print.* Like Chall, Adams emphasized that effective reading instruction is based on "direct instruction in phonics, focusing on the orthographic regularities of English" as well as lots of exposure to reading materials and time to practice reading (Snow, Burns, & Griffin, 1998).

In skills-based learning, phonics skills are taught in isolation with the expectation that once letter-sound relationships are learned, meaning will follow. Emphasis is placed on intensive phonics instruction that is highly sequenced. Children learn letter-sound relationships by sounding out words. They learn letter sounds, consonant blends, and long and short vowels. Typically, this approach uses reading programs that offer stories with controlled vocabulary made up of letter-sound relationships and words with which children are already familiar. Writing instruction follows the same vein; children are asked to write only after having achieved mastery in basic spelling skills or when a correct model is provided for them to copy. This type of instruction was widely used in the 1960s and 1970s and today is being promoted as part of the back-to-basics movement.

Meaning-based approach. The meaning-based approach to reading was highly influenced by the work of Kenneth S. Goodman (Samuels & Kamil, 1984). Goodman was a leader in the development of the psycholinguistic perspective, which asserts that readers rely more on the structure and meaning of language rather than on the graphic information from text. He and others also noted that literacy development parallels language development. Goodman's work in miscue analysis and reading process had a tremendous impact on reading instruction, especially with early readers. (In miscue analysis, children are observed while reading orally and observers note where the children substitute words, make additions or omissions, or change the word order. This information is used to determine the strategies that children are using in their reading and to help develop ideas for remediation.) Goodman developed a reading model that became known as the whole-language approach. This approach became popular in the 1980s and has continued through the 1990s.

In contrast to the emphasis on phonics that is promoted by the skills-based approach to reading, the meaning-based approach to reading emphasizes comprehension and meaning in texts. Children focus on the wholeness of words, sentences, paragraphs, and entire books to derive meaning through context. Whole-language advocates stress the importance of children reading high-quality children's literature and using language in ways that relate to their lives, such as daily journals, trade books, letter writing, and writing workshops. Word-recognition skills are taught in the context of reading and writing. Comprehension takes precedence over skills such as spelling. In fact, invented spellings are encouraged when younger children are learning to write their own stories. Children learn phonics skills while they are immersed in reading; they learn to decode words by their context. Whole language also offers a supportive and tolerant atmosphere in which children learn to read.

A common but mistaken view is that whole-language and skills-based instruction are dichotomous. Many educators believed that the whole-language approach would enable children to learn to read and write naturally without direct instruction if they were immersed in a literacy-rich environment (Manzo, 1999; Sherman, 1998; Routman, 1996). Some teachers erroneously interpreted this idea to mean no phonics. However, whole language was never intended to exclude phonics (Sherman, 1998; Routman, 1996). In fact, the teaching of skills in context is one of the key characteristics of whole-language education (Weaver, 1995). Instead of being taught in isolation, skills such as grammar and spelling are embedded in whole-language reading and writing activities and are based on the words that children encounter. In this framework, skills teaching arises as a result of children's needs: meaning and comprehension are emphasized (Strickland, 1998).

5

rhetorical situations · genres · processes · strategies · research mla/apa · media/ design

For years, the works of skills-based and meaning-based researchers were pitted against each other in a media war over the best way to teach reading. Now is the time to find resolution. Recent research, such as *Preventing Reading Difficulties in Young Children* (Snow, Burns, & Griffin, 1998), confirms that the teaching of reading requires solid skill instruction, including phonics and phonemic awareness (awareness of the separate sounds in words), imbedded in enjoyable reading and writing experiences with whole texts to facilitate the construction of meaning. In other words, balanced reading instruction in the classroom combines the best of phonics instruction and the whole-language approach to teach both skills and meaning and to meet the reading needs of individual children. In this combined approach, notes Diegmueller (1996), "children are explicitly taught the relationship between letters and sounds in a systematic fashion, but they are being read to and reading interesting stories and writing at the same time."

The current revival of phonics as the cure-all to all reading problems is not the answer to improving reading skills. "Phonics should not be taught as a separate 'subject' with an emphasis on drills and rote memorization," notes the National Association for the Education of Young Children (1996). "The key is a balanced approach and attention to each child's individual needs." In order to accomplish this goal, teachers must keep in mind several key points, notes Strickland (cited in Sherman, 1998): First, teaching phonics is not the same as teaching reading; phonics is merely a tool for readers to use. Second, reading and spelling require much more than just phonics; spelling strategies and word-analysis skills are equally important. Third, memorizing phonics rules does not ensure application of those rules; teaching children how to use phonics is different from teaching them about phonics. Fourth, learners need to see the relevance of phonics for themselves in their own reading and writing.

References

Adams, M. J. (1990). *Beginning to read: Thinking and learning about print.* Cambridge, MA: MIT Press.

Chall, J. S. (1967). *Learning to read: The great debate.* New York: McGraw-Hill.

National Association for the Education of Young Children. (1996). *Phonics and whole language learning: A balanced approach to beginning reading* <http://ericps.crc.uiuc.edu/npin/respar/texts/home/phonics.html>

Samuels, S. J., & Kamil, M. L. (1984). Models of the reading process. In P. D. Pearson, R. Barr, M. L. Kamil, & P. Mosenthal (Eds.), *Handbook of reading research* (Vol. 1, pp. 185–224). New York: Longman.

Sherman, L. (1998, Fall). Seeking common ground. *Northwest Education Magazine* <http://www.nwrel.org/nwedu/fall_98/article2.html>

Snow, C. E., Burns, M. S., & Griffin, P. (Eds.). (1998). *Preventing reading difficulties in young children.* Washington, DC: National Academy Press.

Strickland, D. S. (1998). *Teaching phonics today: A primer for educators.* Newark, DE: International Reading Association.

Venezky, R. L. (1984). The history of reading research. In P. D. Pearson, R. Barr, M. L. Kamil, & P. Mosenthal (Eds.), *Handbook of reading research* (Vol. 1, pp. 3–38). New York: Longman.

The writer begins by establishing a context for the discussion and then focuses on her topic: the controversy between phonics and whole language methods of reading instruction. She defines each method, summarizes the most important literature, and then evaluates the role of each method in reading instruction today. Writing for an audience of educators, she follows APA documentation style. (Because it was written in 1999, its documentation of Internet sources does not include retrieval dates, as would be required now.)

Key Features / Reviews of Scholarly Literature

Careful, thorough research.   A review of scholarly literature demands that you research all the major literature on the topic — or at least the major literature available to you, given the time you have.

Accurate, objective summaries of the relevant literature.   Readers expect a literature review to objectively summarize the main ideas or conclusions of the texts reviewed.

Critical evaluation of the literature.   A literature review offers a considered selection of the most important, relevant, and useful sources of

rhetorical situations | genres | processes | strategies | research mla/apa | media/ design

information on its topic, so you must evaluate each source to decide whether it should be included and then to determine how it advances understanding of the topic.

A clear focus. Because a literature review provides an overview of your topic's main issues and explains the main concepts underlying your research, it must be carefully organized and clearly focused on your specific topic.

A BRIEF GUIDE TO WRITING

Considering the Rhetorical Situation

▨ **PURPOSE**	How much information should you provide to explain the scholarly context of your research or argument? What is your primary goal? To show your expertise on the topic? To inform your readers about the literature on a particular topic? To support a topic proposal?	3–4
▨ **AUDIENCE**	How much do your readers know about your subject and its scholarly literature? Will you need to provide any background information? What documentation system will your readers expect you to use?	5–8
▨ **STANCE**	What is the appropriate tone for your purpose and audience? Do you need to demonstrate your authority? make difficult material accessible?	12–14
▨ **MEDIA/DESIGN**	Are you planning to deliver your review in print or online? If you deliver it online, will you provide active links from your review to online literature?	15–17

Generating Ideas and Text

Start early. Selecting, reading, and understanding the most relevant scholarly literature on a topic require time and effort. This is one assignment not to put off until the last minute.

Choose a manageable topic.   Decide what aspect of your topic you're going to research. If you're researching a topic with a vast literature, you'll need to narrow and define the topic to one you can handle. However, you'll also need a topic for which adequate research is available. The narrower your topic, the easier it'll be to do a comprehensive review. After you've done some research, **CLUSTERING** the various facets of your topic may help you narrow your focus.

201–02 ◎

Survey the literature.   Begin by reading—abstracts, first and last paragraphs, charts and graphs—to help decide what's important and what isn't. Look for repeated references to certain studies: the ones that get cited most are probably the most important. The advice in the **READING STRATEGIES** chapter can help you read critically, and you'll also find help in the **EVALUATIONS** chapter developing criteria for deciding what needs to be included and discussed.

313–28 ◆
120–26 ▲

Read easier literature first.   Get to know your way around your topic; understanding its basic terms, techniques, concepts, and controversies will help you tackle more difficult or specialized literature.

Take notes as you read.   While copying and pasting Internet source material can save time, a literature review demands that you summarize and synthesize a lot of material. Consider using a low-tech method: writing notes on 3×5-inch index cards, one card per source, including for each source its thesis or research question, along with a brief **SUMMARY** of its methods or approach, its findings, its conclusions, and **DOCUMENTATION** information. If you gather the documentation information now, you can simply alphabetize the cards and copy their data into your works cited or references section.

366–67 ●
375–449 ●

Look for any patterns, trends, controversies, contradictions.   How do these sources relate to one another? to your topic? Part of your purpose in reviewing the literature is to identify important trends and issues pertaining to your topic—and to summarize such patterns in your review.

Organizing a Review of Scholarly Literature

Reviews of scholarly literature usually organize the literature into sub-groups. See Chapter 31 for help **DIVIDING** your topic into meaningful subtopics.

261–62

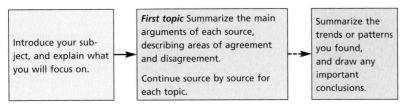

Introduce your subject, and explain what you will focus on. → *First topic* Summarize the main arguments of each source, describing areas of agreement and disagreement.

Continue source by source for each topic. --> Summarize the trends or patterns you found, and draw any important conclusions.

If You Need More Help

See Chapter 23 for guidelines on **DRAFTING**, Chapter 24 on **ASSESSING YOUR DRAFT,** Chapter 25 on **GETTING RESPONSE AND REVISING,** and Chapter 26 on **EDITING AND PROOFREADING.** See Chapter 27 if you are required to submit your review in a writing **PORTFOLIO.**

205–35

20 Résumés and Application Letters

Résumés summarize our education, work experience, and other accomplishments for prospective employers. Application letters introduce us to those employers. When you send a letter and résumé applying for a job, you are making an argument for why that employer should want to meet you, and perhaps hire you. In a way, the two texts together serve as an advertisement selling your talents and abilities to someone who likely has to sift through many applications to decide whom to invite for an interview. That's why résumés and application letters require a level of care that few other documents do. Résumés and application letters are obviously two very different genres—yet they share one common purpose and are done for the same audience. They also go together in the same envelope or email. Thus, they are presented together in this chapter.

RÉSUMÉS

This chapter covers two kinds of résumés, print ones and scannable ones. *Print résumés* are presented on paper to be read by people. You usually design a print résumé to highlight key information typographically, using italic or bold type for headings, for instance. *Scannable résumés* can be delivered on paper or via email, but they are formatted to be read by a computer. Therefore, you need to use a single typeface without any bold or italics or even indents, and you need to write the résumé using keywords that will hopefully match words in the job descriptions the computer is reading for.

Following are two résumés—the first one print and the second one scannable—both done by one college student applying for an internship before his senior year.

rhetorical situations ■ genres ▲ processes ○ strategies ◆ research mla/apa ● media/ design □

Print Résumé

Samuel Praeger
28 Murphy Lane
Springfield, OH 45399
937-555-2640
spraeger22@webmail.com

OBJECTIVE	To obtain an internship with a public relations firm
EDUCATION Fall 2002–present	Wittenberg University, Springfield, OH • B.A. in Psychology expected in May 2006 • Minor in East Asian Studies
EXPERIENCE 2004–present	Department of Psychology, Wittenberg University *Research Assistant* • Collect and analyze data • Interview research participants
Summer 2004	Landis and Landis Public Relations, Springfield, OH *Events Coordinator* • Organized local charity events • Coordinated database of potential donors • Produced two radio spots for event promotion
Summers 2002, 2003	Springfield Aquatic Club, Springfield, OH *Assistant Swim Coach* • Instructed children ages 5–18 in competitive swimming
HONORS 2005	Psi Chi National Honor Society in Psychology
2003–2005	Community Service Scholarship, Wittenberg University
ACTIVITIES	Varsity Swim Team, Ronald McDonald House Fund-raiser
SKILLS	Microsoft Office, SPSS for Windows, Eudora Pro, PowerPoint, Fluency in Japanese language
REFERENCES	Available upon request

Scannable Résumé

Samuel Praeger

Key words: public relations; event coordination; event promotion; sales; independent worker; responsible; collegiate athletics; Japanese language fluency

Address
28 Murphy Lane
Springfield, OH 45399
Phone: 937-555-2640
E-mail: spraeger22@webmail.com

Education
B.A. in Psychology, Minor in East Asian Studies, Wittenberg University, expected May 2006

Experience
Research Assistant, 2004–present
Wittenberg University, Springfield, OH
Data collection from research participants through interviews. Data entry and analysis, using SPSS statistical software.

Events Coordinator, summer 2004
Landis and Landis Public Relations, Springfield, OH
Organizer of charity events. Coordinator of database. Producer of two radio spots.

Assistant Swim Coach, summers 2002 and 2003
Springfield Aquatic Club, Springfield, OH
Instructor of children ages 5–18 in competitive swimming techniques and rules.

Honors
Psi Chi National Honor Society in Psychology, 2005
Community Service Scholarship, Wittenberg University, 2003–2005

Activities
Varsity Swim Team
Ronald McDonald House Fund-raiser

Skills
Microsoft Office; SPSS for Windows; Eudora Pro; PowerPoint, Fluency in Japanese language

References on request

 rhetorical situations
 genres
 processes
 strategies
 research mla/apa
 media/ design

Samuel Praeger's résumé is arranged chronologically, and because he was look-
ing for work in a certain field, the résumé is targeted, focusing on his related
work and skills and leaving out any references to high school (being in college
allows readers to assume graduation from high school, and his past job as a
house painter is not relevant). The print version describes his work respon-
sibilities using action verbs to highlight what he actually did — produced,
instructed, *and so on* — whereas *the scannable version converts the verbs to*
nouns — producer, instructor. *The scannable version is formatted in a single*
standard typeface, with no italics, boldfacing, or other typographic variation.

Key Features / Résumés

An organization that suits your goals and experience.   There are conventional ways of organizing a résumé but no one way. You can organize a résumé chronologically or functionally, and it can be targeted or
not. A *chronological résumé* is the most general, listing pretty much all
your academic and work experience from the most recent to the earliest. A *targeted résumé* will generally announce the specific goal up top,
just beneath your name, and will influence information selectively,
showing only the experience and skills relevant to your goal. A *functional*
résumé is organized around various kinds of experience and is not
chronological. You might write a functional résumé if you wish to
demonstrate a lot of experience in more than one area and perhaps if
you wish to downplay dates.

Succinct.   A résumé should almost always be short — one page if at all
possible. Entries should be parallel but do not need to be written in complete sentences — "Produced two radio spots," for instance, rather than
"I produced two radio spots." *Print résumés* often use action verbs
("instructed," "produced") to emphasize what you accomplished; *scannable*
résumés use nouns instead ("instructor," "producer").

A design that highlights key information.   It's important for a résumé
to look good and to be easy to scan. *On a print résumé,* typography, white

space, and alignment matter. Your name should be bold at the top. Major sections should be labeled with headings, all of which should be in one slightly larger or bolder font. And you need to surround each section and the text as a whole with adequate white space to make the parts easy to read—and to make the entire document look professional. *On a scannable résumé,* you should use one standard typeface throughout and *not* use any italics, boldface, bullets, or indents.

A BRIEF GUIDE TO WRITING

Considering the Rhetorical Situation

3–4

■ **PURPOSE**   Are you seeking a job? an internship? some other position? How will the position for which you're applying affect what you include on your résumé?

5–8

■ **AUDIENCE**   What sort of employee is the company or organization seeking? What experience and qualities will the person doing the hiring be looking for?

12–14

■ **STANCE**   What personal and professional qualities do you want to convey? Think about how you want to come across—as eager? polite? serious? ambitious?—and choose your words accordingly.

15–17

■ **MEDIA / DESIGN**   Are you planning to send your résumé and letter on paper? as an email attachment? in a scannable format? Whatever your medium, be sure both documents are formatted appropriately and proofread carefully.

Generating Ideas and Text for a Résumé

Consider how you want to present yourself.   Begin by gathering the information you will need to include. As you work through the steps of

putting your résumé together, think about the method of organization that works best for your purpose — chronological, targeted, or functional.

- *Contact information.* At the top of your résumé, list your full name, a permanent address (rather than your school address), a permanent telephone number with area code, and your email address (which should sound professional; addresses like *hotbabe334@aol.com* do not make a good first impression on potential employers).

- *Your education.* Start with the most recent: degree (if earned), major (if declared), college attended, and minor (if any). You may want to list your GPA (if it's over 3.0) and any academic honors you've received. If you don't have much work experience, list education first.

- *Your work experience.* As with education, list your most recent job first and work backward. Include job title, organization name, city and state, start and end dates, and responsibilities. Describe them in terms of your duties and accomplishments. If you have extensive work experience in the area in which you're applying, list that first.

- *Community service, volunteer, and charitable activities.* Many high school students are required to perform community service, and many students participate in various volunteer activities that benefit others. List what you've done, and think about the skills and aptitudes that work helped you develop or demonstrate.

- *Other activities, interests, and abilities.* What do you do for fun? What skills do your leisure activities require? (For example, if you play complicated games on the Internet, you probably have a high level of knowledge about computers. You should describe your computer skills in a way that an employer might find useful.)

Define your objective.   Are you looking for a particular job for which you should create a targeted résumé? Are you preparing a generic chronological résumé to use in a search for work of any kind? Defining your objective as specifically as possible helps you decide on the form the résumé will take and the information it will include.

Choose contacts. Whether you list references on your résumé or offer to provide them on request, ask people to serve as references for you before you send out a résumé. It's a good idea to provide each reference with a one-page summary of relevant information about you (for example, give professors a list of courses you took with them, including the grades you earned and the titles of papers you wrote).

Choose your words carefully. Remember, your résumé is a sales document—you're trying to present yourself as someone worth a second look. Focus on your achievements, using action verbs that say what you've done. If, however, you're composing a scannable résumé, use nouns rather than verbs, and use terms that will function as key words. Key words help the computer match your qualifications to the organization's needs. People in charge of hiring search the database of résumés by entering key words relating to the job for which they are seeking applicants. Key words for a lab technician, for example, might include *laboratory, technician, procedures, subjects, experimental*—among many others. To determine what key words to list on your résumé, read job ads carefully, and use the same words the ads do—as long as they accurately reflect your experience. Be honest—employers expect truthfulness, and embellishing the truth can cause you to lose a job later.

Consider key design elements. Make sure your résumé is centered on the page and that it looks clean and clear. It's usually best to use a single, simple **FONT** (serif for print, sans serif for scannable) throughout and to print on white or off-white paper. Limit paper résumés to no more—and no less—than one full page. If you plan to send a scannable résumé or post it on a Web site, create a version that does *not* contain bullets, indents, italics, or underlining, since downloading can cause those elements to get lost or garbled.

454–55 ▢

Edit and proofread carefully. Your résumé must be perfect. Show it to others, and proofread again. You don't want even one typo.

■ ▲ ○ ◆ ● ▢
rhetorical situations | genres | processes | strategies | research mla/apa | media/ design

Ways of Organizing a Résumé

If you don't have much work experience or if you've just gone back to school to train for a new career, put education before work experience; if you have extensive work experience in the area in which you're applying, list work before education.

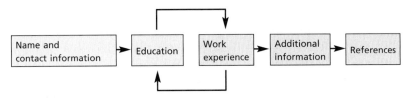

APPLICATION LETTERS

Application letters argue that the writer should be taken seriously as a candidate for a job or some other opportunity. Generally, they are sent together with a résumé, so they don't need to give that much information. They do, however, have to make a favorable impression: the way it's written and presented can get you in for an interview—or not. On the following page is an application letter that Samuel Praeger wrote seeking a position at the end of his junior year. Praeger tailored his letter to one specific reader at a specific organization. The letter cites details, showing that it is not a generic application letter being sent to many possible employers. Rather, it identifies a particular position—the public relations internship—and stresses the fit between his credentials and the position. He also states his availability.

Key Features / Application Letters

A succinct indication of your qualifications. You need to make clear why you're interested in the position or the organization—and at the same time give some sense of why the person you're writing to should at least want to meet you.

street address
city, state zip
date

recipient's name
and title,
organization,
address

salutation,
with a colon

position
identified

match between
experience and
job description

availability

line space

closing

4 lines space for
signature

sender's name,
typed

equal space at
top and bottom
of page, all text
aligning at left
margin

28 Murphy Lane
Springfield, OH 45399
May 19, 2005

Barbara Jeremiah, President   *line space*
Jeremiah Enterprises
44322 Commerce Way
Worthington, OH 45322

Dear Ms. Jeremiah: *line space*

I am writing to apply for the public relations internship advertised
in the Sunday, May 18, *Columbus Dispatch*. The success of your
company makes me eager to work with you and learn from you.

My grasp of public relations goes beyond the theories I have learned   *line space*
in the classroom. I worked last summer at Landis and Landis, the
Springfield public relations firm, where I was responsible for organizing two charity events that drew over two hundred potential donors
each. Since your internship focuses on public relations, my experience in the field should allow me to make a contribution to your
company.

I will be available to begin any time after May 23, when the spring
term at Wittenberg ends. I enclose my résumé, which provides
detailed information about my background. I will phone this week
to see if I might arrange an interview.

Sincerely,

Samuel Praeger

Samuel Praeger

A reasonable and pleasing tone.   When writing to an individual about a job, you need to go beyond simply stating your accomplishments. Through your words, you need to demonstrate that you will be the kind of employee the organization wants. Presentation is also important—your letter should be neat and error free.

A conventional, businesslike format.   Application letters typically follow a prescribed format. The most common is the block format shown here. It includes the writer's address, the date, the recipient's name and address, a salutation, the message, a closing, and a signature.

A BRIEF GUIDE TO WRITING

Generating Ideas and Text for Application Letters

Think about exactly what you hope to accomplish.   When you're writing an application letter, what do you want? Information? An application form? An interview? A referral? Review your RHETORICAL SITUATION.

■ 1–17

Focus.   Application letters are not personal and should not be chatty. Keep them focused: when you're applying for a position, include only information relevant to the position. Don't make your audience wade through irrelevant side issues. Stay on topic.

State the reason for the letter.   Unlike essays, which develop a thesis over several paragraphs, or emails, which announce their topic in a subject line, letters need to explicitly introduce their reason for writing, usually in the first paragraph. When you're applying for something, say so in the first sentence: "I am writing to apply for the Margaret Branscomb Peabody Scholarship for students majoring in veterinary science."

Think of your letter as an argument.   When you're asking for a job, you're making an ARGUMENT. You're making a claim—that you're qualified for a certain position—and you need to support your claim with reasons and evi-

▲ 82–106

dence. Praeger, for example, cites his education and his work experience—and he offers to supply references who will support his application.

Choose an appropriate salutation.　If you know the person's name and title, use it: "Dear Professor Turnigan." If you don't know the person's title, one good solution is to address him or her by first and last name: "Dear Julia Turnigan." If, as sometimes happens, you must write to an unknown reader, your options include "To Whom It May Concern" and the more old fashioned "Dear Sir or Madam." Another option might be to omit the salutation completely in such situations and instead use a subject line, for example: "Subject: Public Relations Internship Application." Whenever possible, though, write to a specific person; call the organization and ask whom to write to.

Proofread.　Few writing situations demand greater perfection than professional letters—especially application letters. Employers receive dozens, sometimes hundreds, of applications, and often can't look at them all. Typos, grammar errors, and other forms of sloppiness prejudice readers against applications: they're likely to think that if this applicant can't take the time and care to **PROOFREAD,** how badly does he or she want this position? To compete, strive for perfection.

222–23 ○

Ways of Organizing a Letter of Application

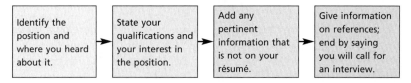

| Identify the position and where you heard about it. | State your qualifications and your interest in the position. | Add any pertinent information that is not on your résumé. | Give information on references; end by saying you will call for an interview. |

If You Need More Help

205–23 ○

See Chapter 23 for guidelines on **DRAFTING,** Chapter 24 on **ASSESSING YOUR DRAFT,** Chapter 25 on **GETTING RESPONSE AND REVISING,** and Chapter 26 on **EDITING.**

rhetorical situations
genres
processes
strategies
research mla/apa
media/ design

part 3

Processes

To create anything, we generally break the work down into a series of steps. We follow a recipe (or the directions on a box) to bake a cake; we break a song down into different parts and the music into various chords to arrange a piece of music. So it is when we write. We rely on various processes to get from a blank page to a finished product. The chapters that follow offer advice on some of these processes—from GENERATING IDEAS to DRAFTING to GETTING RESPONSE to EDITING to COMPILING A PORTFOLIO, and more.

Processes

Collaborating 21

Whether you're working in a group, participating in a Listserv, or exchanging drafts with a classmate for peer review, you likely spend a lot of time collaborating with others. Even if you do much of your writing sitting alone at a computer, you probably get help from others at various stages in the writing process—and provide help as well. The fact is that two heads can be better than one—and learning to work well with a team is as important as anything you'll learn in college. This chapter offers some guidelines for collaborating successfully with other writers.

Some Ground Rules for Working in a Group

- Make sure everyone is facing everyone else and is physically part of the group. Doing that makes a real difference in the quality of the interactions—think how much better conversation works when you're sitting around a table than it does when you're sitting in a row.

- Thoughtfulness, respect, and tact are key, since most writers (as you know) are sensitive and need to be able to trust those commenting on their work. Respond to the writing of others as you would like others to respond to yours.

- Each meeting needs an agenda—and careful attention paid to time. Appoint one person timekeeper to make sure all necessary work gets done in the available time.

- Appoint another person to be group leader or facilitator. That person needs to make sure everyone gets a chance to speak, no one dominates the discussion, and the group stays on task.

- Appoint a third member of the group to keep a record of the group's discussion. He or she should jot down the major points as they come up and afterward write a **SUMMARY** of the discussion that the group members approve.

321–22 ◆

Group Writing Projects

Creating a document with a team is common in business and industry and in some academic fields as well. Collaboration of this kind presents new challenges and different kinds of responsibilities. Here are some tips for making group projects work well:

- *Define the task as clearly as possible,* and make sure everyone understands and agrees with the stated goals.
- *Divide the task into parts.* Decide which parts can be done by individuals, which can be done by a subgroup, and which need to be done by everyone together.
- *Assign each group member certain tasks.* Try to match tasks to each person's skills and interests, and divide the work equally.
- *Establish a deadline for each task.* Allow time for unforeseen problems before the project deadline.
- *Try to accommodate everyone's style of working.* Some people value discussion; others want to get right down to the writing. There's no best way to get work done; everyone needs to be conscious that his or her way is not the only way.
- *Work for consensus — not necessarily total agreement.* Everyone needs to agree that the plan is doable and appropriate — if not exactly the way you would do it if you were working alone.
- *Make sure everyone performs.* In some situations, your instructor may help, but in others the group itself may have to develop a way to make sure that the work gets done well and fairly. During the course of the project, it's sometimes helpful for each member of the group to write an assessment both of the group's work and of individual members' contributions.

Online Collaboration

Sometimes you'll need or want to work with one or more people online. Working together online offers many advantages, including the ability to collaborate without being in the same place at the same time. Nonetheless, working online presents some challenges that differ from those of face-to-face group work. When sharing writing or collaborating with others online, consider the following suggestions:

- As with all online communication, remember that you need to choose your words carefully to avoid flaming another group member or inadvertently hurting someone's feelings. Without facial expressions, gestures, and other forms of body language and without tone of voice, your words carry all the weight.

- Remember that the **AUDIENCE** for what you write may well extend beyond your group — your work might be forwarded to others, there is no telling who else might read it.

5–8

- Decide as a group how best to deal with the logistics of exchanging drafts and comments. You can cut and paste text directly into email, send it as an attachment to a message, or post it to a newsgroup or course bulletin board. You may need to use a combination of methods, depending on each group member's access to equipment and software.

Writing Conferences

Conferences with instructors or writing tutors can be an especially helpful kind of collaboration. These one-on-one sessions often offer the most strongly focused assistance you can get — and truly valuable instruction. Here are some tips for making the most of conference time:

- *Come prepared.* Bring all necessary materials, including the draft you'll be discussing, your notes, any outlines — and, of course, any questions.

- *Be prompt.* Your instructor or tutor has set aside a block of time for you, and once that time is up, there's likely to be another student writer waiting.

- **Listen carefully, take notes, discuss your work seriously, and try not to be defensive.** Your instructor or tutor is only trying to help you produce the best piece possible. If you sense that your work is being misunderstood, explain what you're trying to say. Don't get angry! If a sympathetic reader who's trying to help can't understand what you mean, maybe you haven't conveyed your meaning well enough.

- **Reflect on the conference.** Afterward, think about what you learned. What do you have to do now? What have you learned? Think about questions you will ask at your next conference.

rhetorical situations

genres

processes

strategies

research mla/apa

media/ design

Generating Ideas and Text **22**

All good writing revolves around ideas. Whether you're writing a job-application letter, a sonnet, or an essay, you'll always spend time and effort generating ideas. Some writers can come up with a topic, put their thoughts in order, and flesh out their arguments in their heads, but most of us need to write down our ideas, play with them, tease them out, and examine them from some distance and from multiple perspectives. This chapter offers activities that can help you do just that. *Freewriting, looping, listing*, and *clustering* can help you explore what you know about a subject; *cubing* and *questioning* nudge you to consider a subject in new ways; and *outlining, letterwriting*, and *discovery drafting* offer ways to generate a text.

Freewriting

An informal method of exploring a subject by writing about it, freewriting ("writing freely") can help you generate ideas and come up with materials for your draft. Here's how to do it:

1. Write as quickly as you can without stopping for 5–10 minutes (or until you fill a page or screen).

2. If you have a subject to explore, write it at the top of the page and then start writing, but if you stray, don't worry—just keep writing. If you don't have a subject yet, just start writing and don't stop until the time is up. If you can't think of anything to say, write that ("I can't think of anything to say") again and again until you do—and you will!

3. Once the time is up, read over what you've written, and underline passages that interest you.

4. Then write some more, starting with one of those underlined passages as your new topic. Repeat the process until you've come up with a usable topic.

Looping

Looping is a more focused version of freewriting; it can help you to explore what you know about a subject. You stop, reflect on what you've written, and then write again, developing your understanding in the process. It's good for clarifying your knowledge of a subject and finding a focus. Here's what you do:

1. Write for 5–10 minutes, jotting down whatever you know about your subject. This is your first loop.

2. Read over what you wrote, and then write a single sentence summarizing the most important or interesting idea. You might try completing one of these sentences: "I guess what I was trying to say was . . . " or "What surprises me most in reading what I wrote is . . . " This will be the start of another loop.

3. Write again for 5–10 minutes, using your summary sentence as your beginning and your focus. Again, read what you've written, and then write a sentence capturing the most important idea—in a third loop.

Keep going until you have enough understanding of your topic to be able to decide on a tentative focus—something you can write about.

Listing

Some writers find it useful to keep lists of ideas that occur to them while they are thinking about a topic. Follow these steps:

1. Write a list of potential topics, leaving space to add ideas that might occur to you later. Don't try to limit your list—include anything that interests you.

2. Look for relationships among the items on your list: what patterns do you see?

rhetorical situations

genres

processes

strategies

research mla/apa

media/ design

3. Finally, arrange the items in an order that makes sense for your purpose and can serve as the beginning of an outline for your writing.

Clustering

Clustering is a way of generating and connecting ideas visually. It's useful for seeing how various ideas relate to one another and for developing subtopics. The technique is simple:

1. Write your topic in the middle of a sheet of paper and circle it.

2. Write ideas relating to that topic around it, circle them, and connect them to the central circle.

3. Write down ideas, examples, facts, or other details relating to each idea, and join them to the appropriate circles.

4. Keep going until you can't think of anything else relating to your topic.

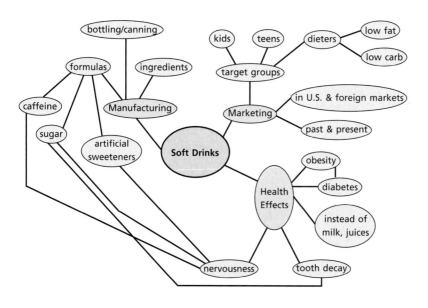

You should end up with various ideas about your topic, and the clusters will allow you to see how they relate. Here's an example of a cluster on the topic of "soft drinks." Note how some ideas link not only to the main topic or related topics but also to other ideas.

Cubing

A cube has six sides. You can examine a topic as you might a cube, looking at it in these six ways:

- **DESCRIBE** it. What's its color? shape? age? size? What's it made of?
- **COMPARE** it to something else. What is it similar to or different from?
- Associate it with other things. What does it remind you of? What connections does it have to other things? How would you **CLASSIFY** it?
- **ANALYZE** it. How is it made? Where did it come from? Where is it going? How are its parts related?
- Apply it. What is it used for? What can be done with it?
- **ARGUE** for or against it. Choose a position relating to your subject, and defend it.

285–93

266–74

260–65

255–59

82–106

Questioning

It's always useful to ask questions, starting with What? Who? When? Where? How? and Why? One method of exploring a topic is asking questions as if the topic were a play. This method is particularly useful for exploring literature, history, the arts, and the social sciences. Start with these questions:

- *What?* What happens? How is it similar to or different from other actions?
- *Who?* Who are the actors? Who are the participants, and who are the spectators? How do the actors affect the action, and how are they affected by it?
- *When?* When does the action take place? How often does it happen? What happens before, after, or at the same time? Would it be different at another time? Does the time have historical significance?

- *Where?* What is the setting? What is the situation, and what makes it significant?
- *Why?* Why did this happen? What are the actors' motives? What end does the action serve?
- *How?* How does the action occur? What are the steps in the process? What techniques are required? What equipment is needed?

Outlining

You may create an *informal outline* by simply listing your ideas and numbering them in the order in which you want to write about them. You might prefer to make a *working outline*, to show the hierarchy of relationships among your ideas. While still informal, a working outline distinguishes your main ideas and your support, often through simple indentation:

First main idea
    Supporting evidence or detail
    Supporting evidence or detail

Second main idea
    Supporting evidence or detail
    Supporting evidence or detail

A *formal outline* shows the hierarchy of your ideas through a system of indenting, numbering, and lettering. Remember that when you divide a point into more specific subpoints, you should have at least two of them—you can't divide something into only one part. Also, try to keep items at each level parallel in structure. Formal outlines work this way:

Thesis statement
  I. First reason
    A. Supporting evidence
      1. Detail of evidence
      2. Detail of evidence
    B. Supporting evidence
  II. Another reason

Writing out a formal outline can be helpful when you're dealing with a complex subject; as you revise your drafts, though, be flexible and ready to change your outline as your understanding of your topic develops.

Letter Writing

Sometimes the prospect of writing a report or essay can be intimidating. You may find that explaining your topic to someone will help you get started. In that case, write a letter to someone you know — your best friend, a parent or grandparent, a sibling — in which you discuss your subject. Explain it in terms that your reader can understand. Use the unsent letter to rehearse your topic; make it a kind of rough draft that you can then revise and develop to suit your actual audience.

Discovery Drafting

Some writers do best by jumping in and writing. Here are the steps to take if you're ready to write a preliminary **DRAFT:**

205–07 ◎

1. Write your draft quickly, in one sitting if possible.

2. Assume that you are writing to discover what you want to say and how you need to say it — and that you will make substantial revisions in a later part of the process.

3. Don't worry about grammatical or factual correctness — if you can't think of a word, leave a blank to fill in later. If you're unsure of a date or spelling, put a question mark in parentheses as a reminder to check it later. Just write.

19–192 ▲

> See also each of the **GENRE** chapters for specific stategies for generating text in each genre.

Drafting 23

At some point, you need to write out a draft. By the time you begin drafting, you've probably written quite a bit—in the form of notes, lists, outlines, and other kinds of informal writing. This chapter offers some hints on how to write a draft—and reminds you that as you draft, you may well need to get more information, rethink some aspect of your work, or follow new ideas that occur to you as you write.

Establishing a Schedule with Deadlines

Don't wait until the last minute to write. Computers crash, printers jam. Life intervenes in unpredictable ways. You increase your chances of success immensely by setting and meeting deadlines: Research done by ___; rough draft done by ___; revisions done by ___; final draft edited, proofread, and submitted by ___. How much time you need varies with each writing task—but trying to compress everything into twenty-four or forty-eight hours before the deadline is asking for trouble.

Getting Comfortable

When are you at your best? When do you have your best ideas? For major writing projects, consider establishing a schedule that lets you write when you stand the best chance of doing good work. Schedule breaks for exercise and snacks. Find a good place to write, a place where you've got a good surface on which to spread out your materials, good lighting, a comfortable chair, and the right tools (pen, paper, computer) for the job. Often, however, we must make do: you may have to do your drafting in a busy computer lab or classroom. The trick is to make yourself as comfortable as you can manage. Sort out what you *need* from what you *prefer*.

Starting to Write

All of the above advice notwithstanding, don't worry so much about the trappings of your writing situation that you don't get around to writing. Write. Start by **FREEWRITING,** start with a first sentence, start with awful writing that you know you'll discard later—but write. That's what gets you warmed up and going.

199–200

Write quickly in spurts.   Write quickly with the goal of writing a complete draft, or a complete section of a longer draft, in one sitting. If you need to stop in the middle, jot down some notes about where you were headed when you stopped so that you can easily pick up your train of thought when you begin again.

Break down your writing task into small segments.   Big projects can be intimidating. But you can always write one section or, if need be, one paragraph or even a single sentence—and then another and another. It's a little like dieting—if I think I need to lose twenty pounds, I get discouraged and head for the doughnuts; but if I decide that I'll lose one pound and I lose it, well, I'll lose another—*that* I can do.

Expect surprises.   Writing is a form of thinking; the words you write lead you down certain roads and away from others. You may end up somewhere you didn't anticipate. Sometimes that can be a good thing—but sometimes you can write yourself into a dead end or out onto a tangent. Just know that this is natural, part of every writer's experience, and it's okay to double back or follow a new path that opens up before you.

Remember that your writing is not carved in stone.   A first sentence, first page, or first draft represents your attempt to organize into words your thoughts, ideas, feelings, research findings, and more. It's likely that

rhetorical situations

genres

processes

strategies

research mla/apa

media/ design

some of that first try will not achieve your goals. That's okay—having writing on paper or on screen that you can change, add to, and cut means you're part of the way there.

Dealing with Writer's Block

You may sit down to write but find that you can't—nothing occurs to you; your mind is blank. Don't panic; here are some ways to get started writing again:

- Think of the assignment as a problem to be solved. Try to capture that problem in a single sentence: "How do I . . . ?" "What is the best way to . . . ?" "What am I trying to do in . . . ?" Think of a solution to the problem, and then stop thinking about it. If you can't solve it, do something else; give yourself time. Many of us find the solution in the shower, after a good night's sleep.

- Stop trying: take a walk, take a shower, do something else. Come back in a half hour, refreshed.

- Open a window, or get a fresh piece of paper and **FREEWRITE,** or try **LOOPING** or **LISTING.** What are you trying to say? Just let whatever comes come—you may write yourself out of your box.

  ⊙ 199–200
  ⊙ 200–01

- Try a different medium: try **CLUSTERING,** or draw a chart of what you want to say; draw a picture; doodle.

  ⊙ 201–02

- Do some **RESEARCH** on your topic to see what others have said about it.

  ● 329–449

- Talk to someone about what you are trying to do; if there's a writing center at your school, talk to a tutor: **GET RESPONSE.** If there's no one to talk to, talk to yourself. It's the act of talking—using your mouth instead of your hands—that can free you up.

  ⊙ 213–14

> See the chapter on **GENERATING IDEAS AND TEXT** if you find you need more material. And once you have a draft, see the chapters on **ASSESSING YOUR OWN WRITING** and **GETTING RESPONSE AND REVISING** for help evaluating your draft.

⊙ 199–204
⊙ 208–18

24 Assessing Your Own Writing

In school and out, our work is continually assessed by others. Teachers determine whether our writing is strong or weak; supervisors decide whether we merit raises or promotions; even friends and relatives size up the things we do in various ways. As writers, we need to assess our work — to step back and see it with a critical eye. By developing standards of our own and being conscious of the standards others use, we can assess — and shape — our writing, making sure it does what we want it to do. This chapter will help you assess your own written work.

Assessing the Writing You Do for Yourself

We sometimes write not for an audience but for ourselves — to generate ideas, reflect, make sense of things. The best advice on assessing it is *don't*. If you're writing to explore your thoughts, understand a subject, record the events of your day or just for the pleasure of putting words on paper, shut off your internal evaluator. Let the words flow without worrying about them. Let yourself wander without censoring yourself or fretting that what you're writing is incorrect or incomplete or incoherent. That's okay.

199–202 ○

One measure of the success of personal writing is its length. FREEWRITING, journal writing, LISTING, CUBING, and other types of informal writing are like warm-up exercises to limber you up and get you thinking. If you don't give those writing exercises enough time and space, they may not do what you want them to. I've found, for example, that my students' best insights most often appear at the end of their journal entries. Had they stopped before that point, they never would have had those good ideas.

A way to study the ideas in your personal writing is to highlight useful patterns in different colors. For example, academic journals usually involve some questioning and speculating, as well as summarizing and paraphrasing. Try color coding each of these, sentence by sentence, phrase by phrase: yellow for summaries or paraphrases, green for questions, blue for speculations. Do any colors dominate? If, for example, your text is mostly yellow, you may be restating the course content too much and per-haps need to ask more of your own questions. If you're generating ideas for an essay, you might assign colors to ideas or themes to see which ones are most promising.

Assessing the Writing You Do for Others

What we write for others must stand on its own because we usually aren't present when it is read—we rarely get to explain to readers why we did what we did and what it means. So we need to make our writing as good as we can before we submit, post, display, or publish it. It's a good idea to assess your writing in two stages, first considering how well it meets the needs of your particular rhetorical situation, then studying the text itself to check its focus, argument, and organization. Sometimes some sim-ple questions can get you started:

> What works?
> What still needs work?
> Where do you need to say more (or less)?

Considering the Rhetorical Situation

■ **PURPOSE** What is your purpose for writing? If you have multiple purposes, list them, and then note which ones are the most important. How does your draft achieve your pur-pose(s)? If you're writing for an assignment, what are the requirements of the assignment and does your draft meet those requirements? 3–4

■ **AUDIENCE** To whom are you writing? What do those readers need and expect, as far as you can tell? Does your draft 5–8 answer their needs? Do you define any terms and explain any concepts they won't know?

9–11 ■ **GENRE**   What is the genre, and what are the key features of that genre? Does your draft include each of those features?

12–14 ■ **STANCE**   Is it clear where you stand on your topic? Does your writing project the personality, voice, and tone that you want? Look at the words you use—how do they represent you as a person?

15–17 ■ **MEDIA / DESIGN**   At this point, your text is not likely to be designed, but think about the medium (print? spoken? electronic?) and whether your writing suits it. What design requirements can you anticipate? Lists? Headings? Charts? Visuals?

Examining the Text Itself

Look carefully at your text to see how well it says what you want it to say. Start with the broadest aspect, its focus, and then examine its reasons and evidence, organization, and clarity, in that order. If your writing lacks focus, the revising you'll do to sharpen the focus is likely to change everything else; if it needs more reasons and evidence, the organization may well change.

Consider your focus.   Your writing should have a clear point, and every part of the writing should support that point. Here are some questions that can help you see if your draft is adequately focused:

251–52 ◆
- What is your **THESIS?** Even if it is not stated overtly, you should be able to summarize it for yourself in a single sentence.
- Is your thesis narrow or broad enough to suit the needs and expectations of your audience?

239–45 ◆
- How does the **BEGINNING** focus attention on your main point?
- Does each paragraph support or develop that point? Do any paragraphs or sentences stray from your focus?

- Does the **ENDING** leave readers thinking about your main point? Is there another way of concluding the essay that would sharpen your focus?

245–48

Consider the support you provide for your argument. Your writing needs to give readers enough information to understand your points, follow your argument, and see the logic of your thinking. How much information is enough will vary according to your audience. If they already know a lot about your subject or are likely to agree with your point of view, you may need to give less detail. If, however, they are unfamiliar with your topic or are skeptical about your views, you will probably need to provide much more information to help them understand your position.

- What **REASONS** and **EVIDENCE** do you give to support your thesis? Where might more information be helpful or useful?

93–94

- What key terms and concepts do you **DEFINE?** Are there any other terms your readers might need to have explained?

275–84

- Where might you want more **DESCRIPTION** or other detail?

285–93

- Do you include any **COMPARISONS?** Especially if your readers will not be familiar with your topic, it can help to compare it with something more familiar.

266–74

- If you include **NARRATIVE,** how is it relevant to your point?

304–12

- See Part IV for other useful **STRATEGIES.**

237–328

Consider the organization. As a writer, you need to lead readers through your text, carefully structuring your material so that they will be able to follow your argument.

- Analyze the structure by **OUTLINING** it. An informal outline will do since you mainly need to see the parts, not the details.

203–04

- Does your genre require an abstract, a works cited list, or any other elements?

- What **TRANSITIONS** help readers move from idea to idea and paragraph to paragraph?

254

- Would **HEADINGS** help orient readers?

456–57

Check for clarity. Nothing else matters if readers can't understand what you write. So clarity matters. Following are some questions that can help you see whether your meaning is clear and your text is easy to read:

250–51
- Does your **TITLE** announce your subject of your text and give some sense of what you have to say? If not, would it strengthen your argument to be more direct?

251–52
- Do you state your **THESIS** directly? If not, how will readers understand your main point? Try stating your thesis outright, and see if it makes your argument easier to follow.

239–49
- Does your **BEGINNING** tell readers what they need to understand your text, and does your **ENDING** help them make sense of what they've just read?

- How does each paragraph relate to the ones before and after? Do you

254
  make those relationships clear — or do you need to add **TRANSITIONS**?

- Do you vary your sentences? If all the sentences are roughly the same length and follow the same subject-verb-object pattern, your text probably lacks any clear emphasis and might even be difficult to read.

458–62
- Are **VISUALS** clearly labeled, positioned near the text they relate to, referred to clearly in the text?

358–69
- If you introduce materials from other **SOURCES**, have you clearly distinguished quoted, paraphrased, or summarized ideas from your own?

- Have a look at the words you use. Concrete words are generally easier to understand than abstract words. If you use too many abstract words, consider changing some of them to concrete terms. Do you

275–84
  DEFINE all the words that your readers may not know?

- Does your punctuation make your writing more or less clear? Incorrect punctuation can make writing difficult to follow or, worse, change the intended meaning. As a best-selling punctuation manual reminds us, there's a considerable difference between "eats, shoots, and leaves" and "eats shoots and leaves."

rhetorical situations

genres

processes

strategies

research mla/apa

media/ design

Getting Response and Revising **25**

If we want to learn to play a song on the guitar, we play it over and over again until we get it right. If we play basketball or baseball, we likely spend hours shooting foul shots or practicing a swing. Writing works the same way. Making our meaning clear can be tricky, and you should plan on revising and if need be rewriting in order to get it right. When we speak with someone face-to-face or on the phone or write an instant message to a friend, we can get immediate response and adjust or restate our message if we've been misunderstood. When we write, that immediate response is missing, so we need to seek out response from readers to help us revise. This chapter includes a list of things for those readers to consider, along with various strategies for then revising and rewriting.

Getting Response

Sometimes the most helpful eyes belong to others: readers you trust, including trained writing-center tutors. They can often point out problems (and strengths) that you simply cannot see in your own work. Ask your readers to consider the specific elements in the list below, but don't restrict them to those elements. Caution: If a reader says nothing about any of these elements, don't be too quick to assume that you needn't think about them yourself.

- What did you think when you first saw the **TITLE?** Is it interesting? informative? appropriate? Will it attract other readers' attention?

  250–51

- Does the **BEGINNING** grab readers' attention? If so, how does it do so? Does it give enough information about the topic? offer necessary background information? How else might the piece begin?

  239–45

- Is there a clear **THESIS?** What is it?

  251–52

94

375–449

- Is there sufficient **SUPPORT** for the thesis? Is there anywhere you'd like to have more detail? Is the supporting material sufficiently **DOCUMENTED?**

- Does the text have a clear pattern of organization? Does each part relate to the thesis? Does each part follow from the one preceding it? Was the text easy to follow? How might the organization be improved?

245–48

- Is the **ENDING** satisfying? What did it leave you thinking? How else might it end?

12-14

- What is the writer's **STANCE?** Can you tell the writer's attitude toward the subject and audience? What words convey that attitude? Is it consistent throughout?

1–17

- How well does the text address the rest of its **RHETORICAL SITUATION?** Does it meet the needs and expectations of its **AUDIENCE?** Where might readers need more information, guidance, or clarification? Does it achieve its **PURPOSE?** Does every part of the text help achieve the purpose? Could anything be cut? Should anything be added? Does it meet the requirements of its **GENRE?** Should anything be added, deleted, or changed to meet those requirements?

Revising

Once you have studied your draft with a critical eye and hopefully gotten response from other readers, it's time to revise. Major changes may be necessary, and you may need to generate new material or do some rewriting. But assume that your draft is good raw material that you can revise to achieve your purposes. Revision should take place on several levels, from global (whole-text issues) to particular (the details). Work on your draft in that order, starting with the elements that are global in nature and gradually moving to smaller, more particular aspects. This allows you to use your time most efficiently and take care of bigger issues first. In fact, as you deal with the larger aspects of your writing, many of the smaller ones will be taken care of along the way.

Give yourself time to revise.   When you have a deadline, set deadlines for yourself that will give you time — preferably several days but as much as your schedule permits—to work on the text before it has to be delivered. Also, get some distance. Often when you're immersed in a project, you can't see the big picture because you're so busy creating it. If you can, get away from your writing for a while and think about something else. When you return to it, you're more likely to see it freshly. If there's not time to put a draft away for several days or more, even letting it sit overnight or for a few hours can help.

As you revise, assume that nothing is sacred. Bring a critical eye to all parts of a draft, not only to those parts pointed out by your reviewers. Content, organization, sentence patterns, individual words—all are subject to improvement. Be aware that a change in one part of the text may require changes in other parts.

Revise to sharpen your focus.   Examine your **THESIS** to make sure it matches your **PURPOSE** as you now understand it. Read each paragraph to ensure that it contributes to your main point; you may find it helpful to **OUTLINE** your draft to help you see all the parts. If any parts of your draft do not advance your thesis, you need either to modify the parts of the draft that don't match or to revise your thesis to reflect your draft's focus. Read your **BEGINNING AND ENDING** carefully; make sure that the first paragraphs introduce your topic and provide any needed contextual information and that the last paragraphs provide a satisfying conclusion.

251–52
3–4
203–04
239–49

Revise to strengthen the argument.   If readers find some of your claims unconvincing, you need to provide more information or more support. You may need to define terms you've assumed they will understand, offer additional examples, or provide more detail by describing, explaining processes, adding dialogue, or using some other **STRATEGIES.** Make sure you show as well as tell! You might try freewriting, clustering, or other ways of **GENERATING IDEAS AND TEXTS.** If you need to provide additional evidence, you might need to do additional **RESEARCH.**

237–328
199–204
329–449

Revise to improve the organization.   If you've outlined your draft, number each paragraph, and make sure each one follows from the one before. If anything seems out of place, move it, or if necessary, cut it completely. Check to see if you've included appropriate **TRANSITIONS** or **HEADINGS** to

254
456–57

help readers move through the text, and add them as needed. Check to make sure your text meets the requirements of the **GENRE** you're writing in.

9–11

Revise for clarity.   Be sure readers will be able to understand what you're saying. Look closely at your **TITLE** to be sure it gives a sense of what the text is about, and at your **THESIS** to be sure readers will recognize your main point. If you don't state a thesis directly, consider whether you should. Be sure you provide any necessary background information and **DEFINE** any key terms. Make sure you've integrated any **QUOTATIONS, PARAPHRASES,** or **SUMMARIES** into your text clearly. Be sure all paragraphs are focused around one main point and that the sentences in each paragraph contribute to that point. Finally, consider whether there are any data that would be more clearly presented in a **CHART, TABLE,** or **GRAPH.**

250–51
251–52
275–84
358–69
458–62

One way to test whether your text is clear is to switch audiences: say what you're trying to say as if you were talking to an eight-year-old. You probably don't want to write that way, but the act of explaining your ideas to a young audience or readers who know nothing about your topic can help you discover any points that may be unclear.

Read and reread and reread.   Take some advice from Donald Murray:

> Nonwriters confront a writing problem and look away from the text to rules and principles and textbooks and handbooks and models. Writers look at the text, knowing that the text itself will reveal what needs to be done and what should not yet be done or may never be done. The writer reads and rereads and rereads, standing far back and reading quickly from a distance, moving in close and reading slowly line by line, reading again and again, knowing that the answers to all writing problems lie within the evolving text.
>
> —Donald Murray, *A Writer Teaches Writing*

Rewriting

Some writers find it useful to try rewriting a draft in various ways or from various perspectives just to explore possibilities. Try it! If you find that

your original plan works best for your purpose, fine. But you may find that another way will work better. Especially if you're not completely satisfied with your draft, consider the following ways of rewriting. Experiment with your rhetorical situation:

- Rewrite your draft from different points of view, through the eyes of different people perhaps or through the eyes of an animal or even from the perspective of an object. See how the text changes (in the information it presents, its perspective, its voice).

- Rewrite for a different **AUDIENCE.** How might an email detailing a recent car accident be written to a friend, the insurance adjuster, a parent?　　5–8

- Rewrite in a different **STANCE.** If the first draft was temperate and judicious, be extreme; if it was polite, be more direct. If the first draft was in standard English, rewrite it in the language your relatives use.　　12–14

- Rewrite the draft in a different **GENRE** or **MEDIUM.** Rewrite an essay as a letter, story, poem, speech. Which genre and medium work best to reach your intended audience and achieve your purpose?　　9–11　15–16

Ways of rewriting a narrative

- Rewrite one scene completely in **DIALOGUE.**　　294–98

- Start at the end of the story and work back to the beginning, or start in the middle and fill in the beginning as you work toward the end.

Ways of rewriting a textual analysis

- **COMPARE** the text you're analyzing with another text (which may be in a completely different genre—film, TV, song lyrics, computer games, poetry, fiction—whatever).　　266–74

- Write a parody of the text you're analyzing. Be as silly and as funny as you can while maintaining the structure of the original text. Alternatively, write a parody of your analysis, using evidence from the text to support an outrageous analysis.

Ways of rewriting a report

5–8

- Rewrite for a different AUDIENCE. For example, explain a concept to your grandparents; describe the subject of a profile to a visitor from another planet.

- Be silly. Rewrite the draft as if for *The Daily Show* or *The Onion*, or rewrite it as if it were written by Bart Simpson.

Ways of rewriting an argument

82–106 ▲

- Rewrite taking another POSITION. Argue as forcefully for that position as you did for your actual one, acknowledging and refuting that position. Alternatively, write a rebuttal to your first draft from the perspective of someone with different beliefs.

304–12 ◆

- Rewrite your draft as a STORY—make it real in the lives of specific individuals. (For example, if you were writing about abortion rights, you could write a story about a young pregnant woman trying to decide what she believes and what to do.) Or rewrite the argument as a fable or parable.

- Rewrite the draft as a letter responding to a hostile reader, trying at least to make him or her understand what you have to say.

- Rewrite the draft as an angry letter to someone, or as a table-thumping dinner-with-the-relatives discussion. Write from the most extreme position possible.

324–27 ◆

- Write an ANALYSIS of your argument in which you identify, as carefully and as neutrally as you can, the various positions people hold on the issue.

Once you've rewritten a draft in any of these ways, see whether there's anything you can use. Read each draft, considering how it might help you achieve your purpose, reach your audience, convey your stance. Revise your actual draft to incorporate anything you think will make your text more effective.

Editing and Proofreading 26

Your ability to produce clear, error-free writing shows something about your ability as a writer and also leads readers to make assumptions about your intellect, work habits, even your character. Readers of job-application letters and résumés, for example, may reject applications if they contain a single error if only because that's an easy way to narrow the field of potential candidates. In addition, they may well assume that applicants who present themselves sloppily in an application will do sloppy work on the job. This is all to say that you should edit and proofread your work carefully.

Editing

Editing is the stage when you work on the details of your paragraphs, sentences, words, and punctuation to make your writing as clear, precise, correct—and effective—as possible. Your goal is not to achieve "perfection" (whatever that may be) so much as to make your writing as effective as possible for your particular purpose and audience. Check a good writing handbook for detailed advice, but the following guidelines can help you check your drafts systematically for some common errors with paragraphs, sentences, and words.

Editing paragraphs

- Does each paragraph focus on one point? Does it have a **TOPIC SENTENCE** 252–53 that announces that point, and if so, where is it located? If it's not the first sentence, should it be? If there's no clear topic sentence, should there be one?

- Does every sentence in the paragraph relate to the main point of that paragraph? If any sentences do not, consider whether they should be deleted, moved, or revised.

- Is there enough detail to develop the main point of the paragraph? How is the point developed—as a narrative? a definition? some other **STRATEGY?**

237–328

- Where have you placed the most important information—at the beginning? the end? in the middle? The most emphatic spot is at the end, so in general that's where to put information you want readers to remember. The second most emphatic spot is at the beginning.

- Are any paragraphs especially long or short? Consider breaking long paragraphs if there's a logical place to do so—maybe an extended example should be in its own paragraph, for instance. If you have paragraphs of only a sentence or two, see if you can add to them or combine them with another paragraph.

- Check the way your paragraphs fit together. Does each one follow smoothly from the one before? Do you need to add any **TRANSITIONS** or other links?

254

- Does the **BEGINNING** paragraph catch readers' attention? In what other ways might you begin your text?

239–45

- Does the final paragraph provide a satisfactory **ENDING?** How else might you conclude your text?

245–48

Editing sentences

- Is each sentence complete? Does it have someone or something (the subject) performing some sort of action or expressing a state of being (the verb)? Does each sentence begin with a capital letter and end with a period, question mark, or exclamation point?

- Check your use of the active voice ("The choir sang 'Amazing Grace.'") and the passive ("'Amazing Grace' was sung by the choir.") Some kinds of writing call for the passive voice, and sometimes it is more appropriate than the active voice, but in general, you'll do well to edit out any use of the passive voice that's not required.

- Check for parallelism. Items in a list or series should be parallel in form — all nouns (lions, tigers, bears), all verbs (hopped, skipped, jumped), all clauses (he came, he saw, he conquered), and so on.

- Do many of your sentences begin with *it* or *there?* Sometimes these words help introduce a topic, but too often they make your text vague or even conceal needed information. Why write "There are reasons we voted for him." when you can say "We had reasons to vote for him."?

- Are your sentences varied? If they all start with a subject or are all the same length, your writing might be dull and maybe even hard to read. Try varying your sentence openings by adding transitions, introductory phrases, or dependent clauses. Vary sentence lengths by adding detail to some or combining some sentences.

Editing words

- Are you sure of the meaning of every word? Use a dictionary; be sure to look up words whose meanings you're not sure about. And remember your audience — do you use any terms they'll need to have **DEFINED?**

275–84

- Is any of your language too general or vague? Why write that you competed in a race, for example, if you could say you ran the 4×200 relay?

- What about the tone? If your stance is serious (or humorous, or critical, or something else), make sure that your words all convey that tone.

- Do all pronouns have clear antecedents? If you write "he" or "they" or "it" or "these," will readers know whom or what the words refer to?

- Have you used any clichés — expressions that are used so frequently that they are no longer fresh? "Live and let live," avoiding something "like the plague," and similar expressions are so predictable that your writing will almost always be better off without them.

- Be careful with the language you use to refer to others. Make sure that your words do not stereotype any individual or group. Mention age, gender, race, religion, sexual orientation, and so on, only if they are relevant to your subject. When referring to an ethnic group, make every effort to use the terms members of the group prefer.

- Edit out language that might be considered sexist. Do you say "he" when you mean "he and she"? Have you used words like *manpower* or *policeman* to refer to people who may be female? If so, substitute less gendered words such as *personnel* or *police officer*. Do your words reflect any gender stereotypes—for example, that all engineers are male, or all schoolteachers female? If you mention someone's gender, is it even necessary? If not, eliminate the unneeded words.

- How many of your verbs are forms of *be*, *do*, and *have*? If you rely too much on these words, try replacing them with more specific verbs. Why write "She did a story" when you could say "She wrote a story"?

- Do you ever confuse *its* and *it's*? Use *it's* when you mean *it is* or *it has*. Use *its* when you mean *belonging to it*.

Proofreading

Proofreading is the final stage of the writing process, the point where you clean up your work to present it to your readers. Proofreading is like checking your appearance in a mirror before going into a job interview: being neat and well groomed looms large in creating a good first impression, and the same principle applies to writing. Misspelled words, missing pages, mixed-up fonts, and other lapses send a negative message about your work—and about you. Most readers excuse an occasional error, but by and large readers are an intolerant bunch: too many errors will lead them to declare your writing—and maybe your thinking—flawed. There goes your credibility. So proofread your final draft with care to ensure that your message is taken as seriously as you want it to be.

Up to this point, you've been told *not* to read individual words on the page and instead to read for meaning. Proofreading demands the opposite: you must slow down your reading so that you can see every word, every punctuation mark.

- Use your computer's grammar checker and spelling checker, but only as a first step, and know that they're not very reliable. Computer pro-

rhetorical situations

genres

processes

strategies

research mla/apa

media/ design

grams don't read writing; instead, they rely on formulas and banks of words, so what they flag (or don't flag) as mistakes may or may not be accurate. If you were to write, "Sea you soon," *sea* would not be flagged as misspelled because it is a word and it's spelled correctly even though it's the wrong word in that sentence.

- To keep your eyes from jumping ahead, place a ruler or piece of paper under each line as you read it. Use your finger or pen or pencil as a pointer.

- Some writers find it helpful to read the text one sentence at a time, beginning with the last sentence and working backward.

- Read your text out loud to yourself—or better, to others, who may *hear* problems you can't see. Alternatively, have someone else read your text aloud to you while you follow along on the page or screen.

- Ask someone else to read your text. The more important the writing is, the more important this step.

- If you find a mistake after you've printed out your text and are unable to print out a corrected version, make the change as neatly as possible in pencil or pen.

27 Compiling a Portfolio

Artists maintain portfolios of their work to show gallery owners, collectors, and other potential buyers. Money managers work with investment portfolios of stocks, bonds, and various mutual funds. And often as part of a writing class, student writers compile portfolios of their work. As with a portfolio of paintings or drawings, a portfolio of writing includes a writer's best work and, sometimes, preliminary and revised drafts of that work, along with a statement by the writer articulating why he or she considers it good. The *why* is as important as the work, for it provides you with an occasion for assessing your overall strengths and weaknesses as a writer. This chapter offers guidelines to help you compile both a *writing portfolio* and a *literacy portfolio*, a project that writing students are sometimes asked to complete as part of a literacy narrative.

Considering the Rhetorical Situation

As with the writing you put in a portfolio, the portfolio itself is generally intended for a particular audience but could serve a number of different purposes. It's a good idea, then, to consider these and the other elements of your rhetorical situation when you begin to compile a portfolio.

<table>
<tr>
<td>3–4</td>
<td>■ **PURPOSE**</td>
<td>Why are you creating this portfolio? To create a record of your writing? As the basis for a grade in a course? To organize your research? To explore your literacy? For something else?</td>
</tr>
<tr>
<td>5–8</td>
<td>■ **AUDIENCE**</td>
<td>Who will read your portfolio? What will your readers expect it to contain? How can you help them understand the context or occasion for each piece of writing you include?</td>
</tr>
</table>

rhetorical situations · genres · processes · strategies · research mla/apa · media/ design

■ **GENRE** What genres of writing should the portfolio contain? Do you want to demonstrate your ability to write a particular type of writing or in a variety of genres? Will your statement about the portfolio be in the form of a letter or an essay?   9–11

■ **STANCE** How do you want to portray yourself in this portfolio? What items should you include to create this impression? What stance do you want to take in your written assessment of its contents? Thoughtful? Enthusiastic? Something else?   12–14

■ **MEDIA / DESIGN** Will your portfolio be in print? Or will it be electronic? Whichever medium you choose, how can you help readers navigate its contents? What design elements will be most appropriate to your purpose and medium?   15–17

A WRITING PORTFOLIO

What to Include in a Writing Portfolio

A portfolio developed for a writing course typically contains examples of your best work in that course, including any notes, outlines, preliminary drafts, and so on, along with your own assessment of your performance in that course. You might include any of the following items:

- freewriting, outlines, and other work you did to generate ideas
- drafts, rough and revised
- in-class writing assignments
- source material—copies of articles, Web sites, observation notes, interview transcripts, and other evidence of your research
- tests and quizzes
- responses to your drafts
- conference notes, error logs, lecture notes, other course materials
- reflections on your work

What you have included will vary depending on what your instructor asks for. You may be asked to include three of your best papers or everything you've written. You may also be asked to choose certain items for evaluation or perhaps to show work in several different genres. In any case, you will need to choose, and to do that you will need to have criteria for making your choices. Don't base your decision solely on grades (unless grades are one criterion); your portfolio should reflect *your* assessment of your work, not your instructor's. What do you think is your best work? your most interesting work? your most ambitious work? Whatever criteria you use, you are the judge.

Organizing a Portfolio

Your instructor may provide explicit guidelines for organizing your portfolio. If not, here are some guidelines. If you set up a way to organize your writing at the start of the course, you'll be able to keep track of it throughout the course, making your job at term's end much easier. Remember that your portfolio presents you as a writer, presumably at your best. It should be neat, well organized, and easy to navigate.

Paper portfolios.   Choose something in which to gather your work. You might use a two-pocket folder, a three-ring binder, or a file folder, or you may need a box, basket, or some other container to accommodate bulky or odd-shaped items. You might also put your drafts on a computer disk, with each file clearly named.

Label everything. Label each piece at the top of the first page, specifying the assignment, the draft, and the date: "Proposal, Draft 1, 2/12/05"; "Text Analysis, Final Draft, 10/10/05"; "Portfolio Self-Assessment, Final Draft, 12/11/05"—and so on. Write this information neatly on the page, or put it on a Post-it note. For each assignment, arrange your materials chronologically, with your earliest material (freewriting, for example) on the bottom, and each successive item (source materials, say, then your outline, then your first draft, and so on) on top of the last, ending with

your final draft on top. That way readers can see how your writing progressed from earliest work to final draft.

Online portfolios.   You might also assemble a Web portfolio that includes a home page with links to your portfolio's contents. Doing this requires that you create Web pages and then make them available on the Web. Some Web-based courseware programs allow you to create a portfolio from the texts you've submitted to the program; others require you to use a Web-authoring program. Microsoft FrontPage, Netscape Composer, or Macromedia Dreamweaver may be available through your school. Road Runner, Tripod, and Yahoo! GeoCities also provide tools for constructing Web pages. You can also use Microsoft Word, Excel, or PowerPoint. The programs available for your use and the requirements for posting your portfolio on the Web vary from school to school and instructor to instructor; ask your instructor or your school's computer help desk for help (and see the chapter on **ELECTRONIC TEXT** for general guidance).

476–84

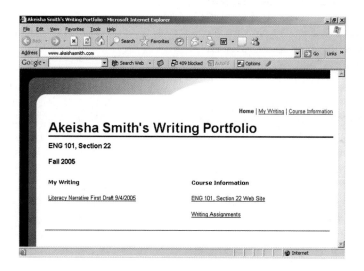

In general, you should first create a basic Web home page using one of those programs. Your home page should include your name, the portfolio's title, the relevant course information, the date, a menu of the contents, and your self-assessment. Below is an example, created with PowerPoint, of the kind of home page you might create early in the course; you can add links as you write new drafts.

Your home page might include a menu of links to each portfolio item, as this one does. Alternatively, you might include links to each piece of writing as you discuss it in your self-assessment—or you could do both. However you guide readers to your writing, be sure to provide a clearly descriptive title for each item. On each page of a final draft, you might create links to preliminary drafts and to work you did generating ideas.

The best way to plan such a portfolio is to make a map of its contents, like the one shown here done for a first-year writing course. Each box represents a different page; each line represents a link from one page to another.

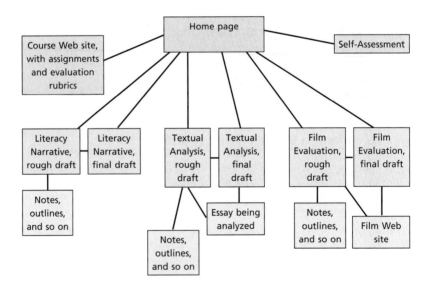

Reflecting on Your Writing Portfolio

The most important part of your portfolio is your written statement reflecting on your work. This is an occasion to step back from the work at hand and examine it with a critical eye. It is also an opportunity to assess your work, and to think about what you're most proud of, what you most enjoyed doing, what you want to improve. It's your chance to think about and say what you've learned. Some instructors may ask you to write out your assessment in essay form; others will want you to put it in letter form, which usually allows for a more relaxed and personal tone. Whatever form it takes, your statement should cover the following ground:

- *An evaluation of each piece of writing in the portfolio.* Consider both strengths and weaknesses, and give examples from your writing to support what you say. What would you change if you had more time? Which is your favorite piece, and why? Which is your least favorite?

- *An assessment of your overall writing performance.* What do you do well? What still needs improvement?

- *A discussion of how the writing you did in this course has affected your development as a writer.* How does the writing in your portfolio compare with writing you did in the past? What do you know now that you didn't know before? What can you do that you couldn't do before?

- *A description of your writing habits and process.* What do you usually do? How well does it work? What techniques seem to help you most, and why? Which seem less helpful? Cite passages from your drafts that support your conclusions.

- *An analysis of your performance in the course.* How did you spend your time? Did you collaborate with others? Did you have any conferences with your instructor? Did you visit the writing center? Consider how these or any other activities contributed to your success.

A SAMPLE SELF-ASSESSMENT

Here is a letter written by Nathaniel Cooney as part of his portfolio for his first-year writing class at Wright State University.

2 June 2004

Dear Reader,

It is my hope that in reading this letter, you will gain an understanding of the projects contained in this portfolio. I enclose three works that I have submitted for an introductory writing class at Wright State University, English 102, Writing in Academic Discourse: an informative report, an argument paper, and a genre project based largely on the content of the argument paper. I selected the topics of these works for two reasons: First, they address issues that I believe to be relevant in terms of both the intended audience (peers and instructors of the course) and the times when they were published. Second, they speak to issues that are important to me personally. Below I present general descriptions of the works, along with my review of their strengths and weaknesses.

My purpose in writing the informative report "Higher Standards in Education Are Taking Their Toll on Students" was to present a subject in a factual manner and to support it with well-documented research. My intent was not to argue a point. However, because I chose a narrowly focused topic and chose information to support a thesis, the report tends to favor one side of the issue over the other. Because as a student I have a personal stake in the changing standards in the formal education system, I chose to research recent changes in higher education and their effects on students. Specifically, I examine students' struggles to reach a standard that seems to be moving farther and farther beyond their grasp.

I believe that this paper could be improved in two areas. The first is a bias that I think exists because I am a student presenting

information from the point of view of a student. It is my hope, however, that my inclusion of unbiased sources lessens this problem somewhat and, furthermore, that it presents the reader with a fair and accurate collection of facts and examples that supports the thesis. My second area of concern is the overall balance in the paper between outside sources supporting my own thoughts and outside sources supporting opposing points of view. Rereading the paper, I notice many places where I may have worked too hard to include sources to support my ideas. I do not necessarily see that as a bad thing, however, because, as I stated earlier, the outside sources work to counterbalance my own bias and provide the reader with additional information. I do think, though, that the paper might be improved if I were to reach a better balance between the amount of space dedicated to the expression of my ideas and the amount of space dedicated to the presentation of source materials.

The second paper, "Protecting Animals That Serve," is an argument intended not only to take a clear position on an issue but also to argue for that position and convince the reader that it is a valid one. That issue is the need for legislation guaranteeing that certain rights of service animals be protected. I am blind and use a guide dog. Thus, this issue is especially important to me. During the few months that I have had him, my guide dog has already encountered a number of situations where intentional or negligent treatment by others has put him in danger. At the time I was writing the paper, a bill was being written in the Ohio House of Representatives that, if passed, would protect service animals and establish consequences for those who violated the law. The purpose of the paper, therefore, was to present the reader with information about service animals, establish the need for the legislation in Ohio and nationwide, and argue for passage of such legislation.

I think that the best parts of my argument are the introduction and the conclusion. In particular, I think that the conclusion does a good job of not only bringing together the various points, but also conveying the significance of the issue for me and for others. In contrast, I think that the area most in need of further attention is the body of the paper. While I think the content is strong, I believe the overall organization could be improved. The connections between ideas are unclear in places, particularly in the section that acknowledges opposing viewpoints. This may be due in part to the fact that I had difficulty understanding the reasoning behind the opposing argument.

The argument paper served as a starting point for the genre project, for which the assignment was to revise one paper written for this class in a different genre. My genre project consists of a poster and a brochure. As it was for the argument paper, my primary goal was to convince my audience of the importance of a particular issue and viewpoint—specifically, to convince my audience to support House Bill 369, the bill being introduced in the Ohio Legislature that would create laws to protect the rights of service animals in the state.

Perhaps both the greatest strength and the greatest weakness of the genre project is my use of graphics. Because of my blindness, I was limited in my use of some graphics. Nevertheless, the pictures were carefully selected to capture the attention of readers, and, in part, to appeal to their emotions as they viewed and reflected on the material.

I noticed two other weaknesses in this project. First, I think that in my effort to include the most relevant information in the brochure, I may have included too many details. Because space is limited, brochures generally include only short, simple facts. Although I tried to keep the facts short and simple, I also tried to use the space that I had to provide as much supporting information as I could. This may have resulted in too much information, given the genre. Second, I dedicated one portion of the poster to a poem I wrote. While the thoughts it conveys are extremely impor-

rhetorical situations

genres

processes

strategies

research mla/apa

media/ design

tant to me, I was somewhat unsatisfied with its style. I tried to avoid a simple rhyme scheme, but the words kept making their way back to that format. I kept the poem as it was on the advice of others, but I still believe that it could be better.

Despite its weakness, the poem also adds strength to the project in its last stanzas. There, I ask readers to take a side step for a moment, to consider what their lives would be like if they were directly affected by the issue, and to reflect on the issue from that perspective. I hope that doing so personalized the issue for readers and thus strengthened my argument.

I put a great deal of time, effort, and personal reflection into each project. While I am hesitant to say that they are finished and while I am dissatisfied with some of the finer points, I am satisfied with the overall outcome of this collection of works. Viewing it as a collection, I am also reminded that writing is an evolving process and that even if these works never become exactly what I envisioned them to be, they stand as reflections of my thoughts at a particular time in my life. In that respect, they need not be anything but what they already are, because what they are is a product of who I was when I wrote them. I hope that you find the papers interesting and informative and that as you read them, you, too, may realize their significance.

Respectfully,

Nathaniel J. Cooney

Enclosures (3)

Cooney describes each of the works he includes and considers their strengths and weaknesses, citing examples from his texts to support his assessment.

A LITERACY PORTFOLIO

As a writing student, you may be asked to think back to the time when you first learned to read and write or to remember significant books or other texts you've read and perhaps to put together a portfolio that chronicles your development as a reader and writer. You may also be asked to put together a literacy portfolio as part of a written narrative assignment.

What you include in such a portfolio will vary depending on what you've kept over the years and what your family has kept. You may have all of your favorite books, stories you dictated to a preschool teacher, notebooks in which you practiced cursive writing. Or you may have almost nothing. What you have or don't have is unimportant in the end: what's important is that you gather what you can and arrange it in a way that shows how you think about your development and growth as a literate person. What has been your experience with reading and writing? What's your earliest memory of learning to write? If you love to read, what led you to love it? Who was most responsible for shaping your writing ability? Those are some of the questions you'll ask if you write a **LITERACY NARRATIVE.** You might also compile a literacy portfolio as a good way to generate ideas and text for that assignment.

21–38 ▲

What to Include in a Literacy Portfolio

- school papers
- drawings and doodles from preschool
- favorite books
- photographs you've taken
- drawings
- poems
- letters

- journals and diaries
- lists
- reading records or logs
- marriage vows
- legal documents
- speeches you've given
- awards you've received

Organizing a Literacy Portfolio

You may wish to organize your material chronologically, but there are other methods of organization to consider as well. For example, you might group items according to where they were written (at home, at school, at work), by genre (stories, poems, essays, letters, notes), or even by purpose (pleasure, school, work, church, and so on). Arrange your portfolio in the way that best conveys who you are as a literate person. Label each item you include, perhaps with a Post-it note, to identify what it is, when it was written or read, and why you've included it in your portfolio.

Reflecting on Your Literacy Portfolio

- Why did you choose each item?
- Is anything missing? Are there any other important materials that should be here?
- Why is the portfolio arranged as it is?
- What does the portfolio show about your development as a reader and writer?
- What patterns do you see? Are there any common themes you've read or written about? Any techniques you rely on? Any notable changes over time?
- What are the most significant items—and why?

part 4

Strategies

Whenever we write, we draw on many different strategies to articulate what we have to say. We may DEFINE key terms, DESCRIBE people or places, and EXPLAIN how something is done. We may COMPARE one thing to another. Sometimes we may choose a pertinent story to NARRATE, and we may even want to include some DIALOGUE. The chapters that follow offer advice on how to use these AND OTHER BASIC STRATEGIES for developing and organizing the texts you write.

Strategies

Beginning and Ending **28**

Whenever we pick up something to read, we generally start by looking at the first few words or sentences to see if they grab our attention, and based on them we decide whether to keep reading. Beginnings, then, are important, both attracting readers and giving them some information about what's to come. When we get to the end of a text, we expect to be left with a sense of closure, of satisfaction—that the story is complete, our questions have been answered, the argument has been made. So endings are important, too. This chapter offers advice on how to write beginnings and endings.

Beginning

How you begin depends on your **RHETORICAL SITUATION,** especially your purpose and audience. Academic audiences generally expect your introduction to establish context, explaining how the text fits into some larger conversation, addresses certain questions, or explores an aspect of the subject. Most introductions also offer a brief description of the text's content, often in the form of a thesis statement. The following opening of an essay about "the greatest generation" does all of this:

■ 1–17

> Tom Brokaw called the folks of the mid-twentieth century the greatest generation. So why is the generation of my grandparents seen as this country's greatest? Perhaps the reason is not what they accomplished but what they endured. Many of the survivors feel people today "don't have the moral character to withstand a depression like that." This paper will explore the Great Depression through the eyes of ordinary Americans in the most impoverished region in the country, the

American South, in order to detail how they endured and how the government assisted them in this difficult era.

> —Jeffrey DeRoven, "The Greatest Generation:
> The Great Depression and the American South"

If you're writing for a nonacademic audience or genre—for a newspaper or a Web site, for example—your introduction may need to entice your readers to read on by connecting your text to their interests through shared experiences, anecdotes, or some other attention-getting device. Cynthia Bass, writing a newspaper article about the Gettysburg Address on its 135th anniversary, connects that date—the day her audience would read it—to Lincoln's address. She then develops the rationale for thinking about the speech and introduces her specific topic: debates about the writing and delivery of the Gettysburg Address:

> November 19 is the 135th anniversary of the Gettysburg Address. On that day in 1863, with the Civil War only half over and the worst yet to come, Abraham Lincoln delivered a speech now universally regarded as both the most important oration in U.S. history and the best explanation—"government of the people, by the people, for the people"—of why this nation exists.
>
> We would expect the history of an event so monumental as the Gettysburg Address to be well established. The truth is just the opposite. The only thing scholars agree on is that the speech is short—only ten sentences—and that it took Lincoln under five minutes to stand up, deliver it, and sit back down.
>
> Everything else—when Lincoln wrote it, where he wrote it, how quickly he wrote it, how he was invited, how the audience reacted—has been open to debate since the moment the words left his mouth.

> —Cynthia Bass, "Gettysburg Address: Two Versions"

Ways of Beginning

Explain the larger context of your topic.   Most essays are part of an ongoing conversation, so you might begin by outlining the positions to which your writing responds, as the following example from an essay about prejudice does:

The war on prejudice is now, in all likelihood, the most uncontroversial social movement in America. Opposition to "hate speech," formerly identified with the liberal left, has become a bipartisan piety. In the past year, groups and factions that agree on nothing else have agreed that the public expression of any and all prejudices must be forbidden. On the left, protesters and editorialists have insisted that Francis L. Lawrence resign as president of Rutgers University for describing blacks as "a disadvantaged population that doesn't have that genetic, hereditary background to have a higher average." On the other side of the ideological divide, Ralph Reed, the executive director of the Christian Coalition, responded to criticism of the religious right by calling a press conference to denounce a supposed outbreak of "name-calling, scapegoating, and religious bigotry." Craig Rogers, an evangelical Christian student at California State University, recently filed a $2.5 million sexual-harassment suit against a lesbian professor of psychology, claiming that anti-male bias in one of her lectures violated campus rules and left him feeling "raped and trapped."

In universities and on Capitol Hill, in workplaces and newsrooms, authorities are declaring that there is no place for racism, sexism, homophobia, Christian-bashing, and other forms of prejudice in public debate or even in private thought. "Only when racism and other forms of prejudice are expunged," say the crusaders for sweetness and light, "can minorities be safe and society be fair." So sweet, this dream of a world without prejudice. But the very last thing society should do is seek to utterly eradicate racism and other forms of prejudice.

—Jonathan Rauch, "In Defense of Prejudice"

State your thesis. Sometimes the best beginning is a clear THESIS stating your position, like the following statement in an essay arguing that under certain circumstances torture is necessary:

251–52

It is generally assumed that torture is impermissible, a throwback to a more brutal age. Enlightened societies reject it outright, and regimes using it risk the wrath of the United States.

I believe this attitude is unwise. There are situations in which torture is not merely permissible but morally mandatory. Moreover, these situations are moving from the realm of imagination to fact.

—Michael Levin, "The Case for Torture"

Forecast your organization.   You might begin by briefly outlining the way in which you will organize your text. The following example offers background on the subject, an analysis of immigration patterns in the United States, and describes the points that the writer's analysis will discuss:

> This paper analyzes the new geography of immigration during the twentieth century and highlights how immigrant destinations in the 1980s and 1990s differ from earlier settlement patterns. The first part of the analysis uses historical U.S. Census data to develop a classification of urban immigrant "gateways" that describes the ebb and flow of past, present, and likely future receiving areas. The remainder of the analysis examines contemporary trends to explore the recent and rapid settlement of the immigrant population in America's metropolitan gateways.
>
> —Audrey Singer, "The Rise of New Immigrant Gateways"

Offer background information.   If your readers may not know as much as you do about your topic, giving them information to help them understand your position can be important, as David Guterson does in an essay on the Mall of America:

> Last April, on a visit to the new Mall of America near Minneapolis, I carried with me the public-relations press kit provided for the benefit of reporters. It included an assortment of "fun facts" about the mall: 140,000 hot dogs sold each week, 10,000 permanent jobs, 44 escalators and 17 elevators, 12,750 parking places, 13,300 short tons of steel, $1 million in cash disbursed weekly from 8 automatic-teller machines. Opened in the summer of 1992, the mall was built on the 78-acre site of the former Metropolitan Stadium, a five-minute drive from the Minneapolis–St. Paul International Airport. With 4.2 million square feet of floor space—including twenty-two times the retail footage of the average American shopping center—the Mall of America was "the largest fully enclosed combination retail and family entertainment complex in the United States."
>
> —David Guterson, "Enclosed. Encyclopedic. Endured: The Mall of America"

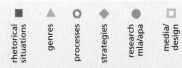

rhetorical situations   genres   processes   strategies   research mla/apa   media/ design

Define key terms or concepts.   The success of an argument often hinges on how key terms are DEFINED. You may wish to provide definitions up front, as this page from an advocacy Web site, *Health Care without Harm,* does in a report on the hazards of fragrances in health-care facilities:

◆ 275–84

> To many people, the word "fragrance" means something that smells nice, such as perfume. We don't often stop to think that scents are chemicals. Fragrance chemicals are organic compounds that volatilize, or vaporize into the air — that's why we can smell them. They are added to products to give them a scent or to mask the odor of other ingredients. The volatile organic chemicals (VOCs) emitted by fragrance products can contribute to poor indoor air quality (IAQ) and are associated with a variety of adverse health effects.
>
> —Health Care without Harm, "Fragrances"

Connect your subject to your readers' interests or values.   You'll always want to establish common ground with your readers, and sometimes you may wish to do so immediately, in your introduction, as in this example:

> We all want to feel safe. Most Americans lock their doors at night, lock their cars in parking lots, try to park near buildings or under lights, and wear seat belts. Many invest in expensive security systems, carry pepper spray or a stun gun, keep guns in their homes, or take self-defense classes. Obviously, safety and security are important issues in American life.
>
> —Andy McDonie, "Airport Security: What Price Safety?"

Start with something that will provoke readers' interest.   Anna Quindlen opens an essay on feminism with the following eye-opening assertion:

> Let's use the F word here. People say it's inappropriate, offensive, that it puts people off. But it seems to me it's the best way to begin, when it's simultaneously devalued and invaluable.
> Feminist. Feminist, feminist, feminist.
>
> —Anna Quindlen, "Still Needing the F Word"

304–12

Start with an anecdote.   Sometimes a brief **NARRATIVE** helps bring a topic to life for readers. See, for example, how an essay on the dozens, a type of verbal contest played by some African Americans, begins:

> Alfred Wright, a nineteen-year-old whose manhood was at stake on Longwood Avenue in the South Bronx, looked fairly calm as another teenager called him Chicken Head and compared his mother to Shamu the whale.
>
> He fingered the gold chain around his thin neck while listening to a detailed complaint about his sister's sexual abilities. Then he slowly took the toothpick out of his mouth; the jeering crowd of young men quieted as he pointed at his accuser.
>
> "He was so ugly when he was born," Wright said, "the doctor smacked his mom instead of him."
>
> —John Tierney, "Playing the Dozens"

Ask a question.   Instead of a thesis statement, you might open with a question about the topic your text will explore, as this study of the status of women in science does:

> Are women's minds different from men's minds? In spite of the women's movement, the age-old debate centering around this question continues. We are surrounded by evidence of de facto differences between men's and women's intellects—in the problems that interest them, in the ways they try to solve those problems, and in the professions they choose. Even though it has become fashionable to view such differences as environmental in origin, the temptation to seek an explanation in terms of innate differences remains a powerful one.
>
> —Evelyn Fox Keller, "Women in Science: A Social Analysis"

Jump right in.   Occasionally you may wish to start a narrative as close to the key action as possible. See how one writer jumps right into his profile of a blues concert:

> Long Tongue, the Blues Merchant, strolls onstage. His guitar rides side-saddle against his hip. The drummer slides onto the tripod seat behind the drums, adjusts the high-hat cymbal, and runs a quick, off-beat tattoo on the tom-tom, then relaxes. The bass player plugs into the ampli-

rhetorical situations
genres
processes
strategies
research mla/apa
media/ design

fier, checks the settings on the control panel, and nods his okay. Three horn players stand off to one side, clustered, lurking like brilliant sorcerer-wizards waiting to do magic with their musical instruments.

—Jerome Washington, "The Blues Merchant"

Ending

Endings are important because they're the last words readers read. How you end a text will depend in part on your RHETORICAL SITUATION. You may end by wrapping up loose ends, or you may wish to give readers something to think about. Some endings do both, as Cynthia Bass does in her report on the disputes over the Gettysburg Address. In her two final paragraphs, she first summarizes the dispute and then shows its implications:

1–17

> What's most interesting about the Lincoln-as-loser and Lincoln-as-winner versions is how they marshal the same facts to prove different points. The invitation asks Lincoln to deliver "a few appropriate remarks." Whether this is a putdown or a reflection of the protocol of the time depends on the "spin"—an expression the highly politicized Lincoln would have readily understood—which the scholar places on it.
>
> These diverse histories should not in any way diminish the power or beauty of Lincoln's words. However, they should remind us that history, even the history of something as deeply respected as the Gettysburg Address, is seldom simple or clear. This reminder is especially useful today as we watch expert witnesses, in an effort to divine what the founders meant by "high crimes and misdemeanors," club one another with conflicting interpretations of the same events, the same words, the same precedents, and the same laws.
>
> —Cynthia Bass, "Gettysburg Address: Two Versions"

Bass summarizes the dispute about Lincoln's Address and then moves on to discuss the role of scholars in interpreting historical events. Writing during the Clinton impeachment hearings, she concluded by pointing out the way in which expert government witnesses often offer conflicting interpretations of events to suit their own needs. The ending combines several strategies to bring various strands of her essay together, leaving readers to interpret her final words themselves.

Ways of Ending

366–67 **Restate your main point.** Sometimes you'll simply **SUMMARIZE** your central idea, as in this example from an essay arguing that we have no "inner" self and that we should be judged by our actions alone:

> The inner man is a fantasy. If it helps you to identify with one, by all means, do so; preserve it, cherish it, embrace it, but do not present it to others for evaluation or consideration, for excuse or exculpation, or, for that matter, for punishment or disapproval.
>
> Like any fantasy, it serves your purposes alone. It has no standing in the real world which we share with each other. Those character traits, those attitudes, that behavior — that strange and alien stuff sticking out all over you — *that's the real you!*
>
> —Willard Gaylin, "What You See Is the Real You"

Discuss the implications of your argument. The following conclusion of an essay on the development of Post-it notes leads readers to consider how failure sometimes leads to innovation:

> Post-it notes provide but one example of a technological artifact that has evolved from a perceived failure of existing artifacts to function without frustrating. Again, it is not that form follows function but, rather, that the form of one thing follows from the failure of another thing to function as we would like. Whether it be bookmarks that fail to stay in place or taped-on notes that fail to leave a once-nice surface clean and intact, their failure and perceived failure is what leads to the true evolution of artifacts. That the perception of failure may take centuries to develop, as in the case of loose bookmarks, does not reduce the importance of the principle in shaping our world.
>
> —Henry Petroski, "Little Things Can Mean a Lot"

304–12 **End with an anecdote,** maybe finishing a **NARRATIVE** that was begun earlier in your text or adding one that illustrates the implications of your argument. See how Sarah Vowell uses a story to end an essay on students' need to examine news reporting critically:

rhetorical situations

genres

processes

strategies

research mla/apa

media/ design

I looked at Joanne McGlynn's syllabus for her media studies course, the one she handed out at the beginning of the year, stating the goals of the class. By the end of the year, she hoped her students would be better able to challenge everything from novels to newscasts, that they would come to identify just who is telling a story and how that person's point of view affects the story being told. I'm going to go out on a limb here and say that this lesson has been learned. In fact, just recently, a student came up to McGlynn and told her something all teachers dream of hearing. The girl told the teacher that she was listening to the radio, singing along with her favorite song, and halfway through the sing-along she stopped and asked herself, "What am I singing? What do these words mean? What are they trying to tell me?" And then, this young citizen of the republic jokingly complained, "I can't even turn on the radio without thinking anymore."

—Sarah Vowell, "Democracy and Things Like That"

Refer to the beginning. One way to bring closure to a text is to bring up something discussed in the beginning; often the reference adds to or even changes the original meaning. See, for example, how Barbara Kingsolver opens an essay arguing that the American flag symbolizes not only patriotism but also the desire for peace and the right to dissent with this anecdote:

My daughter came home from kindergarten and announced, "Tomorrow we all have to wear red, white, and blue."
"Why?" I asked, trying not to sound anxious.
"For all the people that died when the airplanes hit the buildings."
I said quietly, "Why not wear black, then? Why the colors of the flag, what does that mean?"
"It means we're a country. Just all people together."

She returns to this image at the end, where the final sentence takes on a new meaning:

Shortly after the September attacks, my town became famous for a simple gesture in which some eight thousand people wearing red, white, or blue T-shirts assembled themselves in the shape of a flag on a baseball field and had their photograph taken from above. That picture soon began to turn up everywhere, but we saw it first on our newspaper's front page. Our family stood in silence for a minute look-ing at that stunningly beautiful photograph of a human flag, trying to know what to make of it. Then my teenager, who has a quick mind for numbers and a sensitive heart, did an interesting thing. She laid her hand over part of the picture, leaving visible more or less five thou-sand people, and said, "In New York, that many might be dead." We stared at what that looked like—that many innocent souls, parti-colored and packed into a conjoined destiny—and shuddered at the one simple truth behind all the noise, which was that so many beloved, fragile lives were suddenly gone from us. That is my flag, and that's what it means: We're all just people, together.

—Barbara Kingsolver, "And Our Flag Was Still There"

Propose some action, as in the following conclusion of a report on the consequences of binge drinking among college students:

The scope of the problem makes immediate results of any interventions highly unlikely. Colleges need to be committed to large-scale and long-term behavior-change strategies, including referral of alcohol abusers to appropriate treatment. Frequent binge drinkers on college campuses are similar to other alcohol abusers elsewhere in their tendency to deny that they have a problem. Indeed, their youth, the visibility of others who drink the same way, and the shelter of the college community may make them less likely to recognize the problem. In addition to addressing the health problems of alcohol abusers, a major effort should address the large group of students who are not binge drinkers on campus who are adversely affected by the alcohol-related behavior of binge drinkers.

—Henry Wechsler et al., "Health and
Behavioral Consequences of Binge Drinking in College:
A National Survey of Students at 140 Campuses"

Considering the Rhetorical Situation

As a writer or speaker, you need to think about the message that you want to articulate, the audience you want to reach, and the larger context you are writing in.

rhetorical situations

genres

processes

strategies

research mla/apa

media/ design

PURPOSE   Your purpose will affect the way you begin and end. If you're trying to persuade readers to do something, you may want to open by clearly stating your thesis and end by calling for a specific action.   3–4

AUDIENCE   Who do you want to reach, and how does that affect the way you begin and end? You may want to open with an intriguing fact or anecdote to entice your audience to read a profile, for instance, whereas readers of a report may expect it to conclude with a summary of your findings.   5–8

GENRE   Does your genre require a certain type of beginning or ending? Arguments, for example, often provide a statement of the thesis near the beginning; proposals typically end with a call for some solution.   9–11

STANCE   What is your stance, and can your beginning and ending help you convey that stance? For example, beginning an argument on the distribution of AIDS medicine to underdeveloped countries with an anecdote may demonstrate concern for the human costs of the disease, whereas starting with a statistical analysis may suggest the stance of a careful researcher. Ending a proposal by weighing the advantages and disadvantages of the solution you propose may make you seem reasonable.   12–14

MEDIA / DESIGN   Your medium may affect the way you begin and end. A web text, for instance, may open with a home page listing a menu of the site — and giving readers a choice of where they will begin. With a print text, you get to decide how it will begin and end.   15–17

See also the **GUIDES TO WRITING** in chapters 6–9 for ways of beginning and ending a **LITERACY NARRATIVE**, an essay **ANALYZING TEXT**, a **REPORT**, or an **ARGUMENT**.   21–106

29 Guiding Your Reader

Traffic lights, street signs, and lines on the road help drivers find their way. Readers need similar guidance—to know, for example, whether they're reading a report or an argument, an evaluation or a proposal. They also need to know what to expect: What will the report be about? What perspective will it offer? What will this paragraph cover? What about the next one? How do the two paragraphs relate to each other? When you write, you need to provide cues to help your readers navigate your text and understand the points you're trying to make. This chapter offers advice on guiding your reader and, specifically, on using *titles, thesis statements, topic sentences,* and *transitions.*

Titles

A title serves various purposes, naming a text and providing clues to the content. It also helps readers decide whether they want to read further, so it's worth your while to come up with a title that attracts interest. Some titles include subtitles. You generally have considerable freedom in choosing a title but always you'll want to consider the RHETORICAL SITUATION to be sure your title serves your purpose and appeals to the audience you want to reach.

1–17

Some titles simply announce the subject of the text:

"Black Men and Public Space"
"Ain't I a Woman?"
"Why Colleges Shower Their Students with A's"
Nickel and Dimed

rhetorical situations   genres   processes   strategies   research mla/apa   media/design

Some titles provoke readers or otherwise entice them to read:

"Kill 'Em! Crush 'Em! Eat 'Em Raw!"
"Thank God for the Atom Bomb"
"What Are Homosexuals For?"

Sometimes writers add a subtitle to explain or illuminate the title:

Aria: Memoir of a Bilingual Childhood
"Health and Behavioral Consequences of Binge Drinking in College: A
     National Survey of Students at 140 Campuses"
"From Realism to Virtual Reality: Images of America's Wars"

Sometimes when you're starting to write, you'll think of a title that helps you generate ideas and write. More often, though, a title is one of the last things you'll write, when you know what you've written and can craft a suitable name for your text.

Thesis Statements

A thesis identifies the topic of your text along with the claim you are making about it. A good thesis helps readers understand an essay. Working to create a sharp thesis can help you focus both your thinking and your writing. Here are three steps for moving from a topic to a thesis statement:

1. State your topic as a question. You may have an idea for a topic, such as "famine," "gas prices," or "the effects of creatine on athletes." Those may be good topics, but they're not thesis statements, primarily because none of them actually makes a statement. A good way to begin moving from topic to thesis statement is to style your topic as a question:

What can be done to prevent famine in Africa?
What causes fluctuations in gasoline prices?
What are the effects of creatine on athletes?

2. Then turn your question into a position. A thesis statement is an assertion—it takes a stand or makes a claim. Whether you're writing a report or an argument, you are saying, "This is the way I see . . . " or "This is what I believe about . . . " Your thesis statement announces your position on the question you are raising about your topic, so a relatively easy way of establishing a thesis is to answer your own question:

> The most recent famine in Eritrea could have been avoided if certain measures had been taken.
>
> Gasoline prices fluctuate for several reasons.
>
> There are positive as well as negative effects of using creatine to enhance athletic performance.

3. Narrow your thesis. A good thesis is specific, guiding you as you write and showing your audience exactly what your essay will cover. The preceding thesis statements need to be qualified and focused—they need to be made more specific. For example:

> The 1984 famine in Eritrea could have been avoided if farmers had received training in more effective methods and had had access to certain technology and if Western nations had provided more aid more quickly.
>
> Gasoline prices fluctuate because of production procedures, consumer demand, international politics, and oil companies' policies.
>
> When adult athletes use creatine, they become stronger and larger—with no known serious side effects.

Thesis statements are typically positioned at or near the end of the introduction of a text, to let readers know at the outset what you're claiming and what your text will be aiming to prove.

Topic Sentences

Just as a thesis announces your topic and your position, a topic sentence states the subject and focus of a paragraph. Good paragraphs focus on a single point, which is summarized in a topic sentence. Usually, but not always, the topic sentence begins the paragraph:

Graduating from high school or college is an exciting, occasionally even traumatic event. Your identity changes as you move from being a high school teenager to a university student or a worker; your connection to home loosens as you attend school elsewhere, move to a place of your own, or simply exercise your right to stay out later. You suddenly find yourself doing different things, thinking different thoughts, fretting about different matters. As recent high school graduate T. J. Devoe puts it, "I wasn't really scared, but having this vast range of opportunity made me uneasy. I didn't know *what* was gonna happen." Jenny Petrow, in describing her first year out of college, observes, "It's a tough year. It was for all my friends."

—Sydney Lewis, *Help Wanted: Tales from the First Job Front*

Sometimes the topic sentence may come at the end of the paragraph or even at the end of the preceding paragraph, depending on the way the paragraphs relate to one another. Other times a topic sentence will summarize or restate a point made in the previous paragraph, helping readers understand what they've just read as they move on to the next point. See how the linguist Deborah Tannen does this in the first paragraphs of an article on differences in men's and women's conversational styles:

I was addressing a small gathering in a suburban Virginia living room — a women's group that had invited men to join them. Throughout the evening, one man had been particularly talkative, frequently offering ideas and anecdotes, while his wife sat silently beside him on the couch. Toward the end of the evening, I commented that women frequently complain that their husbands don't talk to them. This man quickly concurred. He gestured toward his wife and said, "She's the talker in our family." The room burst into laughter; the man looked puzzled and hurt. "It's true," he explained. "When I come home from work I have nothing to say. If she didn't keep the conversation going, we'd spend the whole evening in silence."

This episode crystallizes the irony that although American men tend to talk more than women in public situations, they often talk less at home. And this pattern is wreaking havoc with marriage.

—Deborah Tannen, "Sex, Lies, and Conversation: Why Is It So Hard for Men and Women to Talk to Each Other?"

Transitions

Transitions help readers move from thought to thought — from sentence to sentence, paragraph to paragraph. You are likely to use a number of transitions as you draft; when you're **EDITING,** you should make a point of checking transitions. Here are some common ones:

219–22 ◐

- **To show causes and effects:** accordingly, as a result, because, consequently, hence, so, then, therefore, thus
- **To show comparisons:** also, in the same way, like, likewise, similarly
- **To show contrasts or exceptions:** although, but, even though, however, in contrast, instead, nevertheless, nonetheless, on the contrary, on the one hand . . . on the other hand, still, yet
- **To show examples:** even, for example, for instance, indeed, in fact, of course, such as
- **To show place or position:** above, adjacent to, below, beyond, elsewhere, here, inside, near, outside, there
- **To show sequence:** again, also, and, and then, besides, finally, furthermore, last, moreover, next, too
- **To show time:** after, as soon as, at first, at the same time, before, eventually, finally, immediately, later, meanwhile, next, simultaneously, so far, soon, then, thereafter
- **To signal a summary or conclusion:** as a result, as we have seen, finally, in a word, in any event, in brief, in conclusion, in other words, in short, in the end, in the final analysis, on the whole, therefore, thus, to summarize

453–63 ▢

> **See also Chapter 47 on PRINT TEXT for ways of creating visual signals for your readers.**

Analyzing Causes and Effects **30**

Analyzing causes helps us think about why something happened, whereas thinking about effects helps us consider what might happen. When we hear a noise in the night, we want to know what caused it. Children poke sticks into holes to see what will happen. Researchers try to understand the causes of diseases. Writers often have occasion to consider causes of effects as part of a larger topic or sometimes as a main focus: in a **PROPOSAL,** we might consider the effects of reducing tuition or the causes of recent tuition increases; in a **MEMOIR,** we might explore why the person we had a date with failed to show up. Often we can only speculate about probable causes or likely effects. In writing about causes and effects, then, we are generally **ARGUING** for those we consider plausible or probable. This chapter will help you analyze causes and effects in writing—and to do so in a way that suits your rhetorical situation.

▲ 160–67
▲ 147–52

▲ 82–106

Determining Plausible Causes and Effects

What causes ozone depletion? sleeplessness? obesity? And what are their effects? Those are of course large, complex topics, but whenever you have reason to ask why something happened or what could happen, there will likely be several possible causes and just as many predictable effects. There may be obvious causes, though often they will be less important than others that are harder to recognize. (Eating too much may be an obvious cause of being overweight, but *why* people eat too much has several less obvious causes: portion size, advertising, lifestyle, and physiological disorders are only a few possibilities.) Similarly, short-term effects are often less important than long-term ones. (A stomachache may be an effect of eating too much candy, but the chemical imbalance that can result from consuming too much sugar is a much more serious effect.)

200–02 ○
203–04 ○
329–449 ●

3–8 ■

LISTING, CLUSTERING, and OUTLINING are useful processes for analyzing causes. And at times you might need to do some RESEARCH to identify possible causes or effects and to find evidence to support your analysis. When you've identified potential causes and effects, you need to analyze them. Which causes and effects are primary? Which seem to be secondary? Which are most relevant to your PURPOSE and are likely to convince your AUDIENCE? You will probably have to choose from several possible causes and effects for your analysis because you won't want or need to include all of them.

Arguing for Causes or Effects

Once you've identified several possible causes or predictable effects, you need to argue that some are more plausible than others. You must provide convincing support for your argument because you cannot prove that X causes Y or that Y will be caused by Z; you can show only, with good reasons and appropriate evidence, that X is likely to cause Y or that Y will likely follow from Z. See, for example, how an essay on the psychological basis for risk taking speculates about two potential causes for the popularity of extreme sports:

> Studies now indicate that the inclination to take high risks may be hardwired into the brain, intimately linked to arousal and pleasure mechanisms, and may offer such a thrill that it functions like an addiction. The tendency probably affects one in five people, mostly young males, and declines with age. It may ensure our survival, even spur our evolution as individuals and as a species. Risk taking probably bestowed a crucial evolutionary advantage, inciting the fighting and foraging of the hunter-gatherer. . . .
>
> As psychologist Salvadore Maddi, PhD, of the University of California at Davis warns, "High-risk takers may have a hard time deriving meaning and purpose from everyday life." Indeed, this peculiar form of dissatisfaction could help explain the explosion of high-risk sports in America and other postindustrial Western nations. In unstable cultures, such as those at war or suffering poverty, people rarely seek out additional thrills. But in a rich and safety-obsessed country like America, land of guardrails, seat belts, and personal-injury lawsuits, everyday life may have

rhetorical situations ■ genres ▲ processes ○ strategies ◆ research mla/apa ● media/design □

become too safe, predictable, and boring for those programmed for risk taking.

—Paul Roberts, "Risk"

Roberts suggests that genetics is one likely cause of extreme sports and that an American obsession with safety is perhaps a cause of their growing popularity. Notice, however, that he presents these as likely or possible, not certain, by choosing his words carefully: "studies now *indicate*," "the inclination to take high risks *may* be hardwired." "Risk taking *probably* bestowed a crucial evolutionary advantage," "this dissatisfaction *could help* explain." Like Roberts, you will almost always need to qualify what you say about causes and effects — to say that something *could explain* (rather than saying it "explains") or that it *suggests* (rather than "shows"). Plausible causes and effects can't be proved definitively, so you need to acknowledge that your argument is not the last word on the subject.

Ways of Organizing an Analysis of Causes and Effects

Your analysis of causes and effects may be part of a proposal or some other genre of writing, or you may write a text whose central purpose is to analyze causes or speculate about effects. While there are many ways to organize an analysis of causes and effects, three common ways are to state a cause and then discuss its effects, to state an effect and then discuss its causes, and to identify a chain of causes and effects.

Identify a cause and then discuss its effects. If you were writing about global warming, you might first show that many scientists fear it will have several effects, including drastic climate changes, the extinction of various kinds of plants, and elevated sea levels.

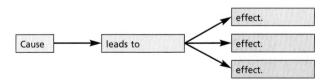

Identify an effect and then trace its causes. If you were writing about school violence, for example, you might argue that it is a result of sloppy dress, informal teacher-student relationships, low academic standards, and disregard for rules.

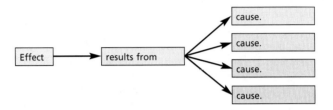

Identify a chain of causes and effects leading from one to another. You may sometimes discuss a chain of causes and effects. If you were writing about the right to privacy, for example, you might consider the case of Megan's law. A convicted child molester raped and murdered a neighborhood child whose name was Megan; the crime caused New Jersey legislators to pass the so-called Megan's law (an effect), which requires that convicted sex offenders be publicly identified. As more states enact versions of Megan's law, concern for the rights of those who are identified is developing—the effect is becoming a cause of further effects.

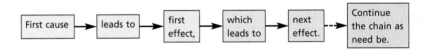

Considering the Rhetorical Situation

As a writer or speaker, you need to think about the message that you want to articulate, the audience you want to reach, and the larger context you are writing in.

3-4

■ **PURPOSE**   Your purpose may be to analyze causes. But sometimes you'll have another goal that calls for such analysis—

a business report, for example, might need to explain what caused a decline in sales.

■ AUDIENCE

Who is your intended audience, and how will analyzing causes help you reach them? Do you need to tell them why some event happened, or what effects resulted?

5–8

■ GENRE

Does your genre require you to analyze causes? Proposals, for example, often need to consider the effects of a proposed solution.

9–11

■ STANCE

What is your stance, and could analyzing causes or effects show that stance? Could it help demonstrate your seriousness, or show that your conclusions are reasonable?

12–14

■ MEDIA / DESIGN

You can rely on words to analyze causes, but sometimes a drawing will help readers *see* how causes lead to effects.

15–17

See also the **PROCESSES** chapters (Chapters 21–27) for help **GENERATING IDEAS, DRAFTING,** and so on if you need to write an entire text whose purpose is to analyze causes or speculate about effects.

193–235

31 Classifying and Dividing

Classification and division are ways of organizing information: various pieces of information about a topic may be classified according to their similarities, or a single topic may be divided into parts. We might classify different kinds of flowers as annuals or perennials, for example, and classify the perennials further as dahlias, daisies, roses, and peonies. We might also divide a flower garden into distinct areas: for herbs, flowers, and vegetables. Writers often use classification and division as ways of developing and organizing material. This book, for instance, classifies comparison, definition, description, and several other common ways of thinking and writing as strategies. It divides the information it provides about writing into seven parts: "Rhetorical Situations," "Genres," "Processes," and so on. Each part further divides its material into various chapters. Even if you never write a book, you will have occasion to classify and divide material in **ANNOTATED BIBLIOGRAPHIES, LITERATURE REVIEWS,** and essays **ANALYZING TEXTS.** This chapter offers advice for classifying and dividing information for various writing purposes—and to do so in a way that suits your own rhetorical situation.

112–19 ▲
174–81 ▲
137–46 ▲

Classifying

When we classify something, we group it with similar things. A linguist would classify French and Spanish and Italian as Romance languages, for example—and Russian, Polish, and Bulgarian as Slavic languages. In a hilarious (if totally phony) news story from *The Onion* about a church bake

rhetorical situations   genres   processes   strategies   research mla/apa   media/ design

sale, the writer classifies the activities observed there as examples of the seven deadly sins:

> GADSDEN, AL—The seven deadly sins—avarice, sloth, envy, lust, gluttony, pride, and wrath—were all committed Sunday during the twice-annual bake sale at St. Mary's of the Immaculate Conception Church.
>
> —*The Onion,* "All Seven Deadly Sins Committed at Church Bake Sale"

The article goes on to categorize the participants' behavior in terms of the sins, describing one parishioner who commits the sin of pride by bragging about her cookies, others who commit the sin of envy by envying the popularity of the prideful parishioner's baked goods (the consumption of which leads to the sin of gluttony). In all, the article notes, "347 individual acts of sin were committed at the bake sale," and every one of them can be classified as one of the seven deadly sins.

Dividing

As a writing strategy, division is a way of breaking something into parts—and a way of making the information easy for readers to follow and understand. See how this example about children's ways of nagging divides their tactics into seven categories:

> James U. McNeal, a professor of marketing at Texas A&M University, is considered America's leading authority on marketing to children. In his book *Kids as Customers* (1992), McNeal provides marketers with a thorough analysis of "children's requesting styles and appeals." He classifies juvenile nagging tactics into seven major categories. A *pleading* nag is one accompanied by repetitions of words like "please" or "mom, mom, mom." A *persistent* nag involves constant requests for the coveted product and may include the phrase "I'm gonna ask just one more time." *Forceful* nags are extremely pushy and may include subtle threats, like "Well, then, I'll go and ask Dad." *Demonstrative* nags are the most high risk, often characterized by full-blown tantrums in public places, breath

holding, tears, a refusal to leave the store. *Sugar-coated* nags promise affection in return for a purchase and may rely on seemingly heartfelt declarations, like "You're the best dad in the world." *Threatening* nags are youthful forms of blackmail, vows of eternal hatred and of running away if something isn't bought. *Pity* nags claim the child will be heartbroken, teased, or socially stunted if the parent refuses to buy a certain item. "All of these appeals and styles may be used in combination," McNeal's research has discovered, "but kids tend to stick to one or two of each that prove most effective . . . for their own parents."

— Eric Schlosser, *Fast Food Nation:*
The Dark Side of the All-American Meal

Here the writer announces the division scheme of "seven major categories." Then he names each tactic and describes how it works. And notice the italics: each nagging tactic is italicized, making it easy to recognize and follow. Take away the italics, and the argument would be less visible.

Creating Clear and Distinct Categories

When you classify or divide, you need to create clear and distinct categories. If you're writing about music, you might divide it on the basis of the genre (hip-hop, rock, classical, gospel), artist (male or female, group or solo), or instruments (violins, trumpets, bongos, guitars). These categories must be distinct, so that no information overlaps or fits into more than one category, and they must include every member of the group you're discussing. The simpler the criteria for selecting the categories, the better. The nagging categories in the example from *Fast Food Nation* are based on only one criterion: a child's verbal behavior.

Highlight your categories.   Sometimes you may want to highlight your categories visually to make them easier to follow. Eric Schlosser does that by italicizing each category: the *pleading* nag, the *persistent* nag, the *forceful* nag, and so on. Other **DESIGN** elements — bulleted lists, pie charts, tables, images — might also prove useful.

451–84

See, for instance, how the humorist Dave Barry uses a two-column list to show two categories of males—"men" and "guys"—in his *Complete Guide to Guys*:

Men	Guys
Vince Lombardi	Joe Namath
Oliver North	Gilligan
Hemingway	Gary Larson
Columbus	Whichever astronaut hit the first golf ball on the moon
Superman	Bart Simpson
Doberman pinschers	Labrador retrievers
Abbott	Costello
Captain Ahab	Captain Kangaroo
Satan	Snidely Whiplash
The pope	Willard Scott
Germany	Italy
Geraldo	Katie Couric

—Dave Barry, *Dave Barry's Complete Guide to Guys: A Fairly Short Book*

Sometimes you might show categories visually, like the illustration on the following page from a news story about the many new varieties of Oreo cookies. In the article, the reporter David Barboza classifies Oreos with words:

There is the Double Delight Oreo . . . , the Uh Oh Oreo (vanilla cookie with chocolate filling), Oreo Cookie Barz, Football Oreos, Oreos Cookies and Creme Pie, Oreos in Kraft Lunchables for kids, and Oreo cookies with a variety of cream fillings (mint, chocolate, coffee) and sizes (six-pack, twelve-pack, snack pack, and more).

**DOUBLE DELIGHT
MINT 'N CREME**
Introduced in 2003

**DOUBLE DELIGHT
PEANUT BUTTER &
CHOCOLATE**
2003

**DOUBLE DELIGHT
COFFEE 'N CREME**
2003

UH OH OREO
(Vanilla cookie, chocolate filling)
2003

CHOCOLATE CREME OREO
2001

FOOTBALL OREO
(Football design on biscuit)
Seasonal

DOUBLE STUFF
1974

ORIGINAL
1912

Piling on the Cookies
In the Oreo's first eight
decades, Nabisco tried only
a handful of variations on the
original. But in recent years, it
has stretched the line to more
than two dozen by varying the
size, the filling, the biscuit
recipe — nearly everything but
the brand name. Here are some
examples now on store shelves.

*David Barboza, "Permutations Push
Oreo Far Beyond Cookie Aisle"*

rhetorical situations

genres

processes

strategies

research mla/apa

media/ design

The illustration, for an article that shows Oreos to be a "hyperevolving, perpetually repackaged, category-migrating" cookie, makes that classification easy to see—and gets our attention in the first place.

Considering the Rhetorical Situation

As a writer or speaker, you need to think about the message that you want to articulate, the audience you want to reach, and the larger context you are writing in.

■ **PURPOSE**   Your purpose for writing will affect how you classify or divide information. Dave Barry classifies males as "men" and "guys" to get a laugh, whereas J. Crew might divide sweaters into cashmere, wool, and cotton to help shoppers find and buy things from their Web site.   *3–4*

■ **AUDIENCE**   Who in your audience do you want to reach, and will classifying or dividing your material help them follow your argument?   *5–8*

■ **GENRE**   Does your genre call for you to categorize or divide information? A long report might need to be divided into sections, for instance.   *9–11*

■ **STANCE**   Your stance may affect the way you classify information. Dave Barry classifies males as "men" and "guys" to reflect a humorist's stance; if he were a psychologist, he might categorize them as "Oedipal," "hormonal," and "libidinal."   *12–14*

■ **MEDIA / DESIGN**   You can classify or divide in paragraph form, but sometimes a pie chart or list will show the categories better.   *15–17*

> See also **CLUSTERING, CUBING,** and **LOOPING,** three methods of **GENERATING IDEAS** that can be especially helpful for classifying material. And see all the **PROCESSES** chapters for guidelines on **DRAFTING, REVISING,** and so on if you need to write a classification essay.
>
> ◎ 200–02
> ◎ 199–204
> ◎ 193–235

32 Comparing and Contrasting

Comparing things looks at their similarities; contrasting them focuses on their differences. It's a kind of thinking that comes naturally and that we do constantly—for example, comparing Houston with Dallas, PCs with Macs, or three paintings by Renoir. And once we start comparing, we generally find ourselves contrasting—Houston and Dallas have differences as well as similarities.

As a student, you'll often be asked to compare and contrast paintings or poems or other things. As a writer, you'll have cause to compare and contrast in most kinds of writing. In a **PROPOSAL,** for instance, you will need to compare your solution with other possible solutions; or in an **EVALUATION,** such as a movie review, you might contrast the film you're reviewing with some other film. This chapter offers advice on ways of comparing and contrasting things for various writing purposes and for your own rhetorical situations.

160–67
120–26

Most of the time, we compare obviously similar things: cars we might purchase, three competing political philosophies, two versions of a film. Occasionally, however, we might compare things that are less obviously similar. See how John McMurtry, an ex–football player, compares football with war in an essay arguing that the attraction football holds for spectators is based in part on its potential for violence and injury:

> The family resemblance between football and war is, indeed, striking. Their languages are similar: "field general," "long bomb," "blitz," "take a shot," "front line," "pursuit," "good hit," "the draft," and so on. Their principles and practices are alike: mass hysteria, the art of intimidation, absolute command and total obedience, territorial aggression, censorship, inflated insignia and propaganda, blackboard maneuvers and strategies, drills, uniforms, marching bands, and train-

rhetorical situations

genres

processes

strategies

research mla/apa

media/ design

ing camps. And the virtues they celebrate are almost identical: hyper-aggressiveness, coolness under fire, and suicidal bravery.

—John McMurtry, "Kill 'Em! Crush 'Em! Eat 'Em Raw!"

McMurtry's comparison helps focus readers' attention on what he's arguing about football in part because it's somewhat unexpected. But the more unlikely the comparison, the more you might be accused of comparing apples and oranges. It's important, therefore, that the things we compare be legitimately compared—as is the case in the following comparison of Ronald Reagan and Arnold Schwarzenegger, two actors who became politicians:

> Like Reagan, Arnold Schwarzenegger made California's governorship his first run for office. Reagan was a few weeks from turning 56 when he took the oath of office in January 1967; Schwarzenegger turned 56 last July. Reagan ousted Democratic Governor Pat Brown; Schwarzenegger's ascent came at the expense of Governor Gray Davis, former chief of staff to Pat's son, Jerry, who succeeded Reagan as governor in 1975.
>
> The parallels go on, like credits at the end of a movie. Reagan evoked "the shining city on the hill"; Schwarzenegger alludes to "the golden dream by the sea" (words probably crafted by the governor's chief wordsmith, Landon Parvin, a Reagan presidential speechwriter). Maybe the eeriest parallel of all: "Arnold" is an anagram of "Ronald."
>
> —Bill Whalen, "Reagan and Schwarzenegger—Parallel Universe?"

No doubt there are contrasts between Reagan and Schwarzenegger as well, but for this piece (which we found on the op-ed page of the *San Francisco Chronicle*), the startling comparisons are the point.

Two Ways of Comparing and Contrasting

Comparisons and contrasts may be organized in two basic ways: block and point by point.

The block method.   One way is to discuss separately each item you're comparing, giving all the information about one item and then all the information about the next item. A report on Seattle and Vancouver, for example, compares the firearm regulations in each city using a paragraph about Seattle and then a paragraph about Vancouver:

> Although similar in many ways, Seattle and Vancouver differ markedly in their approaches to the regulation of firearms. In Seattle, handguns may be purchased legally for self-defense in the street or at home. After a thirty-day waiting period, a permit can be obtained to carry a handgun as a concealed weapon. The recreational use of handguns is minimally restricted.
>
> In Vancouver, self-defense is not considered a valid or legal reason to purchase a handgun. Concealed weapons are not permitted. Recreational uses of handguns (such as target shooting and collecting) are regulated by the province, and the purchase of a handgun requires a restricted-weapons permit. A permit to carry a weapon must also be obtained in order to transport a handgun, and these weapons can be discharged only at a licensed shooting club. Handguns can be transported by car, but only if they are stored in the trunk in a locked box.
>
> —John Henry Sloan et al., "Handgun Regulations, Crime, Assaults, and Homicide: A Tale of Two Cities"

The point-by-point method.   The other way to compare things is to focus on specific points of comparison. A later part of the Seattle-Vancouver study compares the two cities' gun laws and how they're enforced, discussing each point one at a time. (We've underlined each point.) The authors discuss one point, comparing the two cities; then they go on to the next point, again comparing the cities:

> Although they differ in their approach to firearm regulations, both cities aggressively enforce existing gun laws and regulations, and convictions for gun-related offenses carry similar penalties. For example, <u>the commission of a class A felony (such as murder or robbery) with a firearm</u> in Washington State adds a minimum of two years of confinement to the sentence for the felony. In the province of British Columbia, the same offense generally results in one to fourteen years of imprisonment in addition to the felony sentence. <u>Similar percentages of homicides </u>in both communities eventually lead to arrest and

police charges. In Washington, under the Sentencing Reform Act of 1981, <u>murder in the first degree</u> carries a minimum sentence of twenty years of confinement. In British Columbia, first-degree murder carries a minimum sentence of twenty-five years, with a possible judicial parole review after fifteen years. <u>Capital punishment</u> was abolished in Canada during the 1970s. In Washington State, the death penalty may be invoked in cases of aggravated first-degree murder, but no one has been executed since 1963.

Using Graphs and Images to Present Comparisons

Some comparisons can be easier to understand if they're presented visually, as a **CHART, GRAPH,** or **ILLUSTRATION.** See how this chart shows comparative information about Vancouver and Seattle that can be easily understood at a glance and clearly categorized. It would be possible to show the same material in paragraph form, but it's much easier to see and read in this chart:

458–62

Seattle and Vancouver: Basic Demographic Information	Seattle, Washington	Vancouver, British Columbia
Population (1980)	493,846	430,826
Unemployment rate	5.8%	6.0%
High-school graduates	79.0%	66.0%
Median household income (U.S. dollars)	$16,254	$16,681

—John Henry Sloan et al., "Handgun Regulations, Crime, Assaults, and Homicide: A Tale of Two Cities"

The following bar graph, from an economics textbook, compares the incomes of various professions in the United States, both with one another and with the average U.S. income (defined as 100 percent). Again, it would be possible to write out this information in a paragraph—but it is much easier to understand it this way:

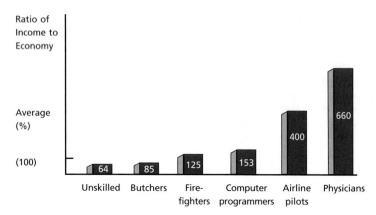

Joseph Stiglitz, *Economics*

Sometimes photographs can make a comparison. The two photos below show a woman before and after she had her hair dyed. The caption suggests that the story is more complicated than the photos alone can tell, however; for the full story, we need words.

"GO BLONDE! *'I tried it before and it came out orange!'* " iVillage.com

Lance Jackson, *San Francisco Chronicle*

And here is a composite photograph that illustrates the comparison of Arnold Schwarzenegger with Ronald Reagan on page 267. Just as the article points out some startling similarities between the two actor-politicians, the photograph makes the comparison visual.

Using Figurative Language to Make Comparisons

Another way we make comparisons is with figurative language: words and phrases used in a nonliteral way to help readers see a point. Three kinds of figurative language that make comparisons are similes, metaphors, and analogies. When Robert Burns wrote that his love was "like a red, red rose," he was comparing his love with a rose and evoking an image—in this case, a simile—that helps us understand his feelings for her. A simile makes a comparison using *like* or *as*. In the following example, from an article in the food section of the *New York Times*, a restaurant critic uses several similes (underlined) to help us visualize an unusual food dish:

> Once upon a time, possibly at a lodge in Wyoming, possibly at a butcher shop in Maurice, Louisiana, or maybe even at a plantation in South Carolina, an enterprising cook decided to take a boned chicken, a boned duck, and a boned turkey, stuff them one inside the other like <u>Russian dolls</u>, and roast them. He called his masterpiece turducken. . . .
>
> A well-prepared turducken is a marvelous treat, a free-form poultry terrine layered with flavorful stuffing and moistened with duck fat. When it's assembled, it looks <u>like a turkey</u> and it roasts <u>like a turkey</u>, but when you go to carve it, you can slice through it <u>like a loaf of bread</u>. In each slice you get a little bit of everything: white meat from the breast; dark meat from the legs, duck, carrots, bits of sausage, bread, herbs, juices, and chicken, too.
>
> —Amanda Hesser, "Turkey Finds Its Inner Duck (and Chicken)"

Metaphors make comparisons without such connecting words as *like* or *as*. See how desert ecologist Craig Childs uses a metaphor to help us understand the nature of water during a flood in the Grand Canyon:

> Water splashed off the desert and ran all over the surface, looking for the quickest way down. It was too swift for the ground to absorb. When water flows like this, it will not be clean tap water. It will be <u>a gravy of debris</u>, snatching everything it finds.
>
> —Craig Childs, *The Secret Knowledge of Water*

Calling the water "a gravy of debris" allows us to see the murky liquid as it streams through the canyon.

Analogies are extended similes or metaphors that compare something unfamiliar with something more familiar. Arguing that corporations should not patent parts of human DNA whose function isn't yet clear, a genetics professor uses the familiar image of a library to explain an unfamiliar concept, the patenting of random gene sequences:

It's like having a library of books and randomly tearing pages out. You may know which books the pages came from but that doesn't tell you much about them.

— Peter Goodfellow, quoted in John Vidal and
John Carvel, "Lambs to the Gene Market"

Sometimes analogies are used for humorous effect as well as to make a point, as in this passage from a critique of history textbooks:

Another history text — this one for fifth grade — begins with the story of how Henry B. Gonzalez, who is a member of Congress from Texas, learned about his own nationality. When he was ten years old, his teacher told him he was an American because he was born in the United States. His grandmother, however, said, "The cat was born in the oven. Does that make him bread?"

— Frances FitzGerald, *America Revised: History
Schoolbooks in the Twentieth Century*

The grandmother's question shows how an intentionally ridiculous analogy can be a source of humor — and can make a point memorably.

Considering the Rhetorical Situation

As a writer or speaker, you need to think about the message that you want to articulate, the audience you want to reach, and the larger context you are writing in.

▨ **PURPOSE**　　Sometimes your purpose for writing will be to compare two or more things. Other times, you may want to compare several things for some other purpose — to compare your views with those of others in an argument essay, or to compare one text with another as you analyze them.　　*3–4*

▨ **AUDIENCE**　　Who is your audience, and will comparing your topic with a more familiar one help them to follow your argument?　　*5–8*

■ **GENRE**
Does your genre require you to compare something? Evaluations often include comparisons—one book to another, in a review; or ten different cell phones, in *Consumer Reports*.

■ **STANCE**
Your stance may affect any comparisons you make. How you compare two things—evenhandedly, or clearly favoring one over the other, for example—will reflect your stance.

■ **MEDIA / DESIGN**
Some things you will want to compare with words alone (lines from two poems, for instance), but sometimes you may wish to make comparisons visually (two images juxtaposed on a page, or several numbers plotted on a line graph).

> See **LOOPING** and **CUBING,** two methods of **GENERATING IDEAS** that can be especially helpful for comparing and contrasting. If you're writing an essay whose purpose is to compare two or more things, see also the **PROCESSES** chapters for help **DRAFTING, REVISING,** and so on.

■ rhetorical situations   ▲ genres   ○ processes   ◆ strategies   ● research mla/apa   □ media/ design

Defining 33

Defining something says what it is — and what it is not. A terrier, for example, is a kind of dog. A fox terrier is a small dog now generally kept as a pet but once used by hunters to dig for foxes. Happiness is a jelly doughnut, at least according to Homer Simpson. All of those are definitions. As writers, we need to define any terms our readers may not know. And sometimes you'll want to stipulate your own definition of a word in order to set the terms of an **ARGUMENT** — as Homer Simpson does with a definition that's not found in any dictionary. This chapter details strategies for using definitions in your writing, to suit your own rhetorical situations.

▲ 82–106

Formal Definitions

Sometimes to make sure readers understand you, you will need to provide a formal definition. If you are using a technical term that readers are unlikely to know or if you are using a term in a specific way, you need to say then and there what the word means. The word *mutual*, for example, has several dictionary meanings:

> **mu•tu•al** . . .
>
> **1a:** directed by each toward the other or the others <*mutual* affection> **b:** having the same feelings one for the other <they had long been *mutual* enemies> **c:** shared in common <enjoying their *mutual* hobby> **d:** joint
> **2:** characterized by intimacy
> **3:** of or relating to a plan whereby the members of an organization share in the profits and expenses; *specifically*: of, relating to, or taking the form of an insurance method in which the policyholders constitute the members of the insuring company
>
> — www.Merriam-Webster.com

The first two meanings are commonly understood and probably require no definition. But if you were to use *mutual* in the third sense, it might—depending on your audience. A general audience would probably need the definition; an audience from the insurance industry would not. A Web site that gives basic financial advice to an audience of non-specialists, for instance, offers a specific definition of the term *mutual fund*:

> *Mutual funds* are financial intermediaries. They are companies set up to receive your money and then, having received it, to make investments with the money.
>
> —Bill Barker, "A Grand, Comprehensive
> Overview to Mutual Funds Investing"

But even writers in specialized fields routinely provide formal definitions to make sure their readers understand the way they are using certain words. See how two writers define the word *stock* as it pertains to their respective (and very different) fields:

> Stocks are the basis for sauces and soups and important flavoring agents for braises. Admittedly, stock making is time consuming, but the extra effort yields great dividends.
>
> —Tom Colicchio, *Think Like a Chef*

> Want to own part of a business without having to show up at its office every day? Or ever? Stock is the vehicle of choice for those who do. Dating back to the Dutch mutual stock corporations of the sixteenth century, the modern stock market exists as a way for entrepreneurs to finance businesses using money collected from investors. In return for ponying up the dough to finance the company, the investor becomes a part owner of the company. That ownership is represented by stock—specialized financial "securities," or financial instruments, that are "secured" by a claim on the assets and profits of a company.
>
> —Fool.com, "Investing Basics: Stocks"

To write a formal definition

- Use words that readers are likely to be familiar with.
- Don't use the word being defined in the definition.

- Begin with the word being defined; include the general category to which the term belongs and the attributes that make it different from the others in that category.

For example:

Term	General Category	Distinguishing Attributes
Stock is	a specialized financial "security"	that is "secured" by a claim.
Photosynthesis is	a process	by which plants use sunlight to create energy.
Astronomers are	scientists	who study celestial objects and phenomena.
Adam Sandler,	a comedian,	has starred in several movies, including *The Wedding Singer* and *Punch-Drunk Love.*

Note that the category and distinguishing attributes cannot be stated too broadly; if they were, the definition would be too vague to be useful. It wouldn't be helpful in most circumstances, for example, to say, "Adam Sandler is a man who has acted" or "Photosynthesis is something having to do with plants."

Extended Definitions

Sometimes you need to provide a more detailed definition. Extended definitions may be several sentences long or several paragraphs long and may include pictures or diagrams. Sometimes an entire essay is devoted to defining a difficult or important concept. Here is one writer's extended definition of stem cells:

> By definition, a stem cell is an unspecialized cell that has the ability to divide and renew itself. Under certain conditions, it can generate large numbers of daughter cells and these go on to mature into cells with

special functions, such as beating heart muscle or new bone to heal a fracture.

Stem cells exist naturally in the body. They're in bone marrow and, although rare, in the blood stream. Stem cells also exist in other tissues and organs, such as the liver, pancreas, brain, and maybe even the heart.

Currently, stem cells come from three sources: blastocysts, which are cells isolated from the inner cell mass of a three-to-five-day-old embryo grown in a petri dish in a lab, also called embryonic stem cells; cord blood cells, which are isolated from blood taken from an umbilical cord saved immediately after birth; and adult stem cells, which are collected from a person's own tissues.

— *Cleveland Clinic Magazine*, "The Miracle of Stem Cells"

That definition includes a description of the distinguishing features of stem cells and tells where they are found and where they come from. We can assume that it's written for a general audience, one that doesn't know anything about stem cells.

Abstract concepts often require extended definitions because by nature they are more complicated to define. There are many ways of writing an extended definition, depending in part on the term being defined and on your audience and purpose. The following examples show some of the methods that can be used for composing extended definitions of *democracy*.

Explore the word's origins. Where did the word come from? When did it first come into use? In the following example, from an essay considering what democracy means in the twenty-first century, the writer started by looking at the word's first known use in English. Though it's from an essay written for a first-year writing course and thus for a fairly general audience, it's a definition that might pique any audience's interest:

According to the *Oxford English Dictionary*, the term *democracy* first appeared in English in a thirteenth-century translation of Aristotle's works—specifically, in his *Politics*, where he stated that the "underlying principle of democracy is freedom" and that "it is customary to say that only in democracies do men have a share in freedom, for that is what every democracy makes its aim." By the sixteenth century, the word was used much as it is now. One writer in 1586, for instance,

rhetorical situations

genres

processes

strategies

research mla/apa

media/ design

defined it in this way: "where free and poore men being the greater number, are lords of the estate."

—Susanna Mejía, "What Does Democracy Mean Now?"

Here's another example, this one written for a scholarly audience, from an essay about women, participation, democracy, and the information age:

The very word *citizenship* carries with it a connotation of place, a "citizen" being, literally, the inhabitant of a city. Over the years the word has, of course, accumulated a number of associated meanings . . . and the word has come to stand in for such concepts as participation, equality, and democracy. The fact that the concept of locality is deeply embedded in the word *citizen* suggests that it is also fundamental to our current understanding of these other, more apparently abstract words.

In Western thought, the concepts of citizenship, equality, and democracy are closely interlinked and can be traced back to a common source, in Athens in the fifth century B.C. Perhaps it is no accident that it was the same culture which also gave us, in its theater, the concept of the unity of time and space. The Greek city-state has been represented for centuries as the ideal model of democracy, with free and equal access for all citizens to decision making. Leaving aside, for the moment, the question of who was included, and who excluded from this notion of citizenship, we can see that the sense of place is fundamental to this model. Entitlement to participate in the democratic process is circumscribed by geography; it is the inhabitants of the geographical entity of the city-state, precisely defined and bounded, who have the rights to citizenship. Those who are not defined as inhabitants of that specific city-state are explicitly excluded, although, of course, they may have the right to citizenship elsewhere.

—Ursula Huws, "Women, Participation, and Democracy in the Information Society"

Provide details. What are its characteristics? What is it made of? See how a historian explores the basic characteristics of democracy in a book written for an audience of historians:

As a historian I am naturally disposed to be satisfied with the meaning which, in the history of politics, men have commonly attributed to the word—a meaning, needless to say, which derives partly from the experience and partly from the aspirations of mankind. So regarded, the term *democracy* refers primarily to a form of government, and it has always meant government by the many as opposed to government by the one—government by the people as opposed to government by a tyrant, a dictator, or an absolute monarch. . . . Since the Greeks first used the term, the essential test of democratic government has always been this: the source of political authority must be and remain in the people and not in the ruler. A democratic government has always meant one in which the citizens, or a sufficient number of them to represent more or less effectively the common will, freely act from time to time, and according to established forms, to appoint or recall the magistrates and to enact or revoke the laws by which the community is governed.

—Carl Becker, *Modern Democracy*

Compare it with other words.   How is this concept like other similar things? How does it differ? What is it *not* like? **COMPARE AND CONTRAST** it. See how a political science textbook defines a *majoritarian democracy* by comparing its characteristics with those of a *consensual democracy*:

266–74

A majoritarian democracy is one

1. having only two major political parties, not many

2. having an electoral system that requires a bare majority to elect one clear winner in an election, as opposed to a proportional electoral system that distributes seats to political parties according to the rough share of votes received in the election

3. a strong executive (president or prime minister) and cabinet that together are largely independent of the legislature when it comes to exercising the executive's constitutional duties, in contrast to an executive and cabinet that are politically controlled by the parties in the legislature and therefore unable to exercise much influence when proposing policy initiatives.

—Benjamin Ginsberg, Theodore J. Lowi, and Margaret Weir,
We the People: An Introduction to American Politics

And here's an example in which democracy is contrasted with various other forms of governments of the past:

> Caesar's power derived from a popular mandate, conveyed through established republican forms, but that did not make his government any the less a dictatorship. Napoleon called his government a democratic republic, but no one, least of all Napoleon himself, doubted that he had destroyed the last vestiges of the democratic republic.
>
> —Carl Becker, *Modern Democracy*

Give examples. See how the essayist E. B. White defines democracy by giving some everyday examples of considerate behavior, humility, and civic participation—all things he suggests constitute democracy:

> It is the line that forms on the right. It is the don't in don't shove. It is the hole in the stuffed shirt through which the sawdust slowly trickles; it is the dent in the high hat. Democracy is the recurrent suspicion that more than half of the people are right more than half of the time. . . . Democracy is a letter to the editor.
>
> —E. B. White, "Democracy"

White's definition is elegant because he uses examples that his readers will know. His characteristics—metaphors, really—define democracy not as a conceptual way of governing but as an everyday part of American life.

Classify it. Often it is useful to divide or CLASSIFY a term. The ways in which democracy unfolds are complex enough to warrant entire textbooks, of course, but the following definition, from the political science textbook, divides democracy into two kinds, representative and direct:

◆ 260–65

> A system of government that gives citizens a regular opportunity to elect the top government officials is usually called a representative democracy or republic. A system that permits citizens to vote directly on laws and policies is often called a direct democracy. At the national level, America is a representative democracy in which citizens select government officials but do not vote on legislation. Some states, how-

ever, have provisions for direct legislation through popular referendum. For example, California voters in 1995 decided to bar undocumented immigrants from receiving some state services.

—Benjamin Ginsberg, Theodore J. Lowi, and Margaret Weir,
We the People: An Introduction to American Politics

Stipulative Definitions

Sometimes a writer will stipulate a certain definition, essentially saying, "This is how I'm defining x." Such definitions are not usually found in a dictionary—and at the same time are central to the argument the writer is making. Here is one example, from an essay by Toni Morrison. Describing a scene from a film in which a newly arrived Greek immigrant, working as a shoe shiner in Grand Central Terminal, chases away an African American competitor, Morrison calls the scene an example of "race talk," a concept she then goes on to define:

> This is race talk, the explicit insertion into everyday life of racial signs and symbols that have no meaning other than pressing African Americans to the lowest level of the racial hierarchy. Popular culture, shaped by film, theater, advertising, the press, television, and literature, is heavily engaged in race talk. It participates freely in this most enduring and efficient rite of passage into American culture: negative appraisals of the native-born black population. Only when the lesson of racial estrangement is learned is assimilation complete. Whatever the lived experience of immigrants with African Americans—pleasant, beneficial, or bruising—the rhetorical experience renders blacks as noncitizens, already discredited outlaws.
>
> All immigrants fight for jobs and space, and who is there to fight but those who have both? As in the fishing ground struggle between Texas and Vietnamese shrimpers, they displace what and whom they can. Although U.S. history is awash in labor battles, political fights and property wars among all religious and ethnic groups, their struggles are persistently framed as struggles between recent arrivals and blacks. In race talk the move into mainstream America always means buying into the notion of American blacks as the real aliens. Whatever the

ethnicity or nationality of the immigrant, his nemesis is understood to be African American.

— Toni Morrison, "On the Backs of Blacks"

In this example below, from a book review of Nancy L. Rosenblum's *Membership and Morals: The Personal Uses of Pluralism in America*, published in the *American Prospect*, a magazine for readers interested in political analysis, a Stanford law professor outlines a definition of "the democracy of everyday life":

Democracy, in this understanding of it, means simply treating people as equals, disregarding social standing, avoiding attitudes of either deference or superiority, making allowances for others' weaknesses, and resisting the temptation to respond to perceived slights. It also means protesting everyday instances of arbitrariness and unfairness—from the rudeness of the bakery clerk to the sexism of the car dealer or the racism of those who vandalize the home of the first black neighbors on the block.

— Kathleen M. Sullivan, "Defining Democracy Down"

Considering the Rhetorical Situation

As a writer or speaker, you need to think about the message that you want to articulate, the audience you want to reach, and the larger context you are writing in.

■ **PURPOSE**	Your purpose for writing will affect any definitions you include. Would writing an extended definition help you explain something? Would stipulating definitions of key terms help you shape an argument? Could an offbeat definition help you entertain your readers?	3–4
■ **AUDIENCE**	What audience do you want to reach, and are there any terms your readers are unlikely to know? Are there terms they might understand differently from the way you're defining them?	5–8

9–11
■ **GENRE** Does your genre require you to define terms? Chances are that if you're reporting information you'll need to define some terms, and some arguments rest on the way you define key terms.

12–14
■ **STANCE** What is your stance, and do you need to define key terms to show that stance clearly? How you define "fetus," for example, is likely to reveal your stance on abortion.

15–17
■ **MEDIA / DESIGN** Your medium will affect the form your definitions take. In a print text, you will need to define terms in your text; if you're giving a speech or presentation, you might also provide images of important terms and their definitions. In an electronic text, you may be able to define terms by linking to an online dictionary definition.

193–235 ○

> See also the **PROCESSES** chapters for help **GENERATING IDEAS, DRAFTING, REVISING,** and so on if you are writing a whole essay dedicated to defining a term or concept.

Describing 34

When we describe something, we indicate what it looks like—and sometimes how it sounds, feels, smells, and tastes. Descriptive details are a way of showing rather than telling, of helping readers see (or hear, smell, and so on) what we're writing about—that the sky is blue, that Miss Havisham is wearing an old yellowed wedding gown, that the chemicals in the beaker have reacted and smell like rotten eggs. You'll have occasion to describe things in most of the writing you do—from describing a favorite hat in a **MEMOIR** to detailing a chemical reaction in a **LAB REPORT**. This chapter will help you work with description—and, in particular, help you think about the use of *detail*, about *objectivity and subjectivity*, about *vantage point*, about creating a clear *dominant impression*, and about using description to fit your rhetorical situation.

▲ 147–52

▲ 127–36

Detail

The goal of using details is to be as specific as possible, providing information that will help your audience imagine the subject or make sense of it. See, for example, how Nancy Mairs, an author with multiple sclerosis, describes the disease in clear, specific terms:

> During its course, which is unpredictable and uncontrollable, one may lose vision, hearing, speech, the ability to walk, control of bladder and/or bowels, strength in any or all extremities, sensitivity to touch, vibration, and/or pain, potency, coordination of movements—the list of possibilities is lengthy and, yes, horrifying. One may also lose one's sense of humor. That's the easiest to lose and the hardest to survive without.
>
> In the past ten years, I have sustained some of these losses. Characteristic of MS are sudden attacks, called exacerbations, followed by remissions, and these I have not had. Instead, my disease has been

slowly progressive. My left leg is now so weak that I walk with the aid of a brace and a cane, and for distances I use an Amigo, a variation on the electric wheelchair that looks rather like an electrified kiddie car. I no longer have much use of my left hand. Now my right side is weakening as well. I still have the blurred spot in my right eye. Overall, though, I've been lucky so far.

—Nancy Mairs, "On Being a Cripple"

Mairs's gruesome list demonstrates, through *specific details*, how the disease affects sufferers generally and her in particular. We know far more after reading this text than we do from the following more general description, from a National Multiple Sclerosis Society brochure:

Multiple sclerosis is a chronic, unpredictable disease of the central nervous system (the brain, optic nerves, and spinal cord). It is thought to be an autoimmune disorder. This means the immune system incorrectly attacks the person's healthy tissue.

MS can cause blurred vision, loss of balance, poor coordination, slurred speech, tremors, numbness, extreme fatigue, problems with memory and concentration, paralysis, and blindness. These problems may be permanent, or they may come and go.

—National Multiple Sclerosis Society, *Just the Facts: 2003–2004*

Specific details are also more effective than labels, which give little meaningful information. Instead of saying that someone is a "moron" or "really smart," it's better to give details so that readers can understand the reasons behind the label: what does this person *do* or *say* that makes him or her deserve this label? See, for example, how the writer of a news story about shopping on the day after Thanksgiving opens with a description of a happy shopper:

Last Friday afternoon, the day ritualized consumerism is traditionally at its most frenetic, Alexx Balcuns twirled in front of a full-length mirror at the Ritz Thrift Shop on West Fifty-seventh Street as if inhabited by the soul of Eva Gabor in *Green Acres*. Ms. Balcuns was languishing in a $795 dyed-mink parka her grandmother had just bought her. Ms. Balcuns is six.

—Ginia Bellafante, "Staying Warm and Fuzzy during Uncertain Times"

rhetorical situations | genres | processes | strategies | research mla/apa | media/ design

The writer might simply have said, "A spoiled child admired herself in the mirror." Instead, she shows her subject twirling and "languishing" in a "$795 dyed-mink parka" and seemingly possessed by the soul of the actress Eva Gabor—all details that create a far more vivid description.

Sensory details help readers imagine sounds, odors, tastes, and physical sensations in addition to sights. In the following example, writer Scott Russell Sanders recalls sawing wood as a child. Note how visual details, odors, and even the physical sense of being picked up by his father mingle to form a vivid scene:

> As the saw teeth bit down, the wood released its smell, each kind with its own fragrance, oak or walnut or cherry or pine—usually pine because it was the softest, easiest for a child to work. No matter how weathered and gray the board, no matter how warped and cracked, inside there was this smell waiting, as of something freshly baked. I gathered every smidgen of sawdust and stored it away in coffee cans, which I kept in a drawer of the workbench. When I did not feel like hammering nails I would dump my sawdust on the concrete floor of the garage and landscape it into highways and farms and towns, running miniature cars and trucks along miniature roads. Looming as huge as a colossus, my father worked over and around me, now and again bending down to inspect my work, careful not to trample my creations. It was a landscape that smelled dizzyingly of wood. Even after a bath my skin would carry the smell, and so would my father's hair, when he lifted me for a bedtime hug.
>
> —Scott Russell Sanders, *The Paradise of Bombs*

Whenever you describe something, you'll select from many possible details you might use. Simply put, to exhaust all of the details to describe something is impossible—and would exhaust your readers as well. To focus your description, you'll need to determine the kinds of details that are appropriate for your subject. They will vary, depending on your **PURPOSE.** ▮ 3–4
See, for example, how the details might differ in three different genres:

- *For a* **MEMOIR** *about an event*, you might choose details that are significant for you, that evoke the sights, sounds, and meaning of your event. ▲ 147–52

153–59 ▲
- For a **PROFILE**, you're likely to select details that will reinforce the dominant impression you want to give, that portray the event from the perspective you want readers to see.

127–36 ▲
- For a **LAB REPORT**, you need to give certain specifics—what equipment was used, what procedures were followed, what exactly were the results.

Deciding on a focus for your description can help you see it better, as you'll look for details that contribute to that focus.

Objectivity and Subjectivity

Descriptions can be written with objectivity, with subjectivity, or with a mixture of both. Objective descriptions attempt to be uncolored by personal opinion or emotion. Police reports and much news writing aim to describe events objectively; scientific writing strives for objectivity in describing laboratory procedures and results. See, for example, the following objective account of what happened at the World Trade Center on September 11, 2001:

> **World Trade Center Disaster—Tuesday, September 11, 2001**
>
> On Tuesday, September 11, 2001, at 8:45 a.m. New York local time, One World Trade Center, the north tower, was hit by a hijacked 767 commercial jet airplane loaded with fuel for a transcontinental flight. Two World Trade Center, the south tower, was hit by a similar hijacked jet eighteen minutes later, at 9:03 a.m. (In separate but related attacks, the Pentagon building near Washington, D.C., was hit by a hijacked 757 at 9:43 a.m., and at 10:10 a.m. a fourth hijacked jetliner crashed in Pennsylvania.) The south tower, WTC 2, which had been hit second, was the first to suffer a complete structural collapse, at 10:05 a.m., 62 minutes after being hit itself, 80 minutes after the first impact. The north tower, WTC 1, then also collapsed, at 10:29 a.m., 104 minutes after being hit. WTC 7, a substantial forty-seven-story office building in its own right, built in 1987, was damaged by the collapsing towers, caught fire, and later in the afternoon also totally collapsed.
>
> —GreatBuildingsOnline.com, "World Trade Center"

Subjective descriptions, on the other hand, allow the writer's opinions and emotions to come through. A house can be described as comfortable, with a lived-in look, or as rundown and in need of a paint job and a new roof.

Here's a subjective description of the planes striking the World Trade Center, as told by a woman watching from a nearby building:

> Incredulously, while looking out [the] window at the damage and carnage the first plane had inflicted, I saw the second plane abruptly come into my right field of vision and deliberately, with shimmering intention, thunder full-force into the south tower. It was so close, so low, so huge and fast, so intent on its target that I swear to you, I swear to you, I felt the vengeance and rage emanating from the plane.
>
> —Debra Fontaine, "Witnessing"

Advertisers regularly use subjective as well as objective description to sell their products, as the ad (on page 290) for a nicotine patch demonstrates. This ad includes an objective description of what makes smoking addictive: "Every time you smoke, the nicotine binds to these little tiny receptors in your brain. Thus, your brain becomes addicted to nicotine." However, it also presents subjective descriptions of the effects of quitting ("if you cut the brain off—well let's just say it gets a little pissed") and the results of buying and using the product: "So your brain's happy. You're happy. Or at least you're happy that your brain's happy."

Vantage Point

Sometimes you'll want or need to describe something from a certain vantage point. Where you locate yourself in relation to what you're describing will determine what you can perceive (and so describe) and what you can't. You may describe your subject from a *stationary vantage point*, from which you (and your readers) see your subject from one angle only, as if you were a camera. This description of one of three photographs that captured a woman's death records only what the camera saw from one angle at one particular moment:

> The first showed some people on a fire escape—a fireman, a woman and a child. The fireman had a nice strong jaw and looked very brave.

The woman was holding the child. Smoke was pouring from the building behind them. A rescue ladder was approaching, just a few feet away, and the fireman had one arm around the woman and one arm reaching out toward the ladder.

—Nora Ephron, "The Boston Photographs"

By contrast, this description of a drive to an Italian villa uses a *moving vantage point*; the writer recounts what he saw as he passed through a gate in a city wall, moving from city to country:

La Pietra—"the stone"—is situated one mile from the Porta San Gallo, an entry to the Old City of Florence. You drive there along the Via Bolognese, twisting past modern apartment blocks, until you come to a gate, which swings open—and there you are, at the upper end of a long lane of cypresses facing a great ocher palazzo; with olive groves spreading out on both sides over an expanse of fifty-seven acres.

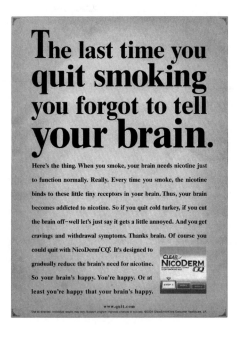

There's something almost comically wonderful about the effect: here, the city, with its winding avenue; there, on the other side of a wall, the country, fertile and gray green.

—James Traub, "Italian Hours"

The description of quarries below uses *multiple vantage points* to capture the quarries from many perspectives.

Dominant Impression

With any description, your aim is to create some dominant impression — the overall feeling that the individual details add up to. The dominant impression may be implied, growing out of the details themselves. For example, Scott Russell Sanders's memory of the smell of sawdust creates a dominant impression of warmth and comfort: the "fragrance . . . as of something freshly baked," sawdust "stored . . . away in coffee cans," a young boy "lifted . . . for a bedtime hug." Sometimes, though, a writer will inform readers directly of the dominant impression, in addition to describing it. In an essay about Indiana limestone quarries, Sanders makes the dominant impression clear from the start: "they are battlefields."

> The quarries will not be domesticated. They are not backyard pools; they are battlefields. Each quarry is an arena where violent struggles have taken place between machines and planet, between human ingenuity and brute resisting stone, between mind and matter. Waste rock litters the floor and brim like rubble in a bombed city. The ragged pits might have been the basements of vanished skyscrapers. Stones weighing tens of tons lean against one another at precarious angles, as if they have been thrown there by some gigantic strength and have not yet finished falling. Wrecked machinery hulks in the weeds, grimly rusting, the cogs and wheels, twisted rails, battered engine housings, trackless bulldozers and burst boilers like junk from an armored regiment. Everywhere the ledges are scarred from drills, as if from an artillery barrage or machine-gun strafing. Stumbling onto one of these abandoned quarries and gazing at the ruins, you might be left wondering who had won the battle, men or stone.
>
> —Scott Russell Sanders, *The Paradise of Bombs*

The rest of his description, full of more figurative language ("like rubble in a bombed city," "like junk from an armored regiment," "as if from an artillery barrage or machine-gun strafing") reinforces the direct "they are battlefields" statement.

Organizing Descriptions

You can organize descriptions in many ways. When your description is primarily visual, you will probably organize it spatially: from left to right, top to bottom, outside to inside. If your description uses the other senses, you may begin with the most significant or noteworthy feature and move outward from that center, as Ephron does, or you may create a chronological description of objects as you encounter them, as Traub does in his description of his drive on page 290. You might even pile up details to create a dominant impression, as Sanders and Mairs do.

Considering the Rhetorical Situation

As a writer or speaker, you need to think about the message that you want to articulate, the audience you want to reach, and the larger context you are writing in.

<table>
<tr>
<td>3–4</td>
<td>■ PURPOSE</td>
<td>Your purpose may affect the way you use description. If you're arguing that a government should intervene in another country's civil war, for example, describing the anguish of refugees from that war could make your argument more persuasive. If you're analyzing a painting, you will likely need to describe it.</td>
</tr>
<tr>
<td>5–8</td>
<td>■ AUDIENCE</td>
<td>Who is your audience, and will they need detailed description to understand your argument?</td>
</tr>
<tr>
<td>9–11</td>
<td>■ GENRE</td>
<td>Does your genre require description? A lab report generally calls for you to describe materials and results;</td>
</tr>
</table>

a memoir about grandma should probably describe her — her smile, her dress, her apple pie.

■ **STANCE**   The way you describe things can help you convey your stance. For example, the details you choose can show you to be objective (or not), careful or casual.   12–14

■ **MEDIA / DESIGN**   Your medium will affect the form your description can take. In a print or spoken text, you will likely rely on words, though you may also include visuals. In an electronic text, you can easily provide links to visuals and so may need fewer words.   15–17

See also **FREEWRITING, CUBING,** and **LISTING.** three methods of **GENERATING IDEAS** that can be especially helpful for developing detailed descriptions. Sometimes you may be assigned to write a whole essay describing something: see the **PROCESSES** chapters for help **DRAFTING, REVISING,** and so on.   199–202   193–235

35 Dialogue

Dialogue is a way of adding people's own words to a text, letting readers hear those people's voices—not just what you say about them. **MEMOIRS** and **PROFILES** often include dialogue, and many other genres do as well: **LITERARY ANALYSES** often quote dialogue from the texts they analyze, and essays **ARGUING A POSITION** might quote an authoritative source as support for a claim. This chapter provides brief guidelines for the conventions of paragraphing and punctuating dialogue and offers some good examples of how you can use dialogue most effectively to suit your own rhetorical situations.

137–59

82–106

Why Add Dialogue?

Dialogue is a way of bringing in voices other than your own, of showing people and scenes rather than just telling about them. It can add color and texture to your writing, making it memorable. Most important, however, dialogue should be more than just colorful or interesting. It needs to contribute to your rhetorical purpose, to support the point you're making. See how dialogue is used in the following excerpt, from a magazine profile of the Mall of America, how it gives us a sense of the place that the journalist's own words could not provide:

> Two pubescent girls in retainers and braces sat beside me sipping coffees topped with whipped cream and chocolate sprinkles, their shopping bags gathered tightly around their legs, their eyes fixed on the passing crowds. They came, they said, from Shakopee—"It's nowhere," one of them explained. The megamall, she added, was "a buzz at first, but now it seems pretty normal. 'Cept my parents are like Twenty Questions every time I want to come here. 'Specially since the shooting."

On a Sunday night, she elaborated, three people had been wounded when shots were fired in a dispute over a San Jose Sharks jacket. "In the *mall*," her friend reminded me. "Right here at megamall. A shooting."

"It's like nowhere's safe," the first added.

— David Guterson, "Enclosed. Encyclopedic. Endured: The Mall of America"

Of course it was the writer who decided whom and what to quote, and Guterson deliberately chose words that capture the young shoppers' speech patterns, quoting fragments ("In the *mall*. Right here at megamall. A shooting"), slang ("a buzz at first," "my parents are like Twenty Questions"), even contractions ('*cept*, '*specially*).

Integrating Dialogue into Your Writing

There are certain conventions for punctuating and paragraphing dialogue:

- **Punctuating.** Enclose each speaker's words in quotation marks, and put any end punctuation — periods, question marks, and exclamation marks — inside the closing quotation mark. Whether you're transcribing words you heard or making them up, you will sometimes need to add punctuation to reflect the rhythm and sound of the speech. See, for example, how Chang-Rae Lee adds a comma after *well* and italicizes *practice* in the last sentence of the example below, to show intonation — and attitude.

- **Paragraphing.** When you're writing dialogue that includes more than one speaker, start a new paragraph each time the speaker changes.

- **Signal phrases.** Sometimes you'll need to introduce dialogue with SIGNAL PHRASES — "I said," "she asked," and so on — to make clear who is speaking. At times, however, the speaker will be clear enough, and you won't need any signal phrases.

367–68

Here is a conversation between a mother and her son that illustrates each of the conventions for punctuating and paragraphing dialogue:

"Whom do I talk to?" she said. She would mostly speak to me in Korean, and I would answer back in English.

"The bank manager, who else?"

"What do I say?"

"Whatever you want to say."

"Don't speak to me like that!" she cried.

"It's just that you should be able to do it yourself," I said.

"You know how I feel about this!"

"Well, maybe then you should consider it *practice*," I answered lightly, using the Korean word to make sure she understood.

—Chang-Rae Lee, "Coming Home Again"

Interviews

Interviews are a kind of dialogue, with different conventions for punctuation. When you're transcribing an interview, give each speaker's name each time he or she speaks, starting a new line but not indenting, and do not use quotation marks. Here are a few lines from an interview that Harold Evans conducted with President Bill Clinton, published in *Talk* magazine shortly before Clinton left office:

Talk: He [Nelson Mandela, president of South Africa and winner of a Nobel Peace Prize] talked to you during impeachment?

Clinton: The whole time, yes. He was very loyal to me. He even came here, came a day early, when Congress gave him the gold medal, and came to the White House and attacked what they were doing to me. He helped me in how to think about it, how to deal with it— something I will never forget.

Talk: He had his own long years in prison. Was his advice pragmatic about getting through, or spiritual?

Clinton: Both. Both. If you read his autobiography, you'll see that. He said basically the only way things like that destroy you is if you give them permission to destroy you.

Talk: You get bitter.

Clinton: He said as long as you don't—if you're not embittered by this, if you're not angry all the time, if you just let it go, and keep going— then you'll be fine.

—Harold Evans, *Talk*

In preparing the interview for publication, Evans had to add punctuation, which of course was not part of the oral conversation, and he probably deleted pauses and verbal expressions such as *um* and *uh*. At the same time, he kept informal constructions, such as incomplete sentences, which are typical answers to questions ("The whole time, yes."), and repetition used for emphasis ("Both. Both.") to maintain the oral flavor of the interview and to reflect the former president's voice. Evans may also have moved parts of the interview around, to eliminate repetition and keep related subjects together. He identifies President Clinton by name, but since he represents *Talk* magazine, he identifies himself by the magazine's name.

Considering the Rhetorical Situation

As a writer or speaker, you need to think about the message that you want to articulate, the audience you want to reach, and the larger context you are writing in.

▪ **PURPOSE**	Your purpose will affect any use of dialogue. Dialogue can help bring a profile to life, and make it memorable. Interviews with experts or first-hand witnesses can add credibility to a report or argument.	3–4
▪ **AUDIENCE**	Whom do you want to reach, and will dialogue help? Sometimes actual dialogue can help readers hear human voices behind facts or reason.	5–8
▪ **GENRE**	Does your genre require dialogue? If you're evaluating or analyzing a literary work, for instance, you may wish to include dialogue from that work. If you're writing a profile of a person or event, dialogue can help you bring your subject to life. Similarly, an interview with an expert or firsthand witness can add credibility to a report or argument.	9–11
▪ **STANCE**	What is your stance, and can dialogue help you communicate that stance? For example, excerpts of an	12–14

interview may allow you to challenge someone's views and make your own views clear.

15–17

■ **MEDIUM / DESIGN** Your medium will affect the way you present dialogue. In a print text, you will present dialogue through written words. In an oral or electronic text, you might include actual recorded dialogue.

351–52 ●

358–69 ●

See also the guidelines on **INTERVIEWING EXPERTS** for advice on setting up and recording interviews and those on **QUOTING, PARAPHRASING,** and **SUMMARIZING** for help deciding how to integrate dialogue into your text.

■ rhetorical situations

▲ genres

○ processes

◆ strategies

● research mla/apa

□ media/ design

Explaining Processes **36**

When you explain a process, you tell how something is (or was) done: how a bill becomes a law, how an embryo develops; or you tell someone how to do something: how to throw a curve ball, how to write a memoir. This chapter focuses on those two kinds of explanations, offering examples and guidelines for explaining a process in writing in a way that works for your rhetorical situation.

Explaining a Process Clearly

Whether the process is simple or complex, you'll need to identify its key stages or steps and explain them one by one, in order. The sequence matters because it allows readers to follow your explanation; it is especially important when you're explaining a process that others are going to follow. Most often you'll explain a process chronologically, from start to finish. **TRANSITIONS** — words like *first, next, then,* and so on — are often necessary, therefore, to show readers how the stages of a process relate to one another and to indicate time sequences. Finally, you'll find that verbs matter; they indicate the actions that take place at each stage of the process.

◆ 254

Explaining How Something Is Done

All processes consist of steps, and when you explain how something is done, you describe each step, generally in order, from first to last. Here, for example, is an explanation of how French fries are made, from an essay published in the *New Yorker*:

Fast-food French fries are made from a baking potato like an Idaho russet, or any other variety that is mealy, or starchy, rather than waxy. The potatoes are harvested, cured, washed, peeled, sliced, and then blanched—cooked enough so that the insides have a fluffy texture but not so much that the fry gets soft and breaks. Blanching is followed by drying, and drying by a thirty-second deep fry, to give the potatoes a crisp shell. Then the fries are frozen until the moment of service, when they are deep-fried again, this time for somewhere around three minutes. Depending on the fast-food chain involved, there are other steps interspersed in this process. McDonald's fries, for example, are briefly dipped in a sugar solution, which gives them their golden-brown color; Burger King fries are dipped in a starch batter, which is what gives those fries their distinctive hard shell and audible crunch. But the result is similar. The potato that is first harvested in the field is roughly 80 percent water. The process of creating a French fry consists, essentially, of removing as much of that water as possible—through blanching, drying, and deep-frying—and replacing it with fat.

—Malcolm Gladwell, "The Trouble with Fries"

Gladwell clearly explains the process of making French fries, showing us the specific steps—how the potatoes "are harvested, cured, washed, peeled, sliced," and so on—and using clear transitions—"followed by," "then," "until," "when"—and action verbs to show the sequence. His last sentence makes his stance clear, pointing out that the process of creating a French fry consists of removing as much of a potato's water as possible "and replacing it with fat."

Explaining How to Do Something

In explaining how to do something, you are giving instruction so that others can follow the process themselves. See how Martha Stewart explains the process of making French fries. She starts by listing the ingredients and then describes the steps:

rhetorical situations   genres   processes   strategies   research mla/apa   media/ design

4 medium baking potatoes
2 tablespoons olive oil
1$\frac{1}{2}$ teaspoons salt
$\frac{1}{4}$ teaspoon freshly ground pepper
malt vinegar (optional)

1. Heat oven to 400 degrees. Place a heavy baking sheet in the oven. Scrub and rinse the potatoes well, and then cut them lengthwise into $\frac{1}{2}$-inch-wide batons. Place the potato batons in a medium bowl, and toss them with the olive oil, salt, and pepper.

2. When baking sheet is hot, about 15 minutes, remove from the oven. Place prepared potatoes on the baking sheet in a single later. Return to oven, and bake until potatoes are golden on the bottom, about 30 minutes. Turn potatoes over, and continue cooking until golden all over, about 15 minutes more. Serve immediately.

—Martha Stewart, *Favorite Comfort Food*

Coming from Martha Stewart, the explanation leaves out no details, giving a clear sequence of steps and descriptive verbs that tell us exactly what to do: "heat," "place," "scrub and rinse," and so on. After she gives the recipe, she even goes on to explain the process of *serving* the fries — "Serve these French fries with a bowl of malt vinegar" — and reminds us that "they are also delicious dipped in spicy mustard, mayonnaise, and, of course, ketchup."

Explaining a Process Visually

Some processes are best explained **VISUALLY**, with diagrams or photographs. See, for example, how a cookbook explains one process of shaping dough into a bagel — giving the details in words and then showing us in a drawing how to do it:

458–62

Roll each piece of dough on an unfloured counter into a 12-inch-long rope. Make a ring, overlapping the ends by 2 inches and joining them by pressing down and rolling on the overlap until it is the same thickness as the rest of the dough ring. There will be a 1-inch hole in the center.

1. Rolling the dough into a 12-inch rope

2. Making a ring by twisting one end of the dough over to overlap the other end by 2 inches

3. Pressing down and rolling the dough

Rose Levy Beranbaum, *The Bread Bible*

Considering the Rhetorical Situation

As a writer or speaker, you need to think about the message that you want to articulate, the audience you want to reach, and the larger context you are writing in.

3–4 ▨ **PURPOSE** Your purpose for writing will affect the way you explain a process. If you're arguing that we should avoid eating fast food, you might explain the process by which chicken nuggets are made. But to give information about how to fry chicken, you would explain the process quite differently.

5–8 ▨ **AUDIENCE** Whom are you trying to reach, and what will you need to provide any special background information? Can they be expected to be interested, or will you first need to interest them in the process?

9–11 ▨ **GENRE** Does your genre require you to explain a process? In a lab report, for example, you'll need to explain the processes used in the experiment. You might want to explain the process in a profile of an activity or the process of a solution you are proposing.

■ **STANCE** If you're giving directions for doing something, you'll want to take a straightforward "do this, then do that" perspective. If you're writing to entertain, you might want to take a clever or amusing stance.

12–14

■ **MEDIA / DESIGN** Your medium will affect the way you explain a process. In a print text or spoken text, you can use both words and images. On the Web, you may have the option of showing an animation of the process as well.

15–17

See also **LAB REPORTS** if you need to explain the process by which an experiment is carried out; and **PROFILES** if you are writing about an activity that needs to be explained. See **NARRATING** for more advice on organizing an explanation chronologically. Sometimes you may be assigned to write a whole essay or report that explains a process; see **PROCESSES** for help **DRAFTING, REVISING,** and so on.

127–136

153–59

304–12

193–235

37 Narrating

82–106 ▲

Narratives are stories. As a writing strategy, a good narrative can lend support to most kinds of writing—in an essay **ARGUING** for Title IX compliance, for example, you might include a brief narrative about an Olympic sprinter who might never have learned to run without Title IX. Or you can

153–59 ▲

bring a **PROFILE** of a favorite coach to life with an anecdote about a pep talk he or she once gave before a championship track meet. Whatever your larger writing purpose, you need to make sure that any narratives you add support that purpose—they should not be inserted simply to tell an interesting story. You'll also need to compose them carefully—to put them in a clear *sequence*, include *pertinent detail*, and make sure they are appropriate to your particular rhetorical situation.

Sequencing

When we write a narrative, we arrange events in a particular sequence. Writers typically sequence narratives in chronological order, reverse chronological order, or as a flashback.

Use chronological order.   Often you may tell the story chronologically, starting at the beginning of an event and working through to the end, as Maya Angelou does in this brief narrative from an essay about her high school graduation:

> The school band struck up a march and all classes filed in as had been rehearsed. We stood in front of our seats, as assigned, and on a signal from the choir director, we sat. No sooner had this been accomplished than the band started to play the national anthem. We rose again and sang the song, after which we recited the pledge of allegiance. We

remained standing for a brief minute before the choir director and the principal signaled to us, rather desperately I thought, to take our seats.

—Maya Angelou, "Graduation"

Use reverse chronological order. You may also begin with the final action and work back to the first, as Aldo Leopold does in this narrative about cutting down a tree:

> Now our saw bites into the 1890s, called gay by those whose eyes turn cityward rather than landward. We cut 1899, when the last passenger pigeon collided with a charge of shot near Babcock, two counties to the north; we cut 1898, when a dry fall, followed by a snowless winter, froze the soil seven feet deep and killed the apple trees; 1897, another drouth year, when another forestry commission came into being; 1896, when 25,000 prairie chickens were shipped to market from the village of Spooner alone; 1895, another year of fires; 1894, another drouth year; and 1893, the year of "the Bluebird Storm," when a March blizzard reduced the migrating bluebirds to near zero.

—Aldo Leopold, *A Sand County Almanac*

RÉSUMÉS are one genre where we generally use reverse chronological order, listing the most recent jobs or degrees first and then working backward. Notice, too, that we usually write these as narratives—telling what we have done rather than just naming positions we have held:

▲ 182–89

Sept. 2004–present	*Student worker*, Department of Information Management, Central State University, Wilberforce, OH. Compile data and format reports using Excel, Word, and university database programs.
June–Sept. 2004	*Intern*, QuestPro Corporation, West Louisville, KY. Assisted in development of software programs.
Sept. 2003–June 2004	*Bagger*, Ace Groceries, Elba, KY. Bagged customer's purchases.

Use a flashback.   You can sometimes put a flashback in the middle of a narrative, to tell about an incident that illuminates the larger narrative. Terry Tempest Williams does this in an essay about the startling incidence of breast cancer in her family: she recalls a dinnertime conversation with her father right after her mother's death from cancer, when she learned for the first time what caused all of the cancer in her family:

> Over dessert, I shared a recurring dream of mine. I told my father that for years, as long as I could remember, I saw this flash of light in the night in the desert. That this image had so permeated my being, I could not venture south without seeing it again, on the horizon, illuminating buttes and mesas.
>
> "You did see it," he said.
>
> "Saw what?" I asked, a bit tentative.
>
> "The bomb. The cloud. We were driving home from Riverside, California. You were sitting on your mother's lap. She was pregnant. In fact, I remember the date, September 7, 1957. We had just gotten out of the Service. We were driving north, past Las Vegas. It was an hour or so before dawn, when this explosion went off. We not only heard it, but felt it. I thought the oil tanker in front of us had blown up. We pulled over and suddenly, rising from the desert floor, we saw it, clearly, this golden-stemmed cloud, the mushroom. The sky seemed to vibrate with an eerie pink glow. Within a few minutes, a light ash was raining on the car."
>
> I stared at my father. This was new information to me.
>
> —Terry Tempest Williams, "The Clan of the One-Breasted Women"

Williams could have simply announced this information as a fact—but see how much more powerful it is when told in narrative form.

Use time markers.   Time markers help readers follow a sequence of events. The most obvious time markers are those that simply label the time, as the narrative entries in a diary, journal, or log might. For example, here is the final part of the narrative kept in a diary by a doomed Antarctic explorer:

> WEDNESDAY, MARCH 21: Got within eleven miles of depot. Monday night; had to lay up all yesterday in severe blizzard. Today forlorn hope, Wilson and Bowers going to depot for fuel.

MARCH 22 and 23: Blizzard bad as ever—Wilson and Bowers unable to start—tomorrow last chance—no fuel and only one or two [days] of food left—must be near the end. Have decided it shall be natural—we shall march for the depot with or without our effects and die in our tracks.

THURSDAY, MARCH 29: Since the 21st we have had a continuous gale from W.S.W. and S.W. We had fuel to make two cups of tea apiece and bare food for two days on the 20th. Every day we have been ready to start for our depot eleven miles away, but outside the door of the tent it remains a scene of whirling drift. I do not think we can hope for any better things now. We shall stick it out to the end, but we are getting weaker, of course, and the end cannot be far. It seems a pity, but I do not think I can write more. . . .

Last Entry: For God's sake look after our people.

—Robert F. Scott, *Scott's Last Expedition: The Journals*

More often you will integrate time markers into the prose itself, as is done in this narrative about a woman preparing and delivering meals to workers at a cotton gin:

She made her plans meticulously and in secret. <u>One early evening</u> to see if she was ready, she placed stones in two five-gallon pails and carried them three miles to the cotton gin. She rested a little, and then, discarding some rocks, she walked in the darkness to the sawmill five miles farther along the dirt road. <u>On her way back</u> to her little house and her babies, she dumped the remaining rocks along the path.

<u>That same night</u> she worked into the early hours boiling chicken and frying ham. She made dough and filled the rolled-out pastry with meat. At last she went to sleep.

<u>The next morning</u> she left her house carrying the meat pies, lard, an iron brazier, and coals for a fire. <u>Just before lunch</u> she appeared in an empty lot behind the cotton gin. <u>As the dinner noon bell rang</u>, she dropped the savors into boiling fat, and the aroma rose and floated over to the workers who spilled out of the gin, covered with white lint, looking like specters.

—Maya Angelou, *Wouldn't Take Nothing for My Journey Now*

Use transitions. Another way to help readers follow a narrative is with **TRANSITIONS,** words like *first, then, meanwhile, at last,* and so on. See how

◆ 254

the following paragraphs from Langston Hughes's classic essay about meeting Jesus use transitions (and time markers) to advance the action:

> <u>Suddenly</u> the whole room broke into a sea of shouting, <u>as</u> they saw me rise. Waves of rejoicing swept the place. Women leaped in the air. My aunt threw her arms around me. The minister took me by the hand and led me to the platform.
>
> <u>When</u> things quieted down, in a hushed silence, punctuated by a few ecstatic "Amens," all the new young lambs were blessed in the name of God. <u>Then</u> joyous singing filled the room. <u>That night,</u> for the last time in my life but one — for I was a big boy twelve years old — I cried.
>
> —Langston Hughes, "Salvation"

Including Pertinent Detail

When you include a narrative in your writing, you must decide which details you need — and which ones you don't need. For example, you don't want to include so much detail that the narrative distracts the reader from the larger text. You must also decide whether you need to include any background, to set the stage for the narrative. The amount of detail you include depends on your audience and purpose: How much detail does your audience need? How much detail do you need to make your meaning clear? In an essay on the suspicion African American men often face when walking at night, a journalist deliberately inserts a story without setting the stage at all:

> My first victim was a woman — white, well dressed, probably in her late twenties. I came upon her late one evening on a deserted street in Hyde Park, a relatively affluent neighborhood in an otherwise mean, impoverished section of Chicago. As I swung onto the avenue behind her, there seemed to be a discreet, uninflammatory distance between us. Not so. She cast back a worried glance. To her, the youngish black man — a broad six feet two inches with a beard and billowing hair, both hands shoved into the pockets of a bulky military jacket — seemed menacingly close. After a few more quick glimpses, she picked up her

pace and was soon running in earnest. Within seconds she disappeared into a cross street.

—Brent Staples, "Black Men and Public Space"

Words like *victim* and phrases like "came upon her" lead us to assume the narrator is scary and perhaps dangerous. We don't know why he is walking on the deserted street because he hasn't told us: he simply begins with the moment he and the woman encounter each other. For his purposes, that's all the audience needs to know at first, and details of his physical appearance that explain the woman's response come later, after he tells us about the encounter. Had he given us those details at the outset, the narrative would not have been nearly so effective. In a way, Staples lets the story sneak up on us, as the woman apparently felt he had on her.

Other times you'll need to provide more background information, as an MIT professor does when she uses an anecdote to introduce an essay about young children's experiences with electronic toys. First the writer tells us a little about Merlin, the computer tic-tac-toe game that the children in her anecdote play with. As you'll see, the anecdote would be hard to follow without the introduction:

Among the first generation of computational objects was Merlin, which challenged children to games of tic-tac-toe. For children who had only played games with human opponents, reaction to this object was intense. For example, while Merlin followed an optimal strategy for winning tic-tac-toe most of the time, it was programmed to make a slip every once in a while. So when children discovered strategies that allowed them to win and then tried these strategies a second time, they usually would not work. The machine gave the impression of not being "dumb enough" to let down its defenses twice. Robert, seven, playing with his friends on the beach, watched his friend Craig perform the "winning trick," but when he tried it, Merlin did not slip up and the game ended in a draw. Robert, confused and frustrated, threw Merlin into the sand and said, "Cheater. I hope your brains break." He was overheard by Craig and Greg, aged six and eight, who salvaged the by-now very sandy toy and took it upon themselves to set Robert straight. "Merlin doesn't know if it cheats," says Craig. "It doesn't know if you break it, Robert. It's not alive." Greg adds, "It's smart enough to make the right kinds of noises. But it doesn't really know if it loses. And when it cheats, it don't even know it's cheating." Jenny, six, interrupts with disdain: "Greg, to cheat you have to know you are cheating. Knowing is part of cheating."

—Sherry Turkle, "Cuddling Up to Cyborg Babies"

Opening and Closing with Narratives

239–45 ◆ Narratives are often useful as **BEGINNINGS** to essays and other kinds of writing. Everyone likes a good story, so an interesting or pithy narrative can be a good way to get your audience's attention. In the following introductory paragraph, a historian tells a gruesome but gripping story to attract our attention to a subject that might not otherwise merit our interest, bubonic plague:

> In October 1347, two months after the fall of Calais, Genoese trading ships put into the harbor of Messina in Sicily with dead and dying men at the oars. The ships had come from the Black Sea port of Caffa (now Feodosiya) in the Crimea, where the Genoese maintained a trading post. The diseased sailors showed strange black swellings about the size of an egg or an apple in the armpits and groin. The swellings oozed blood and pus and were followed by spreading boils and black blotches on the skin from internal bleeding. The sick suffered severe pain and died quickly, within five days of the first symptoms. As the disease spread, other symptoms of continuous fever and spitting of blood appeared instead of the swellings or buboes. These victims coughed and sweated heavily and died even more quickly, within three days or less, sometimes in twenty-four hours. In both types everything that issued from the body—breath, sweat, blood from the buboes and lungs, bloody urine, and blood-blackened excrement—smelled foul. Depression and despair accompanied the physical symptoms, and before the end "death is seen seated on the face."
>
> —Barbara Tuchman, "This Is the End of the World: The Black Death"

Imagine how different the preceding paragraph would be if it weren't in the form of a narrative. Imagine, for example, that Tuchman began by

defining bubonic plague. Would that have gotten your interest? The piece was written for a general audience; how might it have been different if it had been written for scientists? Would they need (or appreciate) the story told here?

Narrative can be a good way of ENDING a text, too, by winding up a discussion with an illustration of the main point. Here, for instance, is a concluding paragraph from an essay on American values and Las Vegas weddings.

◆ 245–48

> I sat next to one . . . wedding party in a Strip restaurant the last time I was in Las Vegas. The marriage had just taken place; the bride still wore her dress, the mother her corsage. A bored waiter poured out a few swallows of pink champagne ("on the house") for everyone but the bride, who was too young to be served. "You'll need something with more kick than that," the bride's father said with heavy jocularity to his new son-in-law; the ritual jokes about the wedding night had a certain Panglossian character, since the bride was clearly several months pregnant. Another round of pink champagne, this time not on the house, and the bride began to cry. "It was just as nice," she sobbed, "as I hoped and dreamed it would be."
>
> —Joan Didion, "Marrying Absurd"

No doubt Didion makes her points about American values clearly and cogently in the essay. But concluding with this story lets us *see* (and hear) what she is saying about Las Vegas wedding chapels, which sell "'niceness,' the facsimile of proper ritual, to children who do not know how else to find it, how to make the arrangements, how to do it 'right.'"

Considering the Rhetorical Situation

As a writer or speaker, you need to think about the message that you want to articulate, the audience you want to reach, and the larger context you are writing in.

■ **PURPOSE**   Your purpose will affect the way you use narrative. For example, in an essay about seat belt laws, you might

3–4

tell about the painful rehabilitation of a teenager who was not wearing a seat belt and was injured in an accident in order to persuade readers that seat belts should be mandatory.

■ **AUDIENCE** Whom do you want to reach, and do you have an anecdote or other narrative that will help them understand your topic or persuade them that your argument has merit?

■ **GENRE** Does your genre require you to include narrative? A memoir about an important event might be primarily narrative, whereas a reflection about an event might focus more on the significance of the event than on what happened.

■ **STANCE** What is your stance, and do you have any stories that would help you convey that stance? A funny story, for example, can help create a humorous stance.

■ **MEDIA / DESIGN** In a print or spoken text, you will likely be limited to brief narratives, perhaps illustrated with photos or other images. In an electronic text, you might have the option of linking to full-length narratives or visuals available on the Web.

> See also the **PROCESSES** chapters if you are assigned to write a narrative essay and need help **DRAFTING, REVISING,** and so on. Two special kinds of narratives are **LAB REPORTS** (which use narrative to describe the steps in an experiment from beginning to end) and **RÉSUMÉS** (which essentially tell the story of the work we've done, at school and on the job).

Reading Strategies

We read newspapers to learn about the events of the day. We read cookbooks to find out how to make brownies and textbooks to learn about history, chemistry, and other academic topics. We read short stories for pleasure — and, in literature classes, to analyze plot, setting, character, and theme. And as writers, we read our own drafts to make sure they say what we mean, and we proofread our final drafts to make sure they're correct. In other words, we read in various ways for many different purposes. This chapter offers a number of strategies for reading with a critical eye — from previewing a text to annotating as you read, identifying meaningful patterns, analyzing an argument, and more.

Reading Strategically

Academic reading is challenging because it makes several demands on you at once. Textbooks present new vocabulary and concepts, and picking out the main ideas can be difficult. Scholarly articles present content and arguments you need to understand, and they often assume because readers understand key concepts and vocabulary, they don't generally provide background information. As you read more texts in an academic field and participate in its conversations, the reading will become easier, but in the meantime you can develop strategies that will help you to read carefully and critically.

Different texts require different kinds of effort. Some texts can be read fairly quickly, if you're reading to get a general overview. Most of the time, though, you need to read carefully, matching the pace of your reading to the difficulty of the text. To read with a critical eye, you can't be in too much of a hurry. You'll likely need to skim the text for an overview of the basic ideas and then read carefully. And then you may read the text again. That is true for visual as well as verbal texts—you'll often need to get an overview of a text and then to pay close attention to its details.

Previewing a Text

It's usually a good idea to start by skimming a text: read the title and subtitle, any headings, the first and last paragraphs, the first sentences of all the other paragraphs. Study any illustrations and other visuals. Your goal is to get a sense of where the text is heading. At this point, don't stop to look up unfamiliar words; just underline them or put a mark in the margin, and look them up later.

Considering the Rhetorical Situation

3–4	■ **PURPOSE**	What is the purpose? To entertain? inform? persuade readers to think something or take some action?
5–8	■ **AUDIENCE**	Who is the intended audience? Are you a member of that group? If not, should you expect that you'll need to look up unfamiliar terms or concepts or that you'll run into assumptions you don't necessarily share?
9–11	■ **GENRE**	What is the genre? Is it a report? an argument? an analysis? something else? Knowing the genre can help you anticipate certain key features.
12–14	■ **STANCE**	Who is the writer, and what is his or her stance? Critical? Curious? Opinionated? Objective? Passionate? Indifferent? Something else? Knowing the stance affects the way you understand a text, whether you're inclined to agree or disagree, to take it seriously, and so on.
15–17	■ **MEDIA / DESIGN**	What is the medium, and how does it affect the way you read? If it's a print text, do you know anything about the publisher? If it's on the Web, who sponsors the site, and when was it last updated? Are there any

design elements — such as headings, summaries, color, or boxes — that highlight key parts of the text?

Thinking about Your Initial Response

It's usually good to read a text first just to get a sense of it. Some readers find it helps to jot down brief notes about their first response to a text, noting their reaction and thinking a little about why they reacted as they did:

- *What are your initial reactions?* Describe both your intellectual reaction and any emotional reaction. Identify places in the text that caused you to react as you did. If you had no particular reaction, note that.

- *What accounts for your reaction?* Do you agree or disagree with the writer or have a different perspective? Why? Are your reactions rooted in personal experiences? positions you hold? particular beliefs? some personal philosophy? As much as possible, you want to keep your opinions from coloring your analysis, so it's important to try to identify those opinions up front — and to give some thought to where they come from.

Annotating

Many readers find it helps to annotate as they read: highlighting key words, phrases, sentences; connecting ideas with lines or symbols; writing comments or questions in the margin; noting anything that seems noteworthy or questionable. Annotate as if you're having a conversation with the author, someone you take seriously but whose words you do not accept without question. Put your part of the conversation in the margin, asking questions, talking back: "What's this mean?" "So what?" "Says who?" "Where's evidence?" "Yes!" "Whoa!" even ☺ or ☹.

What you annotate depends on your **PURPOSE** or what you're most interested in. If you're analyzing an argument, you would probably underline any **THESIS STATEMENT** and then the reasons and evidence that support the statement. It might help to restate those ideas in your own words,

■ 3–4

◆ 251–52

in the margins—in order to put them in your own words, you need to understand them! If you are looking for meaningful patterns, you might highlight each pattern in a different color and write any questions or notes about it in that color. If you are analyzing a literary text to look for certain elements or themes or patterns, you might highlight key passages that demonstrate those things.

Annotating forces you to read for more than just the surface meaning. Especially when you are going to be writing about or responding to a text, annotating creates a record of things you may want to refer to.

There are some texts that you cannot annotate, of course: library books, materials you read on the Web, and so on. Then you will need to make notes elsewhere, and you might find it useful to keep a reading log for that purpose.

On pages 317–18 is an annotated passage from Lawrence Lessig's essay "Some Like It Hot," included in Chapter 9: These annotations rephrase key definitions, identify the essay's thesis and main ideas, ask questions, and comment on issues raised in the essay. Annotating the entire essay, which appears on pages 85–89, would provide a look at Lessig's ideas and a record of the experience of reading the essay—useful for both understanding it and analyzing it.

Playing the Believing and Doubting Game

200–01
199–200

One way to think about your response to a text is to **LIST** or **FREEWRITE** as many reasons as you can think of for believing what the writer says and then as many as you can for doubting it. First, write as if you agree with everything in the writer's argument; look at the world from his or her perspective, trying to understand the writer's premises and reasons for arguing as he or she does even if you strongly disagree. Then, write as if you doubt everything in the text: try to find every flaw in the argument, every possible way it can be refuted—even if you totally agree with it. Developed by writing theorist Peter Elbow, the believing and doubting game helps you consider new ideas and question ideas you already have—and at the same time see where you stand in relation to the ideas in the text you're reading.

rhetorical
situations   genres   processes   strategies   research
mla/apa   media/
design

If piracy means using the creative property of others without their permission, then the history of the content industry is a history of piracy.
Every important sector of big media today—film, music, radio, and
cable TV—was born of a kind of piracy. The consistent story is how
each generation welcomes the pirates from the last. Each generation—
until now.

The Hollywood film industry was built by fleeing pirates. Creators
and directors migrated from the East Coast to California in the early
twentieth century in part to escape controls that film patents granted
the inventor Thomas Edison. These controls were exercised through the
Motion Pictures Patents Company, a monopoly "trust" based on Edison's creative property and formed to vigorously protect his patent
rights.

California was remote enough from Edison's reach that filmmakers like Fox and Paramount could move there and, without fear of the
law, pirate his inventions. Hollywood grew quickly, and enforcement
of federal law eventually spread west. But because patents granted
their holders a truly "limited" monopoly of just seventeen years (at
that time), the patents had expired by the time enough federal marshals appeared. A new industry had been founded, in part from the
piracy of Edison's creative property.

Meanwhile, the record industry grew out of another kind of piracy.
At the time that Edison and Henri Fourneaux invented machines for
reproducing music (Edison the phonograph; Fourneaux the player
piano), the law gave composers the exclusive right to control copies
and public performances of their music. Thus, in 1900, if I wanted a
copy of Phil Russel's 1899 hit, "Happy Mose," the law said I would have
to pay for the right to get a copy of the score, and I would also have
to pay for the right to perform it publicly.

But what if I wanted to record "Happy Mose" using Edison's   5
phonograph or Fourneaux's player piano? Here the law stumbled. If I
simply sang the piece into a recording device in my home, it wasn't
clear that I owed the composer anything. And more important, it

---

*Piracy—
unauthorized use
of the artistic
work of others.*

*"Content
industry"—new
term. Film, music,
and so on?
Doesn't include
books and maga-
zines?*

*Thesis: "Big
media" are all
based on piracy.*

*Hollywood film
industry started
in order to avoid
Edison's patents.
What were they
for? Cameras and
projectors? Is this
true?*

*Record-industry
piracy.*

Player pianos?

wasn't clear whether I owed the composer anything if I then made copies of those recordings. Because of this gap in the law, I could effectively use someone else's song without paying the composer anything. The composers (and publishers) were none too happy about this capacity to pirate.

In 1909, Congress closed the gap in favor of the composer and the recording artist, amending copyright law to make sure that composers would be paid for "mechanical reproductions" of their music. But rather than simply granting the composer complete control over the right to make such reproductions, Congress gave recording artists a right to record the music, at a price set by Congress, after the composer allowed it to be recorded once. This is the part of copyright law that makes cover songs possible. Once a composer authorizes a recording of his song, others are free to record the same song, so long as they pay the original composer a fee set by the law. So, by limiting musicians' rights—by partially pirating their creative work—record producers and the public benefit.

—Lawrence Lessig, "Some Like It Hot"

Is copyright law different for books and other printed matter?

Partial piracy? Not sure about this—when artists use a song, they pay a fee but don't need permission. The composer doesn't have complete control. So it's piracy, but not completely?

rhetorical situations · genres · processes · strategies · research mla/apa · media/ design

Thinking about How the Text Works:
What It Says, What It Does

Sometimes you'll need to think about how a text works, how its parts fit together. You may be assigned to analyze a text, or you may just need to make sense of a difficult text, to think about how the ideas all relate to one another. Whatever your purpose, a good way to think about a text's structure is by OUTLINING it, paragraph by paragraph. If you're interested in analyzing its ideas, look at what each paragraph *says*; if, on the other hand, you're concerned with how the ideas are presented, pay attention to what each paragraph *does*.

◗ 203–04

What it says. Write a sentence that identifies what each paragraph says. Once you've done that for the whole text, look for patterns in the topics the writer addresses. Pay attention to the order in which the topics are presented. Also look for gaps, ideas the writer has left unsaid. Such paragraph-by-paragraph outlining of the content can help you see how the writer has arranged ideas and how that arrangement builds an argument or develops a topic. Here, for example, is such an outline of Lawrence Lessig's essay (the numbers on the left refer to the paragraphs):

1	Every major type of media bases its development on piracy, the unauthorized use of artists' work.
2, 3	To escape patents that restricted the copying of innovations in filmmaking, the movie industry moved from the East Coast to California.
4, 5	Copyright law gave composers control over the performance of their music—but because it didn't cover the recording of music and the sale of copies of the recordings, it allowed piracy in the record industry.
6	Congress eventually changed the law, allowing musicians to record a song without the composer's permission if they paid the composer a fee.
7–11	When a radio station plays a song, it pays the composer but not the recording artist, thus pirating the recording artist's work.

12, 13	Cable TV has pirated works, too, by paying networks nothing for their broadcasts—despite protests by broadcasters and copyright owners.
14	Congress eventually extended the copyright law to cable TV, forcing the cable companies to pay for their broadcasts at a price controlled by Congress in order to protect the innovations of the cable industry.
15	The history of the major media industries suggests that piracy is not necessarily "plainly wrong."
16, 17	Peer-to-peer file sharing, like the earlier media-industry innovations, is being used to share artistic content and avoid industry controls, but it differs from the early cable industry in that it is not selling any content.
18	P2P file sharing provides access to music that can no longer be purchased, music that copyright holders want to share, and music that is no longer copyrighted.
19	P2P file sharing, like the earlier innovations, is the result of new technology, and it raises similar questions: how can it best be used without penalizing the artists whose works are "pirated"?
20	Copyright law must balance the protection of artists' works with the innovation in technologies, a process that takes time.

What it does.   Identify the function of each paragraph. Starting with the first paragraph, ask, What does this paragraph do? Does it introduce a topic? provide background for a topic to come? describe something? define something? entice me to read further? Something else? What does the second paragraph do? the third? As you go through the text, you may identify groups of paragraphs that have a single purpose. For an example, look at this functional outline of Lessig's essay (again, the numbers on the left refer to the paragraphs):

1	Defines the key term, *piracy,* and illustrates the thesis using the history of four media industries in the United States.
2, 3	Tells the history of the first medium, film, by focusing on piracy as a major factor in its development.
4–6	Tells the history of the second medium, the recording industry, again by focusing on the role of piracy in its development.

7–11   Tells the history of the third medium, radio, focusing on the role of piracy in its development.

12–14   Tells the history of the fourth medium, cable TV, focusing on the role of piracy in its development.

15   Offers conclusions about piracy based on the similar roles played by piracy in the histories of the four media.

16, 17 Compares the current controversy over piracy in peer-to-peer file sharing on the Internet with the role of piracy in the earlier media.

18   Describes the benefits of P2P file sharing.

19, 20 Compares those benefits with those of the other media and offers a conclusion in the form of a problem to be solved.

Summarizing

Summarizing a text can help you both to see the relationships among its ideas and to understand what it's saying. When you **SUMMARIZE,** you restate a text's main ideas in your own words, leaving out most examples and other details. Here's a summary of Lawrence Lessig's essay:

● 366–67

> The development of every major media industry is based on piracy, the unauthorized use of artists' or inventors' work. First, the film industry flourished by evading restrictions on the copying of innovations in film-making. Then, the recording industry benefited from copyright laws that gave composers control over the performance of their music but not over the recording of it or the sale of the recordings. A law passed in 1909 in effect allows musicians to record a song without the composer's permission if they pay the composer a fee. Radio broadcasters benefit from piracy, too, every time they play a song recorded by someone other than the composer: they pay the composer a fee but not the recording artist. Finally, when it first started operating, cable TV benefited from piracy—by paying the networks nothing for their broadcasts. Congress eventually extended the copyright law, forcing cable companies to pay for the content they broadcast—but at a price controlled by Congress so that the networks wouldn't be able to drive the cable companies out of business. Peer-to-peer file sharing, like the early media industries, is being used to share artistic content and avoid indus-

try controls on that sharing. It benefits the public by allowing access to music that is out of print, that copyright holders want to share, and that is no longer copyrighted. Therefore, the public needs to figure out how to make it work without penalizing musicians by pirating their songs. Copyright law must balance the protection of artists' work with the encouragement of technological innovation.

Identifying Patterns

Look for notable patterns in the text: recurring words and their synonyms, as well as repeated phrases, metaphors and other images, and types of sentences. Some writers find it helps to highlight patterns in various colors. Does the author rely on any particular writing **STRATEGIES**: narration? comparison? Something else?

237–328 ◆

It might be important to consider the kind of evidence offered: Is it more opinion than fact? nothing but statistics? If many sources are cited, is the information presented in any predominant patterns: as **QUOTATIONS**? **PARAPHRASES**? **SUMMARIES**? Are there repeated references to certain experts or sources?

358–69 ●

In visual texts, look for patterns of color, shape, and line. What's in the foreground, and what's in the background? What's completely visible, partly visible, or invisible? In both verbal and visual texts, look for omissions and anomalies: What isn't there that you would expect to find? Is there anything that doesn't really fit in?

If you discover patterns, then you need to consider what, if anything, they mean in terms of what the writer is saying. What do they reveal about the writer's underlying premises and beliefs? What do they tell us about the writer's strategies for persuading us to accept the truth of what he or she is saying?

See how color coding William Safire's essay on the Gettysburg Address reveals several patterns in the language Safire uses. In this excerpt from the essay, which appears in full in Chapter 7, religious references are colored yellow; references to a "national spirit," green; references to life, death, and rebirth, blue; and places where he directly addresses the reader, gray.

But the selection of this poetic political sermon as the oratorical centerpiece of our observance need not be only an exercise. . . . now, as
then, a national spirit rose from the ashes of destruction.

Here is how to listen to Lincoln's all-too-familiar speech with new
ears.

In those 266 words, you will hear the word *dedicate* five times.
. . .

Those five pillars of dedication rested on a fundament of religious
metaphor. From a president not known for his piety — indeed, often
criticized for his supposed lack of faith — came a speech rooted in the
theme of national resurrection. The speech is grounded in conception,
birth, death, and rebirth.

Consider the barrage of images of birth in the opening sentence. . . .

Finally, the nation's spirit rises from this scene of death: "that this
nation, under God, shall have a new birth of freedom." Conception,
birth, death, rebirth. The nation, purified in this fiery trial of war, is
resurrected. Through the sacrifice of its sons, the sundered nation
would be reborn as one. . . .

Do not listen on Sept. 11 only to Lincoln's famous words and comforting cadences. Think about how Lincoln's message encompasses but
goes beyond paying "fitting and proper" respect to the dead and the
bereaved. His sermon at Gettysburg reminds "us the living" of our
"unfinished work" and "the great task remaining before us" — to
resolve that this generation's response to the deaths of thousands of
our people leads to "a new birth of freedom."

The color coding helps us to see patterns in Safire's language, just as Safire
reveals patterns in Lincoln's words. He offers an interpretation of Lincoln's
address as a "poetic political sermon," and the words he uses throughout
support that interpretation. At the end, he repeats the assertion that Lincoln's address is a sermon, inviting us to consider it differently. Targeting
different textual elements, such as commands to the reader ("Consider,"
"Do not listen," "Think about"), offers additional information on how Safire
wishes to position himself in relation to his readers.

Count up the parts.   This is a two-step process: first, you count things:
how many of this, how many of that. Look for words, phrases, or sentences that seem important, or select a few typical paragraphs on which

to focus. After you count, see what you can conclude about the writing. You may want to work with others, dividing up the counting.

- **Count words.** Count one-, two-, three-syllable words, repeated words, active and passive verbs, prepositions, jargon or specialized terms.
- **Count sentences.** Count the number of words in each sentence, the average number of words per sentence; figure the percentage of sentences above and below average; count the number of sentences in each paragraph; count the number of simple sentences, compound sentences, complex sentences, fragments; mark the distinct rhythms (tap out the beat as you read aloud); count repeated phrases.
- **Count paragraphs.** Count the number of paragraphs, the average number of words and sentences per paragraph, the shortest and longest paragraphs; consider the position of the longest and shortest paragraphs; find parallel paragraph structures.
- **Count images.** List, circle, or underline verbal or visual images, similes, metaphors, and other figures of speech. Categorize them by meaning as well as type.

What do your findings tell you about the text? What generalizations can you make about it? Why did the author choose the words or images he or she used and in those combinations? What do those words tell you about the writer—or about his or her stance? Do your findings suggest a strategy, a plan for your analysis? For instance, Safire counts the number of times Lincoln uses *dedicate* and images of birth, death, and rebirth to argue something about Lincoln's speech and what it should mean to Safire's audience on the anniversary of 9/11.

Analyzing the Argument

All texts make some kind of argument, claiming something and then offering reasons and evidence as support for the claim. As a critical reader, you need to look closely at the argument a text makes—you need to recognize all the claims it makes, consider the support it offers for those claims, and decide how you want to respond. What do you think, and why? Here

are some of the aspects of a text you'll need to consider when you analyze an argument:

- *What is the claim?* What is the main point the writer is trying to make?
  Is there a clearly stated **THESIS,** or is it merely implied?

251–52

- *What support does the writer offer for the claim?* What **REASONS** are given
  to support the claim? What **EVIDENCE** backs up those reasons? Facts?
  Statistics? Testimonials by authorities? Examples? Pertinent anecdotes? Are the reasons plausible and sufficient?

93
94

- *How evenhandedly does the writer present the issues?* Is there any mention of counterarguments? If so, how does the writer deal with them?
  By refuting them? By acknowledging them and responding to them
  reasonably? Does the writer treat other arguments respectfully? dis-
  missively? Are his or her own arguments appropriately qualified?

- *What authorities or sources of outside information does the writer use?*
  How are they used? How credible are they? Are they in any way biased
  or otherwise unreliable? Are they current?

- *How does the writer address you as the reader?* Does the writer assume
  that readers know something about what is being discussed? Does his
  or her language include you or exclude you? (Hint: If you see the word
  we, do you feel included?) Do you sense that you and the author share
  any beliefs or attitudes?

Check for fallacies.   Fallacies are arguments that involve faulty reasoning. Because they often seem plausible, they can be persuasive. It is important, therefore, that you question the legitimacy of such reasoning when
you run across it.

Philosophers and rhetoricians have identified many kinds of faulty
reasoning; here are some of the most common kinds:

- **Ad hominem** arguments attack someone's character rather than
  addressing the issues. (*Ad hominem* is Latin for "to the man.") It is an
  especially common fallacy in political discourse and elsewhere: "Jack
  Turner has no business talking about the way we run things in this
  city. He's lived here only five years and is just another flaky liberal."

The length of time Turner has lived in the city has no bearing on the worth of his argument; neither does his political stance, which his opponent characterizes unfairly.

- **Bandwagon appeals** argue that because others think or do something, we should, too. For example, an advertisement for a rifle association suggests that "67 percent of voters support laws permitting concealed weapons. You should, too." It assumes that readers want to be part of the group and implies that an opinion that is popular must be correct.

- **Begging the question** is a circular argument. It assumes as a given what is trying to be proved, essentially supporting an assertion with the assertion itself. Consider this statement: "Affirmative action can never be fair or just because you cannot remedy one injustice by committing another." This statement begs the question because to prove that affirmative action is unjust, it assumes that it is an injustice.

- **Either-or** arguments, also called *false dilemmas*, are oversimplifications. Either-or arguments assert that there can be only two possible positions on a complex issue. For example, "Those who oppose our actions in this war are enemies of freedom" inaccurately assumes that if someone opposes the war in question, he or she opposes freedom. In fact, people might have many other reasons for opposing the war.

- **False analogies** compare things that resemble each other in some ways but not in the most important respects. For example: "Trees pollute the air just as much as cars and trucks do." Although it's true that plants emit hydrocarbons, and hydrocarbons are a component of smog, they also produce oxygen, whereas motor vehicles emit gases that combine with hydrocarbons to form smog. Vehicles pollute the air; trees provide the air that vehicles' emissions pollute.

- **Faulty causality,** also known as *post hoc, ergo propter hoc* (Latin for "after this, therefore because of this"), assumes that because one event followed another, the first event caused the second—for example, "Legalizing same-sex marriage in Sweden led to an increase in the number of children born to unwed mothers." The statement contains no evidence to show that the first event caused the second. The birth rate

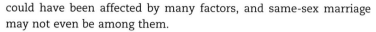

could have been affected by many factors, and same-sex marriage may not even be among them.

- *Hasty generalizations* are conclusions based on insufficient or inappropriately qualified evidence. This summary of a research study is a good example: "Twenty randomly chosen residents of Brooklyn, New York, were asked whether they found graffiti tags offensive; fourteen said yes, five said no, and one had no opinion. Therefore, 70 percent of Brooklyn residents find tagging offensive." In Brooklyn, a part of New York City with a population of over two million, twenty residents is far too small a group from which to draw meaningful conclusions. To be able to generalize, the researcher would have had to survey a much greater percentage of Brooklyn's population.

- *Slippery slope* arguments assert that one event will inevitably lead to another, often cataclysmic event without presenting evidence that such a chain of causes and effects will in fact take place. Here's an example: "If the state legislature passes this 2 percent tax increase, it won't be long before all the corporations in the state move to other states and leave thousands unemployed." According to this argument, if taxes are raised, the state's economy will be ruined — not a likely scenario, given the size of the proposed increase.

Considering the Larger Context

All texts are part of ongoing conversations with other texts that have dealt with the same topic. An essay arguing for handgun trigger locks is part of an ongoing conversation about gun control, which is itself part of a conversation on individual rights and responsibilities. Academic texts document their sources in part to show their relationship to the ongoing scholarly conversations on a particular topic. Academic reading usually challenges you to become aware of those conversations. And in fact, any time you're reading to learn, you're probably reading for some larger context. Whatever your reading goals, being aware of that larger context can help you better understand what you're reading. Here are some specific aspects of the text to pay attention to:

- **Who else cares about this topic?** Especially when you're reading in order to learn about a topic, the texts you read will often reveal which people or groups are part of the conversation — and might be sources of further reading. For example, an essay describing the formation of Mammoth Cave could be of interest to geologists, spelunkers, travel writers, or tourists. If you're reading such an essay while doing research on the cave, you should consider how the audience addressed determines the nature of the information provided — and its suitability as a source for your research.

- **Ideas.** Does the text refer to any concepts or ideas that give you some sense that it's part of a larger conversation? An argument on airport security measures, for example, is part of larger conversations about government response to terrorism, the limits of freedom in a democracy, and the possibilities of using technology to detect weapons and explosives, among others.

- **Terms.** Is there any terminology or specialized language that reflects the writer's allegiance to a particular group or academic discipline? If you run across words like *false consciousness*, *ideology*, and *hegemony*, for example, you might guess the text was written by a Marxist scholar.

- **Citations.** Whom does the writer cite? Do the other writers have a particular academic specialty, belong to an identifiable intellectual school, share similar political leanings? If an article on politics cites Michael Moore and Barbara Ehrenreich in support of its argument, you might assume the writer holds liberal opinions; if it cites Rush Limbaugh and Sean Hannity, the writer is likely a conservative.

354–57 ●
208–23 ○

> See also the chapter on **EVALUATING SOURCES** for help analyzing the reliability of a text, and see the chapters on **ASSESSING YOUR OWN WRITING, GETTING RESPONSE AND REVISING,** and **EDITING AND PROOFREADING** for advice on reading your own writing.

part 5

Doing Research

We do research all the time, for many different reasons. We search the Web for information about a new computer, ask friends about the best place to get coffee, try on several pairs of jeans before deciding which ones to buy. You have no doubt done your share of library research before now, and you probably visited a number of schools' Web sites before deciding which college you wanted to attend. Research, in other words, is something you do every day. The following chapters offer advice on the kind of research you'll need to do for your academic work and, in particular, for research papers and other written documents.

Doing Research

Developing a Research Plan **39**

When you need to do research, it's sometimes tempting to jump in and start looking for information right away. To do research well, however—to find appropriate sources and use them wisely—you need to work systematically. You need a research plan. This chapter will help you establish such a plan and then get started.

Establishing a Schedule

Doing research is complex and time-consuming, so it's good to establish a schedule for yourself. Research-based writing projects usually require you to come up with a topic (or to analyze the requirements of an assigned topic). You'll need to do preliminary research to come up with a research question to guide your research efforts. Once you do some serious, focused research to find the information you need, you'll be ready to turn your research question into a tentative thesis and sketch out a rough outline. After doing whatever additional research you need to fill in your outline, you'll write a draft—and get some response to that draft. Perhaps you'll need to do additional research before revising. Finally, you'll need to edit and proofread. And so you'll want to start by establishing a schedule, perhaps using the form on the next page.

Getting Started

Once you have a schedule, you can get started. The sections that follow offer advice on considering your rhetorical situation, coming up with a topic, and thinking about what you already know about it; doing prelim-

rhetorical situations

genres

processes

strategies

research mla/apa

media/ design

Scheduling a Research Project

Complete by:

Analyze your rhetorical situation.	_____
Choose a possible topic.	_____
Do preliminary research.	_____
Come up with a research question.	_____
Schedule interviews and other field research.	_____
Find and read library and Web sources.	_____
Do any field research.	_____
Come up with a tentative thesis and outline.	_____
Write out a draft.	_____
Get response.	_____
Do any additional research.	_____
Revise.	_____
Prepare a list of works cited.	_____
Edit.	_____
Prepare the final draft.	_____
Proofread.	_____
Submit the final draft.	_____

inary research, and creating a working bibliography; developing a research question, devising a tentative thesis and a rough outline, and keeping track of your sources. The chapters that follow offer guidelines for **FINDING SOURCES** and **EVALUATING SOURCES**.

340–53 ●
354–57 ●

Considering the Rhetorical Situation

As with any writing task, you need to start by considering your purpose, your audience, and the rest of your rhetorical situation:

rhetorical situations   genres   processes   strategies   research mla/apa   media/ design

▦ **PURPOSE**	Is this project part of an assignment—and if so, does it specify any one purpose? If not, what is your broad purpose? To inform? argue? entertain? A combination?	3–4
▦ **AUDIENCE**	To whom are you writing? What does your audience likely know about your topic, and is there any background information you'll need to provide? What opinions or attitudes do your readers likely hold? What kinds of evidence will they find persuasive? How do you want them to respond to your writing?	5–8
▦ **GENRE**	Are you writing to report on something? to compose a profile? to make a proposal? an argument? What are the requirements of your genre in terms of the number and kind of sources you must use?	9–11
▦ **STANCE**	What is your attitude toward your topic? What accounts for your attitude? How do you want to come across? Curious? Critical? Positive? Something else?	12–14
▦ **MEDIA / DESIGN**	What medium will you use? Print? Spoken? Electronic? Will you need to compose any charts, photographs, video, presentation software slides, or other visuals?	15–17

Coming Up with a Topic

If you need to choose a topic, consider your interests. What do you want to learn about? What do you have questions about? What topics from your courses have you found intriguing? What community, national, or global issues do you care about? If your topic is assigned, you still need to make sure you understand exactly what it asks you to do. Read the assignment carefully, looking for key words: does it ask you to **ANALYZE, COMPARE, EVALUATE, SUMMARIZE?** If the assignment offers broad guidelines but allows you to choose within them, identify the requirements and the range of possibilities, and define your topic within those constraints. For

◆ 255–59
◆ 266–74
▲ 120-26
● 366–67

example, in an American history course, your instructor might ask you to "discuss social effects of the Civil War." To define a suitable topic, you might choose to explore such topics as poverty among Confederate soldiers or former slaveholders, the migration of members of those groups to Mexico or northern cities, the establishment of independent black churches, the growth of sharecropping among former slaves, or the spread of the Ku Klux Klan—to name a few possibilities. Once you have a broad topic, you might try **FREEWRITING, LOOPING, LISTING,** or **CLUSTERING** to find an angle to research.

199–202

Narrow the topic.   As you consider possible topics, look to narrow your focus on a topic to make it specific enough for you to research and cover in a paper. For example:

Too general: the environment

Still too general: chemicals harmful to the environment

Better: chemicals in gasoline that harm the environment

More specific: the effects of the gasoline additive MTBE on water purity

If you limit your topic, you can address it with specific information that you'll be more easily able to find and manage. In addition, a limited topic will be more likely to interest your audience than a broad subject that forces you to use abstract, general statements. For example, it's much harder to write well about "the environment" than it is to address a topic that covers a single environmental issue.

Think about what you know about your topic.   Chances are you already know something about your topic, and articulating that knowledge can help you see possible ways to focus your topic or come up with potential sources of information. **FREEWRITING, LISTING, CLUSTERING,** and **LOOPING** are all good ways of tapping your knowledge of your topic. Consider where you might find information about it: Have you read about it in a textbook? heard stories about it on the news? visited Web sites focused on it? Do you know anyone who knows about this topic?

199–202

rhetorical situations · genres · processes · strategies · research mla/apa · media/design

Doing Some Preliminary Research

Doing some preliminary research can save you time in the long run. Scholarly sources usually focus on narrow, specialized aspects of subjects. To define the focus for your research, you first need to explore sources that will provide an overview of your topic.

344–45

One way to begin is to look at **REFERENCE WORKS** — sources that deal with the general topic and that include summaries or overviews of the scholarship in a field. General encyclopedias can give you some background, but they aren't suitable as sources for college work; use them as a starting point, to give you some basic information about your topic and help you see some of the paths you might follow. The same is true of the results you're likely to get from skimming Web sites on the subject. Discipline-specific encyclopedias can be more helpful, as they usually present subjects in much greater depth and provide more scholarly references that might provide starting points for your research. Even if you know a lot about a subject, doing research can open you to new ways of seeing and approaching it, increasing your options for developing and narrowing your topic.

At this stage, pay close attention to the terms used to discuss your topic. These terms could be keywords that you can use to search for information on your topic in library catalogs, in databases, and on the Web.

Keeping a Working Bibliography

A working bibliography is a record of all the sources you consult. You should keep such a record so that you can find sources easily when you need them and then cite any that you use. You can keep a working bibliography on index cards or in a notebook, or in many cases you can print out or photocopy the data you need. To save time later, include all the bibliographic information you'll need to document the sources you use. If possible, follow the **DOCUMENTATION** style you'll use when you write.

375–449

On the next page is most of the basic information you'll want to include for each source in your working bibliography. Go to wwnorton.com/write/fieldguide for templates you can use to keep track of this information.

Information for a working bibliography

FOR A BOOK

Library call number
Author(s) or editor(s)
Title and subtitle
Publication information: city, publisher, year of publication
Other information: edition, volume number, translator, and so on
If your source is a chapter in a book, include its author, title, and page numbers.

FOR AN ARTICLE IN A PERIODICAL

Author(s)
Title and subtitle
Name of periodical
Volume number, issue number, date
Page numbers

FOR A WEB SOURCE

URL
Author(s) or editor(s) if available
Name of site
Sponsor of site
Date site was first posted or last updated
Date you accessed site
If the source is an article or book reprinted on the Web, include its title, the title and publication information of the periodical or book where it was first published, and any page numbers.

FOR A SOURCE FROM AN ELECTRONIC DATABASE

Publication information for the source
Name of database
Item number, if there is one
Name of subscription service and its URL
Library where you accessed source
Date you accessed source

Coming Up with a Research Question

Once you've surveyed the territory of your topic, you'll likely find that your understanding of your topic has become broader and deeper. You may find that your interests have changed and your research has led to surprises and additional research. That's okay: as a result of exploring avenues you hadn't anticipated, you may well come up with a better topic than the one you'd started with. At some point, though, you need to come up with a research question—a specific question that you will then work to answer through your research.

To write a research question, review your analysis of the **RHETORICAL SITUATION,** to remind yourself of any time constraints or length considerations. Generate a list of questions beginning with What? When? Where? Who? How? Why? Would? Could? and Should? Here, for example, are some questions about the tentative topic "the effects of the gasoline additive MTBE on water purity":

1–17

> *What* are the effects of MTBE on humans and animals?
>
> *When* did MTBE become commonly used as a gasoline additive?
>
> *Where* has MTBE entered the water table?
>
> *Who* wants to ban MTBE, and *who* would benefit from banning it?
>
> *How* widespread is groundwater pollution by MTBE?
>
> *Why* do environmental groups oppose the use of MTBE?
>
> *Would* it be appropriate for the EPA to regulate the use of MTBE?
>
> *Could* substitutes for MTBE maintain clean air without pollution?
>
> *Should* the use of MTBE as a gasoline additive be banned?

Select one question from your list that you find interesting and that suits your rhetorical situation. Use the question to guide your research.

Drafting a Tentative Thesis

Once your research has led you to a possible answer to your research question, try formulating that answer as a tentative **THESIS.** You need not be

251–52

committed to the thesis; in fact, you should not be. The object of your research should be to learn about your topic, not to find information that simply supports what you already think you believe. Your tentative thesis may (and probably will) change as you learn more about your subject, consider the many points of view on it, and reconsider your topic and, perhaps, your goal: what you originally planned to be an informational report may become an argument, or the argument you planned to write may become a report. However tentative, a thesis allows you to move forward by clarifying your purpose for doing research. Here are some tentative thesis statements on the topic of MTBE:

> The EPA should regulate the use of MTBE.
>
> Substitutes for MTBE can maintain clean air without causing pollution.
>
> The use of MTBE as a gasoline additive should be banned.

As with a research question, a tentative thesis should guide your research efforts—but be ready to revise it as you learn still more about your topic. Research should be a process of inquiry, in which you approach your topic with an open mind, ready to learn and possibly change. If you hold too tightly to a tentative thesis, you risk selecting only that research and evidence that supports your view, making your writing biased and unconvincing.

Creating a Rough Outline

203–04 ○

After you've created a tentative thesis, write out a rough **OUTLINE** for your research paper. Your rough outline can be a simple list of topics you want to explore, something that will help you structure your research efforts and organize your notes and other materials. As you read your sources, you can use your outline to keep track of what you need to find and where the information you do find fits into your argument. Then you'll be able to see if you've covered all the ideas you intended to explore—or whether you need to rethink the categories on your outline.

rhetorical
situations

genres

processes

strategies

research
mla/apa

media/
design

Keeping Track of Your Sources

- *Staple together copies and printouts of print materials.* It's easy for individual pages to get shuffled or lost on a desk or in a backpack. Keep a stapler handy, and fasten pages together as soon as you copy them or print them out.

- *Store Web site URLs* as *favorites* (in Internet Explorer) or *bookmarks* (in Netscape Navigator).

- *Label everything.* Label your copies with the source's author and title.

- *Highlight sections you plan to use.* When you sit down to draft, your goal will be to find what you need quickly, so as soon as you decide you might use a source, highlight the paragraphs or sentences that you think you'll use. If your instructor wants copies of your sources to see how you used them, you've got them ready.

- *Use your rough outline to keep track of what you've got.* In the margin of each highlighted section, write the number or letter to which the section corresponds. (It's a good idea to write it in the same place consistently so you can flip through a stack of copies and easily see what you've got.) Alternatively, attach sticky notes to each photocopy, using a different color for each main heading in your outline.

- *Keep everything in a file folder or box.* That way, even though your research material may not look organized, it will all be in one place—and if you highlight, number, and use sticky notes, your material will be organized and you'll be better prepared to write a draft. This folder or box will also serve you well if you are required to create a portfolio that includes your research notes, photocopies of sources, and drafts.

See the guidelines on **FINDING SOURCES** once you're ready to move on to in-depth research and those on **EVALUATING SOURCES** for help thinking critically about the sources you find.

340–57

40 Finding Sources

To analyze media coverage of the 2004 Democratic National Convention, you examine news stories and blogs published at the time. To write an essay interpreting a poem by Maya Angelou, you study the poem and read several critical interpretations in literary journals. To write a report on career opportunities in psychology, you interview a graduate of your university who is working in a psychology clinic. In each of these cases, you go beyond your own knowledge to consult additional sources of information.

This chapter offers guidelines for locating a range of sources—print and online, general and specialized, published and firsthand. Keep in mind that as you do research, finding and **EVALUATING SOURCES** are two activities that usually take place simultaneously. So this chapter and the next one go hand in hand.

354–57 ●

Kinds of Sources

Primary and secondary sources.   Your research will likely lead you to both primary and secondary sources. *Primary sources* include historical documents, literary works, eyewitness accounts, field reports, diaries, letters, and lab studies, as well as any original research you do through interviews, observation, experiments, or surveys. *Secondary sources* include scholarly books and articles, reviews, biographies, textbooks, and other works that interpret or discuss primary sources. Novels and poems are

rhetorical situations   genres   processes   strategies   research mla/apa   media/ design

primary sources; articles interpreting them are secondary sources. The Declaration of Independence is a primary historical document; a historian's description of the events surrounding the Declaration's writing is secondary. A published report of scientific findings is primary; a critique of that report is secondary.

Whether a work is considered primary or secondary sometimes depends on your topic and purpose: if you're analyzing a poem, a critic's article interpreting the poem is a secondary source — but if you're investigating that critic's work, the article would be a primary source for your study.

Primary sources are useful because they offer firsthand accounts, whereas secondary sources can help you understand and evaluate primary source material.

Print and online sources.   Some sources are available only in print; some are available only online. But many print sources are also available on the Web. You'll find print sources in your school's library, but chances are that many of the books in your library's reference section will also be available online. And when it comes to finding sources, it's likely that you'll *search* for most sources online, through the library's Web site. In general, there are four kinds of sources you'll want to consult, each of which is discussed in this chapter:

GENERAL REFERENCE WORKS, for encyclopedias, dictionaries, and the like ⬤ 344

THE LIBRARY CATALOG, for books ⬤ 345–46

INDEXES AND DATABASES, for periodicals ⬤ 346–49

SEARCH ENGINES AND SUBJECT DIRECTORIES, for material on the Web ⬤ 349–50

On the next page is a sample search page from the catalog of one university library. This catalog, like most, allows you to search by book title, journal title, author, subject, call number, and keyword. In addition, the links at the top of the page permit you to search through various indexes and databases and take advantage of interlibrary loan (for materials that your library doesn't have) and various tutorials.

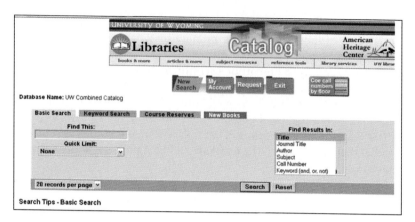

Part of a library catalog search page.

Searching Electronically

Whether you're searching for books, articles in periodicals, or material available on the Web, chances are you'll conduct much of your search electronically. Most materials produced since the 1980s can be found electronically, most library catalogs are online, and most periodical articles can be found by searching electronic indexes and databases. In each case, you can search for authors, titles, or subjects.

When you're searching for subjects, you'll need to come up with *keywords* that will lead you to the information you're looking for. Usually if you start with only one keyword, you'll end up with far too many results — tens of thousands of references when you're searching the Web — so the key to searching efficiently is to come up with keywords that will focus your searches on the information you need. Some search engines will let you enter more than one word and will identify only those sources that contain all the words you entered. Other search engines will let you type in more than one word and will identify those sources that contain at least one of those words but not necessarily all of them. Most search engines

have "advanced search" options that will help you focus your research. Specific commands will vary among search engines and within databases, but here are some of the most common ones:

- Type quotation marks around words to search for an exact phrase — "Thomas Jefferson" — unless you're using a search engine that includes a field to search for exact phrases, in which case you won't need the quotation marks. If your exact-phrase search doesn't yield good results, try removing the quotation marks.

- Type AND to find sources that include more than one keyword: Jefferson AND Adams. Some search engines require a plus sign instead: +Jefferson+Adams.

- Type OR if you're looking for sources that include one of several terms: Jefferson OR Adams OR Madison.

- Type NOT to find sources *without* a certain word: Jefferson NOT Adams. Some search engines call for a minus sign (actually, a hyphen) instead: +Jefferson-Adams will result in sources in which the name Jefferson appears but the name Adams does not.

- Type an asterisk — or some other symbol — to search for words in different forms — teach* will yield sources containing *teacher* and *teaching*, for example. Check the search engine's search tips to find out what symbol to use.

- Some search engines allow you to ask questions in conversational language: What did Thomas Jefferson write about slavery?

- Be more general (*education Japan* instead of *secondary education Japan*) when you get too few sources; be more specific (*homeopathy* instead of *medicine*) when you get far too many sources.

- If you don't get results with one set of keywords, substitute synonyms (if *folk medicine* doesn't generate much information, try *home remedy*). Or look through the sources that turn up in response to other terms to see what keywords you might use in subsequent searches. Searching requires flexibility, in the words you use and the methods you try.

Reference Works

The reference section of your school's library is the place to find encyclopedias, dictionaries, atlases, almanacs, bibliographies, and other reference works in print. Many of these sources are also online and can be accessed from any computer that is connected to the Internet. Others are available only in the library. Remember, though, that whether in print or online, reference works are only a starting point, a place where you can get an overview of your topic.

General reference works. Consult encyclopedias for general background information on a subject, dictionaries for definitions of words, atlases for maps and geographic data, and almanacs for statistics and other data on current events. These are some works you might consult:

The New Encyclopaedia Britannica

The Columbia Encyclopedia

Webster's Third New International Dictionary

Oxford English Dictionary

National Geographic Atlas of the World

Statistical Abstract of the United States

The World Almanac and Book of Facts

Specialized reference works. You can also go to specialized reference works, which provide in-depth information on a single field or topic. These may also include authoritative bibliographies, leading you to more specific works. A reference librarian can refer you to specialized encyclopedias in particular fields; but you'll find a list of some at wwnorton.com/write/fieldguide.

Bibliographies. Bibliographies provide an overview of what has been published on a topic, listing published works along with the information you'll need to find each work. Some are annotated with brief summaries of each work's contents. You'll find bibliographies at the end of scholarly articles and books, and you can also find book-length bibliographies, both

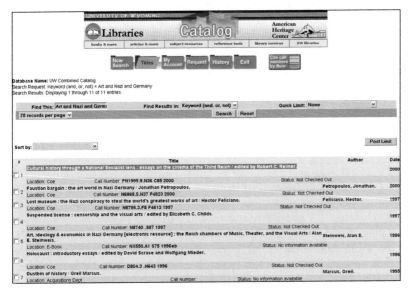

in the reference section of your library and online. Check with a reference librarian for bibliographies on your research topic.

Books / Searching the Library Catalog

The library catalog is your primary source for finding books. Most library catalogs are computerized and can be accessed through the library's Web site. You can search by author, title, subject, or keyword. The image below shows the result of a keyword search for material on art in Nazi Germany. This search revealed that the library has nineteen books on the topic; to access information on each one, the researcher must simply click on the title. The second image shows complete information for one source: bibliographic data about author, title, and publication; call

List of books on a library catalog screen.

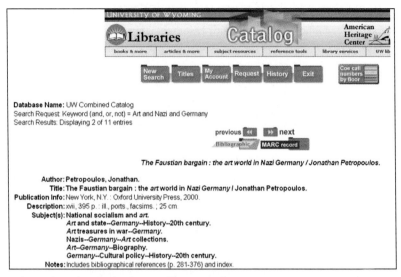

Information about a book on a library catalog screen.

number (which identifies the book's location on the library's shelves); related subject headings (which may lead to other useful materials in the library)—and more.

Periodicals / Searching Indexes and Databases

To find journal and magazine articles, you will need to search periodical indexes and databases. Indexes provide listings of articles organized by topics; databases provide the full texts. Some databases also include indexes of bibliographic citations, which you may use to track down the actual articles. Some indexes are in print and can be found in the reference section of the library; many are online. Some databases are available for free; most of the more authoritative ones, however, are available only by subscription and so must be accessed through a library.

Print indexes.   You'll need to consult print indexes to find articles published before the 1980s. Here are six useful ones:

> *The Readers' Guide to Periodical Literature* (print, 1900 –; online, 1983 –)
>
> *Magazine Index* (print, 1988 –; online via InfoTrac, 1973 –)
>
> *The New York Times Index* (print and online, 1851–)
>
> *Humanities Index* (print, 1974 –; online, 1984 –)
>
> *Social Sciences Index* (print, 1974 –; online, 1983 –)
>
> *General Science Index* (print, 1978 –; online, 1984 –)

General electronic indexes and databases.   A reference librarian can help you determine which databases will be most helpful to you, but here are some useful ones:

> *Academic Search Premier* is a multidisciplinary index and database containing the full text of articles in more than 3,600 journals and indexing of over 8,000 journals, with abstracts of their articles.
>
> *EBSCOhost* provides interlinked databases of abstracts and full-text articles from a variety of periodicals.
>
> *FirstSearch* offers access to more than 10 million full-text, full-image articles in dozens of databases covering many disciplines.
>
> *InfoTrac* offers over 15 million full-text articles in a broad spectrum of disciplines and on a wide variety of topics from over 5,000 scholarly and popular periodicals, including the *New York Times*.
>
> *JSTOR* archives scanned copies of entire publication runs of scholarly journals in many disciplines, but it does not include current issues of the journals.
>
> *LexisNexis Academic Universe* contains full-text publications and articles from a large number of sources—newspapers, business and legal resources, medical texts, and reference sources such as *The World Almanac* and the Roper public opinion polls.
>
> *MasterFile Premier* provides full-text articles from more than 1,900 general reference, business, consumer health, general science, and multicultural periodicals as well as indexing of another 2,510 periodicals and abstracts of their articles.

ProQuest provides access to full-text articles from thousands of periodicals and newspapers from 1986 to the present, with many entries updated daily.

SIRS Researcher contains records of articles from selected domestic and international newspapers, magazines, journals, and government publications.

Single-subject indexes and databases.   These are just a sample of what's available; check with a reference librarian for indexes and databases in the subject you're researching.

America: History and Life indexes scholarly literature on the history of the United States and Canada.

American Humanities Index contains bibliographic references to more than 1,000 journals dealing with the humanities.

BIOSIS Previews provides abstracts and indexes for more than 5,500 sources on biology, botany, zoology, environmental studies, and agriculture.

ERIC is the U.S. Department of Education's Educational Resource Information Center database.

Historical Abstracts includes abstracts of articles on the history of the world, excluding the United States and Canada, since 1450.

MLA International Bibliography indexes scholarly articles on modern languages, literature, folklore, and linguistics.

PsychINFO indexes scholarly literature in a number of disciplines relating to psychology.

Web-based indexes and databases.   The following are freely available on the Internet:

Infomine contains "useful Internet resources such as databases, electronic journals, electronic books, bulletin boards, mailing lists, online library card catalogs, articles, directories of researchers, and many other types of information."

rhetorical situations

genres

processes

strategies

research mla/apa

media/ design

Librarians' Index to the Internet is "a searchable, annotated subject directory of more than 14,000 Internet resources selected and evaluated by librarians for their usefulness to users of public libraries."

The World Wide Web Virtual Library is a catalog of Web sites on a wide range of subjects, compiled by volunteers with expertise in particular subject areas.

CSA: Hot Topics Series provides comprehensive information on current issues in biomedicine, engineering, the environment, the social sciences, and the humanities, with an overview of each subject, key citations with abstracts, and links to Web sites.

The Voice of the Shuttle: Web Site for Humanities Research offers information on subjects in the humanities, organized to mirror the way the humanities are organized for research and teaching as well as the way they are adapting to social, cultural, and technological changes.

The Library of Congress offers online access to information on a wide range of subjects, including academic subjects, as well as prints, photographs, and government documents.

Education Index is an annotated guide to education-related sites on the Web, sorted by subject and life stage.

JURIST is a university-based online gateway to authoritative legal instruction, information, and scholarship.

The Web

The Web provides access to countless sites containing information posted by governments, educational institutions, organizations, businesses, and individuals. Web sites are different from other sources in several ways: (1) they often provide entire texts, not just citations of texts, (2) their content varies greatly in its reliability, and (3) they are not stable: what you see on a site today may be different (or gone) tomorrow. Anyone who wants to can post texts on the Web, so you need to **EVALUATE** carefully what you find there.

● 354–57

Because it is so vast and dynamic, finding what you want on the Web can be a challenge. The primary way of finding information on the Web is with a search engine. There are several ways of searching the Web:

- *Keyword searches.* Google, HotBot, AltaVista, Lycos, and Yahoo! all scan the Web looking for keywords that you specify.

- *Subject directories.* Google, Yahoo! and some other search engines offer directories that arrange information by topics, much like a library cataloging system. Such directories allow you to broaden or narrow your search if you need to—for example, a search for "birds" can be broadened to "animals" or narrowed to "blue-footed booby."

- *Metasearches.* MetaCrawler, Vivísimo, SurfWax, and Dogpile are metasearch engines that allow you to use several search engines simultaneously.

- *Academic searches.* You may find more suitable results for academic writing at Google Scholar (scholar.google.com), a search engine that finds scholarly literature, including peer-reviewed papers, technical reports, and abstracts, or at Scirus (scirus.com), which finds peer-reviewed documents on scientific, technical, and medical topics.

Each search engine and metasearch engine has its own protocols for searching; most have an "advanced search" option that will help you search more productively. Remember, though, that you need to be careful about evaluating sources that you find on the Web because the Web is unregulated and no one independently verifies the information posted on its sites.

Doing Field Research

Sometimes you'll need to do your own research, to go beyond the information you find in published sources and gather data by doing field research. Two kinds of field research you might want to consider are interviews and observations.

Interviewing experts.   Some kinds of writing — a profile of a living person, for instance — almost require that you conduct an interview. And sometimes you may just need to find information that you haven't been able to find in published sources. To get firsthand information on the experience of serving as a soldier in Iraq, you might interview your cousin who served a tour of duty there, or to find current research on pesticide residues in food, you might need to interview a toxicologist. Whatever your goal, you can conduct interviews face-to-face, over the telephone, or by mail or email. In general, you will want to use interviews to find information you can't find elsewhere. Below is some advice on planning and conducting an interview.

Before the interview

1. Once you identify someone you want to interview, email or phone to ask for an appointment, stating your **PURPOSE** for the interview and what you hope to learn.

   3–4

2. Once you've set up the appointment, send a note or email confirming the time and place. If you wish to record the interview, be sure to ask for permission to do so. If you plan to conduct the interview by mail or email, state when you will send your questions.
3. Write out questions. Plan questions that invite extended response: "What accounts for the recent spike in gasoline prices?" forces an explanation, whereas "Is the recent spike in gas prices a direct result of global politics?" is likely to elicit only a yes or a no.

At the interview

4. Record the full name of the person you interview, along with the date, time, and place of the interview; you'll need this information to cite and document the interview accurately.
5. Take notes, even if you are recording the interview.
6. Keep track of time: don't take more than you agreed to beforehand unless both of you agree to keep talking. End by saying thank you and offering to provide a copy of your final product.

After the interview

7. Flesh out your notes with details as soon as possible after the interview, while you still remember them.
8. Be sure to send a thank-you note or email.

Observation.   Some writing projects are based on information you get by observing something. For a sociology paper, you may observe how students behave in large lectures. For an education course, you may observe one child's progress as a writer over a period of time. The following advice can help you conduct observations.

Before observing

3–4

1. Think about your research **PURPOSE:** What are you looking for? What do you expect to find? How will your presence as an observer affect what you observe? What do you plan to do with what you find?
2. If necessary, set up an appointment. You may need to ask permission of the people you wish to observe. Be honest and open about your goals and intentions; college students doing research assignments are often welcomed where others may not be.

While observing

3. You may want to divide each page of your notepaper down the middle vertically and write only on the left side of the page, reserving the right side for information you will fill in later.

285–88 ◆

4. Note **DESCRIPTIVE** details about the setting. What do you see? What do you hear? Do you smell anything? Get down details about color, shape, size, sound, and so on. Consider photographing or making a sketch of what you see.

285–93 ◆

5. Who is there, and what are they doing? **DESCRIBE** what they look like, and make notes about what they say. Note any significant demographic details—about gender, race, occupation, age, dress, and so on.

304–12 ◆

6. What is happening? Who's doing what? What's being said? Note down these kinds of **NARRATIVE** details.

rhetorical situations | genres | processes | strategies | research mla/apa | media/ design

After observing

7. As soon as possible after you complete your observations, use the right side of your pages to fill in gaps and note additional details.

8. **ANALYZE** your notes, looking for patterns. Did some things appear or happen more than once? Did anything stand out? surprise or puzzle you? What did you learn?

◆ 255–59

See **EVALUATING SOURCES** for help determining their usefulness. See also Chapter 42 for help taking notes on your sources.

● 354–57

41 Evaluating Sources

Searching the *Health Source* database for information on the incidence of meningitis among college students, you find seventeen articles. A Google search on the same topic produces over ten thousand hits. How do you decide which sources to read? This chapter presents advice on evaluating sources—first to determine whether a source is useful for your purposes and then to read with a critical eye the ones you choose.

Considering the Reliability of Print and Online Sources

Books and journals that have been published in print have most likely been evaluated by editors, publishers, or expert reviewers before publication. Magazines and newspapers have probably been fact-checked; not so most Web sites—anyone who wishes to post something on the Web can do so. In addition, Web sources come and go, and are easily changed. So print sources are always more stable and often more trustworthy.

Considering Whether a Source Serves Your Purpose

3–4

Think about your PURPOSE. Are you trying to persuade readers to believe or do something? To inform them about something? If the former, it will be especially important to find sources representing various stances; if the latter, you may need sources that are more factual or informative. Reconsider your **AUDIENCE.** What kinds of sources will they find persuasive? If you're writing for readers in a particular field, what counts as evidence in that field? Following are some questions that can help you select useful sources:

5–8

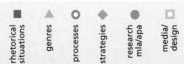

rhetorical situations / genres / processes / strategies / research mla/apa / media/ design

- **Is it relevant?** How does the source relate to your purpose? What will it add to your work? Look at the title and at any introductory material — a preface, abstract, or introduction — to see what it covers.

- **What are the author's credentials?** What are the author's qualifications to write on the subject? Is he or she associated with a particular position on the issue? If the source is a book or a periodical, see whether it mentions other works this author has written. If it's a Web site, see whether an author is identified. If one is, you might do a Web search to see what else you can learn about him or her.

- **What is the stance?** Consider whether a source covers various points of view or advocates one particular point of view. Does its title suggest a certain slant? If it's a Web site, you might check to see whether it includes links to other sites of one or many perspectives. You'll want to consult sources with a variety of viewpoints.

- **Who is the publisher?** If it's a book, what kind of company published it; if an article, what kind of periodical did it appear in? Books published by university presses and articles in scholarly journals are reviewed by experts before they are published. Books and articles written for general audiences typically do not undergo rigorous review — and they may lack the kind of in-depth discussion that is useful to the researcher of an academic work.

- **If it's a Web site, who is the sponsor?** Is the site maintained by an organization? an interest group? a government agency? an individual? If the site doesn't give this information, look for clues in the URL: *edu* is used mostly by colleges and universities, *gov* by government agencies, *org* by nonprofit organizations, *mil* by the military, and *com* by commercial organizations.

- **What is the level?** Can you understand the material? Texts written for a general audience might be easier to understand but are not likely to be authoritative enough for academic work. Texts written for scholars will be more authoritative but may be hard to comprehend.

- **When was it published?** See when books and articles were published. Check to see when Web sites were last updated. (If the site lists no date, see if links to other sites still work.) Recent does not necessarily mean better—some topics may require very current information whereas others may call for older sources.

- **Is it available?** Is it a source you can get hold of? If it's a book and your school's library doesn't have it, can you get it through interlibrary loan?

- **Does it include other useful information?** Is there a bibliography that might lead you to other sources? How current are the sources it cites?

Reading Sources with a Critical Eye

82–106 ▲

- **What ARGUMENTS does the author make?** Does the author present a number of different positions, or does he or she argue for a particular position? Do you need to **ANALYZE THE ARGUMENT?**

324–27 ◆

- **How persuasive do you find the argument?** What reasons and evidence does the author provide in support of any position(s)? Are there citations or links—and if so, are they credible? Is any evidence presented without citations? Do you find any of the author's assumptions questionable? How thoroughly does he or she consider opposing arguments?

12–14 ■

- **What is the author's STANCE?** Does the author strive for objectivity, or does the language reveal a particular bias? Is the author associated with a special interest that might signal a certain perspective? Does he or she consider opposing views? Do the sources cited reflect multiple viewpoints, or only one?

- **Does the publisher bring a certain stance to the work?** Book publishers, periodicals, or Web sites that are clearly liberal or conservative or advance a particular agenda will likely express views reflecting their

12–14 ■

STANCE.

- **Do you recognize ideas you've run across in other sources?** Does it leave out any information that other sources include?

- **Does this source support or challenge your own position—or does it do both?** Does it support your thesis? offer a different argument altogether? Does it represent a position you may need to **ACKNOWLEDGE** or

100–01 ▲

REFUTE? Don't reject a source that challenges your views; your sources should reflect a variety of views on your topic, showing that you've considered the subject thoroughly.

▲ 101

- *What can you tell about the intended* AUDIENCE *and* PURPOSE? Are you a member of the audience addressed—and if not, does that affect the way you interpret what you read? Is the main purpose to inform readers about a topic or to argue a certain point?

■ 3–8

See QUOTING, PARAPHRASING, AND SUMMARIZING for help in taking notes on your sources and deciding how to use them in your writing. See also ACKNOWLEDGING SOURCES, AVOIDING PLAGIARISM for advice on giving credit to the sources you use.

● 358–74

42 Quoting, Paraphrasing, and Summarizing

In an oral presentation about the rhetoric of Abraham Lincoln, you quote a memorable line from the Gettysburg Address. For an essay on the Tet Offensive in the Vietnam War, you paraphrase arguments made by several commentators and summarize some key debates about that war. Like all writers, you work with the ideas and words of others. This chapter will help you with the specifics of quoting, paraphrasing, and summarizing source materials that you wish to use in your writing.

Taking Notes

When you find material you think will be useful, take careful notes. How do you determine how much or how little to record? You need to write down enough information so that when you refer to it later, you will be reminded of the main points, and you need to keep a precise record of where the information comes from.

- *Use index cards, a computer file, or a notebook,* labeling each entry with the information that will allow you to keep track of where it comes from — author, title, and the pages or the URL. You needn't write down full bibliographic information (you can abbreviate author's name and title) since you'll include that information in your **WORKING BIBLIOGRAPHY.**

335–36

- *Take notes in your own words, and use your own sentence patterns.* If you make a note that is a detailed **PARAPHRASE,** label it as such so that you'll know to provide appropriate **DOCUMENTATION** if you use it.

363–66
375–449

rhetorical situations   genres   processes   strategies   research mla/apa   media/ design

- *If you find wording that you'd like to quote,* be sure to enclose it in quotation marks to distinguish your source's words from your own. Double-check your notes to be sure any quoted material is accurately quoted — and that you haven't accidentally **PLAGIARIZED** your sources.

370–74

- *Label each note with a subject heading.*

Here's an example of one writer's notes:

Source: Steingraber, "Pesticides" (976)
—1938: pathbreaking experiments showed that dogs exposed to aromatic amines developed cancer of the bladder.
—aromatic amines: chemicals used in coal-derived synthetic dyes
—Mauve the first synthetic dye—invented in 1854—then synthetic dyes replaced most natural dyes made with plants
—Bladder cancer common among textile workers who used dyes
—Steingraber: "By the beginning of the twentieth century, bladder cancer rates among this group of workers had skyrocketed, and the dog experiments helped unravel this mystery."
—1921: International Labor Organization labels a.a. as carcinogenic (before experiments)
—Dog experiments also helped explain: early 20th century: metal workers, machinists, and workers in the tire industry developed bladder cancer—cutting oils contained aromatic amines to inhibit rust used a.a. accelerants.
—Sandra Steingraber: biologist and ecologist

Deciding Whether to Quote, Paraphrase, or Summarize

When it comes time to **DRAFT**, you'll need to decide *how* to use the sources you've found — in other words, whether to quote, paraphrase, or summarize. You might follow this rule of thumb: **QUOTE** texts when the wording is worth repeating or makes a point so well that no rewording will do it

205–07

360–63

justice, when you want to cite the exact words of a known authority on your topic, when his or her opinions challenge or disagree with those of others, or when the source is one you want to emphasize. **PARAPHRASE** sources that are not worth quoting but contain details you need to include. **SUMMARIZE** longer passages whose main points are important but whose details are not.

363–66 ⬤

366–67 ⬤

Quoting

Quoting a source is a way of weaving someone else's exact words into your text. You need to reproduce the source exactly, though you can modify it to omit unnecessary details (with ellipses) or to make it fit smoothly into your text (with brackets). You also need to distinguish quoted material from your own by enclosing short quotations in quotation marks and setting off longer quotes as a block.

Incorporate short quotations into your text, enclosed in quotation marks. If you are following MLA style, this rule holds for four typed lines or fewer; if you are following APA style, short means no more than forty words.

> Gerald Graff argues that colleges make the intellectual life seem more opaque than it needs to be, leaving many students with "the misconception that the life of the mind is a secret society for which only an elite few qualify."

If you are quoting three lines or less of poetry, run them in with your text, enclosed in quotation marks. Separate lines with slashes, leaving one space on each side of the slashes.

> Emma Lazarus almost speaks for the Statue of Liberty with the words inscribed on its pedestal: "Give me your tired, your poor, / Your huddled masses yearning to breathe free, / The wretched refuse of your teeming shore."

Set off long quotations block style. If you are using MLA style, set off quotations of five or more typed lines by indenting the quote one inch (or ten spaces) from the left margin. If you are using APA style, indent quotes of forty or more words one-half inch (or five spaces) from the left margin. In either case, do not use quotation marks, and put any parenthetical citation *after* any end punctuation.

> Nonprofit organizations such as Oxfam and Habitat for Humanity rely on visual representations of the poor. What better way to get our attention, asks Diana George:
>
>> In a culture saturated by the image, how else do we convince Americans that — despite the prosperity they see all around them — there is real need out there? The solution for most nonprofits has been to show the despair. To do that they must represent poverty as something that can be seen and easily recognized: fallen down shacks and trashed out public housing, broken windows, dilapidated porches, barefoot kids with stringy hair, emaciated old women and men staring out at the camera with empty eyes. (210)

If you are quoting four or more lines of poetry, they need to be set off block style in the same way.

Indicate any omissions with ellipses. You may sometimes delete words from a quotation that are unnecessary for your point. Insert three ellipsis marks (leaving a space before the first and after the last one) to indicate the deletion. If you omit a sentence or more in the middle of a quotation, put a period before the three ellipsis dots.

> Faigley points out that Gore's "Information Superhighway" metaphor "associated the economic prosperity of the 1950s and . . . 1960s facilitated by new highways with the potential for vast . . . commerce to be conducted over the Internet" (253).

> According to Welch, "Television is more acoustic than visual. . . . One can turn one's gaze way from the television, but one cannot turn one's ears from it without leaving the area where the monitor leaks its aural signals into every corner" (102).

Indicate additions or changes with brackets.   Sometimes you'll need to change or add words in a quote—to make the quote fit grammatically within your sentence, for example, or to add a comment. In the following example, the writer changes the passage "one of our goals" to fit the grammar of her sentences:

> Writing about the dwindling attention among some composition scholars to the actual teaching of writing, Susan Miller notes that "few discussions of writing pedagogy take it for granted that one of [their] goals is to teach how to write" (480).

Here's an example of brackets used to add explanatory words to a quotation:

> Barbosa observes that even Buarque's lyrics have long included "many a metaphor of *saudades* [yearning] so characteristic of *fado* music" (207).

A note about punctuating quotes.   When you incorporate a quotation into your text, you have to think about the end punctuation in the quoted material and also about any punctuation you need to add when you insert the quote into your own sentence.

Periods and commas.   With brief quotations, put periods or commas inside the quotation marks, except when you have a parenthetical citation at the end, in which case you put the period after the parentheses.

> "Country music," Tichi says, "is a crucial and vital part of the American identity" (23).

With long quotes set off block style, however, there are no quotation marks, so the period goes *before* the citation, as shown in the example on page 361.

Question marks and exclamation points.   These go *inside* closing quotation marks if they are part of the quoted material but outside when they are not. Notice, however, that when there's a parenthetical citation at the end, it is followed by a period.

> Speaking at a Fourth of July celebration in 1852, Frederick Douglass asked, "What have I, or those I represent, to do with your national independence?" (35).

Who can argue with W. Charisse Goodman's observation that media images persuade women that "thinness equals happiness and fulfillment"? (53).

Colons and semicolons. These always go outside the quotation marks.

It's hard to argue with W. Charisse Goodman's observation that media images persuade women that "thinness equals happiness and fulfillment"; nevertheless, American women today are more overweight than ever (53).

Paraphrasing

When you paraphrase, you restate information from a source in your own words, using your own sentence structures. Paraphrase when the source material is important but the original wording is not. Because it includes all the main points of the source, a paraphrase is usually about the same length as the original.

Here is a paragraph about synthetic dyes and cancer, followed by three example paraphrases. The first two demonstrate some of the challenges of paraphrasing:

ORIGINAL SOURCE

In 1938, in a series of now-classic experiments, exposure to synthetic dyes derived from coal and belonging to a class of chemicals called aromatic amines was shown to cause bladder cancer in dogs. These results helped explain why bladder cancers had become so prevalent among dyestuffs workers. With the invention of mauve in 1854, synthetic dyes began replacing natural plant-based dyes in the coloring of cloth and leather. By the beginning of the twentieth century, bladder cancer rates among this group of workers had skyrocketed, and the dog experiments helped unravel this mystery. The International Labor Organization did not wait for the results of these animal tests, however, and in 1921 declared certain aromatic amines to be human carcinogens. Decades later, these dogs provided a lead in understanding why tire-industry workers, as well as machinists and metalworkers, also began falling victim to bladder cancer: aromatic amines had been added to rubbers and cutting oils to serve as accelerants and antirust agents.

—Sandra Steingraber, "Pesticides, Animals, and Humans"

UNACCEPTABLE PARAPHRASE: WORDING TOO CLOSE

<u>Now-classic experiments</u> in 1938 showed that when dogs were exposed to aromatic amines, chemicals used in <u>synthetic dyes derived from coal</u>, they developed bladder cancer. Similar cancers were <u>prevalent among dyestuffs workers</u>, and <u>these</u> experiments <u>helped</u> to <u>explain why</u>. Mauve, a synthetic dye, was invented in 1854, after which <u>cloth and leather</u> manufacturers replaced most of the natural plant-based dyes with synthetic dyes. <u>By the</u> early <u>twentieth century</u>, <u>this group of workers had skyrocketing</u> rates of bladder cancer, a <u>mystery the dog experiments helped to unravel</u>. As early as 1921, though, before the test results proved the connection, the International Labor Organization had labeled <u>certain aromatic amines</u> carcinogenic. Even so, <u>decades later</u> many metalworkers, machinists, and tire-industry workers began developing bladder cancer. The animal tests helped researchers understand that <u>rubbers and cutting oils</u> contained aromatic amines <u>as accelerants and antirust agents</u> (Steingraber 976).

This paraphrase borrows too much of the language of the original or changes it only slightly, as the underlined words and phrases show.

UNACCEPTABLE PARAPHRASE: SENTENCE STRUCTURE TOO CLOSE

In 1938, several pathbreaking experiments showed that being exposed to synthetic dyes that are made from coal and belong to a type of chemicals called aromatic amines caused dogs to get bladder cancer. These results helped researchers identify why cancers of the bladder had become so common among textile workers who worked with dyes. With the development of mauve in 1854, synthetic dyes began to be used instead of dyes based on plants in the dyeing of leather and cloth. By the end of the nineteenth century, rates of bladder cancer among these workers had increased dramatically, and the experiments using dogs helped clear up this oddity. The International

rhetorical situations   genres   processes   strategies   research mla/apa   media/ design

Labor Organization anticipated the results of these tests on animals, though, and in 1921 labeled some aromatic amines carcinogenic. Years later these experiments with dogs helped researchers explain why workers in the tire industry, as well as metalworkers and machinists, also started dying of bladder cancer: aromatic amines had been put into rubbers and cutting oils as rust inhibitors and accelerants (Steingraber 976).

This paraphrase uses original language but follows the sentence structure of Steingraber's text too closely.

ACCEPTABLE PARAPHRASE

Steingraber explains that pathbreaking experiments in 1938 demonstrated that dogs exposed to aromatic amines (chemicals used in coal-derived synthetic dyes) developed cancers of the bladder that were similar to cancers common among dyers in the textile industry. After mauve, the first synthetic dye, was invented in 1854, leather and cloth manufacturers replaced most natural dyes made from plants with synthetic dyes, and by the early 1900s textile workers had very high rates of bladder cancer. The experiments with dogs proved the connection, but years before, in 1921, the International Labor Organization had labeled some aromatic amines carcinogenic. Even so, years later many metalworkers, machinists, and workers in the tire industry started to develop unusually high rates of bladder cancer. The experiments with dogs helped researchers understand that the cancers were caused by aromatic amines used in cutting oils to inhibit rust and in rubbers as accelerants (976).

Some guidelines for paraphrasing

- *Use your own words and sentence structure.* It is acceptable to quote a word or phrase from the original (in quotation marks), but for the most part the words and sentence structures should be your own.

- *Put in quotation marks any of the source's wording that you use.* Quotation marks distinguish the source's words from your own.

375–88

417–25

370–74

- *Indicate the source of your paraphrase.*   Although the wording may be yours, the ideas and information come from another source; be sure to name the author and include an **IN-TEXT CITATION** to avoid the possibility of PLAGIARISM.

Summarizing

A summary states the main ideas found in a source concisely and in your own words. Unlike a paraphrase, a summary does *not* present all the details so it is generally as brief as possible. Summaries may boil down an entire book or essay into a single sentence, or they may take a paragraph or more to present the main ideas. Here, for example, is a summary of the Steingraber paragraph:

> Steingraber explains that experiments with dogs demonstrated that aromatic amines, chemicals used in synthetic dyes, cutting oils, and rubber, cause bladder cancer (976).

In the context of an essay, the summary might take this form:

> Medical researchers have long relied on experiments using animals to expand understanding of the causes of disease. For example, biologist and ecologist Sandra Steingraber notes that in the second half of the nineteenth century, the rate of bladder cancer soared among textile workers. According to Steingraber, experiments with dogs demonstrated that synthetic chemicals in dyes used to color the textiles caused the cancer (976).

Some guidelines for summarizing

- *Include only the main ideas; leave out the details.* A summary should include just enough information to give the reader the gist of the original. It is always much shorter than the original, sometimes even as brief as one sentence.

- *Use your own words.* If you use any words from the original, enclose them in quotation marks.
- *Indicate the source.* Although the wording may be yours, the ideas and information come from another source. Name the author, either in a signal phrase or parentheses, and include an appropriate **IN-TEXT CITATION** to avoid the possibility of **PLAGIARISM.**

375–88
417–25
370–74

Incorporating Source Materials into Your Text

You need to introduce quotations, paraphrases, and summaries clearly, letting readers know who the author is — and, if need be, something about his or her credentials. Consider this sentence:

> Professor and textbook author Elaine Tyler May argues that many high school history books are too bland to interest young readers (531).

The beginning ("Professor and textbook author Elaine Tyler May argues") functions as a *signal phrase*, telling readers who is making the assertion and why she has the authority to speak on the topic — and making clear that everything between the signal phrase and the parenthetical citation comes from that source. Since the signal phrase names the author, the parenthetical citation includes only the page number; had there been no mention of the author, she would have been named in the parentheses as in the following example:

> Even some textbook authors believe that many high school history books are too bland to interest young readers (May 531).

Signal phrases.   A signal phrase tells readers who says or believes something. The verb you use can be neutral — *says* or *thinks* — or it can suggest something about the **STANCE** — the source's or your own. The above example about the textbook author uses the verb *claims*, suggesting that what she says is arguable (or that the writer believes it is). How

12–14

would it change your understanding if the signal verb were *observes* or *suggests?*

Some common signal verbs

acknowledges	claims	disagrees	observes
admits	comments	disputes	points out
advises	concludes	emphasizes	reasons
agrees	concurs	grants	rejects
argues	confirms	illustrates	reports
asserts	contends	implies	responds
believes	declares	insists	suggests
charges	denies	notes	thinks

Verb tenses.   MLA and APA have different conventions regarding the verbs that introduce signal phrases. MLA requires present-tense verbs (*writes, asserts, notes*) in signal phrases to introduce a work you are quoting, paraphrasing, or summarizing.

> In *Poor Richard's Almanack*, Benjamin Franklin <u>notes</u>, "He that cannot obey, cannot command" (739).

If, however, you are referring to the act of writing something rather than simply quoting someone's words, you might not use the present tense. The writer of the following sentence focuses on the year in which the source was written—therefore, the verb is necessarily in the past tense:

> Back in 1941, Kenneth Burke <u>wrote</u> that "the ethical values of work are in its application of the competitive equipment to cooperative ends" (316).

If you are following APA style, use the past tense or present-perfect tense to introduce sources composed in the past.

> Dowdall, Crawford, and Wechsler (1998) <u>observed</u> that women attending women's colleges are less likely to engage in binge drinking than are women who attend coeducational colleges (p. 713).

rhetorical situations   genres   processes   strategies   research mla/apa   media/ design

APA requires the present tense, however, to discuss the results of an experiment or to explain conclusions that are generally agreed on.

> The findings of this study <u>suggest</u> that excessive drinking has serious consequences for college students and their institutions.

> The authors of numerous studies <u>agree</u> that smoking and drinking among adolescents are associated with lower academic achievement.

See the section on **ACKNOWLEDGING SOURCES, AVOIDING PLAGIARISM** for help in giving credit to the sources you use. See also the **SAMPLE RESEARCH PAPERS** to see how sources are cited in MLA and APA styles.

370–74

407–16

438–49

43 Acknowledging Sources, Avoiding Plagiarism

Whenever you do research-based writing, you find yourself entering a conversation—reading what many others have had to say about your topic, figuring out what you yourself think, and then putting what you think in writing—"putting in your oar," as the rhetorician Kenneth Burke once wrote. As a writer, you need to *acknowledge* any words and ideas that come from others—to give credit where credit is due, to recognize the various authorities and many perspectives you have considered, to show readers where they can find your sources, and to situate your own arguments in the ongoing conversation. Using other people's words and ideas without acknowledgment is *plagiarism,* a serious academic and ethical offense. This chapter will show you how to acknowledge the materials you use and avoid plagiarism.

Acknowledging Sources

When you insert in your text information that you've obtained from others, your reader needs to know where your source's words or ideas begin and end. Therefore, you should introduce a source by naming the author in a **SIGNAL PHRASE**, and follow it with a brief parenthetical **IN-TEXT CITATION** or by naming the author in a parenthetical citation. (You need only a brief citation here, since your readers will find full bibliographic information in your list of **WORKS CITED** [MLA] or **REFERENCES** [APA].)

367–68
375–88
417–25
388–407
426–38

Sources that need acknowledgment.   You almost always need to acknowledge any information that you get from a specific source. Material you should acknowledge includes the following:

rhetorical situations ▪ genres ▲ processes ○ strategies ◆ research mla/apa ● media/ design ◻

- *Direct quotations.* Any words that you quote from another source must be enclosed in quotation marks, cited with brief bibliographic information in parentheses, and introduced with a signal phrase that tells who wrote it and provides necessary contextual information, as in the following sentence:

  > In a dissenting opinion on the issue of racial preferences in college admissions, Supreme Court justice Ruth Bader Ginsburg argues, "The stain of generations of racial oppression is still visible in our society, and the determination to hasten its removal remains vital" (*Gratz v. Bollinger*).

- *Arguable statements and information that may not be common knowledge.* If you state something about which there is disagreement or for which arguments can be made, cite the source of your statement. If in doubt about whether you need to give the source of an assertion, provide it. As part of an essay on "fake news" programs like *The Daily Show*, for example, you might make the following assertion:

  > The satire of *The Daily Show* complements the conservative bias of Fox News, since both have abandoned the stance of objectivity maintained by mainstream news sources, notes Michael Hoyt, executive editor of the *Columbia Journalism Review* (43).

  Others might argue with the contention that the Fox News Channel offers biased reports of the news, so the source of this assertion needs to be acknowledged. In the same essay, you might present information that should be cited because it's not widely known, as in this example:

  > According to a report by the Pew Research Center, 21 percent of Americans under thirty got information about the 2004 presidential campaign primarily from "fake news" and comedy shows like *The Daily Show* and *Saturday Night Live* (2).

- *The opinions and assertions of others.* When you present the ideas, opinions, and assertions of others, cite the source. You may have rewritten the concept in your own words, but the ideas were generated by someone else and must be acknowledged, as they are here:

> Social philosopher David Boonin, writing in the *Journal of Social Philosophy,* asserts that logically, laws banning marriage between people of different races are not discriminatory since everyone of each race is affected equally by them. Laws banning same-sex unions are discriminatory, however, since they apply only to people with a certain sexual orientation (256).

- *Any information that you didn't generate yourself.* If you did not do the research or compile the data yourself, cite your source. This goes for interviews, statistics, graphs, charts, visuals, photographs — anything you use that you did not create. If you create a chart using data from another source, you need to cite that source.

- *Collaboration with and help from others.* In many of your courses and in work situations, you'll be called on to work with others. You may get help with your writing at your school's writing center or from fellow students in your writing courses. Acknowledging such collaboration or assistance, in a brief informational note, is a way of giving credit—and saying thank you. See guidelines for writing notes in the **MLA** and **APA** sections of this book.

388
425

Sources that don't need acknowledgment. Widely available information and common knowledge do not require acknowledgment. What constitutes common knowledge may not be clear, however. When in doubt, provide a citation, or ask your instructor whether the information needs to be cited. You generally do not need to cite the following sources:

- *Information that most readers are likely to know.* You don't need to acknowledge information that is widely known or commonly accepted as fact. For example, in a literary analysis, you wouldn't cite a source saying that Harriet Beecher Stowe wrote *Uncle Tom's Cabin;* you can assume your readers already know that. On the other hand, you should cite the source from which you got the information stating that the book was first published in installments in a magazine and then, with revisions, in book form, because that information isn't common knowledge. As you do research in areas you're not familiar with, be aware that what constitutes common knowledge isn't always clear; the history of the novel's publication would be known to Stowe scholars and would likely need no acknowledgment in an essay written for them. In this case, too, if you aren't sure whether to acknowledge information, do so.

- *Information and documents that are widely available.* If a piece of information appears in several sources or reference works or if a document has been published widely, you needn't cite a source for it. For example, the date when astronauts Neil Armstrong and Buzz Aldrin landed a spacecraft on the moon can be found in any number of reference works. Similarly, the Declaration of Independence and the Gettysburg Address are reprinted in thousands of sources, so the ones where you found them need no citation.

- *Well-known quotations.* These include such famous quotations as Lady Macbeth's "Out, damned spot!" and John F. Kennedy's "Ask not what your country can do for you; ask what you can do for your country." Be sure, however, that the quotation is correct; Winston Churchill is said to have told a class of schoolchildren, "Never, ever, ever, ever, ever, ever, ever give up. Never give up. Never give up. Never give up." His actual words, however, taken from a longer speech, are much different and begin "Never give in."

- *Material that you created or gathered yourself.* You need not cite photographs that you took, graphs that you composed, or material from an interview or data from an experiment or survey that you conducted—though you should make sure readers know that the work is yours.

A good rule of thumb: *when in doubt, cite your source.* You're unlikely to be criticized for citing too much—but you may invite charges of plagiarism by citing too little.

Avoiding Plagiarism

When you use the words or ideas of others, you need to acknowledge who and where the material came from; if you don't credit those sources, you are guilty of plagiarism. Plagiarism is often committed unintentionally — as when a writer paraphrases someone else's ideas in language that is close to the original. It is essential, therefore, to know what constitutes plagiarism: (1) using another writer's words or ideas without in-text citation and documentation, (2) using another writer's exact words without quotation marks, and (3) paraphrasing or summarizing someone else's ideas using language or sentence structures that are too close to theirs.

358–59
To avoid plagiarizing, take careful **NOTES** as you do your research, clearly labeling as quotations any words you quote directly and being careful to use your own words and sentence structures in paraphrases and summaries. Be sure you know what source material you must **DOCUMENT**, 375–449 and give credit to your sources, both in the text and in a list of **REFERENCES** 426–38 or **WORKS CITED**. Be especially careful with material found online — copy- 388–407 ing source material right into a document you are writing is all too easy to do. You must acknowledge information you find on the Web just as you must acknowledge all other source materials.

And you must recognize that plagiarism has consequences. Scholars' work will be discredited if it too closely resembles another's. Journalists found to have plagiarized lose their jobs, and students routinely fail courses or are dismissed from their school when they are caught cheating — all too often by submitting as their own essays that they have purchased from online "research" sites. If you're having trouble completing an assignment, seek assistance. Talk with your instructor, or if your school has a writing center, go there for advice on all aspects of your writing, including acknowledging sources and avoiding plagiarism.

rhetorical situations   genres   processes   strategies   research mla/apa   media/ design

Documentation **44**

In everyday life, we are generally aware of our sources: "I read it in the *Post*." "Amber told me it's your birthday." "If you don't believe me, ask Mom." Saying how we know what we know and where we got our information is part of establishing our credibility and persuading others to take what we say seriously.

The goal of a research project is to study a topic, combining what we learn from sources with our own thinking and then composing a written text. When we write up the results of a research project, we cite the sources we use, usually by quoting, paraphrasing, or summarizing, and we acknowledge those sources, telling readers where the ideas came from. The information we give about sources is called documentation, and we provide it not only to establish our credibility as researchers and writers but also so that our readers, if they wish to, can find the sources themselves.

UNDERSTANDING DOCUMENTATION STYLES

The Norton Field Guide covers the documentation styles of the Modern Language Association (MLA) and the American Psychological Association (APA). MLA style is used chiefly in the humanities; APA is used mainly in the social sciences. Both are two-part systems, consisting of (1) brief in-text parenthetical documentation for quotations, paraphrases, or summaries and (2) more-detailed documentation in a list of sources at the end of the text. MLA and APA require that the end-of-text documentation provide the following basic information about each source you cite:

- author, editor, or organization providing the information
- title of work
- place of publication
- name of organization or company that published it
- date when it was published
- for online sources, date when you accessed the source

MLA and APA are by no means the only documentation styles. Many other publishers and organizations have their own style, among them the University of Chicago Press and the Council of Science Editors. We focus on MLA and APA here because those are styles that college students are often required to use. On the following page are examples of how the two parts—the brief parenthetical documentation in your text and the more detailed information at the end—correspond. The top of the page shows the two parts according to the MLA system; the bottom, the two parts according to the APA system.

As the examples show, when you cite a work in your text, you can name the author either in a signal phrase or in parentheses. If you name the author in a signal phrase, give the page number(s) in parentheses; when the author's name is not given in a signal phrase, include it in parentheses.

The examples here and throughout this book are color-coded to help you see the crucial parts of each citation: tan for author and editor, yellow for title, and green for publication information: city of publication, name of publisher, year of publication, page number(s), and so on. Comparing the MLA and APA styles of listing works cited or references reveals some differences: MLA includes an author's first name while APA gives only the initial; MLA puts the date at the end while APA places it right after the author's name; MLA underlines titles of long works while APA italicizes them; MLA capitalizes most of the words in the title and subtitle while APA capitalizes only the first words of each. Overall, however, the styles provide similar information: each gives author, title, and publication data.

author   title   publication

MLA Style

IN-TEXT DOCUMENTATION

As Lester Faigley puts it, "The world has become a bazaar from which to shop for an individual 'lifestyle' " (12).

As one observer suggests, "The world has become a bazaar from which to shop for an individual 'lifestyle' " (Faigley 12).

WORKS-CITED DOCUMENTATION

Faigley, Lester. Fragments of Rationality: Postmodernity and the Subject of Composition. Pittsburgh: U of Pittsburgh P, 1992.

APA Style

IN-TEXT DOCUMENTATION

As Faigley (1992) suggested, "The world has become a bazaar from which to shop for an individual 'lifestyle'" (p. 12).

As one observer has noted, "The world has become a bazaar from which to shop for an individual 'lifestyle'" (Faigley, 1992, p. 12).

REFERENCE-LIST DOCUMENTATION

Faigley, L. (1992). *Fragments of rationality: Postmodernity and the subject of composition.* Pittsburgh, PA: University of Pittsburgh Press.

45 MLA Style

Modern Language Association style calls for (1) brief in-text documentation and (2) complete documentation in a list of works cited at the end of your text. The models in this chapter draw on the *MLA Handbook for Writers of Research Papers*, 6th edition, by Joseph Gibaldi (2003). Additional information is available at www.mla.org.

A DIRECTORY TO MLA STYLE

author   title   publication

author   title   publication

MLA IN-TEXT DOCUMENTATION

Brief documentation in your text makes clear to your reader what you took from a source and where in the source you found the information.

In your text, you have three options for citing a source: quoting, paraphrasing, and summarizing. As you cite each source, you will need to decide whether or not to name the author in a signal phrase—"as Toni Morrison writes"—or in parentheses—"(Morrison 24)."

The first examples in this chapter show basic in-text citations of a work by one author. Variations on those examples follow. All of the examples are color-coded to help you see how writers using MLA style work authors and page numbers—and sometimes titles—into their texts. The examples also illustrate the MLA style of using quotation marks around titles of short works and underlining titles of long works. (Your instructor may prefer italics to underlining; find out if you're not sure.)

1. AUTHOR NAMED IN A SIGNAL PHRASE

If you mention the author in a signal phrase, put only the page number(s) in parentheses. Do not write *page* or *p*.

> McCullough describes John Adams as having "the hands of a man accustomed to pruning his own trees, cutting his own hay, and splitting his own firewood" (18).

> McCullough describes John Adams's hands as those of someone used to manual labor (18).

2. AUTHOR NAMED IN PARENTHESES

If you do not mention the author in a signal phrase, put his or her last name in parentheses along with the page number(s). Do not use punctuation between the name and the page number(s).

> Adams is said to have had "the hands of a man accustomed to pruning his own trees, cutting his own hay, and splitting his own firewood" (McCullough 18).

> One biographer describes John Adams as someone who was not a stranger to manual labor (McCullough 18).

Whether you use a signal phrase and parentheses or parentheses only, try to put the parenthetical citation at the end of the sentence or as close as possible to the material you've cited without awkwardly interrupting the sentence. Notice that in the first example above, the parenthetical reference comes after the closing quotation marks but before the period at the end of the sentence.

3. TWO OR MORE WORKS BY THE SAME AUTHOR

If you cite multiple works by one author, you have four choices. You can mention the author in a signal phrase and give the title and page reference in parentheses. Give the full title if it's brief; otherwise, give a short version.

> Kaplan insists that understanding power in the Near East requires "Western leaders who know when to intervene, and do so without illusions" (Eastward 330).

You can mention both author and title in a signal phrase and give only the page reference in parentheses.

> In Eastward to Tartary, Kaplan insists that understanding power in the Near East requires "Western leaders who know when to intervene, and do so without illusions" (330).

You can indicate author, title, and page reference only in parentheses, with a comma between author and title.

> Understanding power in the Near East requires "Western leaders who
> know when to intervene, and do so without illusions" (Kaplan,
> Eastward 330).

Or you can mention the title in a signal phrase and give the author and
page reference in parentheses.

> Eastward to Tartary argues that understanding power in the Near East
> requires "Western leaders who know when to intervene, and do so
> without illusions" (Kaplan 330).

4. AUTHORS WITH THE SAME LAST NAME

If your works-cited list includes works by authors with the same last name,
you need to give the author's first name in any signal phrase or the
author's first initial in the parenthetical reference.

> Edmund Wilson uses the broader term imaginative, whereas Anne Wilson
> chooses the narrower adjective magical.

> Imaginative applies not only to modern literature (E. Wilson) but also to
> writing of all periods, whereas magical is often used in writing about
> Arthurian romances (A. Wilson).

5. AFTER A BLOCK QUOTATION

When quoting more than three lines of poetry, more than four lines of
prose, or dialogue from a drama, set off the quotation from the rest of
your text, indenting it one inch (or ten spaces) from the left margin. Do
not use quotation marks. Place any parenthetical documentation *after* the
final punctuation.

> In Eastward to Tartary, Kaplan captures ancient and contemporary
> Antioch for us:
>> At the height of its glory in the Roman-Byzantine age, when
>> it had an amphitheater, public baths, aqueducts, and sewage
>> pipes, half a million people lived in Antioch. Today the

population is only 125,000. With sour relations between Turkey
and Syria, and unstable politics throughout the Middle East,
Antioch is now a backwater—seedy and tumbledown, with
relatively few tourists. I found it altogether charming. (123)

6. TWO OR MORE AUTHORS

For a work by two or three authors, name all the authors, either in a signal phrase or in the parentheses.

Carlson and Ventura's stated goal is to introduce Julio Cortázar, Marjorie
Agosín, and other Latin American writers to an audience of
English-speaking adolescents (v).

For a work with four or more authors, you have the option of mentioning
all their names or just the name of the first author followed by *et al.*, which
means "and others."

One popular survey of American literature breaks the contents into sixteen
thematic groupings (Anderson, Brinnin, Leggett, Arpin, and Toth A19-24).

One popular survey of American literature breaks the contents into
sixteen thematic groupings (Anderson et al. A19-24).

7. ORGANIZATION OR GOVERNMENT AS AUTHOR

If the author is an organization, cite the organization either in a signal
phrase or in parentheses. It's acceptable to shorten long names.

The U.S. government can be direct when it wants to be. For example, it
sternly warns, "If you are overpaid, we will recover any payments not
due you" (Social Security Administration 12).

8. AUTHOR UNKNOWN

If you don't know the author of a work, as you won't with many reference
books and with most newspaper editorials, use the work's title or a short-
ened version of the title in the parentheses.

author   title   publication

The explanatory notes at the front of the literature encyclopedia point out that writers known by pseudonyms are listed alphabetically under those pseudonyms (Merriam-Webster's vii).

A powerful editorial in last week's paper asserts that healthy liver donor Mike Hurewitz died because of "frightening" faulty postoperative care ("Every Patient's Nightmare").

9. LITERARY WORKS

When referring to literary works that are available in many different editions, cite the page numbers from the edition you are using, followed by information that will let readers of any edition locate the text you are citing.

NOVELS

Give the page and chapter number.

> In Pride and Prejudice, Mrs. Bennett shows no warmth toward Jane and Elizabeth when they return from Netherfield (105; ch. 12).

VERSE PLAYS

Give the act, scene, and line numbers; separate them with periods.

> Macbeth continues the vision theme when he addresses the Ghost with "Thou hast no speculation in those eyes / Which thou dost glare with" (3.3.96-97).

POEMS

Give the part and the line numbers (separated by periods). If a poem has only line numbers, use the word line(s) in the first reference.

> Whitman sets up not only opposing adjectives but also opposing nouns in "Song of Myself" when he says, "I am of old and young, of the foolish as much as the wise, / . . . a child as well as a man" (16.330-32).

> One description of the mere in Beowulf is "not a pleasant place!" (line 1372). Later, the label is "the awful place" (1378).

10. WORK IN AN ANTHOLOGY

If you're citing a work that is included in an anthology, name the author(s) of the work, not the editor of the anthology—either in a signal phrase or in parentheses.

> "It is the teapots that truly shock," according to Cynthia Ozick in her essay on teapots as metaphor (70).

> In In Short: A Collection of Creative Nonfiction, readers will find both an essay on Scottish tea (Hiestand) and a piece on teapots as metaphors (Ozick).

11. SACRED TEXT

When citing sacred texts such as the Bible or the Qur'an, give the title of the edition used, and in parentheses give the book, chapter, and verse (or their equivalent), separated by periods. MLA style recommends that you abbreviate the names of the books of the Bible in parenthetical references.

> The wording from The New English Bible follows: "In the beginning of creation, when God made heaven and earth, the earth was without form and void, with darkness over the face of the abyss, and a mighty wind that swept over the surface of the waters" (Gen. 1.1-2).

12. MULTIVOLUME WORK

If you cite more than one volume of a multivolume work, each time you cite one of the volumes, give the volume *and* the page numbers in parentheses, separated by a colon.

> Sandburg concludes with the following sentence about those paying last respects to Lincoln: "All day long and through the night the unbroken line moved, the home town having its farewell" (4: 413).

If your works-cited list includes only a single volume of a multivolume work, the only number you need to give in your parenthetical reference is the page number.

13. TWO OR MORE WORKS CITED TOGETHER

If you're citing two or more works closely together, you will sometimes need to provide a parenthetical citation for each one.

> Tanner (7) and Smith (viii) have looked at works from a cultural perspective.

If the citation allows you to include both in the same parentheses, separate the references with a semicolon.

> Critics have looked at both <u>Pride and Prejudice</u> and <u>Frankenstein</u> from a cultural perspective (Tanner 7; Smith viii).

14. SOURCE QUOTED IN ANOTHER SOURCE

When you are quoting text that you found quoted in another source, use the abbreviation *qtd. in* in the parenthetical reference.

> Charlotte Brontë wrote to G. H. Lewes: "Why do you like Miss Austen so very much? I am puzzled on that point" (qtd. in Tanner 7).

15. WORK WITHOUT PAGE NUMBERS

For works without page numbers, give paragraph or section numbers, using the abbreviation *par.* or *sec.* If you are including the author's name in the parenthetical reference, add a comma.

> Russell's dismissals from Trinity College at Cambridge and from City College in New York City are seen as examples of the controversy that marked the philosopher's life (Irvine, par. 2).

16. AN ENTIRE WORK

If your text is referring to an entire work rather than a part of it, identify the author in a signal phrase or in parentheses. There's no need to include page numbers.

> Kaplan considers Turkey and Central Asia explosive.

> At least one observer considers Turkey and Central Asia explosive (Kaplan).

NOTES

Sometimes you may need to give information that doesn't fit into the text itself—to thank people who helped you, provide additional details, or refer readers to other sources not cited in your text. Such information can be given in a *footnote* (at the bottom of the page) or an *endnote* (on a separate page with the heading *Notes* just before your works-cited list. Put a superscript number at the appropriate point in your text, signaling to readers to look for the note with the corresponding number. If you have multiple notes, number them consecutively throughout your paper.

TEXT

> This essay will argue that small liberal arts colleges should not recruit
> athletes and, more specifically, that giving student athletes preferential
> treatment undermines the larger educational goals.[1]

NOTE

> [1]I want to thank all those who have contributed to my thinking on
> this topic, especially my classmates and my teachers Marian Johnson and
> Diane O'Connor.

MLA LIST OF WORKS CITED

A works-cited list provides full bibliographic information for every source cited in your text. The list should be alphabetized by authors' last names (or sometimes by editors' or translators' names). Works that do not have an identifiable author or editor are alphabetized by title. See pages 415–16 for a sample works-cited list.

Books

BASIC FORMAT FOR A BOOK

For most books, you'll need to provide information about the author; the title and any subtitle; and the place of publication, publisher, and date. You'll find this information on the book's title page and copyright page.

author   title   publication

Greenblatt, Stephen. <u>Will in the World: How Shakespeare Became Shakespeare</u>. New York: Norton, 2004.

A FEW DETAILS TO NOTE

- **TITLES**: capitalize the first and last words of titles, subtitles, and all principal words. Do not capitalize *a*, *an*, *the*, *to*, or any prepositions or coordinating conjunctions unless they begin a title or subtitle.
- **PLACE OF PUBLICATION**: If more than one city is given, use only the first.
- **PUBLISHER**: Use a shortened form of the publisher's name (Norton for W. W. Norton & Company, Princeton UP for Princeton University Press).
- **DATES**: If more than one year is given, use the most recent one.

1. ONE AUTHOR

Author's Last Name, First Name. <u>Title</u>. Publication City: Publisher, Year of publication.

Miller, Susan. <u>Assuming the Positions: Cultural Pedagogy and the Politics of Commonplace Writing</u>. Pittsburgh: U of Pittsburgh P, 1998.

When the title of a book itself contains the title of another book (or other long work), do not underline that title.

Walker, Roy. <u>Time Is Free: A Study of</u> Macbeth. London: Dakers, 1949.

Include the author's middle name or initials. When the title of a book contains the title of a short work, the title of the short work should be enclosed in quotation marks, and the entire title should be underlined.

Thompson, Lawrance Roger. <u>"Fire and Ice": The Art and Thought of Robert Frost</u>. New York: Holt, 1942.

2. TWO OR MORE WORKS BY THE SAME AUTHOR(S)

Give the author's name in the first entry, and then use three hyphens in the author slot for each of the subsequent works, listing them alphabetically by the first important word of each title (see page 390).

Author's Last Name, First Name. Title That Comes First Alphabetically. Publication City: Publisher, Year of publication.

---. Title That Comes Next Alphabetically. Publication City: Publisher, Year of publication.

Kaplan, Robert D. The Coming Anarchy: Shattering the Dreams of the Post Cold War. New York: Random, 2000.

---. Eastward to Tartary: Travels in the Balkans, the Middle East, and the Caucasus. New York: Random, 2000.

3. TWO AUTHORS

First Author's Last Name, First Name, and Second Author's First and Last Names. Title. Publication City: Publisher, Year of publication.

Malless, Stanley, and Jeffrey McQuain. Coined by God: Words and Phrases That First Appear in the English Translations of the Bible. New York: Norton, 2003.

4. THREE AUTHORS

First Author's Last Name, First Name, Second Author's First and Last Names, and Third Author's First and Last Names. Title. Publication City: Publisher, Year of publication.

Sebranek, Patrick, Verne Meyer, and Dave Kemper. Writers INC: A Guide to Writing, Thinking, and Learning. Burlington: Write Source, 1990.

5. FOUR OR MORE AUTHORS

You may give each author's name or the name of the first author only, followed by *et al.*, Latin for "and others."

First Author's Last Name, First Name, Second Author's First and Last Names, Third Author's First and Last Names, and Final Author's First and Last Names. Title. Publication City: Publisher, Year of publication.

Anderson, Robert, John Malcolm Brinnin, John Leggett, Gary Q. Arpin, and Susan Allen Toth. <u>Elements of Literature: Literature of the United States</u>. Austin: Holt, 1993.

First Author's Last Name, First Name, et al. <u>Title</u>. Publication City: Publisher, Year of publication.

Anderson, Robert, et al. <u>Elements of Literature: Literature of the United States</u>. Austin: Holt, 1993.

6. ORGANIZATION OR GOVERNMENT AS AUTHOR

Sometimes the author is a corporation or government organization.

Organization Name. <u>Title</u>. Publication City: Publisher, Year of publication.

Diagram Group. <u>The Macmillan Visual Desk Reference</u>. New York: Macmillan, 1993.

National Assessment of Educational Progress. <u>The Civics Report Card</u>. Princeton: ETS, 1990.

7. ANTHOLOGY

Editor's Last Name, First Name, ed. <u>Title</u>. Publication City: Publisher, Year of publication.

Hall, Donald, ed. <u>The Oxford Book of Children's Verse in America</u>. New York: Oxford UP, 1985.

If there is more than one editor, list the first editor last-name-first and the others first-name-first.

Kitchen, Judith, and Mary Paumier Jones, eds. <u>In Short: A Collection of Brief Creative Nonfiction</u>. New York: Norton, 1996.

8. WORK(S) IN AN ANTHOLOGY

> Author's Last Name, First Name. "Title of Work." Title of Anthology.
> Ed. Editor's First and Last Names. Publication City: Publisher, Year of
> publication. Pages.

> Achebe, Chinua. "Uncle Ben's Choice." The Seagull Reader: Literature.
> Ed. Joseph Kelly. New York: Norton, 2005. 23-27.

To document two or more selections from one anthology, list each selection by author and title, followed by a cross-reference to the anthology. In addition, include on your works-cited list an entry for the anthology itself (see no. 7 on page 391).

> Author's Last Name, First Name. "Title of Work." Anthology Editor's Last
> Name. Pages.

> Hiestand, Emily. "Afternoon Tea." Kitchen and Jones. 65-67.

> Ozick, Cynthia. "The Shock of Teapots." Kitchen and Jones. 68-71.

9. AUTHOR AND EDITOR

Start with the author if you've cited the text itself.

> Author's Last Name, First Name. Title. Ed. Editor's First and Last Names.
> Publication City: Publisher, Year of publication.

> Austen, Jane. Emma. Ed. Stephen M. Parrish. New York: Norton, 2000.

Start with the editor if you've cited his or her work.

> Editor's Last Name, First Name, ed. Title. By Author's First and Last Names.
> Publication City: Publisher, Year of publication.

> Parrish, Stephen M., ed. Emma. By Jane Austen. New York: Norton, 2000.

10. NO AUTHOR OR EDITOR

> Title. Publication City: Publisher, Year of publication.

> 2004 New York City Restaurants. New York: Zagat, 2003.

author   title   publication

11. TRANSLATION

Start with the author to emphasize the work itself.

> Author's Last Name, First Name. <u>Title</u>. Trans. Translator's First and Last
>   Names. Publication City: Publisher, Year of publication.

> Dostoevsky, Fyodor. <u>Crime and Punishment</u>. Trans. Richard Pevear and
>   Larissa Volokhonsky. New York: Vintage, 1993.

Start with the translator to emphasize the translation.

> Translator's Last Name, First Name, trans. <u>Title</u>. By Author's First and Last
>   Names. Publication City: Publisher, Year of publication.

> Pevear, Richard, and Larissa Volokhonsky, trans. <u>Crime and Punishment</u>.
>   By Fyodor Dostoevsky. New York: Vintage, 1993.

12. FOREWORD, INTRODUCTION, PREFACE, OR AFTERWORD

> Part Author's Last Name, First Name. Name of Part. <u>Title of Book</u>.
>   By Author's First and Last Names. Publication City: Publisher, Year
>   of publication. Pages.

> Tanner, Tony. Introduction. <u>Pride and Prejudice</u>. By Jane Austen.
>   London: Penguin, 1972. 7-46.

13. MULTIVOLUME WORK

If you cite all the volumes of a multivolume work, give the number of volumes after the title.

> Author's Last Name, First Name. <u>Title of Complete Work</u>. Number of vols.
>   Publication City: Publisher, Year of publication.

> Sandburg, Carl. <u>Abraham Lincoln: The War Years</u>. 4 vols. New York:
>   Harcourt, 1939.

If you cite only one volume, give the volume number after the title.

> Sandburg, Carl. <u>Abraham Lincoln: The War Years</u>. Vol. 2. New York:
>   Harcourt, 1939.

14. BOOK IN A SERIES

> Editor's Last Name, First Name, ed. <u>Title of Book</u>. By Author's First and Last Names. Series Title abbreviated. Publication City: Publisher, Year of publication.

> Hunter, J. Paul, ed. <u>Frankenstein</u>. By Mary Shelley. Norton Critical Ed. New York: Norton, 1996.

15. SACRED TEXT

If you have cited a specific edition of a religious text, you need to include it in your works-cited list.

> <u>Title</u>. Editor's First and Last Names, ed. (if any) Publication City: Publisher, Year of publication.

> <u>The New English Bible with the Apocrypha</u>. New York: Oxford UP, 1971.

> <u>The Torah: A Modern Commentary</u>. W. Gunther Plaut, ed. New York: Union of American Hebrew Congregations, 1981.

16. EDITION OTHER THAN THE FIRST

> Author's Last Name, First Name. <u>Title</u>. Name or number of ed. Publication City: Publisher, Year of publication.

> Gibaldi, Joseph. <u>MLA Handbook for Writers of Research Papers</u>. 6th ed. New York: MLA, 2003.

> Hirsch, E. D., Jr., ed. <u>What Your Second Grader Needs to Know: Fundamentals of a Good Second-Grade Education</u>. Rev. ed. New York: Doubleday, 1998.

17. REPUBLISHED WORK

Give the original publication date after the title, followed by the publication information of the republished edition.

> Author's Last Name, First Name. <u>Title</u>. Year of original edition.
>   Publication City: Current Publisher, Year of republication.

Bierce, Ambrose. <u>Civil War Stories</u>. 1909. New York: Dover, 1994.

Periodicals

BASIC FORMAT FOR AN ARTICLE

For most articles, you'll need to provide information about the author, the article title and any subtitle, the periodical title, any volume or issue number, the date, and inclusive page numbers.

> Weinberger, Jerry. "Pious Princes and Red-Hot Lovers: The Politics of
>   Shakespeare's <u>Romeo and Juliet</u>." <u>Journal of Politics</u> 65 (2003): 370-75.

A FEW DETAILS TO NOTE

- **AUTHORS**: If there is more than one author, list the first author last-name-first and the others first-name-first.

- **TITLES**: Capitalize the first and last words of titles and subtitles and all principal words. Do not capitalize *a*, *an*, *the*, *to*, or any prepositions or coordinating conjunctions unless they begin a title or subtitle. For periodical titles, omit any initial *A*, *An*, or *The*.

- **DATES**: Abbreviate the names of months except for May, June, or July: Jan., Feb., Mar., Apr., Aug., Sept., Oct., Nov., Dec. Journals paginated by volume or issue call only for the year (in parentheses).

- **PAGES**: If an article does not fall on consecutive pages, give the first page with a plus sign (55+).

18. ARTICLE IN A JOURNAL PAGINATED BY VOLUME

> Author's Last Name, First Name. "Title of Article." <u>Title of Journal</u>
>   Volume (Year): Pages.

> Bartley, William. "Imagining the Future in <u>The Awakening</u>." <u>College</u>
>   <u>English</u> 62 (2000): 719-46.

19. ARTICLE IN A JOURNAL PAGINATED BY ISSUE

Author's Last Name, First Name. "Title of Article." Title of Journal
      Volume.Issue (Year): Pages.

Weaver, Constance, Carol McNally, and Sharon Moerman. "To
      Grammar or Not to Grammar: That Is Not the Question!" Voices
      from the Middle 8.3 (2001): 17-33.

20. ARTICLE IN A MONTHLY MAGAZINE

Author's Last Name, First Name. "Title of Article." Title of Magazine
      Month Year: Pages.

Fellman, Bruce. "Leading the Libraries." Yale Alumni Magazine
      Feb. 2002: 26-31.

21. ARTICLE IN A WEEKLY MAGAZINE

Author's Last Name, First Name. "Title of Article." Title of Magazine
      Day Month Year: Pages.

Cloud, John. "Should SATs Matter?" Time 12 Mar. 2001: 62+.

22. ARTICLE IN A DAILY NEWSPAPER

Author's Last Name, First Name. "Title of Article." Name of Newspaper
      Day Month Year: Pages.

Springer, Shira. "Celtics Reserves Are Whizzes vs. Wizards." Boston Globe
      14 Mar. 2005: D4+.

If you are documenting a particular edition of a newspaper (indicated on
the front page), specify the edition (late ed., natl. ed., etc.) in between the
date and the section and page reference.

Margulius, David L. "Smarter Call Centers: At Your Service?" New York
      Times 14 Mar. 2002, late ed.: G1+.

author   title   publication

23. UNSIGNED ARTICLE

"Title of Article." Name of Publication Day Month Year: Page(s).

"Laura Bush Ponders Trip to Afghanistan." New York Times 2 Dec. 2003: A22.

24. EDITORIAL

"Title." Editorial. Name of Publication Day Month Year: Page.

"Gas, Cigarettes Are Safe to Tax." Editorial. Lakeville Journal 17 Feb. 2005: A10.

25. LETTER TO THE EDITOR

Author's Last Name, First Name. "Title (if any)." Letter. Name of Publication Day Month Year: Page.

Testa, Roger. "Social Security: Another Phony Crisis." Letter. Lakeville Journal 17 Feb. 2005: A10.

26. REVIEW

Author's Last Name, First Name. "Title (if any) of Review." Rev. of Title of Work, by Author's First and Last Names. Title of Periodical Day Month Year: Pages.

Lahr, John. "Night for Day." Rev. of The Crucible, by Arthur Miller. New Yorker 18 Mar. 2002: 149-51.

Electronic Sources

BASIC FORMAT FOR AN ELECTRONIC SOURCE

Not every electronic source gives you all the data that MLA would like to see in a works-cited entry. Ideally, you will be able to list the author's name, the title, any information about print publication, information about electronic publication (title of site, editor, date of first electronic publication and / or most recent revision, name of the sponsoring institution), date of access, and URL. Of those nine pieces of information, you will find seven in the following example.

> Johnson, Charles W. "How Our Laws Are Made." <u>Thomas: Legislative Information on the Internet</u> 31 Jan. 2000. Lib. of Congress. 5 Apr. 2005 <http://thomas.loc.gov/home/holam.txt>.

A FEW DETAILS TO NOTE

- **AUTHORS**: If there is more than one author, list the first author last-name-first and the others first-name-first.

- **TITLES**: Capitalize the first and last words of titles and subtitles, and all principal words. Do not capitalize *a, an, the, to,* or any prepositions or coordinating conjunctions unless they begin a title or subtitle. For periodical titles, omit any initial *A, An,* or *The.*

- **DATES**: Abbreviate the names of months except for May, June, or July: Jan., Feb., Mar., Apr., Aug., Sept., Oct., Nov., Dec. Although MLA asks for the date when materials were first posted or most recently updated, you won't always be able to find that information. You'll also find that it will vary—you may find only the year, not the day and month. The date you must include is the date on which you accessed the electronic source.

- **URL**: Give the address of the Web site in angle brackets. When a URL will not fit on one line, break it only after a slash (and do not add a hyphen). If a URL is very long, consider giving the URL of the site's home page or search page instead. Also keep in mind that if you are accessing an online source through a library's subscription to a database provider (such as EBSCO), you may not see the URL itself. In that case, end your documentation with a period after your access date.

27. PROFESSIONAL WEB SITE

> <u>Title of Site</u>. Ed. Editor's First and Last Names. Date posted or last updated. Sponsoring Institution. Day Month Year of access <URL>.

author   title   publication

Stanford Encyclopedia of Philosophy. Ed. Edward N. Zalta. 2003.
Metaphysics Research Lab, Center for the Study of Language and
Information, Stanford U. 25 July 2004 <http://plato.stanford.edu>.

28. PERSONAL WEB SITE

Author's Last Name, First Name. Home page. Date posted or last
updated. Day Month Year of access <URL>.

Chomsky, Noam. Home page. 25 July 2004 <http://web.mit.edu/
linguistics/www.chomsky.home.html>.

29. HOME PAGE FOR AN ACADEMIC DEPARTMENT

Academic Department. Dept. home page. School. Day Month Year of
access <URL>.

English Language and Literatures. Dept. home page. Wright State U
College of Liberal Arts. 12 Mar. 2003 <http://www.cola.wright.edu/
Dept/ENG/Index.htm>.

30. ONLINE BOOK OR PART OF A BOOK

Author's Last Name, First Name. "Title of Short Work." Title of
Long Work. Original year of publication. Database. Date of
electronic publication. Day Month Year of access <URL>.

Anderson, Sherwood. "The Philosopher." Winesburg, Ohio. 1919.
Bartleby.com: Great Books Online. 1999. 7 Apr. 2002 <http://
www.bartleby.com/156/5.html>.

31. ARTICLE IN AN ONLINE PERIODICAL OR DATABASE

If a source does not number pages or paragraphs, follow the year with a
period instead of a colon. Some periodicals have dates; others have volume
and issue numbers instead—volume 10, issue 3 should be listed as 10.3, followed by the year (in parentheses). See the next page for examples.

FROM A PERIODICAL'S WEB SITE

Author's Last Name, First Name. "Title of Article." <u>Title of Periodical</u> Date or Volume.Issue (Year): Pages or pars. Day Month Year of access <URL>.

Landsburg, Steven E. "Putting All Your Potatoes in One Basket: The Economic Lessons of the Great Famine." <u>Slate</u> 13 Mar. 2001. 15 Mar. 2001 <http://slate.msn.com/Economics/01-03-13/ Economics.asp>.

FROM A DATABASE PROVIDER

Author's Last Name, First Name. "Title of Article." <u>Title of Periodical</u> Date or Volume.Issue (Year): Pages or pars. <u>Database</u>. Database provider. Library. Day Month Year of access <URL>.

Bowman, James. "Moody Blues." <u>American Spectator</u> June 1999: 64-65. <u>Academic Search Premier</u>. EBSCO. Paul Laurence Dunbar Lib., Wright State U. 15 Mar. 2005 <http://epnet.com>.

32. DOCUMENT ACCESSED THROUGH AOL OR OTHER SUBSCRIPTION SERVICE

Note the *keyword* you used or the *path* you followed.

Author's Last Name, First Name. "Title of Document." <u>Title of Longer Work</u>. Date of work. Service. Day Month Year of access. Keyword: Word.

Stewart, Garrett. "Bloomsbury." <u>World Book Online</u>. 2003. America Online. 13 Mar. 2003. Keyword: Worldbook.

Author's Last Name, First Name. "Title of Document." <u>Title of Longer Work</u>. Date of work. Service. Day Month Year of access. Path: Sequence of Topics.

author title publication

Hamashige, Hope. "New Pope's Election to Be Shrouded in Ritual,
Secrecy." <u>National Geographic News</u>. 1 Apr. 2005. America Online.
25 Apr. 2005. Path: Research and Learning; History; History of Pope
Selection.

33. EMAIL

Writer's Last Name, First Name. "Subject Line." Email to the author. Day
Month Year of message.

Smith, William. "Teaching Grammar—Some Thoughts." Email to the
author. 19 Nov. 2004.

34. POSTING TO AN ELECTRONIC FORUM

Writer's Last Name, First Name. "Title of Posting." Online posting.
Day Month Year of posting. Name of Forum. Day Month Year
of access <URL>.

Schafer, Judith Kelleher. "Re: Manumission." Online posting. 27 Jan.
2004. H-Net List on Slavery. 29 Jan. 2004 <http://h-net.msu.edu/
cgi-bin/logbrowse.pl?trx=lm&list=H-Slavery>.

35. CD-ROM

FOR A SINGLE-ISSUE CD-ROM

<u>Title</u>. CD-ROM. Any pertinent information about the edition, release, or
version. Publication City: Publisher, Year of publication.

<u>Othello</u>. CD-ROM. Princeton: Films for the Humanities and Sciences, 1998.

If you are citing only part of the CD-ROM, name the part as you would a
part of a book.

"Snow Leopard." <u>Encarta Encyclopedia 1999</u>. CD-ROM. Seattle: Microsoft,
1998.

FOR A PERIODICAL ON A CD-ROM

Author's Last Name, First Name. "Title of Article." Title of Periodical.
　　Date or Volume.Issue (Year): Page. Database. CD-ROM. Database
　　provider. Month Year of CD-ROM.

Hwang, Suein L. "While Many Competitors See Sales Melt, Ben &
　　Jerry's Scoops Out Solid Growth." Wall Street Journal. 25 May 1993:
　　B1. ABI-INFORM. CD-ROM. Proquest. June 1993.

Other Kinds of Sources

This section shows how to prepare works-cited entries for categories other
than books, periodicals, and writing found on the Web and CD-ROMs. The
categories are in alphabetical order. Two of them — art and cartoon — cover
works that do not originate on the Web but make their way there. From
these examples, you can figure out a documentation style for any texts
that you may come across on the Web.

A FEW DETAILS TO NOTE

- **AUTHORS**: If there is more than one author, list the first author last-
  name-first and the others first-name-first. Do likewise if you begin an
  entry with performers, speakers, and so on.
- **TITLES**: Capitalize the first and last words of titles and subtitles, and
  all principal words. Do not capitalize *a, an, the, to,* or any prepositions
  or coordinating conjunctions unless they begin a title or subtitle. For
  periodical titles, omit any initial *A, An,* or *The.*
- **DATES**: Abbreviate the names of months except for May, June, or July:
  Jan., Feb., Mar., Apr., Aug., Sept., Oct., Nov., Dec. Journals paginated
  by volume or issue need only the year (in parentheses).

36. ADVERTISEMENT

Product or Company. Advertisement. Title of Periodical Date or
　　Volume.Issue (Year): Page.

Empire BlueCross BlueShield. Advertisement. Fortune 8 Dec. 2003: 208.

author　　　title　　　publication

37. ART

> Artist's Last Name, First Name. <u>Title of Art</u>. Year. Institution, City.

> Van Gogh, Vincent. <u>The Potato Eaters</u>. 1885. Van Gogh Museum,
> Amsterdam.

ART ON THE WEB

> Warhol, Andy. <u>Self-Portrait</u>. 1979. J. Paul Getty Museum, Los Angeles.
> 29 Mar. 2005 <http://getty.edu/art/collections/objects/oll4421.html>.

38. CARTOON

> Artist's Last Name, First Name. "Title of Cartoon (if titled)." Cartoon. <u>Title
> of Periodical</u> Date or Volume.Issue (Year): Page.

> Chast, Roz. "The Three Wise Men of Thanksgiving." Cartoon. <u>New Yorker</u>
> 1 Dec. 2003: 174.

CARTOON ON THE WEB

> Fairrington, Brian. Cartoon. <u>Arizona Republic</u> 6 Apr. 2002. 7 Apr. 2002
> <http://cagle.slate.msn.com/politicalcartoons/pccartoons/archives/
> fairrington.asp???Action=Get!>.

39. DISSERTATION

Treat a published dissertation as you would a book, but after its title, add
the abbreviation *Diss.*, the name of the institution, and the date of the dissertation. If the dissertation is published by University Microfilms International (UMI), include the order number, as in the example below.

> Author's Last Name, First Name. <u>Title</u>. Diss. Institution, Year.
> Publication City: Publisher, Year.

> Goggin, Peter N. <u>A New Literacy Map of Research and Scholarship in
> Computers and Writing</u>. Diss. Indiana U of Pennsylvania, 2000. Ann
> Arbor: UMI, 2001. 9985587.

For unpublished dissertations, put the title in quotation marks and end with the degree-granting institution and the year.

> Kim, Loel. "Students Respond to Teacher Comments: A Comparison of Online Written and Voice Modalities." Diss. Carnegie Mellon U, 1998.

40. FILM, VIDEO, OR DVD

> <u>Title</u>. Dir. Director's First and Last Names. Perf. Lead Actors' First and Last Names. Distributor, Year of release.

> <u>Casablanca</u>. Dir. Michael Curtiz. Perf. Humphrey Bogart, Ingrid Bergman, and Claude Rains. Warner, 1942.

If it's a video or DVD, give that information before the name of the distributor.

> <u>Easter Parade</u>. Dir. Charles Walters. Perf. Judy Garland and Fred Astaire. DVD. MGM, 1948.

41. INTERVIEW

BROADCAST INTERVIEW

> Subject's Last Name, First Name. Interview. <u>Title of Program</u>. Network. Station, City. Day Month Year.

> Gates, Henry Louis, Jr. Interview. <u>Fresh Air</u>. NPR. WNYC, New York. 9 Apr. 2002.

PUBLISHED INTERVIEW

> Subject's Last Name, First Name. Interview. or "Title of Interview." <u>Title of Periodical</u> Date or Volume.Issue (Year): Pages.

> Brzezinski, Zbigniew. "Against the Neocons." <u>American Prospect</u> Mar. 2005: 26-27.

> Stone, Oliver. Interview. <u>Esquire</u> Nov. 2004: 170.

PERSONAL INTERVIEW

Subject's Last Name, First Name. Personal interview. Day Month Year.

Berra, Yogi. Personal interview. 17 June 2001.

42. LETTER

UNPUBLISHED LETTER

Author's Last Name, First Name. Letter to the author. Day Month Year.

Quindlen, Anna. Letter to the author. 11 Apr. 2002.

PUBLISHED LETTER

Letter Writer's Last Name, First Name. Letter to First and Last Names.
   Day Month Year of letter. Title of Book. Ed. Editor's First and
   Last Names. Publication City: Publisher, Year of publication. Pages.

White, E. B. Letter to Carol Angell. 28 May 1970. Letters of E. B. White.
   Ed. Dorothy Lobarno Guth. New York: Harper, 1976. 600.

43. MAP

Title of Map. Map. Publication City: Publisher, Year of publication.

Toscana. Map. Milan: Touring Club Italiano, 1987.

44. MUSICAL COMPOSITION

Composer's Last Name, First Name. "Title of Short Composition." or Title
   of Long Composition. Year of composition (optional).

Ellington, Duke. "Mood Indigo." 1931.

If you are identifying a composition by form, number, key, and opus, do
not underline that information or enclose it in quotation marks.

Beethoven, Ludwig van. String quartet no. 13 in B flat, op. 130. 1825.

45. MUSIC RECORDING

> Artist's Last Name, First Name. <u>Title of Long Work</u>. Other pertinent
> details about the artists. Manufacturer, Year of release.

> Beethoven, Ludwig van. <u>Missa Solemnis</u>. Perf. Westminster Choir and
> New York Philharmonic. Cond. Leonard Bernstein. Sony, 1992.

Whether you list the composer, conductor, or performer first depends on
where you want to place the emphasis. If you are citing a specific song,
put it in quotation marks before the name of the recording, which should
be underlined.

> Brown, Greg. "Canned Goods." <u>The Live One</u>. Red House, 1995.

46. ORAL PRESENTATION

> Speaker's Last Name, First Name. "Title of Lecture." Sponsoring
> Institution. Site, City. Day Month Year.

> Cassin, Michael. "Nature in the Raw—The Art of Landscape Painting."
> Berkshire Institute for Lifetime Learning. Clark Art Institute,
> Williamstown. 24 Mar. 2005.

47. PAPER FROM PROCEEDINGS OF A CONFERENCE

> Author's Last Name, First Name. "Title of Paper." <u>Title of Conference
> Proceedings</u>. Date, City. Ed. Editor's First and Last Names.
> Publication City: Publisher, Year. Pages.

> Zolotow, Charlotte. "Passion in Publishing." <u>A Sea of Upturned Faces:
> Proceedings of the Third Pacific Rim Conference on Children's
> Literature</u>. 1986, Los Angeles. Ed. Winifred Ragsdale. Metuchen:
> Scarecrow P, 1989. 236-49.

48. PERFORMANCE

> <u>Title</u>. By Author's First and Last Names. Other appropriate details about
> the performance. Site, City. Day Month Year.

<u>Medea</u>. By Euripedes. Dir. Jonathan Kent. Perf. Diana Rigg. Longacre
    Theatre, New Haven. 10 Apr. 1994.

49. TELEVISION OR RADIO PROGRAM

"Title of Episode." <u>Title of Program</u>. Other appropriate information
    about the writer, director, actors, etc. Network. Station, City.
    Day Month Year of broadcast.

"Stirred." <u>The West Wing</u>. Writ. Aaron Sorkin. Dir. Jeremy Kagan. Perf.
    Martin Sheen. NBC. WPTV, West Palm Beach. 3 Apr. 2002.

SAMPLE RESEARCH PAPER, MLA STYLE

Dylan Borchers wrote the following essay, which reports information, for
a first-year writing course. It is formatted according to the guidelines of
the *MLA Handbook for Writers of Research Papers*, 6th edition (2003). While
the MLA guidelines are used widely in literature and other disciplines in
the humanities, exact documentation requirements may vary from discipline to discipline and course to course. If you're unsure about what your
instructor wants, ask for clarification.

½"

1"

Dylan Borchers

Professor Bullock

English 102, Section 4

20 January 2004

Against the Odds:

Harry S. Truman and the Election of 1948

"Thomas E. Dewey's Election as President Is a Foregone

Conclusion," read a headline in the New York Times during the

presidential election race between incumbent Democrat Harry S.

Truman and his Republican challenger, Thomas E. Dewey. Earlier,

Life magazine had put Dewey on its cover with the caption "The

Next President of the United States" (qtd. in "1948 Truman-Dewey

Election"). In a Newsweek survey of fifty prominent political writers,

each one predicted Truman's defeat, and Time correspondents

declared that Dewey would carry 39 of the 48 states (Donaldson

210). Nearly every major media outlet across the United States

endorsed Dewey and lambasted Truman. As historian Robert H.

Ferrell observes, even Truman's wife, Bess, thought he would be

beaten (270).

The results of an election are not so easily predicted, as the

famous photograph on page 2 shows. Not only did Truman win the

election, but he won by a significant margin, with 303 electoral

votes and 24,179,259 popular votes, compared to Dewey's 189

electoral votes and 21,991,291 popular votes (Donaldson 204-07). In

fact, many historians and political analysts argue that Truman

Put your last name and the page number in the upper-right corner of each page.

Center the title.

Double-space throughout.

If you name the author of a source in a signal phrase, give the page numbers in parentheses.

1"   1"   1"

Borchers 2

Fig. 1. President Harry S. Truman holds up an Election Day edition of the <u>Chicago Daily Tribune</u>, which mistakenly announced "Dewey Defeats Truman." St. Louis, 4 Nov. 1948 (Rollins).

Insert illustrations close to the text to which they relate. Label with figure number, caption, and parenthetical source citation.

would have won by an even greater margin had third-party Progressive candidate Henry A. Wallace not split the Democratic vote in New York State and Dixiecrat Strom Thurmond not won four states in the South (McCullough 711). Although Truman's defeat was heavily predicted, those predictions themselves, Dewey's passiveness as a campaigner, and Truman's zeal turned the tide for a Truman victory.

In the months preceding the election, public opinion polls predicted that Dewey would win by a large margin. Pollster Elmo Roper stopped polling in September, believing there was no reason to continue, given a seemingly inevitable Dewey landslide. Although the margin narrowed as the election drew near, the other

Indent paragraphs $\frac{1}{2}$-inch or 5 spaces.

Give the author and page numbers in parentheses when no signal phrase is used.

pollsters predicted a Dewey win by at least 5 percent (Donaldson 209). Many historians believe that these predictions aided the president in the long run. First, surveys showing Dewey in the lead may have prompted some of Dewey's supporters to feel overconfident about their candidate's chances and therefore to stay home from the polls on Election Day. Second, these same surveys may have energized Democrats to mount late get-out-the-vote efforts ("1948 Truman-Dewey Election"). Other analysts believe that the overwhelming predictions of a Truman loss also kept at home some Democrats who approved of Truman's policies but saw a Truman loss as inevitable. According to political analyst Samuel Lubell, those Democrats may have saved Dewey from an even greater defeat (Hamby, Man of the People 465). Whatever the impact on the voters, the polling numbers had a decided effect on Dewey.

Historians and political analysts alike cite Dewey's overly cautious campaign as one of the main reasons Truman was able to achieve victory. Dewey firmly believed in public opinion polls. With all indications pointing to an easy victory, Dewey and his staff believed that all he had to do was bide his time and make no foolish mistakes. Dewey himself said, "When you're leading, don't talk" (qtd. in McCullough 672). Each of Dewey's speeches was well-crafted and well-rehearsed. As the leader in the race, he kept his remarks faultlessly positive, with the result that he failed to deliver a solid message or even mention Truman or any of Truman's policies. Eventually, Dewey began to be perceived as aloof and stuffy. One

If you quote text quoted in another source, cite that source in a parenthetical reference.

Borchers   4

observer compared him to the plastic groom on top of a wedding
cake (Hamby, "Harry S. Truman"), and others noted his stiff, cold
demeanor (McCullough 671-74).

As his campaign continued, observers noted that Dewey
seemed uncomfortable in crowds, unable to connect with ordinary
people. And he made a number of blunders. One took place at a
train stop when the candidate, commenting on the number of
children in the crowd, said he was glad they had been let out of
school for his arrival. Unfortunately for Dewey, it was a Saturday
("1948: The Great Truman Surprise"). Such gaffes gave voters the
feeling that Dewey was out of touch with the public.

Again and again through the autumn of 1948, Dewey's
campaign speeches failed to address the issues, with the candidate
declaring that he did not want to "get down in the gutter" (qtd. in
McCullough 701). When told by fellow Republicans that he was
losing ground, Dewey insisted that his campaign not alter its
course. Even Time magazine, though it endorsed and praised him,
conceded that his speeches were dull (McCullough 696). According
to historian Zachary Karabell, they were "notable only for taking
place, not for any specific message" (244). Dewey's numbers in the
polls slipped in the weeks before the election, but he still held a
comfortable lead over Truman. It would take Truman's famous
whistle-stop campaign to make the difference.

Few candidates in U.S. history have campaigned for the
presidency with more passion and faith than Harry Truman. In the

If you cite two or
more works
closely together,
provide a paren-
thetical citation
for each one.

autumn of 1948, he wrote to his sister, "It will be the greatest campaign any President ever made. Win, lose, or draw, people will know where I stand" (91). For thirty-three days, Truman traveled the nation, giving hundreds of speeches from the back of the Ferdinand Magellan railroad car. In the same letter, he described the pace: "We made about 140 stops and I spoke over 147 times, shook hands with at least 30,000 and am in good condition to start out again tomorrow for Wilmington, Philadelphia, Jersey City, Newark, Albany and Buffalo" (91). McCullough writes of Truman's campaign:

> No President in history had ever gone so far in quest of support from the people, or with less cause for the effort, to judge by informed opinion. . . . As a test of his skills and judgment as a professional politician, not to say his stamina and disposition at age sixty-four, it would be like no other experience in his long, often difficult career, as he himself understood perfectly. More than any other event in his public life, or in his presidency thus far, it would reveal the kind of man he was. (655)

He spoke in large cities and small towns, defending his policies and attacking Republicans. As a former farmer and relatively late bloomer, Truman was able to connect with the public. He developed an energetic style, usually speaking from notes rather than from a prepared speech, and often mingled with the crowds that met his train. These crowds grew larger as the campaign

Set off quotations of four or more lines by indenting 1 inch (or 10 spaces).

Put parenthetical references after final punctuation in block quotations.

progressed. In Chicago, over half a million people lined the streets as he passed, and in St. Paul the crowd numbered over 25,000. When Dewey entered St. Paul two days later, he was greeted by only 7,000 supporters ("1948 Truman-Dewey Election"). Reporters brushed off the large crowds as mere curiosity seekers wanting to see a president (McCullough 682). Yet Truman persisted, even if he often seemed to be the only one who thought he could win. By going directly to the American people and connecting with them, Truman built the momentum needed to surpass Dewey and win the election.

If you cite a work with no known author, use the title in your parenthetical reference.

The legacy and lessons of Truman's whistle-stop campaign continue to be studied by political analysts, and politicians today often mimic his campaign methods by scheduling multiple visits to key states, as Truman did. He visited California, Illinois, and Ohio 48 times, compared with 6 visits to those states by Dewey. Political scientist Thomas M. Holbrook concludes that his strategic campaigning in those states and others gave Truman the electoral votes he needed to win (61, 65).

The 1948 election also had an effect on pollsters, who, as Elmo Roper admitted, "couldn't have been more wrong" (qtd. in Karabell 255). Life magazine's editors concluded that pollsters as well as reporters and commentators were too convinced of a Dewey victory to analyze the polls seriously, especially the opinions of undecided voters (Karabell 256). Pollsters assumed that undecided voters would vote in the same proportion as decided voters -- and that turned out to be a false assumption (Karabell 258). In fact, the lopsidedness of the polls might have led voters who supported Truman to call themselves undecided out of an unwillingness to associate themselves with the losing side, further skewing the polls' results (McDonald, Glynn, Kim, and Ostman 152). Such errors led pollsters to change their methods significantly after the 1948 election.

In a work by four or more authors, either cite them all or name the first one followed by et al.

After the election, many political analysts, journalists, and historians concluded that the Truman upset was in fact a victory for the American people, who, the New Republic noted, "couldn't be ticketed by the polls, knew its own mind and had picked the rather unlikely but courageous figure of Truman to carry its banner" (qtd. in McCullough 715). How "unlikely" is unclear, however; Truman biographer Alonzo Hamby notes that "polls of scholars consistently rank Truman among the top eight presidents in American history" (Man of the People 641). But despite Truman's high standing, and despite the fact that the whistle-stop campaign is now part of our political landscape, politicians have increasingly imitated the style of the Dewey campaign, with its "packaged candidate who ran so as not to lose, who steered clear of controversy, and who made a good show of appearing presidential" (Karabell 266). The election of 1948 shows that voters are not necessarily swayed by polls, but it may have presaged the packaging of candidates by public relations experts, to the detriment of public debate on the issues in future presidential elections.

Works Cited

Donaldson, Gary A. <u>Truman Defeats Dewey</u>. Lexington: UP of
    Kentucky, 1999.

Ferrell, Robert H. <u>Harry S. Truman: A Life</u>. Columbia: U of Missouri P,
    1994.

Hamby, Alonzo L., ed. "Harry S. Truman (1945-1953)."
    <u>AmericanPresident.org</u>. 11 Dec. 2003. Miller Center of Public
    Affairs, U of Virginia. 12 Jan. 2004 <http://
    www.americanpresident.org/history/harrytruman>.

---. <u>Man of the People: A Life of Harry S. Truman</u>. New York: Oxford
    UP, 1995.

Holbrook, Thomas M. "Did the Whistle-Stop Campaign Matter?" <u>PS:</u>
    <u>Political Science and Politics</u> 35 (2002): 59-66.

Karabell, Zachary. <u>The Last Campaign: How Harry Truman Won the</u>
    <u>1948 Election</u>. New York: Knopf, 2000.

McCullough, David. <u>Truman</u>. New York: Simon, 1992.

McDonald, Daniel G., Carroll J. Glynn, Sei-Hill Kim, and Ronald E.
    Ostman. "The Spiral of Silence in the 1948 Presidential
    Election." <u>Communication Research</u> 28 (2001): 139-55.

"1948 Truman-Dewey Election." <u>Electronic Government Project:</u>
    <u>Eagleton Digital Archive of American Politics</u>. 2004. Eagleton
    Inst. of Politics, Rutgers, State U of New Jersey. 11 Jan. 2004
    <http://www.eagleton.rutgers.edu/>.

1"

Center the
heading.

Double-space
throughout.

Alphabetize the
list by authors'
last names or by
title for works
with no author.

Begin each entry
at the left mar-
gin; indent sub-
sequent lines
$\frac{1}{2}$-inch or 5
spaces.

If you cite more
than one work
by a single
author, list them
alphabetically by
title, and use 3
hyphens instead
of repeating the
author's name
after the first
entry.

"1948: The Great Truman Surprise." <u>Media and Politics Online Projects: Media Coverage of Presidential Campaigns</u>. 29 Oct. 2003. Dept. of Political Science and International Affairs, Kennesaw State U. 11 Jan. 2004 <http://www.kennesaw.edu/pols.3380/pres/1948.html>.

Rollins, Byron. Untitled photograph. "The First 150 Years: 1948." <u>AP History</u>. Associated Press. 10 Jan. 2004 <http://www.ap.org/pages/history/timeline/1948.htm>.

Truman, Harry S. "Campaigning, Letter, October 5, 1948." <u>Harry S. Truman</u>. Ed. Robert H. Ferrell. Washington: CQ P, 2003. 91.

Check to be sure that every source you use is on the list of works cited.

APA Style **46**

American Psychological Association (APA) style calls for (1) brief documentation in parentheses near each in-text citation and (2) complete documentation in a list of references at the end of your text. The models in this chapter draw on the *Publication Manual of the American Psychological Association*, 5th edition (2001). Additional information is available at www.apastyle.org.

A DIRECTORY TO APA STYLE

417

author   title   publication

APA IN-TEXT DOCUMENTATION

Brief documentation in your text makes clear to your reader precisely what you took from a source and, in the case of a quotation, precisely where (usually, on which page) in the source you found the text you are quoting.

Paraphrases and summaries are more common than quotations in APA-style projects. The chapter on quoting, paraphrasing, and summarizing covers all three kinds of citations. It also includes a list of words you can use in signal phrases to introduce quotations, paraphrases, and summaries. As you cite each source, you will need to decide whether to name the author in a signal phrase — "as McCullough (2001) wrote" — or in parentheses — "(McCullough, 2001)."

The first examples in this chapter show basic in-text documentation for a work by one author. Variations on those examples follow. All of the examples are color-coded to help you see how writers using APA style work authors and page numbers — and sometimes titles — into their texts.

1. AUTHOR NAMED IN A SIGNAL PHRASE

If you are quoting, you must give the page number(s). You are not required to give the page number(s) with a paraphrase or a summary, but APA encourages you to do so, especially if you are citing a long or complex work; most of the models in this chapter do include page numbers. Check with your instructors to find out their preferences.

AUTHOR QUOTED

Put the date in parentheses right after the author's name; put the page in parentheses as close to the quotation as possible.

> McCullough (2001) described John Adams as having "the hands of a man accustomed to pruning his own trees, cutting his own hay, and splitting his own firewood" (p. 18).

> John Adams had "the hands of a man accustomed to pruning his own trees, cutting his own hay, and splitting his own firewood," according to McCullough (2001, p. 18).

Notice that in the first example, the parenthetical reference with the page number comes *after* the closing quotation marks but *before* the period at the end of the sentence.

AUTHOR PARAPHRASED

Put the date in parentheses right after the author's name; follow the date with the page.

> McCullough (2001, p. 18) described John Adams's hands as those of someone used to manual labor.

> John Adams's hands were those of a laborer, according to McCullough (2001, p. 18).

2. AUTHOR NAMED IN PARENTHESES

If you do not mention an author in a signal phrase, put his or her name, a comma, and the year of publication in parentheses as close as possible to the quotation, paraphrase, or summary.

AUTHOR QUOTED

Give the author, date, and page in one parentheses, or split the information between two parentheses.

> Adams is said to have had "the hands of a man accustomed to pruning his own trees, cutting his own hay, and splitting his own firewood" (McCullough, 2001, p. 18).

> One biographer (McCullough, 2001) has said John Adams had "the hands of a man accustomed to pruning his own trees, cutting his own hay, and splitting his own firewood" (p. 18).

AUTHOR PARAPHRASED OR SUMMARIZED

Give the author, date, and page in one parentheses toward the beginning or the end of the paraphrase.

> One biographer (McCullough, 2001, p. 18) described John Adams as someone who was not a stranger to manual labor.

> John Adams's hands were those of a laborer (McCullough, 2001, p. 18).

3. AUTHORS WITH THE SAME LAST NAME

If your reference list includes more than one person with the same last name, include initials in all documentation to distinguish the authors from one another.

> Eclecticism is common in contemporary criticism (J. M. Smith, 1992, p. vii).

> J. M. Smith (1992, p. vii) has explained that eclecticism is common in contemporary criticism.

4. AFTER A BLOCK QUOTATION

If a quotation runs forty or more words, set it off from the rest of your text and indent it one-half inch (or five spaces) from the left margin without quotation marks. Place the page number(s) in parentheses *after* the end punctuation.

> Kaplan (2000) captured ancient and contemporary Antioch for us:
>> At the height of its glory in the Roman-Byzantine age, when it had an amphitheater, public baths, aqueducts, and sewage pipes, half a million people lived in Antioch. Today the population is only 125,000. With sour relations between Turkey and Syria, and unstable politics throughout the Middle East, Antioch is now a backwater—seedy and tumbledown, with relatively few tourists. I found it altogether charming. (p. 123)

5. TWO AUTHORS

Always mention both authors. Use *and* in a signal phrase, but use an ampersand (&) in parentheses.

> Carlson and Ventura (1990, p. v) wanted to introduce Julio Cortázar, Marjorie Agosín, and other Latin American writers to an audience of English-speaking adolescents.

> According to the Peter Principle, "In a hierarchy, every employee tends to rise to his level of incompetence" (Peter & Hull, 1969, p. 26).

6. THREE OR MORE AUTHORS

In the first reference to a work by three to five persons, name all contributors. In subsequent references, name the first author followed by *et al.* Whenever you refer to a work by six or more contributors, name only the first author, followed by *et al.* Use *and* in a signal phrase, but use an ampersand (&) in parentheses.

> Faigley, George, Palchik, and Selfe (2004, p. xii) have argued that where there used to be a concept called *literacy*, today's multitude of new kinds of texts has given us *literacies*.

> It's easier to talk about a good movie than a good book (Sebranek, Meyer, & Kemper, 1990, p. 143).

author   title   publication

Peilen et al. (1990, p. 75) supported their claims about corporate corruption with startling anecdotal evidence.

7. ORGANIZATION OR GOVERNMENT AS AUTHOR

If an organization has a long name that is recognizable by its abbreviation, give the full name and the abbreviation the first time you cite the source. In subsequent citations, use only the abbreviation. If the organization does not have a familiar abbreviation, use the full name each time you refer to it.

FIRST CITATION

(American Psychological Association [APA], 2001)

SUBSEQUENT CITATIONS

(APA, 2001)

8. AUTHOR UNKNOWN

With reference books and newspaper editorials, among other things, you may not know the author of a work. Use the complete title if it is short; if it is long, use the first few words of the title under which the work appears in the reference list.

Webster's New Biographical Dictionary (1988) identifies William James as "American psychologist and philosopher" (p. 520).

A powerful editorial asserted that healthy liver donor Mike Hurewitz died because of "frightening" faulty postoperative care ("Every Patient's Nightmare," 2002).

9. TWO OR MORE CITATIONS IN ONE PARENTHESES

If you need to cite multiple works in the same parentheses, list them in the same order that they appear in your reference list, separated by semicolons.

Many researchers have argued that what counts as "literacy" is not necessarily learned at school (Heath, 1983; Moss, 2003).

10. SOURCE QUOTED IN ANOTHER SOURCE

When you need to cite a source that was quoted in another source, let the reader know that you used a secondary source by adding the words *as cited in.*

> During the meeting with the psychologist, the patient stated repeatedly that he "didn't want to be too paranoid" (as cited in Oberfield & Yasik, 2004, p. 294).

11. WORK WITHOUT PAGE NUMBERS

Instead of page numbers, some electronic works have paragraph numbers, which you should include if you are referring to a specific part of such a source. Use the ¶ symbol or the abbreviation *para.* In sources with neither page nor paragraph numbers, refer readers to a particular part of the source if possible, perhaps indicating a heading and the paragraph under the heading.

> Russell's dismissals from Trinity College at Cambridge and from City College in New York City have been seen as examples of the controversy that marked the philosopher's life (Irvine, 2002, para. 2).

12. AN ENTIRE WORK

You do not need to give a page number if you are directing readers' attention to an entire work. Identify the author in a signal phrase or in parentheses, and cite the year of publication in parentheses.

> Kaplan (2000) considered Turkey and Central Asia explosive.

13. PERSONAL COMMUNICATION

Cite email, telephone conversations, interviews, personal letters, and other personal texts as *personal communication*, along with the person's initial(s), last name, and the date. You do not need to include such personal communications in your reference list.

The author and editors seriously considered alternative ways of demonstrating documentation styles (F. Weinberg, personal communication, November 14, 2003).

L. Strauss (personal communication, December 6, 2003) told about visiting Yogi Berra when they both lived in Montclair, New Jersey.

NOTES

APA recognizes that there are instances when writers of research papers may need to use *content notes* to give an explanation or information that doesn't fit into the paper proper. To signal a content note, place a superscript numeral in your text at the appropriate point. Your readers will know to look for a note beginning with the same superscript numeral on a separate page with the heading *Notes*, after your paper but before the reference list. If you have multiple notes, number them consecutively throughout your paper. Indent the first line of each note five spaces, and flush all subsequent lines left.

Here is an example showing text and an accompanying content note from a book called *In Search of Solutions: A New Direction in Psychotherapy* (2003).

TEXT WITH SUPERSCRIPT

An important part of working with teams and one-way mirrors is taking the consultation break, as at Milan, BFTC, and MRI.[1]

CONTENT NOTE

[1] It is crucial to note here that, while working within a team is fun, stimulating, and revitalizing, it is not necessary for successful outcomes. Solution-oriented therapy works equally well when working solo.

APA REFERENCE LIST

A reference list provides full bibliographic information for every source cited in your text with the exception of personal communication. This list should be alphabetized by authors' last names (or sometimes by editors' names). Works that do not have an identifiable author or editor are alphabetized by title. See pages 448–49 for a sample reference list.

Books

BASIC FORMAT FOR A BOOK

For most books, you'll need to provide information about the author; the date of publication; the title and any subtitle; and the place of publication and publisher. You'll find this information on the book's title page and copyright page.

> Diamond, J. (1997). *Guns, germs, and steel: The fates of human societies.* New York: Norton.

A FEW DETAILS TO NOTE

- **DATES:** If more than one year is given, use the most recent one.
- **TITLES:** Capitalize only the first word and proper nouns and proper adjectives in titles and subtitles.
- **PLACE OF PUBLICATION:** Give city followed by state (abbreviated) or province or country (for example, Dubuque, IA). Omit state, province, or country for larger cities such as London, New York, and Tokyo. If more than one city is given, use the first.
- **PUBLISHER:** Use a shortened form of the publisher's name (Little, Brown for Little, Brown and Company), but retain *Association*, *Books*, and *Press* (American Psychological Association, Princeton University Press).

1. ONE AUTHOR

> Author's Last Name, Initials. (Year of publication). *Title.* Publication City: Publisher.

Young, K. S. (1998). *Caught in the net: How to recognize the signs of Internet addiction — and a winning strategy for recovery.* New York: Wiley.

2. TWO OR MORE WORKS BY THE SAME AUTHOR

If the works were published in different years, list them chronologically.

Lewis, B. (1995). *The Middle East: A brief history of the last 2,000 years.* New York: Scribner.

Lewis, B. (2003). *The crisis of Islam: Holy war and unholy terror.* New York: Modern Library.

If the works were published in the same year, list them alphabetically by title, adding "a," "b," and so on to the years.

Kaplan, R. D. (2000a). *The coming anarchy: Shattering the dreams of the post cold war.* New York: Random House.

Kaplan, R. D. (2000b). *Eastward to Tartary: Travels in the Balkans, the Middle East, and the Caucasus.* New York: Random House.

3. TWO OR MORE AUTHORS

For two to six authors, use this format.

First Author's Last Name, Initials, Next Author's Last Name, Initials, & Last Author's Last Name, Initials. (Year of publication). *Title.* Publication City: Publisher.

Malless, S., & McQuain, J. (2003). *Coined by God: Words and phrases that first appear in the English translations of the Bible.* New York: Norton.

Sebranek, P., Meyer, V., & Kemper, D. (1990). *Writers INC: A guide to writing, thinking, and learning.* Burlington, WI: Write Source.

For a work by seven or more authors, name just the first six authors. After the sixth name, add the abbreviation *et al.*

4. ORGANIZATION OR GOVERNMENT AS AUTHOR

Sometimes a corporation or government organization is both author and publisher. If so, use the word *Author* as the publisher.

> Organization Name or Government Agency. (Year of publication). *Title.*
> Publication City: Publisher.

> Catholic News Service. (2002). *Stylebook on religion 2000: A reference
> guide and usage manual.* Washington, DC: Author.

> U.S. Social Security Administration. (2003). *Social Security: Retirement
> benefits.* Washington, DC: Author.

5. AUTHOR AND EDITOR

> Author's Last Name, Initials. (Year of edited edition). *Title.* (Editor's
> Initials Last Name, Ed.). Publication City: Publisher. (Original work[s]
> published year[s])

> Douglass, F. (1994). *Autobiographies.* (H. L. Gates, Jr., Ed.). New York:
> Library of America. (Original works published 1845–1893)

6. EDITED COLLECTION

> First Editor's Last Name, Initials, Next Editor's Last Name, Initials, & Final
> Editor's Last Name, Initials. (Eds.). (Year of edited edition). *Title.*
> Publication City: Publisher.

> Raviv, A., Oppenheimer, L., & Bar-Tal, D. (Eds.). (1999). *How children
> understand war and peace: A call for international peace education.*
> San Francisco: Jossey-Bass.

7. WORK IN A COLLECTION

> Author's Last Name, Initials. (Year of publication). Title of article or
> chapter. In Initials Last Name (Ed.), *Title* (pp. pages). Publication
> City: Publisher.

author   title   publication

Harris, I. M. (1999). Types of peace education. In A. Raviv, L. Oppenheimer, & D. Bar-Tal (Eds.), *How children understand war and peace: A call for international peace education* (pp. 46–70). San Francisco: Jossey-Bass.

8. UNKNOWN AUTHOR

Title. (Year of publication). Publication City: Publisher.

Webster's new biographical dictionary. (1988). Springfield, MA: Merriam-Webster.

If the title page of a work lists the author as *Anonymous*, treat the reference-list entry as if the author's name were Anonymous, and alphabetize it accordingly.

9. EDITION OTHER THAN THE FIRST

Author's Last Name, Initials. (Year). *Title* (name or number ed.). Publication City: Publisher.

Diamond, R. J. (2002). *Instant psychopharmacology* (2nd ed.). New York: Norton.

10. ONE VOLUME OF A MULTIVOLUME WORK

Author's Last Name, Initials. (Year). *Title of whole work: Vol. number. Title of volume*. Publication City: Publisher.

Spiegelman, A. (1986). *Maus: Vol. 1. My father bleeds history*. New York: Random House.

Periodicals

BASIC FORMAT FOR AN ARTICLE

For most articles, you'll need to provide information about the author; the date; the article title and any subtitle, the periodical title; and any volume or issue number and inclusive page numbers. Here is an example of an entry for an article in a journal.

Ferguson, N. (2005). Sinking globalization. *Foreign Affairs, 84*(2), 64–77.

A FEW DETAILS TO NOTE

- **AUTHORS**: Give each author's last name first followed by initials. When there are seven or more authors, name the first six and add *et al.* after the sixth name.

- **DATES**: For journals, give year only. For magazines and newspapers, give year followed by a comma and then month or month and day. Do not abbreviate months.

- **TITLES**: Capitalize only the first word and proper nouns and proper adjectives in titles and subtitles of articles. Capitalize the first and last words and all principal words of periodical titles. Do not capitalize *a, an, the,* or any prepositions or coordinating conjunctions unless they begin the title of the periodical.

- **VOLUME AND ISSUE**: For journals and magazines, give volume or volume and issue, as explained in more detail below. For newspapers, do not give volume or issue.

- **PAGES**: For a journal or magazine article, do not use *p.* or *pp.* even though you do use that designation for a newspaper article. If an article does not fall on consecutive pages, give all the page numbers (for example, 45, 75–77 for a journal or magazine; pp. C1, C3, C5–C7 for a newspaper).

11. ARTICLE IN A JOURNAL PAGINATED BY VOLUME

Author's Last Name, Initials. (Year). Title of article. *Title of Journal, volume,* pages.

Yaffe, K., Fox, P., Newcomer, R., Sands, L., Lindquist, K., Dane, K., et al. (2002). Patient and caregiver characteristics and nursing home placement in patients with dementia. *Journal of American Medical Association, 287,* 2090–2097.

12. ARTICLE IN A JOURNAL PAGINATED BY ISSUE

> Author's Last Name, Initials. (Year). Title of article. *Title of Journal,*
> *volume*(issue), pages.

> Weaver, C., McNally, C., & Moerman, S. (2001). To grammar or not to
> grammar: That is *not* the question! *Voices from the Middle, 8*(3),
> 17–33.

13. ARTICLE IN A MAGAZINE

If a magazine is published weekly, include the day and the month. If there
is a volume number, include it after the magazine title.

> Author's Last Name, Initials. (Year, Month Day). Title of article. *Title of*
> *Magazine, volume,* page(s).

> Wagner, R., & Schiermeier, Q. (2002, April 18). Conservationists under fire
> in the Philippines. *Nature, 416,* 669.

If a magazine is published monthly, include the month(s) only.

> Webster, D. (2002, May). Drawn from prehistory. *Smithsonian, 33,*
> 100–107.

14. ARTICLE IN A NEWSPAPER

If page numbers are consecutive, separate them with a dash. If not, separate them with a comma.

> Author's Last Name, Initials. (Year, Month Day). Title of article. *Title of*
> *Newspaper,* p(p). page(s).

> Schneider, G. (2005, March 13). Fashion sense on wheels. *The Washington*
> *Post,* pp. F1, F6.

15. ARTICLE BY AN UNKNOWN AUTHOR

List an article whose author is unknown by the title of the article.

IN A MAGAZINE

Title of article. (Year, Month Day). *Title of Magazine, volume,* page(s).

Hot property: From carriage house to family compound. (2004, December). *Berkshire Living, 1,* 99.

IN A NEWSPAPER

Title of article. (Year, Month Day). *Title of Newspaper,* p(p). page(s).

Accept terror threat, Homeland chief says. (2005, March 15). *The Cincinnati Enquirer,* p. A5.

16. REVIEW

IN A JOURNAL

Author's Last Name, Initials. (Year). Title of review [Review of *Title of Work*]. *Title of Journal, volume*(issue), page(s).

Geller, J. L. (2005). The cock and bull of Augusten Burroughs [Review of the books *Running with scissors, Dry: A memoir,* and *Magical thinking*]. *Psychiatric Services, 56,* 364–365.

IN A MAGAZINE

Author's Last Name, Initials. (Year, Month Day). Title of review [Review of *Title of Work*]. *Title of Magazine, volume,* page(s).

Brandt, A. (2003, October). Animal planet [Review of the book *Intelligence of apes and other rational beings*]. *National Geographic Adventure, 5,* 47.

author   title   publication

IN A NEWSPAPER

Author's Last Name, Initials. (Year, Month Day). Title of review [Review
of *Title of Work*].*Title of Newspaper*, p(p). page(s).

Morris, C. A. (2005, March 24). Untangling the threads of the Enron
fraud [Review of the book *Conspiracy of fools: A true story*]. *The
New York Times*, p. B9.

If the review does not have a title, include just the bracketed information
about the work being reviewed.

Jarratt, S. C. (2000). [Review of the book *Lend me your ear:
Rhetorical constructions of deafness*]. *College Composition
and Communication, 52*, 300–302.

Electronic Sources

BASIC FORMAT FOR AN ELECTRONIC SOURCE

Not every electronic source gives you all the data that APA would like
to see in a reference entry. Ideally, you will be able to list author's
or editor's name, date of first electronic publication or most recent
revision, title of document, information about print publication if
any, information about electronic publication (title of site, date of your
access of the site or retrieval of the document, name of the sponsoring institution), and URL (address of document or site). Of those
eight pieces of information, you will find seven in the following
example.

Johnson, C. W. (2000). How our laws are made. In *Thomas: Legislative
information on the Internet*. Retrieved March 5, 2005, from
the Library of Congress Web site: http://thomas.loc.gov/home/
holam.txt

A FEW DETAILS TO NOTE

- **AUTHORS**: List all authors last-name-first and initials. When there's more than one author, use an ampersand (&). When there are seven or more authors, name the first six and add *et al.* after the sixth name.

- **TITLES**: For Web sites and electronic documents, articles, or books, capitalize only the first word of titles and subtitles, proper nouns, and proper adjectives; for titles of periodicals, capitalize the first and last words and all principal words of the periodical title, but do not capitalize *a*, *an*, *the*, *to*, or any prepositions or coordinating conjunctions unless they begin a title or subtitle.

- **DATES**: After the author, give the year of the document's original publication on the Web or of its most recent revision. If neither of those years is clear, use *n.d.* to mean "no date"; the date you *must* include comes toward the end of the entry—month (not abbreviated), day, and year that you retrieved the document.

- **URL**: If you do not identify the sponsoring institution ("the Library of Congress Web site" in the example on page 433), you do not need a colon before the URL. Don't include any punctuation at the end of the URL.

17. NONPERIODICAL WEB SITE

COMPLETE SITE

Author's or Editor's Last Name, Initials. (Ed. if appropriate). (Year). *Title of site*. Retrieved Month Day, Year, from URL

Ockerbloom, J. M. (Ed.). (2005). *The online books page*. Retrieved March 28, 2005, from http://digital.library.upenn.edu/books

If you cannot find an author's or editor's name, use the name of the organization that created the Web site. Alternatively, begin with the title of the site, placing it before the year, as in the following example. For the year give the most recent update. The URL should lead to the site's home page.

Mental help net. (2001). Retrieved March 28, 2005, from http://mentalhelp.net

PART OF SITE

Author's Last Name, Initials. (Year). Title of page or article. In *Title of site*. Retrieved Month Day, Year, from URL

Tucker-Ladd, C. E. (2000). Happiness, depression and self-concept. In *Psychological self-help*. Retrieved March 28, 2005, from http://mentalhelp.net/psyhelp/chap6/

LARGE AND COMPLEX SITE

Introduce the URL by naming the host organization and the relevant collection, department, or institute within the organization.

Author's or Editor's Last Name, Initials. (Ed. if appropriate). (Year). *Title of site*. Retrieved Month Day, Year, from Host Organization Web site: URL

Salda, M. N. (Ed.). (1995). *The little red riding hood project*. Retrieved March 12, 2003, from University of Southern Mississippi, De Grummond Children's Literature Research Collection Web site: http://www.usm.edu/english/fairytales/lrrh/lrrhhome.htm

18. ARTICLE IN AN ONLINE PERIODICAL OR DATABASE

AN ONLINE ARTICLE WITH NO PRINT VERSION

Author's Last Name, Initials. (Year, Month Day). Title of article. *Title of Periodical*. Retrieved Month Day, Year, from URL

Landsburg, S. E. (2001, March 13). Putting all your potatoes in one basket: The economic lessons of the Great Famine. *Slate*. Retrieved March 5, 2005, from http://slate.msn.com/id/102180

AN ARTICLE IN PRINT AND ONLINE

If an article appears online in the same format and with the same content as its print version, simply add *[Electronic version]*; you do not need to give the URL. See the next page for an example.

> Author's Last Name, Initials. (Year, Month Day). Title of article [Electronic
> version]. *Title of Newspaper*, p(p). page(s).

> Dowd, M. (2002, April 7). Sacred cruelties [Electronic version]. *The New
> York Times*, p. A30.

Give the retrieval date and the URL if the online version of a periodical
article differs from the print version.

> Author's Last Name, Initials. (Year, Month Day). Title of article. *Title of
> Newspaper*, p. page. Retrieved Month Day, Year, from URL

> Dowd, M. (2002, April 7). Sacred cruelties. *The New York Times*, p. A30.
> Retrieved April 8, 2002, from http://www.nytimes.com/2002/04/07/
> opinion/07DOWD.html

AN ONLINE ARTICLE ACCESSED THROUGH A DATABASE

Follow the format for a journal (as below), magazine, newspaper, or other
source, but instead of giving the URL, end your retrieval statement with
the name of the database.

> Author's Last Name, Initials. (Year). Title of article. *Title of Journal,
> volume*(issue). Retrieved Month Day, Year, from Name of database.

> White, D. E. (1999). The "Joineriana": Anna Barbauld, the Aikin
> family circle, and the dissenting public sphere. *Eighteenth-Century
> Studies, 32*(4). Retrieved March 3, 2002, from Project Muse
> database.

19. ELECTRONIC DISCUSSION SOURCES

List online postings only if they are archived and can be retrieved.

> Author's Last Name, Initials. (Year, Month Day). Subject line of message
> [Msg number, if any]. Message posted to Name of Organization
> electronic mailing list, archived at URL

Baker, J. (2005, February 15). Huffing and puffing [Msg 89].
Message posted to the American Dialect Society electronic
mailing list, archived at http://listserv.linguistlist.org/archives/
ads-1.html

Do not include email or other nonarchived discussions in your list of
references. Simply cite the sender's name in your text. See no. 13 on
page 424 for guidelines on identifying such sources in your text.

Other Kinds of Sources

20. FILM

Last Name, Initials (Producer), & Last Name, Initials (Director). (Year). *Title*
[Motion picture]. Country: Studio.

Wallis, H. B. (Producer), & Curtiz, M. (Director). (1942). *Casablanca*
[Motion picture]. United States: Warner.

21. MUSIC RECORDING

Composer's Last Name, Initials. (Year of copyright). Title of song. On *Title
of album* [Medium]. City: Label.

Veloso, C. (1997). Na baixado sapateiro. On *Livros* [CD]. Los Angeles:
Nonesuch.

If the music is performed by someone other than the composer, put
that information in brackets following the title. When the recording
date is different from the copyright date, put it in parentheses after
the label.

Cahn, S., & Van Heusen, J. (1960). The last dance [Recorded by F. Sinatra].
On *Sinatra reprise: The very good years* [CD]. Burbank, CA: Reprise
Records. (1991)

22. PROCEEDINGS OF A CONFERENCE

Author's Last Name, Initials. (Year of publication). Title of paper. In
Proceedings Title (pp. pages). Publication City: Publisher.

Heath, S. B. (1997). Talking work: Language among teens. In *Symposium
about Language and Society–Austin* (pp. 27–45). Austin: Department
of Linguistics at the University of Texas.

23. TELEVISION PROGRAM

Last Name, Initials (Writer), & Last Name, Initials (Director). (Year). Title
of episode [Descriptive label]. In Initials Last Name (Producer), *Series
title*. City: Network.

Sorkin, A. (Writer), & Kagan, J. (Director). (2002). Stirred [Television series
episode]. In A. Sorkin (Executive Producer), *The west wing*. New
York: NBC.

SAMPLE RESEARCH PAPER, APA STYLE

Carolyn Stonehill wrote the following paper for a first-year writing course.
It is formatted according to the guidelines of the *Publication Manual of the
American Psychological Association*, 5th edition (2001). While APA guidelines
are used widely in linguistics and the social sciences, exact requirements
may vary from discipline to discipline and course to course. If you're unsure
about what your instructor wants, ask for clarification.

Insert a short-ened title and page number in the upper-right corner of each page, including the title page.

It's in Our Genes:

The Biological Basis of Human Mating Behavior

Karen Stonehill

English 102, Section 22

Professor Bertsch

February 24, 2003

Center the full title, your name, the name and section number of the course, your instructor's name, and the date, unless your instructor requires different information.

It's in Our Genes   2

Abstract

While cultural values and messages certainly play a part in the process of mate selection, the genetic and psychological predispositions developed by our ancestors play the biggest role in determining to whom we are attracted. Women are attracted to strong, capable men with access to resources to help rear children. Men find women attractive based on visual signs of youth, health, and, by implication, fertility. While perceptions of attractiveness are influenced by cultural norms and reinforced by advertisements and popular media, the persistence of mating behaviors that have no relationship to societal realities suggests that they are part of our biological heritage.

Unless your instructor specifies another length, limit your abstract to 120 words or fewer.

It's in Our Genes   3

It's in Our Genes: ●·· *Center the title.*

The Biological Basis of Human Mating Behavior   ●············ *Double-space the entire paper.*

Consider the following scenario: It's a sunny afternoon on campus, and Jenny is walking to her next class. Out of the corner of her eye, she catches sight of her lab partner, Joey, parking his car. She stops to admire how tall, muscular, and stylishly dressed he is, and she does not take her eyes off him as he walks away from his shiny new BMW. As he flashes her a pearly white smile, Jenny melts, then quickly adjusts her skirt and smoothes her hair.

This scenario, while generalized, is familiar: Our attraction to   ●············ *Indent each new paragraph 5 to 7 spaces ($\frac{1}{2}$-inch).*
people—or lack of it—often depends on their physical traits. But why this attraction? Why does Jenny respond the way she does to her handsome lab partner? Why does she deem him handsome at all? Certainly Joey embodies the stereotypes of physical attractiveness prevalent in contemporary American society. Advertisements, television shows, and magazine articles all provide Jenny with signals telling her what constitutes the ideal American man. Yet she is also attracted to Joey's new sports car even though she has a new car herself. Does Jenny find this man striking because of the influence of her culture, or does her attraction lie in a more fundamental part of her constitution? Evolutionary psychologists, who apply principles of evolutionary biology to research on the human mind, would say that Jenny's responses in this situation are due largely to mating strategies developed by her prehistoric ancestors. Driven by the need to reproduce and

propagate the species, these ancestors of ours formed patterns of mate selection so effective in providing for their needs and those of their offspring that they are mimicked even in today's society. While cultural values and messages clearly play a part in the process of mate selection, the genetic and psychological predispositions developed by our ancestors play the biggest role in determining to whom we are attracted.

Provide headings to help readers follow the organization.

Women's Need to Find a Capable Mate

Pioneering evolutionary psychologist Trivers (as cited in Allman, 1993) observed that having and rearing children requires women to invest far more resources than men because of the length of pregnancy, the dangers of childbirth, and the duration of infants' dependence on their mothers (p. 56). According to Fisher (as cited in

Refer to authors by last name. In general, use the past tense or the present perfect in signal phrases.

Frank, 2001), one of the leading advocates of this theory, finding a capable mate was a huge preoccupation of all prehistoric reproductive women, and for good reason: "A female couldn't carry a baby in one arm and sticks and stones in the other arm and still feed and protect herself on the very dangerous open grasslands, so she began to need a mate to help her rear her young" (p. 85). So because of this it became advantageous for the woman to find a strong, capable man with access to resources, and it became suitable for the man to find a healthy, reproductively sound woman to bear and care for his offspring. According to evolutionary psychologists, these are the bases upon which modern mate selection is founded, and there are many examples of this phenomenon to be found in our own society.

It's in Our Genes   5

One can see now why Jenny might be attracted by Joey's display of resources — his BMW. In our society, men with good job prospects, a respected social position, friends in high places, or any combination thereof have generally been viewed as more desirable mates than those without these things because they signal to women that the men have resources (Buss & Schmitt, 1993, p. 226). Compared with males, females invest more energy in bearing and raising children, so it is most advantageous for females to choose mates with easy access to resources, the better to provide for their children.

Men's Need to Find a Healthy Mate

For men, reproductive success depends mainly on the reproductive fitness of their female counterpart: No amount of available resources can save a baby miscarried in the first month of gestation. Because of this need for a healthy mate, men have evolved a particular attraction "radar" that focuses on signs of a woman's health and youth, markers that are primarily visual (Weiten, 2001, p. 399). Present-day attractiveness ratings are based significantly on this primitive standard: "Some researchers have suggested that cross-cultural standards of beauty reflect an evolved preference for physical traits that are generally associated with youth, such as smooth skin, good muscle tone, and shiny hair" (Boyd & Silk, 2000, p. 625). This observation would explain why women of our time are preoccupied with plastic surgery, makeup, and — in Jenny's case — a quick hair check as a potential date

Use ampersands in parenthetical references — but use and in signal phrases.

If the author is not named in a signal phrase, include the name in parentheses, along with the date and (if the work is quoted), the page number.

If an author is named in a signal phrase, include the publication date in parentheses after the name.

approaches. As Cunningham, Roberts, Barbee, Druen, and Wu (1995) noted, "A focus on outer beauty may have stemmed from a need for desirable inner qualities," such as health, strength, and fertility, and "culture may build on evolutionary dynamics by specifying grooming attributes that signal successful adaptation" (pp. 262–263).

The Influence of the Media on Mate Selection

There is, however, a good deal of opposition to evolutionary theory. Some critics say that the messages fed to us by the media are a larger influence on the criteria of present-day mate selection than any sort of ancestral behavior. Advertisements and popular media have long shown Americans what constitutes a physically ideal mate: In general, youthful, well-toned, symmetrical features are considered more attractive than aging, flabby, or lopsided ones. Evolutionary psychologists argue that research has not determined what is cause and what is effect. Cosmides and Tooby (1997) offered the following analogy to show the danger of assigning culture too powerful a causal role:

Indent quotations of 40 or more words 5 to 7 spaces, about $\frac{1}{2}$-inch from the left margin.

> For example, people think that if they can show that there is information in the culture that mirrors how people behave, then *that* is the cause of their behavior. So if they see that men on TV have trouble crying, they assume that their example is *causing* boys to be afraid to cry. But which is cause and which effect? Does the fact that men don't cry much on TV *teach* boys to not cry, or does it merely *reflect* the way boys normally develop? In the absence of research on the particular topic,

It's in Our Genes 7

there is no way of knowing. ("Nature and Nurture: An Adaptationist Perspective," para. 16)

We can hypothesize, then, that rather than media messages determining our mating habits, our mating habits determine the media messages. Advertisers rely on classical conditioning to interest consumers in their product. For instance, by showing an image of a beautiful woman while advertising a beauty product, advertisers hope that consumers will associate attractiveness with the use of that particular product (Weiten, 2001). In order for this method to be effective, however, the images depicted in conjunction with the beauty product must be ones the general public already finds attractive, and an image of a youthful, clear-skinned woman would, according to evolutionary psychologists, be attractive for reasons of reproductive fitness. In short, what some call media influence is not an influence at all but merely a mirror in which we see evidence of our ancestral predispositions.

If Not Media, Then What?

Tattersall (2001), a paleoanthropologist at the American Museum of Natural History, offered another counterargument to the evolutionary theory of mate selection. First, he argued that the behavior of organisms is influenced not only by genetics, economics, and ecology working together (p. 663). Second, he argued that no comparisons can be made between modern human behavior and that of our evolutionary predecessors because the appearance of *Homo sapiens* presented a sudden, qualitative change

To cite a specific part of an unpaginated Web site, count paragraphs from the beginning of the document or, as is done here, from a major heading.

from the Neanderthals — not a gradual evolution of behavioral traits:

> As a cognitive and behavioral entity, our species is truly unprecedented. Our consciousness is an emergent quality, not the result of eons of fine-tuning of a single instrument. And, if so, it is to this recently acquired quality of uniqueness, not to the hypothetical "ancestral environments," that we must look in the effort to understand our often unfathomable behaviors. (p. 665)

The key to Tattersall's argument is this "emergent quality" of symbolic thought; according to his theories, the ability to think symbolically is what separates modern humans from their ancestors and shows the impossibility of sexual selection behaviors having been passed down over millions of years. Our sexual preferences, Tattersall said, are a result of our own recent and species-specific development and have nothing whatsoever to do with our ancestors.

Opponents of the evolutionary theory, though, fail to explain how "unfathomable" mating behaviors can exist in our present society for no apparent or logical reason. Though medicine has advanced to the point where fertility can be medically enhanced, Singh (1993) observed that curvy women are still viewed as especially attractive because they are perceived to possess greater fertility — a perception that is borne out by several studies of female fertility, hormone levels, and waist-to-hip ratio (p. 304). Though more and more women are attending college and achieving high-paying positions, women are still "more likely than men to consider economic prospects a high priority in a mate" (Sapolsky, 2001–2002, p. 18). While cultural norms and economic conditions influence our taste in mates, as Singh (1993) showed in observing that "the degree of affluence of a society or of an ethnic group within a society may, to a large extent, determine the prevalence and admiration of fatness [of women]" (pp. 304–305), we still react to potential mates in ways determined in Paleolithic times. The key to understanding our mating behavior does not lie only in an emergent modern quality, nor does it lie solely in the messages relayed to us by society; rather, it involves as well the complex mating strategies developed by our ancestors.

It's in Our Genes   10

References

Allman, W. F. (1993, July 19). The mating game [Electronic version]. *U.S. News & World Report,* 56–63. Retrieved January 27, 2003, from SIRS database.

Boyd, R., & Silk, J. B. (2000). *How humans evolved.* (2nd ed.). New York: Norton, 2000.

Buss, D. M., & Schmitt, D. P. (1993). Sexual strategies theory: An evolutionary perspective on human mating. *Psychological Review, 100,* 204–232.

Cosmides, L., & Tooby, J. (1997, January 13). *Evolutionary psychology: A primer.* Retrieved February 2, 2003, from University of California, Santa Barbara, Center for Evolutionary Psychology Web site: http://www.psych.ucsb.edu/research/cep/primer.html

Cunningham, M. R., Roberts, A. R., Barbee, A. P., Druen, P. B., & Wu, C.-H. (1995). "Their ideas of beauty are, on the whole, the same as ours": Consistency and variability in the cross-cultural perception of female physical attractiveness. *Journal of Personality and Social Psychology, 68,* 261–279.

Frank, C. (2001, February). Why do we fall in — and out of — love? Dr. Helen Fisher unravels the mystery. *Biography,* 85–87, 112. Retrieved January 31, 2003, from Academic Search Premier database.

Sapolsky, R. M. (2001–2002, December–January). What do females want? *Natural History,* 18–21. Retrieved January 26, 2003, from Academic Search Premier database.

Begin list of references on a new page; center the heading.

Alphabetize the list by author's last name.

Indent all lines after the first line of each entry 5 spaces or $\frac{1}{2}$-inch.

Be sure every source listed is cited in the text; don't list sources consulted but not cited.

It's in Our Genes   11

Singh, D. (1993). Adaptive significance of female physical
  attractiveness: Role of waist-to-hip ratio. *Journal of Personality
  and Social Behavior, 65,* 293–307.

Tattersall, I. (2001). Evolution, genes, and behavior. *Zygon: Journal of
  Religion & Science, 36,* 657–666. Retrieved February 3, 2003, from
  the Psychology and Behavioral Sciences Collection database.

Weiten, W. (2001). *Psychology: Themes & variations.* (5th ed.). San
  Bernardino, CA: Wadsworth.

part 6

Media / Design

Consciously or not, we design all the texts we write, choosing typefaces, setting up text as lists or charts, deciding whether to add headings—and then whether to center them or flush them left. Sometimes our genre calls for certain design elements—essays begin with titles, letters begin with salutations ("Dear Auntie Em"). Other times we design texts to meet the demands of particular audiences, formatting documentation in MLA or APA or some other style, setting type larger for young children, and so on. And always our designs will depend upon our medium. A memoir might take the form of an essay in a book, be turned into a bulleted list for a PowerPoint presentation, or include links to images or other pages if presented on a Web site. The chapters in this part offer advice for working with PRINT texts, SPOKEN texts, and ELECTRONIC texts.

Media / Design

USA Today reports on a major news story with an article that includes a large photo and a colorful graph; the *New York Times* covers the same story with an article that is not illustrated but has a large headline and a pull quote highlighting one key point. Your psychology textbook includes many photos, tables, charts, and other visuals to help readers understand the subject matter. When you submit an essay for a class, you choose a typeface and you may make the type larger—or smaller—as need be. In all these instances, the message is in some way "designed." This chapter offers advice on designing print texts to suit your purpose, audience, genre, and subject. Much of the advice also holds for **ELECTRONIC TEXTS** and for visuals that accompany **SPOKEN TEXTS.**

476–84

464–75

Considering the Rhetorical Situation

As with all writing tasks, your rhetorical situation affects the way you design a print text.

PURPOSE   Consider how you can design your text to help achieve your purpose. If you're reporting certain kinds of information, for instance, you may want to present some data in a chart or table; if you're trying to get readers to care about an issue, a photo or pull quote might help you do so.

3–4

AUDIENCE   Do you need to do anything designwise for your intended audience? Change the type size? Add headings? tables? color?

5–8

rhetorical situations · genres · processes · strategies · research mla/apa · media/ design

9–11
■ **GENRE** Does your genre have any design requirements? Must (or can) it have headings? illustrations? tables or graphs? a certain size paper?

12–14
■ **STANCE** How can your design reflect your attitude toward your audience and subject? Do you need a businesslike typeface? Will plotting out statistics on a bar graph make them seem more important than they would seem in the middle of a paragraph? Can you use color?

Some Elements of Design

Whatever your text, you have various design decisions to make. What typeface(s) should you use? How should you arrange your text on the page? Should you include any headings? The following guidelines will help you consider each of these questions.

12–14

1–17
456–58

Type. You can choose from among many typefaces, and the one you choose will affect your text—how well readers can read it and how they will perceive your tone and STANCE. Times Roman will make a text look businesslike or academic; Comic Sans will make it look playful. For most academic writing, you'll want to use 10- or 11- or 12-point type, and you'll usually want to use a serif face (such as Times Roman or Bookman); which is generally easier to read than a sans serif face (such as Arial, Verdana, or Century Gothic). It's usually a good idea to use a serif face for your main text, reserving sans serif for headings and parts you want to highlight. Decorative typefaces (such as Magneto, Amaze, Chiller, and Jokerman) should be used sparingly and only when they're appropriate for your audience, purpose, and the rest of your RHETORICAL SITUATION. If you use more than one typeface in a text, use each one consistently: one face for HEADINGS, one for captions, one for the main body of your text. And don't go overboard—you won't often have reason to use more than two or, at most, three typefaces in any one text.

Every typeface has regular, **bold**, and *italic* fonts. In general, choose regular for the main text, bold for major headings, and italic for titles of books and other long works and, occasionally, to emphasize words or brief phrases. Avoid italicizing or boldfacing entire paragraphs. If you are following MLA, APA, or some other style, be sure your use of fonts conforms to its requirements.

● 378–416
◐ 417–49

Finally, consider the line spacing of your text. Generally, academic writing is double-spaced, whereas LETTERS and RÉSUMÉS are usually single-spaced. Some kinds of REPORTS may call for single-spacing; check with your instructor if you're not sure. In addition, you'll often need to add an extra space to set off parts of a text—items in a list, for instance, or headings.

▲ 182–92
▲ 127–36

Layout.   Layout is the way text is arranged on a page. An academic essay, for example, will usually have a title centered at the top, one-inch margins all around, and double-spacing. A text can be presented in paragraphs—or in the form of LISTS, TABLES, CHARTS, GRAPHS, and so on. Sometimes you need to include other elements as well: headings, images and other graphics, captions, lists of works cited.

▫ 455–56
458–60

Paragraphs.   Dividing text into paragraphs focuses information for readers and helps them process the information by dividing it into manageable chunks. If you're writing a story for a newspaper with narrow columns, for example, you'll divide your text into shorter paragraphs than you would if you were writing an academic essay. In general, indent paragraphs five spaces when your text is double-spaced; either indent or skip a line between paragraphs that are single-spaced.

Lists.   Put information into list form that you want to set off and make easily accessible. Number the items in a list when the sequence matters (in instructions, for example); use bullets when the order is not important. Set off lists with an extra line of space above and below, and add extra space between the items on a list if necessary for legibility. Here's an example:

Darwin's theory of how species change through time derives from three postulates, each of which builds on the previous one:

1. The ability of a population to expand is infinite, but the ability of any environment to support populations is always finite.

2. Organisms within populations vary, and this variation affects the ability of individuals to survive and reproduce.

3. The variations are transmitted from parents to offspring.

—Robert Boyd and Joan B. Silk, *How Humans Evolved*

Do not set off text as a list unless there's a good reason to do so, however. Some lists are more appropriately presented in paragraph form, especially when they give information that is not meant to be referred to more than once. In the following example, there is no reason to highlight the information by setting it off in a list—and bad news is softened by putting it in paragraph form:

> I regret to inform you that the Scholarship Review Committee did not approve your application for a Board of Rectors scholarship, for the following reasons: your grade-point average did not meet the minimum requirements; your major is not among those eligible for consideration; and the required letter of recommendation was not received before the deadline.

Presented as a list, that information would be needlessly emphatic.

Headings.   Headings make the structure of a text easier to follow and help readers find specific information. Some genres require standard headings—announcing an **ABSTRACT,** for example, or a list of **WORKS CITED.** Other times you will want to use heads to provide an overview of a section of text. You may not need any headings with brief texts, and when you do, you'll probably want to use one level at most, just to announce major topics. Longer texts and information-rich genres, such as pamphlets or detailed **REPORTS,** may require several levels of headings. If you decide to include headings, you will need to decide how to phrase them, what typefaces and fonts to use, and where to position them.

107–11 ▲
415–16 ●

127–36 ▲

Phrase headings concisely.   Make your headings succinct and parallel in structure. You might make all the headings nouns (**Mushrooms**), noun phrases (**Kinds of Mushrooms**), gerund phrases (**Recognizing Kinds of Mushrooms**), or questions (**How Do I Identify Mushrooms?**). Whatever form you decide on, use it consistently for each heading. Sometimes your

phrasing will depend on your purpose. If you're simply helping readers find information, use brief phrases:

Head	**Forms of Social Groups among Primates**
Subhead	***Solitary Social Groups***
Subhead	***Monogamous Social Groups***

If you want to address your readers directly with the information in your text, consider writing your headings as questions:

How can you identify morels?
Where can you find morels?
How can you cook morels?

Make headings visible.　Headings need to be visible, so consider printing them in a bold, italic, or underlined font — or use a different typeface. For example, you could print your main text in a serif font like Times Roman and your headings in a sans serif font like Arial or make the headings larger than the regular text. When you have several levels of headings, use capitalization, boldface, and italics to distinguish among the various levels. For example:

FIRST-LEVEL HEAD
Second-Level Head
Third-Level Head

Be aware, though, that APA and MLA formats expect headings to be in the same typeface as the main text; APA requires that each level of heading appear in a specific style: all uppercase, uppercase and lowercase, italicized uppercase and lowercase, and so on.

Position headings appropriately.　If you're following APA format, center first- and second-level headings. If you're following MLA format, align headings at the left margin without any extra space above or below. If you are not following a prescribed format, you get to decide where to position your headings: centered, flush with the left margin, or even alongside the text, in a wide left-hand margin. Position each level of head consistently throughout your text.

417–49
378–416

White space.   Use white space to separate the various parts of a text. In general, use one-inch margins for the text of an essay or report. Unless you're following MLA or APA format, include space above headings, above and below lists, and around photos, graphs, and other images to set them apart from the rest of the text. See the two **SAMPLE RESEARCH PAPERS** in this book for examples of the formats required by MLA and APA.

407–16
438–49

Visuals

Visuals can sometimes help you to make a point in ways that words alone cannot. Be careful, however, that any visuals you use contribute to your point — not simply act as decoration. This section discusses how to use photos, graphs, charts, tables, and diagrams effectively.

Select visuals that are appropriate for your rhetorical situation.   There are various kinds of visuals: photographs, line graphs, bar graphs, pie charts, tables, diagrams, flowcharts, drawings, and more. Which ones you use, if any, will depend on your content, your **GENRE**, and your **RHETORICAL SITUATION**. A newspaper article on housing prices might include a bar graph or line graph, and also some photographs; a report on the same topic written for an economics class would probably have graphs but no photos. See the examples on the facing page, along with advice for using each one.

19–192
1–17

Some guidelines for using visuals

- Use visuals as part of your text's content, one that is as important as your words to your message. Therefore, avoid clip art, which is usually intended as decoration.
- Position visuals in your text as close as possible to your discussion of the topic to which they relate.
- Number all visuals, using a separate sequence for figures (photos, graphs, and drawings) and tables: *Figure 1, Figure 2; Table 1, Table 2.*
- Refer to the visual before it appears, identifying it and summarizing its point. For example: "As Figure 1 shows, Japan's economy grew dramatically between 1965 and 1980."

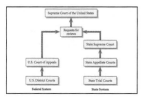

Photographs can support an argument, illustrate events and processes, present alternative points of view, and help readers "place" your information in time and space.

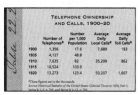

Line graphs are a good way of showing changes in data over time. Each line here shows a different set of data; plotting the two lines together allows readers to compare the data at different points in time.

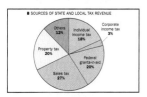

Bar graphs are useful for comparing quantitative data. The bars can be horizontal or vertical.

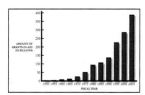

Pie charts can be used for showing how a whole is divided into parts or how something is apportioned.

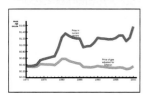

Tables are useful for displaying information concisely, especially when several items are being compared.

Diagrams, flowcharts, and drawings are ways of showing relationships and processes.

- Provide a title or caption for each visual to identify it and explain its significance for your text. For example: "Table 1. Japanese economic output, 1965–80."

375–77 ●

- **DOCUMENT** the source of any visuals you found in another source: "Figure 1. Two Tokyo shoppers display their purchases. (Ochiro, 1967)." Document any tables you create with data from another source. You need not document visuals you create yourself or data from your own experimental or field research.

- Obtain permission to use any visuals you found in another source that will appear in texts you publish in any form other than for a course.

- Label visuals to ensure that your audience will understand what they show. For example, label each section of a pie chart to show what it represents.

When you choose visuals and integrate them into your texts, follow the same procedures you use with other source materials.

Evaluate visuals as you would any text. Make sure visuals relate directly to your subject, support your assertions, and add information that words alone can't provide as clearly or easily. Evaluate visuals as you would other source materials: Is the photographer named? Do charts and graphs identify the source of the data they portray? Where was the visual published? How was the visual used in its original context? Does the information in the visual match, complement, or contradict the information in your other sources?

Include any necessary source information. Make sure visuals are accompanied by background and citation information: graphs and tables should cite the source of the data they present, and captions of photos should identify the photographer and date.

Use visuals ethically. You may want to crop a photograph, cutting it to show only part. See, for example, the photo on the facing page of a young couple in the 1940s and the cropped version that shows only the man's head.

You might have reason to crop the photo to accompany a profile or memoir about the man, but you would not want to eliminate the young woman (who later became his wife) from the photo in an account of the

man's life. If you crop or otherwise alter a photograph, keep your purpose in mind.

But altering photographs in a way that misrepresents someone or something is a serious breach of ethics. In 1997, when O. J. Simpson was arrested for the murder of his ex-wife, both *Time* and *Newsweek* used the same mug shot on their covers. *Time*, however, digitally darkened Simpson's skin, making him look "blacker." This sort of manipulation misleads readers, creating visual lies that can inappropriately influence how readers interpret both the text and the subject. If you alter a photo, be sure the image represents the subject accurately—and tell your readers how you have changed it.

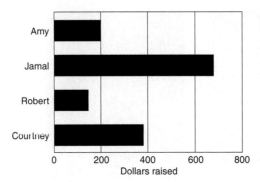

Fig. 1. Fund-raising results for the class gift.

Charts and graphs can mislead, too. Changing the scale on a bar graph, for example, can change the effect of the comparison, making the quantities being compared seem very similar or very different, as the two bar graphs of identical data show in figures 1 and 2.

Depending on the fund-raising goal implied by each bar graph ($800 or $5,000) and the increments of the dollars raised ($200 or $1,000), the two graphs send very different messages, though the dollars raised by each fund-raiser remain the same. Just as you shouldn't edit a quotation or a photograph in a way that might misrepresent its meaning, you should not present data in a way that could mislead readers.

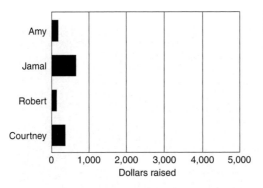

Fig. 2. Fund-raising results for the class gift.

Evaluating a Design

Does the design suit its PURPOSE? Do the typeface and any visuals help to convey the text's message, support its argument, or present information? Is there any key information that should be highlighted in a list or chart?

3–4

How well does the design meet the needs of its AUDIENCE? Will the overall appearance of the text appeal to the intended readers? Is the typeface large enough for them to read? Are there headings to help them find their way through the text? Are there the kind of visuals they are likely to expect? Are the visuals clearly labeled and referred to in the main text so that readers know why they're there?

5–8

How well does the text meet the requirements of its GENRE? Can you tell by looking at the text that it is an academic essay, a lab report, a résumé? Do its typeface, margins, headings, and page layout meet the requirements of MLA, APA, or whatever style being followed? Are visuals appropriately labeled and cited?

19–11

378–416

417–49

How well does the design reflect the writer's STANCE? Do the page layout and typeface convey the appropriate tone — serious, playful, adventuresome, conservative, and so on? Do the visuals reveal anything about the writer's position or beliefs? For instance, does the choice of visuals show any particular bias?

12–14

48 Spoken Text

In a marketing class, you give a formal presentation as part of a research project. As a candidate for student government, you deliver several speeches to various campus groups. At a good friend's wedding, you make a toast to the married couple. In school and out, you may be called on to speak in public, to compose and deliver spoken texts. This chapter offers guidelines to help you prepare and deliver effective spoken texts, along with the visual aids you often need to include. We'll start with two good examples.

ABRAHAM LINCOLN

Gettysburg Address

Given by the sixteenth president of the United States, at the dedication of the Gettysburg battlefield as a memorial to those who died in the Civil War, this is one of the most famous speeches ever delivered in the United States.

Four score and seven years ago our fathers brought forth on this continent, a new nation, conceived in Liberty, and dedicated to the proposition that all men are created equal.

Now we are engaged in a great civil war, testing whether that nation, or any nation so conceived and so dedicated, can long endure. We are met on a great battle-field of that war. We have come to dedicate a portion of that field, as a final resting place for those who here gave their lives that that nation might live. It is altogether fitting and proper that we should do this.

But, in a larger sense, we can not dedicate—we can not consecrate—we can not hallow—this ground. The brave men, living and

rhetorical situations genres processes strategies research mla/apa media/design

dead, who struggled here, have consecrated it, far above our poor power to add or detract. The world will little note, nor long remember what we say here, but it can never forget what they did here. It is for us the living, rather, to be dedicated here to the unfinished work which they who fought here have thus far so nobly advanced. It is rather for us to be here dedicated to the great task remaining before us — that from these honored dead we take increased devotion to that cause for which they gave the last full measure of devotion — that we here highly resolve that these dead shall not have died in vain — that this nation, under God, shall have a new birth of freedom — and that government of the people, by the people, for the people, shall not perish from the earth.

You won't likely be called on to deliver such an address, but the techniques Lincoln used — brevity, rhythm, recurring themes — are ones you can use in your own spoken texts. The next example represents the type of spoken text we are sometimes called on to deliver at important occasions in the lives of our families.

JUDY DAVIS

Ours Was a Dad . . .

This short eulogy was given at the funeral of the writer's father, Walter Boock. Judy Davis lives in Davis, California, where she is the principal of North Davis Elementary School.

Elsa, Peggy, David, and I were lucky to have such a dad. Ours was a dad who created the childhood for us that he did not have for himself. The dad who sent us airborne on the soles of his feet, squealing with delight. The dad who built a platform in the peach tree so we could eat ourselves comfortably into peachy oblivion. The dad who assigned us chores and then did them with us. The dad who felt our pain when we skinned our knees.

Ours was the dad who took us camping, all over the U.S. and Canada, but most of all in our beloved Yosemite. The one who awed us with his ability to swing around a full pail of water without spilling a drop and let us hold sticks in the fire and draw designs in the night air with hot orange coals.

Our dad wanted us to feel safe and secure. On Elsa's eighth birthday, we acquired a small camping trailer. One very blustery night in Minnesota, Mom and Dad asleep in the main bed, David suspended in the hammock over them, Peggy and Elsa snuggled in the little dinette bed, and me on an air mattress on the floor, I remember the most incredible sense of well-being: our family all together, so snug, in that little trailer as the storm rocked us back and forth. It was only in the morning that I learned about the tornado warnings. Mom and Dad weren't sleeping; they were praying that when morning came we wouldn't find ourselves in the next state.

Ours was the dad who helped us with homework at the round oak table. He listened to our oral reports, taught us to add by looking for combinations of 10, quizzed us on spelling words, and when our written reports sounded a little too much like the *World Book* encyclopedia, he told us so.

Ours was the dad who believed our round oak table that seated 5 twelve when fully extended should be full at Thanksgiving. Dad called the chaplain at the airbase, asked about homesick boys, and invited them to join our family. Or he'd call International House in Berkeley to see if someone from another country would like to experience an American Thanksgiving. We're still friends with the Swedish couple who came for turkey forty-five years ago. Many people became a part of our extended family around that table. And if twelve around the table were good, then certainly fourteen would be better. Just last fall, Dad commissioned our neighbor Randy to make yet another leaf for the table. There were fourteen around the table for Dad's last Thanksgiving.

Ours was a dad who had a lifelong desire to serve. He delivered Meals on Wheels until he was eighty-three. He delighted in picking up the day-old doughnuts from Mr. Rollen's shop to give those on his route an extra treat. We teased him that he should be receiving those meals himself! Even after walking became difficult for him, he continued to drive and took along an able friend to carry the meals to the door.

Our family, like most, had its ups and downs. But ours was a dad who forgave us our human failings as we forgave him his. He died in

peace, surrounded by love. Elsa, Peggy, David, and I were so lucky to have such a dad.

This eulogy, in honor of the writer's father, provides concrete and memorable details that give the audience a clear image of the kind of man he was. The repetition of the phrase "ours was a dad" provides a rhythm and unity that moves the text forward, and the use of short, conventional sentences makes the text easy to understand — and deliver.

Key Features / Spoken Text

A clear structure.   Spoken texts need to be clearly organized so that your audience can follow what you're saying. The **BEGINNING** needs to engage their interest, make clear what you will be talking about, and perhaps forecast the main parts of your talk. The main part of the text should focus on a few main points and only as many as your listeners can be expected to handle. (Remember, they can't go back to reread!) The **ENDING** is especially important: it should leave your audience with something to remember, think about, or do. Davis ends as she begins, saying that she and her sisters and brother "were so lucky to have such a dad." Lincoln ends by challenging his audience to "the great task remaining before us . . . that we . . . resolve that these dead shall not have died in vain — that this nation, under God, shall have a new birth of freedom — and that government of the people, by the people, for the people, shall not perish from the earth."

239–45

245–48

Signpost language to keep your audience on track.   You may need to provide cues to help your listeners follow your text, especially **TRANSITIONS** that lead them from one point to the next. Sometimes you'll also want to stop and **SUMMARIZE** a complex point to help your audience keep track of your ideas and follow your narrative.

254

366–67

A tone to suit the occasion.   Lincoln spoke at a serious, formal event, the dedication of a national cemetery, and his address is formal and even solemn. Davis's eulogy is more informal in tone, as befits a speech given for friends and loved ones. In a presentation to a panel of professors, you probably would want to take an academic tone, avoiding too much slang and speaking in complete sentences. If you had occasion to speak on the very same topic to a neighborhood group, however, you would likely want to speak more casually.

Sound. Remember that spoken texts have the added element of sound. Be aware of how your words and phrases sound. Even if you're never called on to deliver a Gettysburg Address, you will find that repetition and parallel structure can lend power to a presentation, making it easier to follow — and more likely to be remembered. "We can not dedicate, we can not consecrate — we can not hallow": these are words said more than one hundred years ago, but who among us does not know where they're from? The repetition of "we can not" and the parallel forms of the three verbs are one reason they stay with us. These are structures any writer can use. See how the repetition of "ours was a dad" in Davis's eulogy creates a rhythm that engages listeners and at the same time unifies the text.

Visual aids. Many times you will want or need to use visuals — PowerPoint or other presentation software, transparencies, flip charts, and so on — to present certain information and to highlight key points for your audience.

Considering the Rhetorical Situation

As with any writing, you need to consider your purpose, audience, and the rest of your rhetorical situation:

3–4
■ **PURPOSE**   What is your primary purpose? To inform? persuade? entertain? evoke an emotional response? Something else?

5–8
■ **AUDIENCE**   Think about whom you'll be addressing and how well you know your audience. Will they be interested, or

rhetorical situations   genres   processes   strategies   research mla/apa   media/ design

will you need to get them interested? Are they likely to be friendly? How can you get and maintain their attention, and how can you establish common ground? Will they know about your subject, or will you need to provide background and define key terms?

GENRE   The genre of your text will affect the way you structure it. If you're making an argument, for instance, you'll need to consider counterarguments — and to anticipate questions from members of the audience who hold other opinions. If you're giving a report, you may have reason to prepare handouts with detailed information you don't have time to cover.   9–11

STANCE   Consider the attitude you want to express — is it serious? thoughtful? passionate? well-informed? funny? something else? — and choose your words accordingly.   12–14

Delivering a Spoken Text

The success of a spoken text often hinges on how you deliver it. As you practice delivering your spoken texts, bear in mind the following points.

Speak clearly.   When delivering a spoken text, your first goal is to be understood by your audience. If listeners miss important words or phrases because you don't form your words distinctly, your talk will not succeed. Make sure your pace matches your audience's needs — sometimes you may need to speak slowly to explain complex material; other times you may need to speed up to keep an audience's attention.

Pause for emphasis.   In writing, you have white space and punctuation to show readers where an idea or discussion ends. When speaking, you need to be the one to pause to signal the end of a thought, to give listeners a moment to consider something you've said, or to get them ready for a surprising or amusing statement.

Avoid reading your presentation.   Speech textbooks often advise that you never read your speech. For some of us, though, that's just not possible. If you can speak well from notes or an outline, great—you're likely to do well. If you must have a complete text in front of you, though, try to write it as if you were talking. Then, practice by reading it into a tape recorder; listen for spots that sound as if you're reading, and work on your delivery to sound more relaxed.

Stand up straight, and look at your audience.   Try to maintain some eye contact with your audience. If that's uncomfortable, fake it: pick a spot on the wall just above the head of a person in the last row of chairs, and focus on it. You'll appear as if you're looking at your audience even if you're not looking them in the eye. And if you stand up straight, you'll project the sense that you have confidence in what you're saying. If you appear to believe in your words, others will, too.

Use gestures for emphasis.   If you're not used to speaking in front of a group, you may let your nervousness show by holding yourself stiffly, elbows tucked in. To overcome some of that nervousness, take some deep breaths, try to relax, move your arms as you would if you were talking to a friend. Use your hands for emphasis. Most public speakers use one hand to emphasize points and both to make larger gestures. Watch politicians on C-SPAN to see how people who speak on a regular basis use their hands and bodies as part of their overall delivery.

Practice.   Practice, practice, and then practice some more. Pay particular attention to how much time you have—and don't go over your time limit.

Visual Aids

When you give an oral presentation, you'll often want or need to include some visuals to help listeners follow what you're saying. Especially when you're presenting complex information, it helps to let them see it as well as hear it. Remember, though, that visuals are a means of conveying information, not mere decoration.

Deciding on the appropriate visual. Presentation software, overhead transparencies, flip charts, and posters are some of the most common kinds of visuals. Presentation software and overhead transparencies are useful for listing main points and for projecting illustrations, tables, and graphs. Overhead transparencies, like whiteboards and chalkboards, allow you to create visuals as you speak. Sometimes you'll want to distribute handouts to provide lists of works cited or copies of any slides you show.

Whatever you decide to use, make sure that the necessary equipment is available—and that it works. If at all possible, check out the room and the equipment before you give your presentation. If you bring your own equipment, make sure electrical outlets are in reach of your power cords.

Also make sure that your visuals will be seen. You may have to rearrange the furniture or the screen in the room to make sure everyone can see. And finally: *have a backup plan.* Computers fail; projector bulbs burn out; marking pens run dry. Whatever visuals you plan, have an alternative plan in case any of these things happen.

Using presentation software. Programs such as Microsoft PowerPoint allow you to create slides that you then project via a computer. These programs enable you to project graphs, charts, photographs, sound—and plain text. Here are some tips for using presentation software effectively:

- *Use* LISTS *rather than paragraphs.* Use slides to emphasize your main points, not to reproduce your talk onscreen. Be aware that you can project the list all at once or one item at a time.   ☐ 455–56

- *Don't put too much information on a slide.* How many bulleted points you include will depend on how long each one is, but you want to be sure that you don't include more words than listeners will be able to read as you present each slide.

- *Be sure your* TYPE *is large enough for your audience to read it.* In general, you don't want to use any type smaller than 18 points, and you'll want something larger than that for headings. Projected slides are easier to read in sans serif fonts like Arial, Helvetica, and Tahoma instead of serif fonts like Times Roman. Avoid using all caps—all-capped text is hard to read.   ☐ 454–55

- *Choose colors carefully.* Your text must contrast strongly with the background. Dark text on a light background is easier to read than the reverse. And remember that not everyone sees all colors; be sure your audience does not need to recognize colors in order to get your meaning. Red-green contrasts are especially hard to see and should be avoided.

- *Use bells and whistles sparingly, if at all.* Presentation software offers lots of decorative backgrounds, letters that fade in or dance across the screen, and, literally, bells and whistles. These can be more distracting than helpful; avoid using them unless they help you make your point.

- *Mark your text.* In your notes, mark each place where you need to click a mouse to call up the next slide.

On the facing page are two slides from a PowerPoint presentation that Dylan Borchers created for an oral presentation based on his essay exploring the U.S. presidential election campaign of 1948 (see pages 408–16). These slides offer an outline of Borchers' main points; the speech itself fills in the details. The design is simple and uncluttered, and the large font and high contrast between type and background make the slides easy to read, even from across a large room.

Overhead transparencies.   Transparency slides can hold more information than slides created with presentation software, but someone must place each transparency on the projector one at a time. To minimize the number of slides you will need, you can place a lot of information on each transparency and use a blank sheet of paper to cover and reveal each point as you discuss it (see an example on page 474). Here are some tips for using overhead transparencies effectively:

- *Use a white background and large type.* If you're typing your text, use black type. Use type that is at least 18 points, and use larger type for headings. As with presentation software, fonts like Arial and Tahoma are easiest to read from a distance. If you're making handwritten transparencies, you might write in several colors.

Dewey

- Appeared overconfident
- Ran a lackluster, "safe" campaign
- Was perceived as stuffy and aloof
- Made several blunders
- Would not address issues

Truman

- Conducted whistle-stop campaign
- Made hundreds of speeches
- Spoke energetically
- Connected personally with voters
- Focused on key states

Slides made with presentation software

Dewey

- Appeared overconfident
- Ran a lackluster, "safe" campaign
- Was perceived as stuffy and aloof
- Made several blunders
- Would not address issues

Truman

- Conducted whistle-stop campaign
- Made hundreds of speeches
- Spoke energetically
- Connected personally with voters
- Focused on key states

An overhead transparency

- *Write legibly and large.* If you want to write as you speak and have trouble writing in a straight line, place a sheet of lined paper under the blank slide. Use a blank sheet to cover any unused part of the slide so that you don't smudge the ink on the slide as you write.
- *Position slides carefully.* You might want to mark the top right corner of each transparency to make sure you put it where it needs to go on

the projector. And have someplace to put the transparencies before and after you use them.

See the sample transparency slide on page 474. You might compare it with the PowerPoint slides on page 473—you'll see that it provides identical information.

Handouts. When you want to give your audience information they can refer to later—reproductions of your visuals, bibliographic information about your sources, printouts of your slides—do so in the form of a handout. Refer to the handout in your presentation, but unless it includes material your audience needs to consult as you talk, don't distribute the handouts until you are finished. Clearly label everything you give out, including your name and the date and title of the presentation.

See also the guidelines in Chapter 47 on **DESIGNING PRINT TEXT** for additional help creating visuals. If you are working with a group, see Chapter 21 on **COLLABORATING.**

453–63

195–98

49 Electronic Text

College singing groups create Web sites to publicize their concerts and sell their CDs. Political commentators post their opinions on blogs; readers of the blogs post responses. Job seekers post scannable résumés. And almost everyone sends email, every day, rain or shine. These are just some of the electronic texts you may have occasion to write. These texts differ in a few obvious ways from print texts—Web sites open with home pages rather than with plain introductory paragraphs, for instance—but like print texts, they have certain key features and are composed in the context of particular rhetorical situations. This chapter offers some very basic advice for thinking about the rhetorical situations and key features of texts that you post online.

Considering the Rhetorical Situation

As with any writing task, you need to consider your particular rhetorical situation when you write something to post online. In fact, you may need to consider it especially carefully, since the makeup of an online audience is pretty much impossible to predict—there's no telling who might read what you write or how efficient your readers' computer systems will be at dealing with different types and sizes of files.

3–4   ■ **PURPOSE**   Why are you writing—to fulfill an assignment? answer a question? find or provide information? get in touch with someone? In email, you may want to state your topic, and even your purpose, in the subject line. On a Web site, you will need to make the site's purpose clear on its home page.

476

■ AUDIENCE

What kind of readers are you aiming to reach, and what might they be expecting from you? What are they likely to know about your topic, and what information will you need to provide? What are their technical limitations — can they receive files the size of the one you want to send? If you're constructing a Web site, what kind of home page will appeal to your intended audience?

What do you want them to do — read what you write? forward what you write to others? write something themselves? Remember, however, that you can never be sure where your original readers will forward your email or who will visit a Web site; don't put any writing online that you don't feel comfortable having lots of different people read.

5–8

■ GENRE

Are you reporting information? evaluating something? arguing a point? proposing an action?

9–11

■ STANCE

What overall impression do you want to convey? If you're constructing a Web site for a group, how does the group wish to be seen? Should the site look academic? hip? professional? If you want to demonstrate a political stance, remember that the links you provide can help you to do so. (Remember too that if you want to show a balanced political stance, the links should reflect a range of different viewpoints.)

12–14

■ DESIGN

Your medium will affect your design choices. If you're writing email, you'll want to format it to be as simple as possible — different colors and fonts are not necessarily recognized by every email program, so it's best to write in black type using a standard font. It's best also to keep your paragraphs short so readers can see each point without a lot of scrolling. If you're constructing a Web site, you'll need to create a consistent design scheme using color and type to signal key parts of the site.

15–17

Key Features / Email

Email is such a constant form of communicating that it can feel and read more like talking than writing. But writing it is, and it has certain features and conventions that readers expect and that writers need to be aware of.

An explicit subject line.   Your subject line should state your topic clearly: "Reminder: emedia meeting at 2" rather than "Meeting" or "Hi." People get so much email that they need to see a reason to read yours. In addition, most computer viruses are sent via unsolicited email messages, so many people delete all messages from unknown senders or with suspicious or vague subject lines. A clear subject line increases the chances that your message will be read.

A tone appropriate to the situation.   Email messages should be written in the same tone you'd use if you were writing the same text on paper. You can be informal when writing to friends, but you should be more formal when writing to people you don't know, especially in professional or academic contexts (to your boss or your instructor). Be aware that your tone starts with your salutation (*Hi Lisa* to a friend, *Dear Professor Alikum* to a teacher). And of course your tone is reflected in the register and conventions of your writing. You can use email shorthand with friends (gtg, cul8r), but professional and academic email should observe professional and academic conventions (complete sentences, correct spelling and punctuation).

Brevity.   Email works best when it's brief. Short paragraphs are easier to read on screen than long ones—you don't want readers to have to do too much scrolling to see the point you're trying to make. When you need to email a longer text, you may want to send it as an attachment that readers can open separately. If you don't know for sure whether your recipients will be able to open an attachment, check with them first before sending it.

Speed and reach.   This one's not a textual feature as much as it is a reminder to be careful before you hit *send*. Email travels so fast—and can be so easily forwarded to people you never imagined would read what

rhetorical situations   genres   processes   strategies   research mla/apa   media/ design

you've written—that you want to be good and sure that your email neither says something you'll regret later (don't send email when you're angry!) nor includes anything you don't want the whole world, or at least part of it, reading (don't put confidential or sensitive information in email).

Key Features / Web Sites

The writing you do for the Web differs from that which you do on paper, in the way that you organize and present it—and in the way your readers will approach what you write. Here are some of the features that characterize most Web sites, along with general advice to help you think about each feature when you write for the Web.

A home page. The home page functions much like the first page of an essay, giving the name of the site, indicating something about its purpose, and letting readers know what they'll find on the site. It also gives the name of the site's author or sponsor and includes information about when the site was last updated. Plan the text for a home page so that it fits on one screen, and make it simple enough graphically that it downloads quickly.

A clear organizational structure. Web texts are presented as a number of separate pages, and when you compose a Web site you need to organize the pages so that readers can get to them. Unlike print text, in which the writer determines where a text begins and ends and what order it follows in between, most Web texts are organized so that readers can choose which pages they'll look at and in what order. There's no sure way that you can know what sequence they'll follow. Here are three common ways of organizing a Web site:

As a sequence. A simple way to organize a site is as a linear sequence of pages.

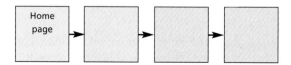

Use this organization if you want readers to view pages in a specific sequence. Though it still doesn't guarantee that they'll follow your sequence, it certainly increases the chances that they'll do so.

As a hierarchy.   A hierarchical design groups related Web pages in the same way an outline organizes related topics in an essay.

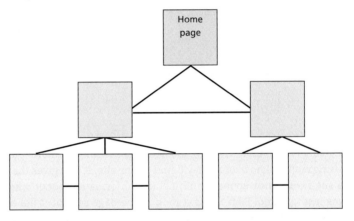

Use a hierarchy to guide readers through complex information while allowing them to choose what to read within categories.

As a web.   A web design allows readers to view pages in just about any order they wish.

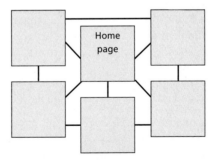

Use a web design when you want to present information that readers can browse for themselves, with little or no guidance from you.

rhetorical situations   genres   processes   strategies   research mla/apa   media/ design

An explicit navigation system.   Just as a book has a table of contents, so a Web site has a navigation menu. The navigation menu shows what's on your site, usually in a menu of the main parts that readers can click on to get to the pages. The navigation menu should appear in the same place on every page. One item on the menu should be a button that lets readers return to the home page.

A consistent design.   Design is important—for creating a visual tone for the site, highlighting features or information, and providing a clear focus and emphasis. You need to create a clear color scheme (all links in one color, for example, to distinguish them from the rest of the text) and a consistent **PAGE DESIGN** (for example, a navigation bar at the top of each page and a background color that stays the same and doesn't detract from the content); in addition, you need to use **TYPE** consistently (for example, one font for the main text, another for the headings).

□ 454–58

□ 454–55

You can also use color and type to create emphasis or to highlight particular types of information. Though you can't know which pages readers will go to, careful site design can help you control what's on the page they'll see first. You can also include **IMAGES**—drawings, photos, maps, and the like. Be sure, however, that the illustrations you include support or add to your point, and that they are not mere decoration. Take care also that you don't include so many graphics that the site takes a long time to open.

□ 458–62

Finally, your design should reflect the appropriate tone and **STANCE.** Formal, informal, academic, whimsical, whatever—your choice of type and color and images can convey this stance.

■ 12–14

Links.   Web sites include links among the pages on the site as well as to material elsewhere on the Web. Links allow you to bring material from other sources into your text—you can link to the **DEFINITION** of a key term, for instance, rather than defining it yourself, or you can link to a **SOURCE** rather than summarizing or paraphrasing it. You can also provide a list of links to related sites. When you're writing a text for a Web site, you can link to some of the details, giving readers the choice of whether they want or need to see an illustration, detailed description, map, and so on. For example, page 482 shows how my literacy narrative (on pages 25–27) might look as a Web text.

◆ 275–84

● 340–53

Amanda K. Hartman was born in 1882 in West Virginia. She left home at 14 for Cleveland, Ohio, where she worked as a seamstress. In her 30's she married Frederick Hartman, a German immigrant. Together they had one child, Louise. After her husband's death in 1955, Amanda obtained a realtor's license and sold real estate for many years.

She read widely, preferring Greek and Roman history and philosophy. Between 1952 and 1956, she and her husband shared a large house with my parents, giving her ample opportunity to read to me. She taught me to read by reading to me for hours on end, every day. She died at the age of 93.

My family was blue-collar, working-class, and — my grandmother excepted — not very interested in books or reading. But my parents took pride in my achievement and told stories about my precocious literacy, such as the time at a restaurant when the waitress bent over as I sat in my booster chair and asked, "What would you like, little boy?" I'm told I gave her a withering look and said, "I'd like to see a menu."

There was a more serious aspect to reading so young, however. At that time the murder trial of Dr. Sam Sheppard, a physician whose wife had been bludgeoned to death in their house, was the focus of lurid coverage in the Cleveland newspapers. Daily news stories recounted the grisly details of both the murder and the trial testimony, in which Sheppard maintained his innocence. (The story would serve as the inspiration for the TV series and Harrison Ford movie, The Fugitive.)

Sample Web text, with links

How text on the Web links to details from other sources.   As the text on the facing page shows, links from my narrative might include a brief biography of my grandmother, *Court TV*'s account of the Sheppard murder case, a site presenting excerpts of news coverage of the trial, and a poster from *The Fugitive*. Such links allow me to stay focused on my own narrative while offering readers the opportunity to explore issues mentioned in my story in as much depth as they want.

A Sample Site

Here and on page 484 are examples from a home page, a content page, and a linked page from a Web site created by Colleen James, a student at Illinois State University, as part of an online portfolio of work for a course in hypertext.

Home page

High contrast between text and simple background makes reading easy.

Careful organization: Text has been divided into brief sections grouped logically.

Table of contents contains links to each section, permitting easy navigation within sections.

Illustration and title clearly describe the site's contents.

Contents page

Explicit navigation system: Links to pages in the site appear at the same place on each page.

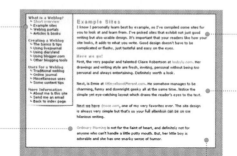

Color is used to show headings and links.

Text has been divided into brief sections, with headings.

Links to other Web sites are integrated into the text.

Background doesn't interfere with reading.

Linked page

Consistent design helps readers know where they are and how to navigate the site.

Links to other parts of the site help readers navigate.

High contrast between text and simple background makes reading easy.

english.ilstu.edu/students/cejames/final/

See Chapter 47, **PRINT TEXT**, for more information on text design elements, such as fonts and effective use of white space. When writing electronic texts, be aware that the way you use various **STRATEGIES** may change—for example, you may create a link to a dictionary definition of a term instead of defining it within the text.

453–63 ◻

237–328 ◆

rhetorical situations ▲ genres ○ processes ◆ strategies ● research mla/apa ◻ media/ design

Acknowledgments

IMAGE ACKNOWLEDGMENTS

Every effort has been made to gain permission for images used in this book. Unless otherwise noted, all images not cited in this section have been provided by the editor and authors of this publication. Please contact the publishers with any updated information.

40: Courtesy Alfred Leslie; 45: From Scholes, Robert, and Nancy R. Comley. *The Practice of Writing.* 3rd ed. New York: St. Martin's Press, 1989; 47: Courtesy Unilever; 48: Courtesy Pfizer; 67: Bettmann/Corbis; 71: From *The 9/11 Commission Report.* New York: Norton; 87: (both) Bettmann/Corbis; 227: screen shot recreated by Kim Yi; 264: Naum Kazhdan/The *New York Times*; 270: (top) From Stiglitz, Joseph. *Economics.* New York: Norton; 270: (bottom) www.ivillage.com; 271: Lance Jackson/The *San Francisco Chronicle*; 290: Courtesy Glaxo Smith Kline; 302: From Beranbaum, Rose Levy. *The Bread Bible.* New York: Norton; 342, 345, 346: Courtesy of the University of Wyoming Library; 409: Bettman/Corbis; 459: (top) Peter Turnley/Corbis; 459: (second image) From Stiglitz and Walsh. *Principles of Microeconomics.* 3rd ed. New York: Norton; 459: (third image) From Ginsberg, Lowi, Weir, *We the People.* 5th ed. New York: Norton; 459: (fourth image) From Stiglitz, Joseph. *Economics.* New York: Norton; 459: (fifth image) From Maier, Smith, Keyssar, Kevles. *Inventing America.* New York: Norton; 459: (sixth image) From Ginsberg, Lowi, Weir, *We the People.* 5th ed. New York: Norton; 461: (top two) Courtesy of the author; 461: (bottom two) AP/Wide World Photos; 482: (top) Courtesy of the author; 482: (top middle) AP/Wide World Photos; 482: (bottom middle) Courtesy of Dr. R. Standler; 482: (bottom) Warner Bros./Photofest; 483, 484: Courtesy Illinois State University, Claire Robertson, www.loobylu.com.

TEXT ACKNOWLEDGMENTS

Dave Barry: From *Dave Barry's Complete Guide to Guys* by Dave Barry, copyright © 1995 by Dave Barry. Used by permission of Random House, Inc.

Michael Benton, Mark Dolan, and Rebecca Zisch: From "Teen Film$," *The Journal of Popular Film and Television,* Vol. 25, No. 2, Summer 1997. Reprinted with permission of the Helen Dwight Reid Educational Foundation. Published by Heldref Publications, 1319 18th Street, NW, Washington, DC 20036-1802. www.heldref.org. Copyright © 1997.

Dylan Borchers: "Against the Odds: Harry S Truman and the Election of 1948." Reprinted courtesy of the author.

Jennifer Church: "Biodiversity Loss and Its Effect on Medicine." Reprinted courtesy of the author.

Nathaniel Cooney: "Portfolio Self-Assessment Letter." Reprinted courtesy of the author.

Bernard Cooper: "The Fine Art of Sighing." Originally published in *Truth Serum* (1997). Reprinted by permission of the author.

Jeffrey DeRoven: "The Greatest Generation: The Great Depression and the American South." Originally published in *Etude and Techne*, Vol 1. Reprinted courtesy of the author.

Cathi Eastman and Becky Burrell: "The Science of Screams: Laws of Physics Instill Thrills in Roller Coasters," by Catherine Eastman and Becky Burell. Originally published in *The Dayton Daily News*. Reprinted courtesy of the authors.

Amanda Hesser: "Turkey Finds Its Inner Duck (and Chicken)." Originally appeared in *The New York Times* on November 20, 2002. Reprinted by permission of *The New York Times*.

Stephanie Huff: "Metaphors and Society in Shelley's 'Sonnet'." Reprinted courtesy of the author.

Doug Lantry: "Stay Sweet As You Are: An Analysis of Change and Continuity in Advertising Aimed at Women." Reprinted courtesy of the author.

Ben Leever: "In Defense of Dawson's Creek: Teen Heroes Inspire Youths Seeking Answers." Reprinted by permission of the author.

Lawrence Lessig: "Some Like It Hot—Wired Magazine article", from *Free Culture* by Lawrence Lessig, copyright © 2004 by Lawrence Lessig. Used by permission of The Penguin Press, a division of Penguin Group (USA) Inc.

Andy McDonie: "Airport Security: What Price Safety?" Reprinted courtesy of the author.

Shannon Nichols: "Proficiency." Reprinted courtesy of the author.

Anna Quindlen: "Still Needing the F Word." Copyright © 2003 by Anna Quindlen. Reprinted by permission of International Creative Management, Inc.

David S. Rubin: "It's the Same Old Song" from *It's Only Rock and Roll: Rock and Roll Currents in Contemporary Art*. Reprinted courtesy of the author.

William Safire: "A Spirit Reborn." Originally appeared in *The New York Times* on September 9, 2002. Reprinted by permission of *The New York Times*.

Carolyn Stonehill: "Modern Dating, Prehistoric Style." Reprinted courtesy of the author.

Sarah Thomas: "Effect of Biofeedback Training on Muscle Tension and Skin Temperature." Reprinted courtesy of the author.

Bill Whalen: "Reagan and Schwarzenegger—Parallel Universe?" Reprinted courtesy of the author.

Glossary / Index*

abstract A GENRE of writing that summarizes a book, an article, or a paper, usually in 100–200 words. Authors in some academic fields must provide, at the top of a report submitted for publication, an abstract of its content. The abstract may then appear in a journal of abstracts, such as *Psychological Abstracts*. An *informative abstract* summarizes a complete report; a briefer *descriptive abstract* works more as a teaser; a standalone *proposal abstract* (also called a TOPIC PROPOSAL) requests permission to conduct research, write on a topic, or present a report at a scholarly conference. Key Features: SUMMARY of basic information • objective description • brevity

---

*This glossary/index defines key terms and concepts, and directs you to pages in the book where you can find specific information on these and other topics. Please note that words set in SMALL CAPITAL LETTERS are themselves defined in the glossary/index.

ad hominem A logical FALLACY that attacks someone's character rather than addresses the issues.

487

analysis A GENRE of writing that methodically examines a topic or text by breaking it into its parts and noting how they work in relation to one another. *See* LITERARY ANALYSIS and TEXTUAL ANALYSIS.

analyses, *see* literary analysis; textual analysis
analyzing causes and effects, *see* causes and effects
analyzing text, *see* textual analysis
"And Our Flag Was Still There," 247–48

anecdote A brief narrative (*see* NARRATE) used to illustrate a point.

anecdotes
    beginnings and, 244
    endings and, 246–47
    narratives and, 244, 309–10
Angelou, Maya, 304–5, 307

annotated bibliography A GENRE of writing that gives an overview of published research and scholarship on a topic. Each entry includes complete publication information and a SUMMARY or an ABSTRACT for each source. A *descriptive annotation* summarizes the content of a source without commenting on its value; an *evaluative annotation* gives an opinion about the source along with a description of it. Key Features: statement of the scope • complete bibliographic information • relevant commentary • consistent presentation

annotated bibliographies, 112–20
    appropriateness and, 117
    balance and, 117
    careful reading and, 117–18
    complete information, 115
    concise description, 115
    consistency and, 118
    consistent presentation, 116
    credibility and, 117
    descriptive, 112–14

    determining the type of, 117
    evaluating sources, 118
    evaluative, 112, 114, 115
    example of, 112–15
    generating ideas and text, 116–18
    guide to writing, 116–19
    help with, 119
    key features of, 115–16
    organizing, 119
    relevant commentary, 115–16
    researching the writer, 118
    rhetorical situation, 116
    statement of scope, 115
    summarizing the work, 118
    timeliness and, 117
annotating a text, 315–18
    example of, 316–18

APA style A system of documenting sources in the social sciences. APA stands for the American Psychological Association. *See also* DOCUMENTATION.

APA style, 417–49
    in-text documentation, 377, 417, 419–25
    notes, 425
    quotations and, 360–61
    reference list, 377, 418–19, 426–38
        books, 426–30
        electronic sources, 433–37
        other sources, 437–38
        periodicals, 429–33
    sample research paper using, 438–49
    summary of, 375–77
    verb tenses and, 368–69

appendix A section at the end of a written work for supplementary material that would be distracting in the main part of the text.

application letter A letter written to apply for a job or other position. *See also* RÉSUMÉ. Key Features:

succinct indication of qualifications • reasonable and pleasing TONE • conventional, businesslike format

application letters, 182, 189–92
    appropriate salutation, 192
    as an argument, 191–92
    example of, 190
    focus, 191
    format of, 191
    generating ideas and text, 191–92
    guide to writing, 191–92
    help with, 192
    key features of, 189, 191
    organizing, 192
    proofreading, 192
    purpose of, 191
    reason for, 191
    succinct, 189
    tone of, 191

argument A GENRE of writing that uses REASONS and EVIDENCE to support a CLAIM or POSITION and, sometimes, to persuade an AUDIENCE to accept that position. Key Features: clear and arguable position • necessary background • good REASON • convincing support for each reason • appeal to readers' values • trustworthy TONE • careful consideration of other positions

arguments, analyzing, 324–27
    evaluating sources and, 356
arguments (arguing a position), 82–106
    acknowledging sources and, 371
    appeals to readers' values, 94
    background information and, 93
    choosing a topic, 95–96
    clarity and plausibility, 93
    design and, 97, 104–5
    drafting, 103–4
    editing and proofreading, 105–6
    examples of, 82–93
    exploring issues, 97–98
    generating ideas and text, 97–101
    getting response, 105
    good reasons and, 93, 99–100
    guide to writing, 95–106
    key features, 93–94
    organizing, 101–3
    other positions and, 94, 100–1
    prior knowledge and, 97
    research and, 97
    revising, 105
    rewriting, 218
    rhetorical situation, 96–97
    support for reasons, 94
    taking stock of your work, 106
    thesis and, 98–100
    trustworthy tone, 94
    worthiness of, 98
articles, citing
    in APA style, 429–33
        electronic sources, 435–36
    in MLA style, 395–97
        electronic sources, 397–401
art work, citing, 403
assessing your own writing, 208–12
    clarity, 212
    done for others, 209
    focus, 210–11
    organization, 211
    personal writing, 208–9
    portfolios and, 230–34
    rhetorical situations, 209–10
    support for your argument, 211
    text itself, 210–12

audience Those to whom a text is directed—the people who read, listen to, or view the text. Audience is a key part of every text's RHETORICAL SITUATION.

authority People or texts that are cited as support for a writer's ARGUMENT. A structural engineer may be quoted as an authority on bridge construction, for example. *Authority* also refers to a quality conveyed by a writer who is knowledgeable about his or her subject.

bandwagon appeal A logical FALLACY that argues for a thought or an action based on the sole defense that others support it.

begging the question A logical FALLACY that goes in a circle, assuming as a given what the writer is trying to prove.

block quotation In a written work, long quotations are set off indented and without quotation marks. in MLA style: set off text more than four typed lines, indented ten spaces (or one inch) from the left margin; in APA style, set off quotes of forty or more words, indented five spaces (or one-half inch) from the left margin. *See also* QUOTATION.

cause and effect A STRATEGY for analyzing why something occurred or speculating about what its consequences will be. Sometimes cause and effect serves as the ORGANIZING principle for a whole text.

chronological order A way of organizing text that proceeds from the beginning of an event to the end. Reverse chronological order proceeds in the other direction, from the end to the beginning.

citation In a text, the act of giving information from a source. A citation and its corresponding parenthetical DOCUMENTATION or footnote or endnote provide minimal information about the source, and complete bibliographic information appears in a list of WORKS CITED or REFERENCES at the end of the text.

claim A statement that asserts a belief or POSITION. In an ARGUMENT, a claim needs to be stated in a THESIS or clearly implied, and requires support with REASONS and other kinds of EVIDENCE.

classify and divide A STRATEGY that either groups (classifies) numerous individual items by their similarities (for example, classifying cereal, bread, butter, chicken, cheese, ice cream, eggs, and oil as carbohydrates, proteins, and fats) or breaks (divides) one large category into smaller categories (for example, dividing food into carbohydrates, proteins, and fats). Sometimes classification and/or division serves as the ORGANIZING principle for a whole text.

clustering A PROCESS for GENERATING IDEAS AND TEXT, in which a writer visually connects thoughts by jotting them down and drawing lines between related items.

coherence The quality that allows an AUDIENCE to follow a text's meaning and to see the connections among ideas, sentences, and paragraphs. Elements that can help to achieve coherence include the title, a clearly stated or implied THESIS, topic sentences, an easy-to-follow organization with clear TRANSITIONS, and parallelism among comparable ideas.

collaborating The PROCESS of working with others.

common ground Shared values. Writers build common ground with AUDIENCES by acknowledging others' POINTS OF VIEW, seeking areas of compromise, and using language that includes, rather than excludes, those they aim to reach.

compare and contrast A STRATEGY that highlights the similarities and differences between items. Using the *block method* of comparison-contrast, a writer discusses all the points about one item and then all the same points about the next item; using the *point-by-point method,* a writer discusses one point for both items before going on to discuss the next point for both items, and so on. Sometimes comparison and/or contrast serves as the ORGANIZING principle for a whole text.

point-by-point method of, 268–69

rhetorical situation, 273–74

similes, 271–72

as transitions, 254

ways of, 267–69

conference, writing, 197–98

conference proceedings, citing

in APA style, 438

in MLA style, 406

content notes, citing

in APA style, 425

in MLA style, 388

contrasting, *see* comparing and contrasting

Cooney, Nathaniel J., 230–34

Cooper, Bernard, 168–71, 172

counterargument In ARGUMENT, an alternative POSITION or objections to the writer's position. The writer of an argument should not only acknowledge counterarguments but also, if at all possible, accept, accommodate, or refute each counterargument.

credentials of authors, 355

credibility The sense of trustworthiness that a writer conveys through his or her text.

criteria In EVALUATION, the standards against which something is judged.

criteria in evaluations, 122, 124

CSA: Hot Topics Service, 349

cubing A PROCESS for GENERATING IDEAS AND TEXT in which a writer looks at a topic in six ways — to DESCRIBE it, to COMPARE it to something else, to associate it with other things or CLASSIFY it, to analyze it (*see* ANALYSIS), to apply it, and to argue for or against it (*see* ARGUMENT).

databases, 346–49

citing

in APA style, 435–36

in MLA style, 399–400

Dave Barry's Complete Guide to Guys: A Fairly Short Book, 263, 265

Davis, Judy, 465–67

deadlines, 205

"Defining Democracy Down," 283

define A STRATEGY that gets at the meaning of something. Three main kinds of definitions are the *formal definition,* which may identify the category that something belongs to and tell what distinguishes it from other things in that category: for example, defining a worm as an invertebrate (a category) with a long, rounded body and no appendages (distinguishing features); the *extended definition,* which, as its name suggests, is longer: for example, a paragraph explaining why the antagonist of a story is worm-like; and the *stipulative definition,* which gives a writer's own, particular use of a term: for example, using the term *worm* to refer to a kind of gummy candy. Sometimes definition serves as the ORGANIZING principle for a whole text.

definitions, 275–84

beginnings and, 243

dictionary, 275

extended, *see* extended definitions

formal, 275–77

rhetorical situation, 283–84

stipulative, 282–83

"Democracy," 281

"Democracy and Things Like That," 246–47

DeRoven, Jeffrey, 65–70, 75, 77–78, 239–40

describe A STRATEGY that tells how something looks, sounds, smells, feels, or tastes. Effective description creates a clear DOMINANT IMPRESSION built from spe-

describe (cont.)
cific details. Description can be *objective, subjective,* or both. Sometimes description serves as the ORGANIZING principle for a whole text.

descriptions, 285–93
    details, *see* details
    dominant impression and, 291–92
    objective, 288–89, 290
    organizing, 292
    rhetorical situation, 292–93
    subjective, 289
    vantage point and, 289–91
descriptive abstracts, 108
    organizing, 111
    see also abstracts
descriptive annotations, 112–14, 117, 118
    see also annotated bibliographies

design   The way a text is arranged and presented visually. Elements of design include typeface, color, illustration, layout, and white space. One component of any RHETORICAL SITUATION, design plays an important part in reaching a text's AUDIENCE and achieving its PURPOSE.

design, 15–17, 453–63
    abstracts and, 110
    annotated bibliographies and, 116
    arguing a position and, 97, 104–5
    assessing your own writing and, 210
    beginnings and endings and, 249
    causes and effects and, 259
    classifying and dividing and, 265
    comparing and contrasting and, 274
    definition and, 284
    description and, 293
    dialogue and, 298
    evaluation and, 124
    explaining processes and, 303
    identifying your, 16
    lab reports and, 134

    literacy narratives and, 31, 36
    literary analyses and, 141, 145
    memoirs and, 151
    narratives and, 312
    portfolios and, 225
    previewing a text, 315
    profiles and, 156
    proposals and, 164
    reflections and, 172
    reporting information and, 71, 73, 78–79
    research plan and, 333
    résumés and, 185–86, 188
    reviews of scholarly literature and, 179
    textual analysis and, 52, 57
    thinking about, 17
    see also electronic text; print text; spoken text
details, 285–88
    labels versus, 286
    literacy narratives and, 29
    narratives and, 308–10
    sensory, 287–88
    specific, 285–87
diagrams, flowcharts, and drawings, 465

dialogue   A STRATEGY for adding people's own words to a text.

dialogue, 294–98
    interviews, 296–97
    literacy narratives and, 32–33
    paragraphing, 295–96
    punctuating, 295–96
    reasons for, 294–95
    rhetorical situation, 297–98
    signal phrases, 295

Didion, Joan, 311

discovery drafting   A PROCESS of DRAFTING something quickly, mostly for the purpose of discovering what one wants to say.

evidence The data you present to support your reasons. Such data may include statistics, calculations, examples, anecdotes, quotations, case studies, or anything else that will convince your reader that your reasons are compelling. Evidence should be sufficient (enough to show that the reasons have merit) and relevant (appropriate to the argument you're making).

explain a process A STRATEGY for telling how something is done or how to do something. Sometimes an explanation of a process serves as the ORGANIZING principle for a whole text.

fallacy, logical Faulty reasoning that can mislead an AUDIENCE. Fallacies include AD HOMINEM, BANDWAGON APPEAL, BEGGING THE QUESTION, EITHER-OR ARGUMENT (also called false dilemma), false analogy, faulty causality (also called POST HOC, ERGO PROPTER HOC), HASTY GENERALIZATION, and SLIPPERY SLOPE.

false analogy A FALLACY comparing things that do resemble each other but that are not alike in the most important respects.

false dilemma See EITHER-OR ARGUMENT.

faulty causality A FALLACY that mistakenly assumes the first of two events causes the second. This fallacy is also called POST HOC, ERGO PROPTER HOC.

field research The collection of first-hand data through observation, interviews, and questionnaires or surveys.

flashback In narrative (NARRATE), an interruption of the main story in order to show an incident that occurred at an earlier time.

font A variation of a typeface such as italic and bold.

formal writing Writing intended to be evaluated by someone such as an instructor or read by an AUDIENCE expecting academic or businesslike argument and presentation. Formal writing should be carefully revised, edited, and PROOFREAD. See also INFORMAL WRITING.

freewriting A PROCESS for GENERATING IDEAS AND TEXT by writing continuously for several minutes without pausing to read what has been written.

generating ideas and text A set of PROCESSES including CLUSTERING, CUBING, DISCOVERY DRAFTING, FREEWRITING, LETTER WRITING, LISTING, LOOPING, OUTLINING, and QUESTIONING.

genre A kind of text marked by and expected to have certain key features and to follow certain conventions of style and presentation. In the literary world, readers recognize such genres as the short story and novel (which are expected to have plots) and the poem (which may not have a plot but has other characteristics, such as rhythm); in academic and workplace settings, readers and writers focus on other genres, which also meet expectations in content, style, and appearance. Genres covered in the *Norton Field Guide* include ABSTRACTS, ANNOTATED BIBLIOGRAPHIES, APPLICATION LETTERS, ARGUMENTS, EVALUATIONS, LAB REPORTS, LITERACY NARRATIVES, LITERARY ANALYSES, PROFILES, PROPOSALS, REFLECTIONS, RÉSUMÉS, REPORTS, TEXTUAL ANALYSES, and REVIEWS OF SCHOLARLY LITERATURE.

hasty generalization A FALLACY that reaches a conclusion based on insufficient or inappropriately qualified EVIDENCE.

home page The introductory page of a Web site.

informal writing Writing not intended to be evaluated, sometimes not even to be read by others. Informal writing is produced primarily to explore ideas or to communicate casually with friends and acquaintances. *See also* FORMAL WRITING.

interpretation The act of making sense of something or explaining what one thinks it means. Interpretation is the goal of writing a LITERARY ANALYSIS or TEXTUAL ANALYSIS.

literacy portfolio An organized collection of materials showing examples of one writer's progress as a reader and / or writer.

literary analysis A GENRE of writing that argues for a particular INTERPRETATION of a literary text — most often fiction, poetry, or drama. *See also* ANALYSIS and TEXTUAL ANALYSIS. Key Features: arguable THESIS • careful attention to the language of the text • attention to patterns or themes • clear interpretation • MLA style

literature Literary works — including fiction, poetry, drama, and some nonfiction; also, the body of written work produced in a given field.

literature review *See* REVIEW OF SCHOLARLY LITERATURE.

logical fallacy *See* FALLACY, LOGICAL.

looping A PROCESS for GENERATING IDEAS AND TEXT in which a writer writes about a topic quickly for several minutes and summarizes the most important or interesting idea in a sentence, which becomes the beginning of another round of writing and summarizing . . . and so on until finding an angle for a paper.

narrate   A STRATEGY for presenting information as a story, for telling "what happened." It is a pattern most often associated with fiction, but it shows up in all kinds of writing. When used in an essay, a REPORT, or another academic GENRE, a narrative must support a point — not merely tell an interesting story for its own sake. It must also present events in some kind of sequence and include only pertinent detail. Sometimes narrative serves as the ORGANIZING principle for a whole text. See also LITERACY NARRATIVE.

organizing   Arranging parts of a text so that the text as a whole has COHERENCE. The text may use one STRATEGY throughout or may combine several strategies to create a suitable organization.

outlining A PROCESS for GENERATING IDEAS AND TEXT or for examining a text. An *informal outline* simply lists ideas and then numbers them in the order that they will appear; a *working outline* distinguishes support from main ideas by indenting the former; a *formal outline* is arranged as a series of headings and indented subheadings, each on a separate line, with letters and numerals indicating relative levels of importance.

paraphrase A rewording of a text in about the same number of words but without using the word order or sentence structure of the original. A paraphrase is generally used when you want to include the details of a passage but do not need to quote it word for word. Like a quotation, a paraphrase requires DOCUMENTATION.

peer review *See* RESPONDING.

plagiarism Using another person's words, syntax, or ideas without giving appropriate credit and DOCUMENTATION. Plagiarism is a serious breach of ethics.

proofreading   The final PROCESS of writing, when a writer checks for correct spelling and punctuation as well as for page order, missing copy, and consistent use of typefaces and FONTS. *See also* EDITING, REVISING, and REWRITING.

proposal   A GENRE that argues for a solution to a problem or suggests some action. See also TOPIC PROPOSAL. Key Features: well-defined problem • recommended solution • convincing argument for proposed solution • answers to anticipated questions • call to action • appropriate TONE

purpose   A writer's goal: to explore; to express oneself; to entertain; to demonstrate learning; to report; to persuade; and so on. Purpose is one element of the RHETORICAL SITUATION.

questioning A PROCESS of GENERATING IDEAS AND TEXT about a topic — asking, for example, What? Who? When? Where? How? and Why? or other questions.

quotation Someone's words used exactly as they were spoken or written. Quotation is most effective when the wording is worth repeating or makes a point so well that no rewording will do it justice or when you want to cite someone's exact words or to quote someone whose opinions disagree with others. Quotations need to be acknowledged, with DOCUMENTATION.

reason A statement supporting a CLAIM or POSITION. A reason, in turn, requires its own support.

references (APA) The list of sources at the end of a text prepared APA style.

reference list, *see* APA style

responding (to writing) A PROCESS of writing in which a reader responds to a writer's work by giving his or her thoughts about the writer's title, beginning, clarity of THESIS, support and DOCUMENTATION, ORGAN-IZING, STANCE, treatment of AUDIENCE, achievement of PURPOSE, handling of the GENRE, ending, and other matters.

résumé A GENRE that summarizes someone's academic and employment history, generally written to submit to potential employers. DESIGN and word choice depend on whether a résumé is submitted as a print document or in an electronic or scannable form. Key Features: organization that suits goals and experience • succinctness • design that highlights key information (for print) or that uses only one typeface (for scannable)

review of scholarly literature A GENRE in which, for a given topic, a writer summarizes those scholarly publications ("literature") he or she deems most important. *See also* SCHOLARLY LITERATURE. Key Features: careful, thorough research • accurate, objective SUMMARY of the relevant literature • critical EVALUATION of the literature • clear focus

revising The PROCESS of making substantive changes, including additions and cuts, to a draft so that it contains all the necessary information in an appropriate organization. During revision, a writer generally moves from whole-text issues to details with the goals of sharpening the focus and strengthening the argument.

rewriting A PROCESS of composing a new draft from another perspective — from a different POINT OF VIEW, AUDIENCE, STANCE, GENRE, MEDIUM, sequence, and so on.

rhetorical situation   The context within which writing or other communication takes place, including PURPOSE, AUDIENCE, GENRE, STANCE, and MEDIA / DESIGN.

scholarly literature   Writing from a scholarly field. *See also* REVIEW OF SCHOLARLY LITERATURE.

secondary source   An analysis or INTERPRETATION of a PRIMARY SOURCE. In writing about the Revolutionary War, a researcher would likely consider the Declaration of Independence a PRIMARY SOURCE and a textbook's description of the writing of the document a secondary source.

strategy A pattern for organizing text to ANALYZE
CAUSE AND EFFECT, CLASSIFY AND DIVIDE, COMPARE AND
CONTRAST, DEFINE, DESCRIBE, EXPLAIN A PROCESS, NAR-
RATE, and so on.

style In writing, the arrangement of sentences,
phrases, words, and punctuation to achieve a desired
effect; also, the rules of capitalization, punctuation,
and so on recommended for DOCUMENTATION of a
source.

summary A condensation of a text into a briefer
but still faithful version in lieu of a PARAPHRASE or
a QUOTATION.

textual analysis A GENRE of writing in which a
writer looks at what a text says and how it says it.
See also ANALYSIS and LITERARY ANALYSIS. Key Features:
SUMMARY of the text • attention to context • clear
INTERPRETATION or judgment • reasonable support for
your conclusions

thesis A CLAIM or statement of a writer's POSITION or main point.

tone A writer's or speaker's attitude toward his or her readers and subject. A writer's tone reflects his or her STANCE, and may be formal or informal, optimistic or pessimistic, playful, ironic, and so on.

topic proposal A statement of intent to examine a topic; also called a proposal ABSTRACT. Some instructors require a topic proposal in order to assess the feasibility of the writing project that a student has in mind. Key Features: concise discussion of the subject • clear statement of the intended focus • rationale for choosing the subject • mention of resources

transition A word or phrase used to make clear the connection between ideas in a text.

Directory to MLA Style

MLA IN-TEXT DOCUMENTATION

MLA LIST OF WORKS CITED